New Leadership in Health Care Management

The Physician Executive

Second Edition

Edited by Wesley Curry

American College of Physician Executives
4890 West Kennedy Boulevard, Suite 200
Tampa, Florida 33609
813/287-2000

ISBN: 0-924674-30-X

Library of Congress Card Number: 94-72291

Printed in the United States of America by BookCrafters, Fredericksburg, Virginia.

FOREWORD

Since this book was first published in 1988, the membership of the American College of Physician Executives has doubled. By the time this book is printed, the 9,000 mark will be exceeded. Nearly 150 physician executives on average now join the College each month.

As was true in 1988, physician executives may be found in every conceivable environment (hospitals, group practices, managed care organizations, academia, industry, government) and at all levels of management, from CEO to department head. Increasingly, physicians are being asked to take on tough decision-making roles, particularly in the provider sector.

The forces for change in the health care system that were just coming into bloom in 1988 are by now in full flower. And the prospects for the years ahead are for even more, and more rapid, change. The first edition of this book was adequate for its times, but some new concepts and disciplines have developed for health care delivery. It was time, we thought, for an up-date.

Although integrated health systems existed six years ago as a fact, they have only recently become a trend. It seems certain that survival in a reformed health care system will depend on the degree to which individual components of the health care delivery system are linked with others, both similar and complementing. A new chapter in this edition deals with this important subject.

Likewise, computers were already a critical tool in health care management in 1988, but one could have looked for a long time to find the notion of medical informatics treated in the literature of the field. Now there are periodicals devoted to the topic. This edition recognizes this fundamental change in information systems with a chapter by Marshall Ruffin Jr., MD, MPH, MBA, a leading exponent of medical informatics applications.

Quality and costs have long been a major issue in health care, with first one and then the other having the upper hand in the seemingly endless debate over their relationship. Medical quality management has moved from its early concentration on quality assurance to newer concepts of total quality management and continuous quality improvement. Physician executives have, by and large, been assigned primary responsibility for its management. Two chapters in this new edition deal with quality and costs.

It is something more than quiet understatement to assert that physicians generally have been threatened by all this change. And they are even more apprehensive about the changes looming on the horizon. The demise of the dominance of fee-for-service practice has been forecast for years. Now it seems more certain, as managed care and other alternatives grow in influence and stature. In one way or another, physicians of the future are likely to be employees. The job of managing these professionals, which is apt to fall to physician executives, will not be easy. A new chapter helps guide the reader through this minefield.

All the chapters in the previous edition have been up-dated by authors to reflect new realities in medical management. We think that the result is a text that continues to provide the most comprehensive and accurate picture of the content and context of medical management.

Thanks to all of the authors and a special thanks to Wes Curry for a masterful job in doing all the things it takes to bring a book like this to us, the readers.

Roger S. Schenke
Executive Vice President
American College of Physician Executives
Tampa, Florida
July 14, 1994

TABLE OF CONTENTS

The Context of Management

The Ascendancy of Management: National Health Care Reform, Managed Competition and Its Implications for Physician Executives

CHAPTER 1

by Edward F.X. Hughes, MD, MPH, FACPE

At the time of this writing, the United States is involved in a major domestic debate as to how to configure the financing of health care for its citizens. The genesis of the debate has been the rejection by the middle class of the status quo as it pertains to the financing of health care. This rejection has set in motion a process of "social choice" wherein the American people are searching for a better way to finance health care. The principal driver of this process is concern by the citizenry for financial access to health care complemented, and reinforced, by concern for the costs of health care. The bulk of the attention in the media and in the public debate to date has focused on these two aspects of health reform. A little discussed fact, however, is that the process of reform, no matter what the eventual outcome, is accelerating the ascendancy of management in health care. Central to this growing primacy is the critical role for physician managers in the present and future of our nation's health care delivery system.

This chapter will examine the forces driving health care reform, the options for achieving its goals, and the likelihood of compromise among the various options. It will then discuss the option most in the ascendancy, managed competition, and the infrastructure underlying it, namely managed care. It will provide a definition of managed care, discuss its attributes and its implications for the delivery of health care, and elaborate its implications for the importance of physician managers in our health system.

The genesis of health care reforms lies in the rejection by the middle class of the status quo as it pertains to the financing of health care. The middle class has been motivated in this rejection by two factors. The first is genuine social compassion for the well-being of the estimated 38.9 million Americans without private or public health insurance.[1] Even though there are a number of voluntarily uninsured individuals in this population, its size is a well-documented fact. The great bulk of individuals in it are workers or dependents of workers.[2] They can be found disproportionately in industries such as the hospitality industry and agriculture, among lower-wage employees, and employees of small firms.[3] The number of such individuals actually grew last year as a result, in part, of an increased number of small businesses ceasing to cover their employees because of the rising costs of health insurance.[1]

Increasingly, the American middle class has grown to feel that it is inappropriate in a nation as wealthy as ours to have such a large segment of the population remain without private or public health insurance. The many cases of personal bankruptcy caused by health care costs and the human suffering associated with the inability of many individuals to purchase health insurance, even when they possess the required resources and the desire to do so, have coalesced to create a consensus for change.[4,5]

Not only is the compassion of the middle class for the uninsured driving this phenomenon but also contributing, and critically so, is the fear of many in the middle class that they themselves might, at some point, become uninsured. In an effort to regain international as well as domestic competitiveness, the American industrial sector has in recent years eliminated more than a million jobs. Many of these have been white-collar, managerial positions whose occupants have held the position for many years. Even if an individual is able to get another job, it is often of a part-time or consulting nature not carrying health insurance. Similarly, if the individual in question has a preexisting condition, he or she may be denied insurance coverage on the new job, particularly if he or she works for, or is, a small employer. Whereas job loss often entails transient economic insecurity, the inability to purchase health insurance can entail permanent economic catastrophe.

Thus, consensus has emerged within the population for change. To its credit, the Clinton Administration listened to the people; heard the call for change; and, for better or for worse, set in motion the series of events that have brought us where we are today. The process of social choice now under way is similar in its magnitude and in its search for a better way of doing things to the civil rights movement of the early 1960s and the debate over the Vietnam war in the late 1960s and early 1970s. The goal of the process is the attainment of universal financial access to health care. No matter how heartfeltly or stridently certain political leaders advocate this goal, it may most realistically and productively be viewed as an ideal. A more realistic goal may be the progressive expansion of financial access to health care in a deliberate, sustained, and incremental fashion.

What is not generally realized is that there are many ways through which a society can strive to enhance financial access to health care. There is not just one or two. In fact, I have identified 11 of them:

- National health service
- **National health insurance**
- Play or pay (employer mandate)
- Explicit rationing
- Mandated personal health insurance
- Medical IRAs
- Managed competition
- Tinkering with the tax code
- **Reform of the health insurance market**
- **Incremental enhancements**
- Status quo

The list is ordered roughly from the most centralized of options to the least intrusive. The first two options, national health service and national health insurance, are both "single payer" options. Although they share this characteristic, they also differ substantially. Under a system of national health insurance, such as that in Canada, the government is, in essence, the only legal insurance company for the services covered under the federal-provincial partnership.[6,7] The Canadians believe so strongly in the norm of equity that it is illegal to buy or sell private health insurance for services covered by the government plan. One can, however, buy private insurance for services not covered by the government or for the uncovered portion of partially covered services. Physicians are in private practice and paid on a fee-for-service basis within a global budget negotiated between the provincial government and the provincial medical society. Hospitals are, for the most part, community-based, not-for-profit corporations operating under an annual prospective budget negotiated between the hospital and the provincial government.

Under a national health service, as in Great Britain, however, the government is not only the payer of care but, for the most part, the actual owner of health care facilities and the employer of health care professionals. There is an opt-out provision in Britain's National Health Service wherein patients can seek privately paid care from hospital-based consultants in the small proportion of beds set aside within the system for that purpose. One can also purchase private insurance or receive employer-paid insurance for that purpose.

Despite the well-intended advocacy of many of our citizens and the support of a number of our politicians, neither of these options is in the ascendancy in the health care reform debate.[8] An interesting question is, "Why not?" The radical right can always be counted upon to comment that the lack of ascendancy is due to the fact that "the government can't do anything." The fact is that the government can do many things and some of them quite well—air traffic control being one of the latter. Why, then, does not a larger segment of the American people support a government-based, single-payer approach for our health care system? The best critique I have found of government-based approaches is that of Peter Drucker in his book *The New Realities*.[9] In the chapter entitled: "The Limits of Government," Drucker argues that the critical question in assessing the appropriateness of a government-based approach to a social challenge is not "What *should* government do?" which the left and the right debate on a daily basis, but rather "What *can* government do?"

In addressing the latter question, Drucker posits two conditions for successful government programs: a natural monopoly and no alternative in the private sector. He cites as programs fulfilling these criteria the 19th Century American Postal Service and the building of the railroads in Europe. The Panama Canal and the U.S. space program would also appear to be programs that fulfill his criteria. Drucker argues that even if these criteria are fulfilled, over time, the program can be captured to serve social purposes other than those for which it was originally set up. The U.S. Postal Service is, in large part, now serving the social goal of minority employment—a laudable and important social goal but not the one for which it was established, namely the transfer of information. The program has been captured and inefficiencies have resulted. The British National Health Service has also been captured to serve the social goal of employment rather than timely, cost-effective delivery of health care, with the resulting queuing we are all familiar with. The single biggest opponent to reform of the British National Health Service has, at times, been labor unions, which have seen the service's goal as a provision of employment. A similar scenario is now playing itself out in New York City's Health and Hospital Corporation, where Mayor Giuliani's efforts at reasonable system consolidation and privatization are being strongly resisted by the labor unions.[10]

It is, I believe, for these reasons, implicitly and/or explicitly, that the bulk of the American people do not now favor a government-based, single-payer system and are searching for a different way of doing things. Among the options is "play or pay," also known as an employer mandate. Hawaii has had such a system since the early 1970s, antedating the federal ERISA legislation.[11] Its advocates allege that between 93 and 98 percent of the population is now covered by private health insurance as a result of the mandate, without ruinous taxation or costly job loss. Increasingly, however, voices are rising alleging that far less than these percentages of the population is actually covered and that jobs are leaving the islands. Governor Dukakis advocated an employer mandate during his presidential campaign in 1988. Massachusetts legislated and partially enacted such an approach, and Clinton began his campaign advocating such an approach.[3] It served as a mainstay of the Clinton plan, within an overall approach of managed competition.

Many centrist Democrats, let alone Republicans, are opposed to an employer mandate for fear that the requirement that employers pay a large proportion of the health insurance premium of their workers will cost jobs, particularly among small employers.[12] Some job loss will occur. From my perspective, however, the strongest argument against an employer mandate is that there is no such thing as an employer paying for anything. Martin Feldstein has shown that, within a few years, the entire cost of employer-paid health insurance will be borne by employees in the form of foregone earnings.[13] As the cost of health benefits to employers has risen in recent years, the wages they have paid have declined in real terms.[13,14]

Another state has pioneered in yet another mechanism to enhance financial access to health care.[15-18] The citizens of the state of Oregon voted to increase their taxes in the amount of 50 million dollars so that, when these dollars were matched by an equal amount of federal dollars, financial access to health care could be provided to approximately 25 percent of the state's more than 400,000 uninsured through an expanded Medicaid program.[17] Not simply content to expand health care spending, Oregonians desired the highest value for their scarce health care dollars and initiated a process of social choice wherein, in a studied and systematic fashion, medical interventions were ranked by diverse groups on the basis of their efficacy and cost effectiveness.[15] The various rankings were coalesced into a master ranking. Consistent with the desire to maximize the return on their investment in health care, they proceeded down the list of 688 interventions, agreeing to pay for each of them until, on the basis of anticipated costs, the money ran out.[16] They were able to get to item 568, paying for everything above that number but nothing below it. This process has been widely and appropriately designated as one of "rationing." The problem with this appellation, however, is that the program is viewed by many as a "take-away" program. In reality, it is a genuine and well-thought through effort to expand financial access to health care. Interventions not covered include antibiotic therapy for viral upper-respiratory infections, removal of benign moles, and intensive care for terminal illnesses with less than a small percentage chance of survival.[18] Home care and hospice care, however, are provided in the latter conditions. In vitro fertilization is also not covered because of its expense.

Rationing is implicit, one way or the other, in all of the 11 approaches to health care financing being discussed. What the Oregonians did was make it explicit. It is interesting that no other state is emulating the Oregon program. Their approach is unique. My bias, however, is that the Oregon experiment is an extremely valuable approach to have in one's programmatic armamentarium and that, at one level or another, because of one of its distinguishing attributes, it will play an important role in the ultimate resolution of our nation's effort to enhance financial access to health care. That distinguishing attribute separates the Oregon program from almost any other approach to expanding financial access to health care. The distinguishing attribute is that the Oregon plan is honest. The Oregonians had the honesty and the courage to say that they couldn't pay for it all. They could have chosen to raise their taxes $200 million and therein have made an attempt to cover all of the state's uninsured. They made a decision, however, that they could not afford to do so. They acknowledged financial limitations and chose to raise their taxes to the extent to which 25 percent would initially be covered and sought the most efficient use of these newly available dollars. The approach does have provisions for expanding access over time beyond these initial levels.

The Oregon approach differs markedly from that of those who in the most recent presidential campaign stated they would endeavor to expand financial access to all of the 37 million then uninsured and it wouldn't cost the American taxpayer anything. The bulk of the costs would be met through apocryphal savings from Medicare and Medicaid obtained through the alleged reduction in waste in these programs. This approach to the financing of such an expansion of access to health care is the Achilles heel of those advocating it. In fact, it is such a large Achilles heel, it is an Achilles torso. There are not the savings to be had from such an approach to cover the costs.[19,20] The Oregonians have set an enviable standard of integrity and are pioneering a very important course.

Because of the trade-off in health benefit costs and wage increases, many individuals support *mandated personal health insurance* as opposed to an employer mandate.[21] They argue that if individuals were required to purchase their own health insurance they would be far more cost-conscious in the process, selecting options with higher coinsurance and deductibles, as opposed to more expensive first-dollar coverage, in itself a cost-enhancing vehicle. They could use the resulting dollars saved in premiums to pay for the coinsurance and deductibles and the "noninsurable," routine medical occurrences. Such an approach would also enable workers to bargain once again for higher wages and use the money achieved through those wage increases to purchase insurance.

An option featuring elements of both the employer mandate and mandated personal health insurance is *Medical IRAs*.[22] This option retains the centrality of the employer. Rather than the employer purchasing employees' health insurance, however, it provides money to employees so that they can purchase their own health insurance. The money comes in the form of a tax-free account that is portable from job to job and into which the employee is able to plow back whatever annual savings accrue. With a favorable health history over time, the individual can become his or her own insurance company.

Under this option, individuals, by virtue of the ability to retain the savings, have an incentive to be cost-conscious and also retain the advantage of the tax exclusion of the cost of the health benefit.

In order for either the "play or pay" option or the "Medical IRA" option to be feasible, an individual must have a job. For mandated personal health insurance to work, an individual must have the means to purchase health insurance. Many individuals have neither. Therefore, many argue for *tax code tinkering* to provide a financial subsidy, possibly in the form of a voucher, for individuals/families below the federal poverty line and a tax rebate for individuals/families below some multiple of the poverty line. Most of the approaches to enhance financial access to health care entail some variation on the theme of tax code tinkering.[23-25] It is an unobtrusive way to expand the purchasing power of low-income individuals regarding health insurance.

Complementing the above option is reform of the health insurance market. Undertaken in a number of states, such as New York, insurance reform focuses on changing the rules regarding the underwriting and sales practices of private insurance companies: eliminating preexisting condition exclusions, mandating community rating, instituting open enrollment, and monitoring insurance premium increases. New York put such a program in place on April 1, 1993.[26] Premiums for older citizens fell while premiums for the younger rose. The overall impact on the number of insured over the first nine months of the program, however, was paradoxically a net decline of one percent. Even though the program expanded financial access to health care for older citizens, the rise in premium for younger individuals was sufficiently large to bring about the net one percent decline. Despite this paradoxical finding, reform of the private insurance market is seen by many as an unobtrusive mechanism to expand the number of individuals covered by health insurance without negatively affecting the long-term delivery of health care.

Paralleling reform of the private health insurance market is reform of our public insurance programs, specifically in the form of incremental enhancements. One of the most readily implementable enhancements is expanded Medicaid eligibility. In response to the Dukakis advocacy of "play or pay" during the 1988 campaign, the Bush administration realized it needed to do something to expand access. Accordingly, Medicaid eligibility was expanded, beginning with pregnant women and children under the age of one below an eligibility ceiling that was progressively expanded, along with the eligibility age of the child.[27] Eligibility was expanded to such an extent that, when President Bush left office, six million more people were eligible for Medicaid than when he took office.[28] These additional individuals represented a greater than 20 percent increase in the size of the population eligible for the Medicaid program. This increase in Medicaid eligibility was associated with a greater than 100 percent increase in program costs, dramatic evidence that efforts to expand access to health care are associated with substantial increases in the costs of that care.[19]

The last option on the above list is the *status quo*. In other words, do nothing. I call this the John Sununu solution. It was advocated during the Sununu tenure in the White House, with disastrous political consequence for the Bush administration. It is the least intrusive option. Interestingly, when I got to this eleventh option during a presentation to a state medical society, a physician rose to challenge my depiction of it as the least intrusive option. He stated: "How can you call it the least intrusive option? We have all these horrible government programs. They are killing my patients. I can't practice medicine the way I want. We have to get rid of them all." On the spot, I coined a twelfth and new option: *Darwinian survival.* Fortunately, the American people, through the development of the progenitors of Blue Cross and managed care in 1929, long ago rejected this option and, through the passage of Medicare and Medicaid in 1965, sought to establish a new equilibrium of expanded financial access to health care.

The growth of the cost of medical care since the mid-1960s (associated, by the way, with enormous and often-unacknowledged enhancements in the quality of medical care) has caused the growth in the number of the uninsured. With this increase in the number of the uninsured has come another rejection of the status quo and a search for a new and better way of doing things. Out of this search will come some amalgam of the above options. As the debate proceeds, it is becoming apparent that the weight of reform will center around items further down the list rather than those at the top. Whatever the amalgam, it will be organized explicitly or implicitly under the rubric of "managed competition."

I define managed competition as "the structured or regulated competition of managed care plans to achieve universal access to health care of appropriate quality at reasonable cost." There are a number of important concepts within this definition. One would like to think the concept of reasonable cost speaks for itself. By "appropriate quality," I am talking about everything that should be done being done, and everything that should not be done, not being done. Increasingly, we are developing technologies to distinguish appropriate from inappropriate care.

The concept of "structured or regulated competition" is difficult for many individuals to grasp. They ask how it is possible to have competition and regulation simultaneously. It is very easy. Indeed, the entire U.S. domestic economy might be viewed as a regulated competition with, for instance, antitrust legislation as one element of the structure or regulation to level the playing field and enhance the competitiveness of markets. The New York Stock Exchange is another example of a regulated or structured competition with very clear rules for the financial requirements for firms to be able to participate, rules for trading, oversight to ensure that those rules are followed, and clearly defined sanctions if they arc not. The games of organized sports are further examples of regulated competition.

The critical operative phrase in the above definition of managed competition is thus "managed care." What is managed care? Many people use the phrase "managed care" without ever attempting to define it. Indeed, until recently, there were many who believed the phrase could not be defined.[29] When it became obvious that a phrase as important as managed care needed to be defined, individuals attempted to define it in terms of the "things that made up the universe of managed care." Generally, these types of definitions entailed the development of a list that would span the spectrum of the "things" of managed care, arrayed from the least intrusive thing, e.g., indemnity insurance with a preadmission certification rider, to the most centralized of managed care entities, the staff-model HMO. This sort of definition is called an "ostensive definition," in which one defines a concept by pointing out the elements encompassed by that concept. For instance, if, using this approach, one were to attempt to define what is meant by a table to someone who had never seen a table, one could point to a variety of tables and the individual would intuit what a table was. What we need for managed care is a conceptual definition, indeed, even a strategic one, both to enable one to understand the very essence of the concept as well as begin to respond strategically to it—to, at a minimum, reduce the threats it might pose and optimally to capitalize on the opportunities that it presents.

My definition of managed care is as follows: "Managed care is the process of the application of standard business practices to the delivery of health care in the traditions of the American free enterprise system." First and foremost, managed care is a process. It is not a collection of things. Rather, it is change itself. This change is inexorable. There is, and will be, no rollback to a preexisting status quo. This is so because of deep-seated forces in the American business and consumer communities and because of the performance of managed care in meeting the needs of these communities.[30-33] In fact, in endorsing managed care as the centerpiece of his approach to health care reform, President Clinton was moving to endorse reality.

Managed care is a uniquely American invention. And, like other great American inventions, such as blue jeans, fast food, and rock and roll, it will ultimately grow to dominate the world. This is so because there really is no alternative to managed care to rationalize the cost and quality of care. Knowledge is sufficiently imperfect and difficult to come by in the market for health care services to render regulation as the primary vehicle for such rationalization ineffectual. "By the application of standard business practices" is meant the application of the invisible hand of Adam Smith to that sector of our economy that we call health care, currently 14-15 percent of our gross domestic product, to discipline that sector. This sector has heretofore been decentralized and unorganized. If one wished to be pejorative, which I am not, one might also say that this sector has been disorganized. The U.S. health delivery system has, in fact, grown as a result of very specific historical forces and economic incentives that have created the organizational structures and means of financing that we have today.

The disciplining of this sector by the invisible hand of Adam Smith entails squeezing out of it the excess supply and excess profits that are in it so that they may be used for more productive social purposes. This is what markets do in general and is why many reasonable citizens feel they are our best social rationing mechanism. They allow for the collective expression of the preferences of millions upon millions of individuals for the desired quantity of specific products and specific services at specific prices. These specific products and services are thus brought forth in appropriate quantities and appropriate prices such that equilibria are reached and utilities satisfied. Markets are not perfect, however. Hence, the need for regulation to ensure that all individuals are able to participate in them and that socially beneficial rules are followed. Health care is now being disciplined as all other American industries, with one exception, have heretofore been disciplined. That remaining industry is the market for higher education, where college and university tuitions have risen seemingly without any acknowledgements of limits. This market is now also beginning to be disciplined, with consolidations of departments within universities, lay-offs of personnel, etc.

The *sine qua non* of the process of managed care is the presence of management in the health field as it has never before existed. Management to make decisions regarding the appropriate mix of the factors of production to achieve the desired health outcomes of a defined population for which management is now accountable–accountable from both an economic and a quality perspective to produce the desired health outcomes in the most cost-effective manner and at the highest level of quality possible. The essence of managed care is management's choosing among a mix of possible inputs to achieve the highest possible quality of care for the defined population for which it is now accountable at the least possible cost.

Management has existed in health care before. There has been management within an individual physician's office. There has been management within an individual hospital, within an individual nursing home, pharmaceutical firm, ambulatory surgery center, hospice, etc. But never before has there been management looking down over these various factors of production and systematically evaluating the health care production process to chose just the right level of each one of these factors to achieve the desired health outcomes at the least possible cost. What we are talking about is the studied and systematic substitution of a day of hospitalization with an ambulatory visit, a day in the intensive care unit with a day in a hospice, a surgical procedure with a pharmaceutical compound, a visit to a physician specialist with a visit to a primary care physician, a visit to a primary care physician with a visit to an advanced practice nurse, or, if one wants to become truly pyrotechnic, care by a registered nurse with care by a licensed practical nurse.

I stress that this process is "in the traditions of the American free enterprise system" for a number of reasons. The first is to accentuate that there are, and will be, in any capitalistic process, winners and losers. Capitalism is not a warm and fuzzy thing. This fact is becoming increasingly apparent to the citizens of Eastern Europe and the former Soviet Union. In fact, it is quite ironic that in the cradle of democracy of Poland, the Gdansk shipyards, substantial lay-offs are now being experienced. The reason for the lay-offs is no one is buying the ships of inferior quality being produced in those yards. Similarly, a steel mill now in the Czech republic that used to count its workers in the thousands does so now in the tens because no one is buying the inferior quality steel that it is producing. It will have to retool to match the quality of its competitors or will soon be out of business.

As production processes become standardized across an industry and costs approximate each other, the product-differentiating factor determining which organization does or does not survive is quality. This latter attribute of competitive markets is often not appreciated by caregivers, possibly because they are now being buffeted, and in some cases relentlessly so, by the cost-reducing behavior of managed care organizations, possibly because of the nature of their professional education, and possibly because of the fact that, in the past, they have been somewhat shielded from these markets. The American people do not buy junk. One need only look at the history of the American automobile industry in the second half of this century to realize this fact. The personal computer industry also is rife with examples of firms that are no longer in existence because of their inability to match the quality of their competitors.

An important lesson for health care and managed care can be drawn here. As the cost structure of production processes becomes equilibrated across competitors in a given industry, the product-differentiating and survival-determining variable is quality.

This lesson has not yet been learned by all managed care plans and is a source of concern to health care professionals and to many of our citizenry. The plans have not yet learned the lesson because we have not yet begun to approximate the cost-effectiveness equilibrium. The most difficult variable to predict in competitive markets is the variable of time. We don't know how long it will take to reach the new equilibrium, and the road to it is often a bumpy one, with excesses and deficiencies along the way. Regulators often believe that they can mandate that a given equilibrium begin on a specific date. (Refreshingly, increasing numbers of individuals are less sanguine about the stability of regulators to mandate such equilibria.) Such alleged precision is not a property of free markets.

As we perfect our ability to measure outcomes of care and the quality of processes leading to those outcomes, we increasingly will have reliable and valid data on the quality of care within plans widely available to consumers to make informed decisions on quality across health plans. Increasingly, consumers will make their decisions regarding health care plans on the basis of those data.

It is not unusual, when I speak to groups of physicians, to have one state: "But Dr. Hughes, this is all corporate stuff. Where does the compassionate physician in his or her office fit in all this?" The answer is: "Quite centrally!" As the production process is studied and made increasingly more efficient, all managed care organizations (assuming they are employing the same management practices) will ultimately approach the same equilibrium with respect to cost. The product-differentiating attribute of competing managed care plans then becomes quality. Central to this quality is the compassionate physician in his or her office, caring for the medical and personal needs of patients. The survival of any managed care plan is, among other things, a function of increased market share and membership retention. Critical to both of these survival strategies is consumer satisfaction, and central to that is a satisfied and professionally fulfilled caregiver.

If managed care organizations do not now appreciate the importance of satisfied caregivers, and there is ample evidence to suggest that not all of them do, they ultimately will. If they do not, they will be driven out of business. I know of no article in the entire industrial organization or organization behavior literature that suggests that firms with unhappy workers do well.[34] The ultimate success of a managed care organization will be a function of the extent to which it embraces and supports professionalism of its caregivers and their efforts to provide high-quality care, not only along the technical dimension but also along the dimension of humane and compassionate care. Our ability to measure consumer satisfaction and provider satisfaction is becoming increasingly sophisticated and will ultimately be standardized across plans. These data will be widely disseminated, and critical decisions will made on the basis of them.[35]

Given the centrality of quality and cost to the success of health care organizations of the future and the critical management processes that must be undertaken to achieve the highest quality and the lowest cost, the primacy of the physician manager emerges. The physician manager is the one individual who, by virtue of both professional training as a caregiver and management education and experience can adequately assess the trade-offs in cost and quality and move toward the achievement of a new equilibrium where maximum quality will be available at the least possible cost. I stress in the above sentence the critical importance of both clinical and management training, for they are both required for success in the challenge ahead. Combining them effectively in the physician manager creates a new entity at a critical time in the history of American health care when attention needs to be given to both cost and quality as two interrelated phenomena. A well-trained physician manager would appear to be well positioned to accept the social challenge occasioned by the ascendancy of management in health care and to satisfy society's needs for effective decision making in health care.

It is not by chance that some of our most successful managed care organizations now have physician managers as their CEOs (or that others have other caregivers, e.g., pharmacists, as their CEOs). We will increasingly see physicians tapped to lead our nation's health care organizations. As managers, they will not necessarily be any less demanding in their exactitude regarding the requests and preferences of their physician colleagues, but they will be able to assess these requests both intuitively and explicitly in ways not possible by those lacking clinical training.

References

1. Pear, R. "Increase Found in Those without Health Coverage." *New York Times*, Dec. 15, 1993, p. A1.

2. Eckholm, E. "Frayed Nerves of People without Health Coverage: The Uninsured: Who Are They?" *New York Times*, July 11, 1994.

3. Blendon, R., and others. "Caring for the Uninsured and the Underinsured: The Uninsured and the Debate Over the Repeal of the Massachusetts Universal Health Care Law." *JAMA* 267(8):1113-7, Feb. 26, 1992.

4. Dowd, M. "Strong Support for Health Plans." *New York Times*, July 20, 1994, p. A1.

5. Sieb, G., and Rogers, D. "Public, in Health-Care Poll, Disapproves of Performance of Clinton and Congress." *Wall Street Journal*, July 28, 1994, p. A16.

6. Evans, R., and others. "Controlling Health Expenditures—The Canadian Reality." *New England Journal of Medicine* 320(9):571-7, March 2, 1989.

7. Marmor, T., and Godfrey, J. "Canada's Medical System Is a Model. That's a Fact." *New York Times*, July 23, 1992, Editorial Page.

8. "Canada's No Medical Model." *New York Times*, May 26, 1992, p. A14.

9. Drucker, P. *The New Realities: In Government and Politics, in Economics and Business, in Society and World View.* New York, N.Y.: Harper and Row, 1989.

10. McKinley, J. "Giuliani Says Council Undermines Labor Talks." *New York Times*, April 29, 1994, p. B3.

11. Worthington, R. "Hawaii Tries Health Coverage for All." *Chicago Tribune*, Sept. 6, 1992, Sec. 1, p. 23.

12. Hennenberger, M. "Small-Business Owners Shudder About Insurance." *New York Times*, July 21, 1994, p. A1.

13. Feldstein, J. "Clinton's Hidden Health Tax." *Chicago Tribune*, Sept. 6, 1992, Sec. 1, p. 23.

14. Toner, R. "House Democrats Unveil Proposal for Health Bill." *New York Times*, July 30, 1994, p. A1.

15. Steinbrook, R., and Lo, B. "Sounding Board: The Oregon Medicaid Demonstration Project—Will It Provide Adequate Medical Care?" *New England Journal of Medicine* 326(5):340-44, Jan. 30, 1992.

16. "Health Care Overhaul Is Approved in Oregon." *New York Times*, Aug. 6, 1993, p. A18.

17. Chase, M. "Oregon's New Health Rationing Means More Care for Some but Less for Others." *Wall Street Journal*, Jan. 28, 1994, p. B1.

18. Janofsky, M. "Oregon Starts to Extend Health Care." *New York Times*, Feb. 19, 1994, p. A6.

19. Hughes, E. "The Challenges Facing American Medicine: The Search for A New Equilibrium and Its Implications for Physician Executives." In *New Leadership in Health Care Management: The Physician Executive*, First Edition, W. Curry, Ed., Tampa, Fla.: American College of Physician Executives, 1988.

20. Feldstein, M. "The Health Plan's Financing Gap." *Wall Street Journal*, Sept. 29, 1993, p. A12.

21. Becker, G. "Economic Viewpoint: Make Families Cough Up for Medical Coverage." *Business Week*, Sept. 9, 1991, p. 18.

22. Gramm, P. "Why We Need Medical Savings Accounts." *New England Journal of Medicine* 330(24):1752-3, June 16, 1994.

23. "The Details: The State of the Health Care Debate: Five Committees, Four Bills." *New York Times*, July 5, 1994, p. A9.

24. Clymer, A. "Senate's Leader Unveils His Plan for Health Care." *New York Times*, Aug. 3, 1994, p. A1.

25. Borkowski, M. "Compare and Contrast: How the House and Senate Bills Stack Up Against the President's Original Proposal." *New York Times*, Aug. 3, 1994, p. A10.

26. Scism, L. "New York Finds Fewer People Have Health Insurance A Year After Reform." *Wall Street Journal*, May 27, 1994, p. A2.

27. Tolchin, M." "Government Seeks to Extend Eligibility for Some Medicaid." *New York Times*, June 21, 1989, p. A15.

28. "Medicaid Cost Jumped 25 Percent in '92 Fiscal Year, U.S. Says." *New York Times*, March 19, 1993, p. A14.

29. Traska, M. "Defining Managed Care." *HMO Magazine*, Jan.-Feb. 1991, p.7.

30. Winslow, R. "`Managed-Care Networks Show Promise." *Wall Street Journal*, March 24, 1992, p. B1.

31. Lawrence, D. The Market Is Already Doing It." *Wall Street Journal*, March 16, 1994, p. A18.

32. Winslow, R. "Market Forces Are Starting to Produce Significant Cuts in Health-Care Costs." *Wall Street Journal*, June 21, 1994, p. A2.

33. Winslow, R. "Performance of HMOs Is Rated Higher Than Fee-for-Service Plans in Study." *Wall Street Journal*, June 21, 1994, p. A2.

34. Winslow, R. "Major Employers Fear New Restraints: Companies Fret Over Controls, Increased Costs." *Wall Street Journal*, Sept. 13, 1993, p. B1.

35. Winslow, R. "Accreditation Group Releases Its List of the Status of 118 Health-Care Plans." *Wall Street Journal*, June 2, 1994, p. B8.

Edward F.X. Hughes, MD, MPH, FACPE, is Professor of Health Services Management and Management and Strategy in the J.L. Kellogg Graduate School of Management, and Professor of Preventive Medicine, in the Medical School, Northwestern University, Evanston, Illinois. He is the founder of the joint MD/Masters of Management degree program at Northwestern.

The Future of Medicine

*by Eugene Schneller, PhD,
Pamela Hood-Szivek, MHSA,
and Robert G. Hughes, PhD*

Background

To understand the fundamental changes occurring in medicine today, it is essential to understand how the profession reached its current status. The history of the medical profession in the United States is one of an autonomous and predominantly self-regulating group of individuals. Through the sixties and seventies, physicians maintained a virtual monopoly over the provision of services and defined, within the profession, the conditions and content of practice.[1,2,3] Their position of dominance, which had been established earlier in the century, was rarely contested by competing occupations, patients, payers, policy makers, or organizations in which clinical work took place. Confidence in the abilities of the profession and in the abilities of its members to intervene effectively in the illness process helped to maintain medicine's position in society. Professional autonomy and self-regulation were further supported by the belief that medical work differed from other forms of work. Each patient was believed to represent a unique case—and the degree of uncertainty associated with the application of medical knowledge to a particular person meant that accountability for outcomes remained with the individual physician and, to a lesser extent, the physician's peers.

Pressures from both inside and outside the system have contributed to substantial changes in American medicine in the past two decades. The autonomy of physicians in their work and their influence on relationships with their patients and with hospitals have been increasingly challenged. For a variety of reasons detailed in this chapter, the very nature of the hospital as an institution of care has also changed. Although it is impossible to predict with confidence what medical practice will be like in the future, it will certainly be different. Medical practice will also be affected by changes in the structure of the health care delivery system. To date, these changes have occurred primarily in the physician's workplace. We have also seen tremendous changes in the hospital—its organization, mission, and relationship with the human and nonhuman capital necessary to deliver health services.

In the fall of 1993, as this chapter was drafted, the nation appeared to be on the verge of health reform. The newly elected Clinton administration, having successfully passed a controversial tax bill, introduced its plan for a version of health care reform based on managed competition—a regulated free market approach that calls for accountable health plan (AHP) providers to secure contracts for patient services through negotiations with large groups called alliances or health insurance purchasing cooperatives (HIPCs). In the administration's scheme, accountable health plans could be offered by a variety of different sponsors, including HMOs, IPAs, and hospitals. Although there have been many alternatives suggested for financing the emerging system, funding through a payroll tax on employers and employees seems likely. A significant portion of managed competition would be financially supported by employer contributions and structured around a variety of managed care mechanisms that use financial incentives to influence physicians' clinical decisions. The plan is to maintain an employee-based financing system, which will continue to affect the organization of the health care delivery system.

One of the goals of health reform is to provide universal coverage for all Americans through a defined package of care. At this point, the contents for such a plan are very uncertain and controversial. Some are arguing for a bare-bones health plan with no frills, low-cost policies that may include only several days of hospitalization. Others argue for comprehensive care, including coverage for pharmaceuticals, long-term care, and even transplants. Whatever the benefits package, it will likely become the universal minimum, with some employers offering enhancements and additional services available for private paying patients. Whatever health care reform is initiated at the federal level, it will take time for these changes to reshape the structure of health care delivery and ultimately the practice of medicine. Nevertheless, extensive changes in the organization of health care are under way in anticipation of some sort of fundamental reform. Thus, the effects of health care reform have begun, and the changes will definitely affect medical practice. This chapter will demonstrate the trends in medical work and opportunities for the profession in this new uncertain environment.

The purpose of this chapter is to:

■ Highlight the major factors in the historical development of the medical profession.

■ Specify the changes in the system that have led to changes in the relationships between physicians and hospitals.

■ Detail the role of organized patient agents, and the reconceptualization of medical work by these entities.

■ Note how physicians may respond to change and develop new roles to cope with these challenges.

■ Present an alternative view of hospitals and physicians that focuses on resources and their scarcity.

■ Identify a number of alternate managerial structures for hospitals and their physicians for the successful management of health care systems in the next decade.

Physicians and Hospitals: Two Streams of Development

Traditionally, we have thought about physicians and hospitals separately. Physicians are viewed first and foremost as members of a profession. Physicians developed as solo entrepreneurs. Their organizational bases, at least through most of the Nineteenth Century, were their offices or clinics or simply the bags that carried their nostrums and rudimentary instruments. Most of their success or failure as healers and businessmen depended on their ability to attract and retain patients.

Hospitals, on the other hand, are viewed as complex organizations, with a sociological emphasis on their extensive division of labor and complexity and an economic emphasis on their behavior as firms and on the ways their behavior deviates from various normative expectations.[4] Historically, hospitals served the role of isolating the sick and were often supported by philanthropy.[5] These institutions were primarily havens for destitute and marginal members of society who had no alternative places to live and die. They were not viewed as advantageous, nor were they numerous. In 1873, the United States had only 149 hospitals (including mental institutions).

The period between the 1870s and 1915 was a formative one for the American hospital.[6,7,8] Important scientific developments in areas such as sanitation increased the likelihood of actually benefitting patients. By 1923, the United States had 6,763 hospitals, mostly what have become to be known as "community" or "general acute care" facilities. By this time, many physicians were using hospitals as their "workshops," but the profession did not exercise direct control over the organization of hospitals. In general, the hospital was governed by nonphysician community leaders and managed by lay administrators and nurses.

This formative period laid the basic framework of hospital-physician relationships that have persisted until today. The primary structural arrangement between hospitals and physicians was the medical staff, an organizational mechanism that developed to accommodate the interests of both hospitals and physicians. It allowed physicians to conduct their work in hospitals. They could make diagnostic and treatment decisions with the use of hospital resources, charge separately for those services, and work with few constraints imposed by the hospital. Most physicians practiced medicine as solo practitioners, in partnerships, or in small groups. With the exception of hospital-based specialists and the few who joined large groups, the medical staff mechanism allowed physicians to expand their entrepreneurial practice of fee-for-service medicine into the hospital.

For hospitals, the medical staff mechanism fostered the use of their facilities by physicians, which in turn strongly influenced where patients were admitted. The formal hospital medical staff also developed out of a concern for quality by functioning as a means for a hospital to monitor the physicians who used its facilities. For both parties, the traditional, autonomous medical staff provided a flexible organizational structure that allowed many substantive issues to remain informal, and thus more resistant to outside influence.

What factors contributed to the establishment of this unique organizational arrangement between physicians and hospitals? An initial factor was the transfer of authority to admit patients from trustees, who exercised lay authority based on social, economic, and moral criteria as well as the health of the patient, to physicians, who exercised professional authority based on clinical judgment.[8] Second, growth in the system led to excess bed capacity. Physician admission decisions, grounded in medical diagnoses, simultaneously reinforced their professional claim to define illness and to determine the illnesses that required hospital admission.

By the turn of the century, physicians were firmly in control of patient admission decisions. This constituted an important source of power in establishing favorable structural arrangements with hospitals. Hospitals and physicians were to become mutually dependent. As institutions were beginning to need financial support in addition to eleemosynary sources, hospitals needed the patients that physicians controlled. Physicians wanted access to hospitals, in part because it provided the means to practice a brand of medicine that would yield benefits for patients, and in part because such practice also was often more lucrative than office practice. Early on, some physicians exchanged charity care for the opportunity to learn new medical techniques by treating a hospital's indigent patients. As physicians brought their paying patients to the hospital, hospitals began to augment their revenues, but they also allowed physicians to charge separately for their services in the hospital. The insurance arrangements that eventually developed, such as Blue Cross and Blue Shield plans, reinforced this separation by agreeing to separately reimburse hospital and physician services.

Underlying the physician orientation to the hospital at the beginning of the century was a democratic, egalitarian ideology within the profession, as promulgated by the American Medical Association (AMA).[9] Substantial attention has been given to AMA exclusionary activities directed at delineating what constitutes a physician, clearly differentiating the profession from other health occupations and healers. But a complementary theme at this time was the preference for minimizing differences within the profession. This fostered a policy preference for the right of all physicians to admit patients and perform operations. The AMA, strongly influenced by general practitioners, who would be the "losers" in any system that recognized status differentials, did not want specialization within the profession along the lines of hospital and nonhospital physicians, as had occurred in England and European countries.[9] Reinforcing this position was the argument that the doctor-patient relationship was sacrosanct, and thus quality and continuity of care were preserved when the physician could follow the patient into the hospital.

Throughout the century, the relative bargaining power of hospitals and physicians favored physicians. Most potent was physicians' ability to use an alternative facility if one hospital instituted policies not to their liking. Because capital requirements earlier in the century were not large, doctors, in extreme situations, could own their own hospitals. Hospitals, on the other hand, were dependent on physicians for patients and had no similar alternatives. In Hirschman's terms, physicians could exercise both a voice and an exit option in their negotiations with hospitals, the potential of the latter strengthening the former.[10]

The medical staff (the collective group of physicians approved to practice within a given hospital) became an organizational affirmation of practices that were already in use. Physicians who met a set of qualifications could admit patients to a hospital, use its equipment and staff, and charge for services separately. The structural relationships between hospitals and physicians thus avoided the organizational form that was transforming other sectors of society: bureaucracy.[11] Rather than being employed by a hospital and thus part of a single, formal authority structure, the physician could be, and often was, a member of more than one hospital medical staff. These patterns of activity have increased over the years. Now, more than 90 percent of physicians have hospital admitting privileges, and the typical physician is a member of at least two medical staffs.[12] For all office-based physicians, over one-third of patient time is spent in the hospital. The economic benefits derived from hospital practice are reflected in the higher earnings of hospital-based physicians when compared to their office-based colleagues.[13] Overall, it is clear that hospitals and physicians have been interdependent since the emergence of the modern hospital and that their interdependency has increased up through the present.

When hospitals and physicians have been considered together, the emphasis has been on the internal dynamics between them and not on their mutual dependence on external resources. Smith, in a classic article,[14] described the hospital as having two lines of authority: administrative and medical. Subsequent approaches have, in effect, built on this core observation and formulated models of the hospital as a physician's workshop[15] or as actually containing two firms (with the medical staff as the demand firm and the administration as the supply firm) in one organization.[16] Most recently, efforts to understand the factors contributing to high costs resulted in the conclusion that hospitals are characterized by a "power equilibrium" in which physicians dominate.[17] Overall, these and other analyses have examined hospitals and physicians by looking at the internal organization in order to understand the outputs or consequences of their combined behavior along some dimension such as costs,[17] quality,[18] or profit maximization.[15]

The history of physicians and hospitals demonstrates how a set of relationships evolved into two parallel lines of authority. The medical staff became a powerful group that successfully controlled the content and conditions of practice. The management system maintained the doctor's workshop by balancing the books and overseeing the day-to-day management of the plant. Initially, no third party shaped the work of physicians or the behavior of the hospital industry. Physicians, through their control of admission and discharge of patients, defined the utilization patterns that accounted for the vast majority of health care expenditures. Interactions between the two decision systems centered on equipment purchases and space allocations during a time of continued growth. This expansion was supported by a cost-based reimbursement system.

Changes in the System

The system of relationships between hospitals and physicians was destined to change due to external forces. An important step in the change was the expansion and formalization of dependence on third parties.[1] Perhaps this became most salient in the mid-1960s with the government's increased involvement in paying for health care services through Medicare and Medicaid. These programs, representing an infusion of dollars into the ongoing system of medical practice, were intended to make services available to a wider range of the population.[19] Other problems addressed programmatically included a shortage of providers, maldistribution of resources, and duplication of services in many areas of the nation. The initial approaches to correcting these problems included expansion of the physician supply through established and new medical schools, design and implementation of peer review processes to combat fraud, development of alternative settings of care, and development of new health practitioner occupations to increase the flow of services to the medically disadvantaged. All of these initially reinforced the physician's claim to dominance in the system. The programs, which remained in place throughout the seventies and into the beginning of the eighties, laid the foundation for subsequent changes.

Perhaps the most important hint of what was to come was the passing of Public Law 93-641, the Health Planning and Resources Development Act of 1974. This legislation established Health Systems Agencies (HSAs), which implemented certification-of-need legislation that mandated state approval for expensive medical equipment purchases or construction and therefore encouraged the regionalization of health services and a more rational distribution of resources.[20] HSAs did not directly interfere with physicians' work or advocate the growth of alternative services outside the hospital. Inherent in their mandate, however, was the belief that the health care system had inordinate duplication of services and often emphasized services that catered to the demands of the physician, who, after all, would fill available beds and use state-of-the-art (and thus increasingly expensive) technology, and this meant using available beds.[21] HSAs also assumed that hospitals, regardless of their ownership, would act out of self-interest rather than community interest. An important component of this self-interest was providing the "total workshop" for its physicians.[22] If system rationality could not be achieved by collaboration between physicians and hospitals, the "state" would use its regulatory arm to achieve the systemwide balance necessary for an effective health care system. This legislation symbolized a shift in federal policies away from infusing more resources, with few constraints on their use, into a health care system organized to accommodate the historical interests of providers. The future would be one in which the government and other payers attempted to shape the system and influence how resources would be used.

The "crisis of cost," however, continued unabated as the driving force of change. Regulatory responses were quickly joined, and then supplanted, by market-oriented approaches to controlling costs. Krause's[23] "radical" and quickly dismissed statement, that health care would not substantially change until corporate America recognized the financial magnitude of the health care system and its influence on the economy, soon became conventional wisdom. The public and private sectors demanded greater accountability of providers and greater control over the distribution of health care dollars by directly influencing utilization patterns. At first, the demand for cost containment was translated into the design and development of a new variety of "cost-effective" and "cost-conscious" health care delivery organizations—especially the staff-model HMO.[24] Acting on the belief that these settings would give attention to prevention, efficiency, and economy as they attempted to provide comprehensive care on a capitation basis, the federal government provided numerous initiatives for the development of such "alternative health care delivery organizations." At the same time, business coalitions attempted to influence health care policy on both the national and the local levels.

And in some communities, interactions between the business and the health care sectors were characterized by substantial conflict.[25] Nonetheless, these coalitions were not effective in controlling costs.[26]

These actions, alone, did relatively little to change the power of physicians or hospitals. The hospital industry successfully acted, during the Carter Administration, to head off cost containment efforts that would have substantially restricted hospital spending, and physicians continued to control the majority of activity within the system. Increasingly, it became clear that mechanisms that would directly affect the physician's behavior as well as more directly affect the hospital's incentives to constrain costs would be considered and, in some cases, adopted.

The eighties signaled a new domestic policy orientation: the desire to change American medicine. The Reagan administration saw many of the regulatory mechanisms and government programs of the sixties and seventies as having obstructed the principles of the marketplace from accomplishing their purported goal of balancing supply and demand and resulting in "natural" cost containment.[26] The new ideology of competition, deregulation, privatization, and monetarization[27,28] in Washington was supported by many hospital administrators who believed that HSAs had stifled creativity and interfered with their ability to maintain a loyal medical staff. The implicit message from the federal government was that physicians and administrators, under current incentives and multiple, fragmented delivery systems, could not make the truly important resource allocation decisions within the whole system.

During this time, rapid advances in technology went hand in hand with further specialization and subspecialization within medicine. The professional identity of medicine began to fragment as specialties competed for technology and space resources, including hospital beds. AMA membership and support fell as specialty organizations grew. Group practices were organized along specialty lines. Although physicians individually still held enormous power on the wards, their collective power decreased, as did their influence in hospital boardrooms.

Dismantling of controls stimulated a period of renewed entrepreneurial activity for for-profit and not-for-profit hospitals. It was also a period characterized by physicians' beginning to compete vigorously with their own hospitals by providing outpatient care and enhanced competition through technology acquisition by physician groups. HMO providers began to signal to the entire medical community that many of the earlier rules for doing business were about to change. Contracting for patient care was suddenly characterized by intense negotiations over the cost, quality, and content of care.

The eighties were also a period of new sorts of regulation, such as the adoption by Medicare of diagnosis-related groups (DRGs). DRGs, clusters of reasonably closely related diagnoses for hospital admissions, would serve as the basis for Medicare's prospective payment system (PPS). By establishing predetermined fixed payments to the hospital for a given admission—regardless of the patient's length of stay—hospitals presumably had incentives to be more efficient and develop schemes to discharge patients who did not truly need inpatient care. Just as important as the impact on hospital behavior, but often overlooked, was medicine's ability to begin to predict and control what it would spend for hospital care. Other regulatory changes occurred in states such as New York, where prospective pricing was adopted through an all-payer system. Insurers and other payers adopted governmentally developed payment schedules as the basis for their negotiations. The overall cost of medical care, however, continued largely unaffected by these changes. Most insurers sustained a more traditional charge-based reimbursement system for hospital services and introduced few effective controls on physician charges.

The prospective payment system stimulated several unintended consequences. It accelerated and highlighted the practice of cost shifting, or charging some (usually private) payers more to offset lower payments from Medicare. It also encouraged the development of physician practice outside the hospital in keeping with new technology that did not need to be located in the hospital. Although many of these practices were established jointly by physicians and hospitals, physicians increasingly acted unilaterally and became direct competitors with the organizations that had been the sites of their workshops.

Procompetition policies resulted in the dismantling of most health systems agencies and encouraged the growth of alternative health care delivery mechanisms. It was argued that the dynamics of a free marketplace would achieve systemic goals where regulatory efforts had apparently failed. The marketplace that was to emerge in the eighties, however, would be far from what many had envisioned as a classical "free market."[29] The aforementioned programs to constrain institutional behavior did not directly address the behavior of those who controlled the use of resources within the system—physicians. It was recognized that need for services was difficult to determine and the actual efficacy of medical procedures was increasingly difficult to define. By the late seventies, the cumulative evidence of small area variation studies alerted policymakers to the fact that the substantial variation in rates of hospitalization and surgery, patient outcomes, average length of stay, and cost per case were reason for concern.[30] Such observations reinforced the belief that the traditional fee-for-service, retrospective reimbursement system offered few incentives for cost-effective behavior—on the part of physicians or hospitals. Suggested changes for controlling costs focused on the need to constrain the flow of patients and the funds that fueled the growth of medical care. Strategies designed to reshape the behavior of physicians and hospitals included:

- Movement of large numbers of patients and physicians out of the traditional doctor/patient/hospital relationship into managed care systems such as HMOs and PPOs, thereby instituting agents other than patients and physicians to serve the various interests involved.

- Reconceptualization of medical work around a more industrial model and thus restructuring of the basis for reimbursing hospitals for the provision of care.

The eighties were an era in which managed care became the "codeword" in reference to procedures, organizations, and individuals, other than attending physicians, becoming involved in planning and monitoring the health care of patients. At first, managed care could be seen as an active strategy that established a new decision-making framework on the relationships between patients and health care providers by going between patients and their providers to evaluate, plan, and authorize utilization prior to, concurrent with, and following the provision of health care services. This review often was a nursing function, and, as nurses moved into these roles, the power balance shifted and professional tensions between physicians and nurses increased. (It is ironic that this also exacerbated the nursing shortage.) As we shall see below, emerging managerial and policy strategies would become much more radical in their approach to change—leading to a redefinition of the traditional relationships between medical and administrative staffs.

Medical Resources and Their Scarcity

The historical relationships among physicians, hospitals, and patients are logical if hospitals and physicians are the scarce resources around which the system is organized (i.e., the scarcity in the system is in the human and technological resources of the medical care system itself). A fundamental shift has occurred in the U.S. health care system. The predominant pattern of medical care organization, based on the aforementioned hospital-physician nexus of technology and expertise, is replaced by the growing scarcity of paying patients. That is, the resources external to the medical care system that are the "inputs" essential for the medical care system to operate have become scarce relative to providers, and therefore constitute an important limiting factor in medical care organization.[31] The relative scarcity of paying patients strengthens the role of any organized patient agent that represents them in bargaining with providers for services.

Our health care system still needs the resources it has always needed to function. In the past, however, attention has been paid to the supply of physicians, facilities, and knowledge. These were the scarce resources around which the organization of medical care evolved. However, the relative abundance of these resources, especially physicians and facilities, coupled with the increasing scarcity of paying patients, presages new dynamics in the ongoing transformation of the health care system. This suggests that a fresh perspective may be useful in understanding these changes.

Physicians and hospitals have been the primary powers in determining the organization and financing of medical care. When medical insurance first became widespread and Medicare and Medicaid were created, payers had no intention of changing the financing of health services in any significant way. It is ironic that the growth of insurance fueled a growth in the volume of health services provided until cost escalation made basic services unaffordable to the uninsured and led to insurance pricing that resulted in a growing group of individuals, often referred to as the "notch group," with no insurance. This notch group, occupied by those who were employed but not offered insurance through their employers or through other family members as well as others who failed to qualify for Medicaid programs, grew by the early nineties to over 37 million individuals. With no insurance or regular provider of care, members of this group frequently postponed preventive and primary care services until illness was advanced and received their health care in emergency departments and other high cost/inappropriate delivery settings. System costs would not come into control unless access to appropriate care was achieved.

Payers soon realized that the health care industry was growing unrestrained and attempted to affect financing of medical care without intruding on the organization of how that care was delivered. We have shown the interconnection of organization and financing and some of the reasons these attempts by the federal government and industry failed. As payers were reluctant, for a variety of legal, political, and organizational reasons, to come directly between patients and their physicians, intermediaries arose. These organizations were usually sponsored by payers but sometimes by hospitals or physician groups and were to act as patient agents in the financing and organization of health care services.

Managed Care and the Rise of Organized Patient Agents

Patient agents have joined hospitals and physicians as a third source of power in the health care system. Organized patient agents may be any formalized entity that directly or indirectly controls the flow of patients to providers.[32] Medicare took on the role of patient agent with the introduction of PPS. Many employers, insurers, unions, and state and local governments have created or encouraged the creation of such organizations. HMO-enabling legislation set the stage for a proliferation of managed care plans that fall under this definition. In the near future, what the Clinton Administration has labeled "alliances" or health care purchasing cooperatives may take on this role for a large portion of the population. The label "organized patient agents" signifies the important characteristics of these actors:

■ Patient agent organizations usually have contractual relationships with patients, payers, and providers, although they may also fill payer or provider roles themselves. Thus, they manage the relationships among patients, payers, physicians, and hospitals and attempt to balance the incentives in the overall system.

■ Patient agents are organized in some form that is expected to endure and have a means of systematically influencing patient flows to providers (e.g., via payment mechanisms).

■ Patient agent organizations are the organizational analog to the physician role as "patient agent." They will act on behalf of individual patients (which will often coincide with their emerging institutional missions) in the organization and financing of medical care, just as physicians act on behalf of individual patients in the clinical realm.

■ Patient agent organizations are in the business of developing resource allocation and service delivery standards and policies for their populations, rather than making all decisions on a case-by-case basis.

Although some organizations, such as staff-model HMOs, may fulfill both patient agent as well as provider roles, it is important to distinguish between actions that are aimed at managing the flow of patients and the actual structure of the delivery system. Organizations act as patient agents as they provide the mediating structures between the systematic interests of payers, patients, physicians, hospitals, and other provider entities. In somewhat different language, patient agent organizations bring the divergent interests of insurers (including those organized by government), the public, hospitals, and physicians into the spotlight by structuring systems with opposing financial incentives for different actors in the system in an effort to maintain checks and balances in the system. The techniques employed by patient agent organizations include:

- Contractual discounts or fee schedules between payers and providers.

- Cost and risk sharing between payers, patients, and providers through mechanisms such as prospective payment.

- Requirement of prevention, monitoring, and early intervention services by providers to patients.

- Significant utilization review, especially for hospitalization and surgery.

- Coordination of care among multiple providers in complex cases.

- Quality studies, including provider profiling.

- Controlling organizational and financing system complaints from patients, providers (physicians, facilities, and others), and payers.

Concurrent with this power shift from physicians and hospitals to patient agent organization, there have been changes in the resources that each of these actors controls. Hospitals, for example, no longer control as much of the advanced technological equipment that was too costly or complex for individual physicians to acquire. This reversal was fostered by both the changing system of financial incentives (PPS) and advancements in selected technologies that have reduced the financial and volume break-even thresholds for nonhospital acquisition of technology. Because there were new markets for technology acquisition outside the hospital, there has also been rapid technological advancement and growth in physician group practices and home health care agencies to facilitate the safe and efficient use of technologies in the community.

The penetration of managed care and the power of patient agent organizations varies considerably across the United States. In states such as Arizona and Minnesota, with large proportions of the population enrolled in managed care plans, patients are directed to certain providers and away from other providers by patient agent organizations. Because of the growing volume of services controlled by patient care organizations, their ability to negotiate reduced rates or impose their fee schedules on providers is significant. If health care alliances develop as the major purchasing cooperatives in states and regions, the vast majority of the population will be subject to the principles of managed care.

We note that there is a great skepticism about the ability of patient agent organizations to actually make a difference in health care costs and quality. Many patient agent organizations grew out of programs of government or industry, and, as such, follow a bureaucratic model. Conventional insurance companies have traditionally performed a clerical function related to eligibility determination and claims payment and have shouldered the risk and the resultant costs for medical utilization by their insured populations. These insurance companies and other patient agent organizations have most recently transferred more financial risk from payers to patients as well as providers to raise their cost-consciousness and to act as a disincentive to unnecessary services. Patient copayments, after years of falling popularity, are returning as a means to reduce patient demand for unnecessary services.

Patient agent organizations are routinely gathering data on quality of care and utilization indicators from their populations to evaluate physicians and assess the organizational and financial arrangements surrounding clinical care. They are also giving increased attention to the results of outcomes studies. Although many have argued that the current state of such data is at best "crude," the future influence of patient agent organizations on patients may be more directly tied to the discrete episode of illness as well as to the systematic organization of the medical care system in which that care will be provided. Whereas in the past influence was exercised via attempts to modify the behavior of hospitals and physicians (e.g., the imposition of reimbursement by DRGs, contracting for services on the basis of capitation, second opinion requirements, preadmission review, and concurrent utilization review), such patient agent organizations will be more likely to specify or dictate preferred procedures to the physician who was once free to choose from competing approaches.

In summary, the orientations of physicians, hospitals, and patient agent organizations follow from their histories, the resources they control, and the ideologies used to justify their control. Hospitals, which have shown an incredible ability to adapt to changing environments, will continue to adapt to take advantage of their unique and complex community role and the ambiguity of their missions.[33] Many hospitals have already taken on the role of patient agents by forming HMOs, by purchasing physician practices, and, most recently, by working to develop their own community care networks in which local groups of doctors and clinics, organized by hospitals, compete for contracts with group insurers. In these instances, hospitals serve the dual role of patient agent and delivery organization. Likewise, many large multispecialty group practices around the country have begun forming HMOs and other forms of managed care organizations. These groups increasingly are negotiating with employers, insurers, and governments for exclusive care of specific patient populations.

In urban areas where there is a substantial surplus of hospital capacity, new collaborative arrangements, characterized by their vertical integration of services, will be important to the survival of the weakest organizations. Those that do not have the ability to shift their strategy and mission will be those most likely to fail. There will undoubtedly be some hospitals, isolated from a competitive environment, that will continue to have the traditional power they have wielded in their communities. But under the emerging financial realities, it will become increasingly difficult. Patient agent organizations will have the leverage that was formerly associated with the hospital/physician symbiotic relationship.

In the face of change, some physicians will continue to use their clinical dominance to foster organizational and financial arrangements that protect their individual professional autonomy.[34] Others will use their clinical expertise to help create organizations and systems that improve the quality and coordination of patient care. Physicians who avoid organizational alliances and frequently shift financial arrangements in order to avoid the changes that are occurring are vulnerable to being left out entirely in the evolving system. Such isolation of individual physicians and even of large groups of physicians is already noticeable today. These physicians have often been invited and then left behind in the decision-making processes going on in hospitals and patient agent organizations—decisionmaking that is significantly affecting clinical practices but may lack meaningful clinical input. With current trends and power shifts, there is an enormous opportunity for individual professional growth and for consensus seeking within the medical professional through active physician involvement in utilization and quality studies under way, and in the development of practice guidelines.

Reconceptualization of Medical Work

Social scientists have provided important insight into the development of medicine as the model for our understanding of the concept of profession.[2,35,36] Under the professional model of medicine, each patient represents a unique set of circumstances. The clinical judgment of the physician requires a substantial ability to apply "scientific" knowledge under a variety of conditions of uncertainty and indeterminacy. Given this "custom" view of medical work, few have ever believed that medicine would lend itself to a form of social organization characterized by standard operating procedures, bureaucratic rules for the implementation of knowledge, and other features of the industrial sector. Even in nationalized systems of medicine, such as the British National Health Service, physicians have not been asked to abandon a professional principle based on the premise that medicine should itself formulate, control, and evaluate the strategic tasks of doctor's work.[37]

A more thorough understanding of technical control models allows us to understand the currents in the changing U.S. health care work environment. The technical control model described by Edwards is one in which management employs techniques not directly related to the product outcome for the purpose of circumscribing worker discretion. In industry, numeric-controlled machines and robots are applied in situations where work is easily routinized. These settings are characterized by repetitive tasks, predictable sequences of events, and little variation in the planned flow of work. This leads to the employment of assembly lines, piece rates, and automated systems to control labor. As work becomes repetitive and more predictable, workers become more interchangeable, and the labor force and jobs under technical control become more homogeneous. Technical control is not without its downside. In many instances, the dehumanizing aspects of treating workers as a commodity in an efficient system has led to sabotage and other creative diversions by workers. The technical control model has given way in the past decade to a new management philosophy in industry that recognizes and designs for both autonomy and group identity by coupling responsibility and control to accountability and by creating unique and balanced work teams.

As cost containment and competition became important factors in the management of the health care system, the work of physicians was subjected to both technical and bureaucratic control mechanisms[38] formerly employed only in industry.[39] We are not suggesting that the professional model has been replaced by the bureaucratic model of work or that physicians have been proletarianized.[35,40,41] However, techniques from industry have been borrowed and modified for the health care industry in order to improve its effectiveness and efficiency and to slow its rate of growth. DRGs, prior approval programs, second opinion programs, and professional review organizations, however, were designed to question the individual physician's discretionary judgment or behavior and to reorganize the physician's approach to work. Many physicians fear that the interpretation of test results in favor of less treatment and other considerations not directly related to a particular patient have become a part of clinical decision making. At the very least, physicians are being asked to question their own decisions and to justify them in terms of multiple parameters related not only to the individual patient's physical health but to the physician's fiduciary responsibility to the patient, payer, and society. These mechanisms begin to reconceptualize professional work as a series of steps "rationally" related to the production of what is believed to be a known product. Only when this premise is accepted can the medical professional itself rigorously pursue the work of developing clinical decision trees, disseminating guidelines, implementing monitoring and feedback systems, and observing a convergence of clinical judgment within specialties and within the profession.

Today, the professional model is being challenged by a technical control model of work. The goal of standardization is to ensure that the principles of successful and cost-effective patient care outcomes are continuously applied to future medical care. This ideology about the nature of work poses a serious philosophical challenge to a profession whose knowledge base is complex and esoteric. To serve the needs of each "unique" patient under conditions of uncertainty, it is argued that medical work cannot be reduced to easily identifiable component parts. This is a serious implementation challenge, even with the sophisticated information tools available today. Hence, the few protocols that have been developed serve as guidelines to augment, not replace, clinical judgment.

Until now, technical control in medicine has been related to computers and other modern technologies only indirectly. Although those who embrace the technical control model may argue that the inability to capture the essence of professional work has been the key deterrent to progress, others believe that the major problem has been the failure of professionals and health care organizations to agree to standards for clinical and organizational data collection and retrieval. It is entirely possible that consensus-seeking discussions among health care professionals about standards will be an educational process with clinical benefits to the patient. Although it is also possible that only the most routine medical services lend themselves to standardization, the most common conditions account for a majority of patient visits. There is, therefore, potential to affect many lives by setting clinical standards that improve the accuracy of diagnosis and the success of treatments.

As health care reform has been debated, there has been a growing belief in the need for a vast and effective electronic highway across which large quantities of information on patients, providers, and institutions can routinely be transmitted. While there is good reason to question the extent to which advanced information technologies will actually affect clinical outcomes, these information systems may lead to a further "demystification" of professional knowledge.[42] In short, a latent function of describing the physician's work in great detail and in standardized formats is the provision of information to third-party payers and planners who will continue to unbundle medical work into component parts. The availability of this information fosters the application of cost accounting and industrial engineering techniques.

Those who doubt that there are major consequences associated with advanced information systems should note the important effect that DRGs have had on the "repackaging" of medical work. With diagnoses and procedures regrouped into bundles of services identified as DRGs, hospitals engaged in technical control by applying standards of time to be allotted to a given admission. While the intent was to simplify accounting and provide an average reimbursement for similar packages of services, often appropriate services within that package were denied to patients because such services were not individually and additionally reimbursed. The effects of misunderstanding and misuse of DRGs and a lack of solid cost accounting in hospitals frequently led to an indiscriminate assembly line mentality in medicine. Improved efficiency in terms of scheduling and evaluating patients is sadly needed in hospitals and clinics, but significant changes in these areas have not occurred systemwide. We note that many of the organizational and structural issues we have discussed are outside of a physician's area of expertise and are controlled by those trained in management. In some instances, physicians are even rewarded for their collective efficiency (e.g., an HMO sharing surplus with employed physicians). Often, however, physician incentives have been linked to collection rates or other factors beyond the control of the physician, causing frustration all around. Clearly, patient care can benefit from improved organizational efficiency and effectiveness, and this is also a source of immense potential cost savings. Efficiency and effectiveness in test-ordering and prescribing behavior are areas where physicians will be expected to become more knowledgeable in order to make better and more consistent clinical decisions.

A full shift to a form of medical work organization not dominated by the physician will evolve only if the knowledge and skills associated with the profession can be routinized, split down, or taken over by technicians or, as in conventional industry, by machines. This is not a likely scenario for modern medicine. To date, however, the application of industrial control mechanisms in medicine has been supported by a pool of physician/workers who are willing to collaborate and comply with those designing and implementing management control systems. Through reimbursement mechanisms, most physicians comply with requests for information that is eventually employed, through electronic manipulation, to monitor the quality and quantity of output in the health care delivery system. The data that are compiled provide opportunities for laymen to become involved in the evaluation of medical work and provide information and ideas to be employed by organized patient agents in their efforts to influence the organization and financing of medical care delivery systems. These developments have not stimulated strong negative responses from hospitals and physicians, although physicians and hospitals are often opposed to distribution of provider-specific gross quality indicators to the general public. Data collection methodologies and gaps in clinical information call into question the validity of much of the available data, but there is not yet a major movement by providers to improve data collection methodologies.

One result of this manipulation of medical knowledge is an intensified debate over the division of labor of medical work within hospitals and the community. Perhaps this is best described in Andrew Abbott's work,[43] which sees health care work as existing within a "system of professions" that, over the years, has been hammered-out through negotiations that have often resulted in legislation that ensures jurisdictions through restrictive licensure. As knowledge has become more readily available to health care workers throughout the system, however, we witness an "interprofessional division of labor" in which task performance is based more on individual abilities and team design within an individual organization than on the academic or professional degree one has attained and subsequent licensure. What we are suggesting is that, although physicians remain the dominant factor and continue to engage in the most complex tasks, there is an ongoing reevaluation of the scope of medical work and renewed contest among the professions. This is perhaps most clearly seen as health reform opens the door for an enhanced role for the allied health professions (including physician assistants and nurse practitioners) and health occupations that fall outside of allopathic and osteopathic medicine—such as chiropractors. That we have included osteopathic and allopathic physicians together signals the rapid disappearance, in many U.S. communities, in the differentiation between the two models of medicine—especially as more osteopathic physicians choose to serve allopathic residencies and are granted privileges in allopathic hospitals.

Integration of Clinical and Managerial Cultures

The interfacing of clinical and managerial cultures takes place in the face of a wide variety of factors that traditionally distinguish the two groups. Managers and physicians often differ on the basis of occupational values, nature of education, nature of tasks, observability of work, career anchors, life-style, income, professional needs, stratification within the occupational group, and form of quality control.[44] To the extent that medical schools and academic health centers have been highly resistant to change and continue to be controlled by physicians with academic values, student physicians and residents do not have the opportunity to develop an appreciation and understanding of management until they have left these institutional settings.

The United States is entering an era in which the profession of medicine as well as provider organizations are breaking down many of the traditional lines separating administrative and clinical organization and control. Simendinger and Pasmore[45] surveyed administrative physicians and key hospital administrators to identify the most important factors inhibiting enhanced cooperation. Both groups indicated cooperation was inhibited by perceptions of dishonesty, incompetence, and a lack of initiative or enthusiasm on the part of the other. Beyond this, physicians were criticized for refusal to listen, arbitrary decision making, manipulation, and a lack of follow-through, while administrators were criticized for lacking intelligence and/or education, wasting time, and having divided loyalties. In addition to differences in training and perspective, the very structure of the hospital has worked against collaboration between physicians and administrators. Ruelas and Leatt[46] list the following issues faced by physician executives as a result of the typical dual hospital organizational structure: unclear accountability, unclear definition of tasks, lack of adequate information for decision making, and an inadequate reward system for managerial functions.

A number of analysts, including Glandon and Morrisey[47] and Shortell,[48] describe organizational strategies with the potential to resolve the tensions between hospitals and physicians. A principal strategy involves a continued promotion of "shared common interest,"[47] in which physicians maintain autonomy, but the hospital or patient agent educates physicians regarding cost-benefit issues. For example, the hospital or organized patient agent may provide performance feedback by DRG and by individual physician, with the expectation that physicians will compare themselves to the norm and thereby self-correct. This system typically uses committees; requires high physician involvement; and works best with high admitters, surgeons, and physicians in sole community hospitals, all of whom are highly dependent on the hospital.

Given the increased availability of performance data on both hospitals and individual physicians, the shared common interest will, we believe, become increasingly important. Hospitals and patient agent organizations already evaluate physicians in terms of their practicing cost-effective medicine and increasingly evaluate performance of individuals and institutions on a variety of gross outcome measures. The assumption in releasing data and encouraging a "shared common interest" is that a convergence of practice patterns will result in higher quality and more cost-effective care. Although we have suggested that practicing state-of-the-art medicine requires that physicians continue to exercise a great deal of discretionary judgment, studies with large numbers of patients, adequately controlling for case mix, are now demonstrating the effectiveness of one approach over another. Critics argue, of course, that cost data are not easily interpreted while data on effectiveness are neither plentiful nor conclusive. This makes it especially difficult to determine the cost-effectiveness of different practice styles.

Sophistication in outcome study design, however, is rapidly advancing. It will be a mistake for the clinical community to discount the impact that newly acquired knowledge about practice will have on the organization of health care. Patient agent organizations and other quality assurance officials will advocate making decisions on the basis of such data—requiring that hospitals and physicians enter into collaborative arrangements and pay close attention to costs and the documentation of patient benefits derived from care.

Physicians now have an opportunity to ensure that studies are clinically meaningful by joining study design teams. Physicians can often provide insightful explanations for observed data variation by drawing on their medical knowledge and their understanding of referral patterns and case mix. The type of study under discussion is retrospective and epidemiological in nature, drawing on statistics as a tool. This is in contrast to much of the clinical literature, which deals in case descriptions and short-term clinical trials.

The development of practice parameters in the past several years has not met with immediate dissemination and use. Published guidelines with a supporting body of research appear to be insufficient to change practice patterns. Social influence theory suggests strategies to overcome this lack of action.[49] To be successful, information dissemination needs to be coupled with social influences that transfer norms and values that encourage or at least permit the new behaviors. Participation of physicians in guideline development; modeling by opinion leader physicians; academic detailing; orientation programs (i.e., to a new practice setting); and presentation of the information at clinical team meetings, study groups, grand rounds, and other professional educational meetings are suggested as strategies that allow for the personal interaction required for the transfer of social norms and values. For example, the use of targeted education and feedback to individual physicians of their practice patterns compared to their peers in the community, or to other agreed upon standards, has been successful in reducing caesarean section rates. The role of opinion leader physicians in bringing about change is crucial here; feedback from nonphysicians tends to be discredited and is less likely to lead to behavioral change.

Although it has been suggested that the employment of physicians is a sound mechanism for managing hospital-physician relations,[50] it is not at all clear that employed physicians have less autonomy or are more likely to follow clinical protocols.[51,52,53] Certainly Glandon and Morrisey[47] are correct that direct employment of physicians gives hospitals more control over administrative decisions, allows for improved scheduling and coordination, and provides the resources for direct contracting with payers. At the same time, the peer review structures that accompany employment may provide the medical staff with even more power to establish its own standards and operating procedures to meet the profession's views of patient requirements.

Hospitals that have invested heavily in purchasing physician practices should closely examine the pros and cons of their behavior. Some may find themselves with an *even stronger and more organized* group of professional employees. Physician organization may be a key catalyst to helping physicians achieve consensus on clinical issues and clinically related protocols.

Michael Kurtz, in Chapter 6 of this book, presents a more detailed analysis of the usual role of the physician executive. The key point worth repeating here is that it is "important for the physician executive to use this unique position to develop and enhance collaboration and integration of the medical and administrative staffs in the daily management and operations of the organization. Through this mechanism, the chasm of the dual roles [physician and manager] and its concomitant frustration and conflict can be bridged." Thus, the role of a physician executive today is a boundary-spanning one, and, without excellent interpersonal skills, the physician may be unable to bridge the chasm and be rejected and isolated by both sides. There is mounting evidence that formal managerial involvement of physicians is key to the success of health care organizations.[54]

If we are correct that the United States is entering an era where the profession of medicine as well as provider organizations will break down many of the traditional lines separating their organization and control, there is a continued need for the two groups to understand each another and to be prepared to restructure and negotiate their activities on the basis of the multiple realities of worklife.[55] In the United Kingdom, there has been a movement to reorganize hospital care around discrete areas of medical work that are managed by clinicians who have access to increasingly sophisticated information systems that provide an "electronic text" of the hospital.[55] The "clinical directorates" formalize the administrative role for physicians, thereby reducing the erosion of professional power by management, which is at risk as power shifts from physicians to corporate management in efforts to control costs. Clinical directorates also support and extend physicians' existing role in microallocation of resources and may reduce tensions between management and clinicians. This approach provides an avenue to ensure informed input into the design of clinical information systems that will be critical to success in effective and efficient resource allocation and provides a structure for incorporating practice guidelines. Because physician "opinion leaders" are known to be influential in effecting change in their peer group and management theory predicts that physician participation in guidelines will improve their success,[56] the clinical directorate model creates an impetus for clinicians to participate in health services research as a way of clarifying appropriateness of options. Mittman and Siu[49] contend that translating health services research into changes in clinical practice has been problematic. In the long run, the clinical directorate could provide a possible mechanism to incorporate research findings into treatment protocols by acknowledging professionalism and providing opportunity for leadership and control.[57] As a consensus model, it should help to resolve the present conflict among hospital administrators, nurses, and physicians, but, in the short run, greater interaction may bring out existing tensions.

The clinical directorate has a variety of weakness, including the potential to exacerbate professional tensions between nursing and physician groups and tensions between lay management and physicians, particularly if management intent is really only to confer "sham" power. It may also be more costly to the system.[57,58] There is presently insufficient experience with the clinical directorate model to answer the question of the appropriate time commitment physicians need to make to this new role. Finally, to the extent that both lay managers and physicians are socialized to be mistrustful of one another, it remains unclear whether either group is ready to commit to the difficult exercise of reshaping this culture.*

Conclusion

In the 1988 edition of this book, we suggested that it would be difficult to predict how physicians would react to continued changes in their work world. Physicians continue to believe that they should do all they can, within reason, for their patients. In short, they seem to have clung to their role as agents for their patients. There is also little evidence that physicians will engage in blatant sabotage of control systems. Many physicians, however, have used their capital to circumvent involvement in organizations that they feel constrain their judgment by establishing practices that directly compete with hospitals with which they have ongoing relationships. Physicians have also become skilled in their negotiations with patient agent organizations to ensure approval for clinical behavior, to ensure payment for their services, and to promote the well-being of their patients.

---

* We are grateful to students at the University of Colorado Executive MBA Program who provided thoughtful analysis of the clinical directorate concept. Although it is difficult to attribute specific arguments to any one student, Judith Vestrup's analysis was particularly useful.

Over the past decade there has been an increased tendency for physicians to change jobs (settings) to maximize autonomy and minimize control by others. For many years, specialty choice for physicians was set very early in their careers, and change in specialty was fairly rare. Recent studies of physician mobility reveal that physicians scrutinize the marketplace for their services and may, increasingly, react by changing specialties.[59] Although physicians have reported increasing dissatisfaction with the practice of medicine, relatively few physicians have actually left practice altogether for alternative careers. Medical education continues to be a substantial "sunken cost." Even physicians who have undergone extensive training in other occupations and professions find it difficult to abandon medicine. Physician salaries seem somewhat threatened by recent and anticipated trends in reimbursement. Physicians, however, quickly learn that it is difficult to match their salaries if they engage in outright career changes. Perhaps this is why physicians joke about early or partial retirement, but few really plan to retire by a certain age.

In theory, it is predictable that physicians might well begin to articulate central work values and attitudes around their working conditions rather than client-oriented issues. There is concern that those who receive training emphasizing cost containment and the values associated with an entrepreneurial system might emphasize treatment of patients in a customer-like rather than a patient-like manner. Perhaps, in an era of heightened competition for patients, there will be a redesigned relationship between physician and patient—with those who have a "bedside manner" that is seen as providing high-quality service being the most successful.

The concern we expressed in the first edition of this book was that the changes we observed might lead to increased risk to the patient. There is also a concern that physicians might respond to decreasing autonomy and decreasing income with behaviors that compromise care. With the introduction of competitive mechanisms, there has, indeed, been a concern for patients being released from treatment too early. There are, however, no systematic studies to indicate that there is increased patient risk under such situations. Indeed, patients who are exempt from the scrutiny of utilization review may be at greater risk for unnecessary, risky treatments or procedures. Perhaps the greatest risk to patients is the ostrich posture of head in the sand that prevents any real learning or growth in the clinical or organizational realm.

Although there has been a continued incursion by government and management into the work of the physician, physicians have not, as some suggested, significantly embraced collective labor mechanisms to deal with their dissatisfaction. The organization of physicians into relatively small groups works against such action, and the hospital medical staff has rarely organized itself in such a way as to act in the collective economic interests of physicians. Although there is more frequent coupling of the physician's salary with the workplace, most physicians have remained independent from the hospitals in which they practice and continue to act as their own agents. While there is a growing trend to larger group practice size, the majority of practices continue to be "small organizations."

Changes in medical work have not been imposed on totally unwilling physicians. The changes we have identified offer many advantages to some physicians. Predictability of work hours and freedom from the business aspects of establishing and running a practice are valued by some physicians over the autonomy that an independent practice brings. Others have taken on, with great enthusiasm, the goal to compete to reduce costs. Although some physicians have decried the use of alternative providers who engage in work that was formerly performed only by physicians, others argue that the changes allow them more opportunities to focus on the more "esoteric" and challenging aspects of medical work and that structural changes often provide more flexibility in vacations, scheduling, and even changing jobs. It is also clear that expansion of delivery organizations provides many opportunities for physicians who want administrative careers. Within these organizations, some administrative tasks uniquely suited for the physician executive include developing clinical protocols, designing quality outcome studies, and monitoring the work of peers. There is also a growing role for complex-case management, coordinating the multiple subspecialty physicians, health care facilities, and other health care providers involved in a given patient's medical management, as well as a major role for physicians working together within their professional organizations to develop agreement and to disseminate what is agreed upon. Facilitated by regulatory agencies, umbrella organizations have been created in recent years that are coordinating the efforts of many professional organizations. Groups of physicians are learning how to use their own data as feedback for continuing education and medical quality enhancement. Discussions about what factors provider profiling should include in order to be valid and meaningful are supplanting discussions of whether or not to do provider profiling.

The next decade will bring continuing challenges to physicians who choose to be involved in health management and health reform. The nonremunerative nature (or indirect reimbursement) of many administrative functions performed by physicians is an issue for physicians who could be spending their time with patients. The wide income differentials between physicians and others trained to do management tasks is significant for those paying for the work. Effective system change requires measurement and rewards, authority for implementation, policy consistency, planning prior to implementation, good information and information tools, and opportunities for periodic networking to stay in sync with other changes in the organization, community, and nation. Furthermore, change requires patience; it's a developmental process that takes time if it is to have a solid and enduring foundation.

It may be that physicians have not reacted to the changes in the marketplace with greater intensity because physician income has been effectively shielded from most of the cost-containment efforts to date. Physician income growth has outpaced inflation throughout the eighties. Detailed analysis shows this growth to be due to charge and volume increases almost equally. A slightly longer work week was also documented. While physicians have felt an increased bureaucratic influence over components of their work, it is primarily their staffs that deal with the increased administrative load. While hospitals have had to reorganize to respond to regulatory and financial changes, physicians have only seen the tip of the iceberg in terms of changes directly affecting how they practice.

Discussion

Physicians, individually and as a group, have controlled the practice of medicine and shaped the delivery system. That the truly important decisions about medical work would remain within the hands of physicians was affirmed throughout the sixties and seventies and into the eighties. A variety of environmental factors, taken together, are pressing for greatly decreased clinical discretionary power for physicians. The practice of medicine has not historically included many formal mechanisms for coordinated decision making, but the need for them is growing. The widely different perspectives of physicians, hospitals, consumer interest groups, regulators, payers, and others with a financial, professional, or personal interest in health care policy create conflicts as these groups all vie for greater control.

This chapter is written at a period when we are on the threshold of health care reform in the United States. As organized patient agents develop policy, there is a new focus on the health of populations as well as of individuals. As the enormous return on investment for prevention becomes recognized, prevention, which has been given a backseat to curative medicine in medical academia and hence medical practice, also seems to be emerging as a focal point of the future practice of medicine. There is also a movement to reshape the very nature of medical practice by altering the balance between primary care and specialist physicians. Although this may take some time to achieve, a health care delivery system that is driven by primary care physicians with strong training in social and managerial epidemiology will certainly look very different from a system that is based on specialist and curative care. We are, for the first time, focusing "upstream" and rethinking a variety of relationships between health, society, disease, and the profession of medicine.

References

1. Starr, P. *The Social Transformation of American Medicine.* New York, N.Y.: Basic Books, Inc., 1982.

2. Freidson, E. *Profession of Medicine. A Study of the Sociology of Applied Knowledge.* New York, N.Y.: Dodd, Mead and Company, 1970.

3. Freidson, E. *Professional Dominance: The Social Structure of Medical Care.* New York, N.Y.: Atherton Press, Inc., 1970.

4. Ver Stegg, G., and Croog, S. "Hospitals and Related Health Care Delivery Settings." In *Handbook of Medical Sociology,* Third Edition. Englewood Cliffs, N.J.: Prentice-Hall, Inc., 1979.

5. Thomas, J., Hall, M., and Schneller, E. "Principles of Health Care Facilities Organization and Management." In *Health Care Corporate Law Formation and Regulation.* Hall, M., Ed. Toronto, Canada: Little Brown and Co., 1993.

6. Rosner, D. *A Once Charitable Enterprise: Hospitals and Health Care in Brooklyn and New York, 1885-1915.* New York, N.Y.: Cambridge University Press, 1982.

7. Vogel, M. *The Invention of the Modern Hospital, Boston, 1870-1930.* Chicago, Ill.: University of Chicago Press, 1980.

8. Rosenberg, C. "Inward Vision and Outward Glance: The Shaping of the American Hospital, 1880-1914." In *Social History and Social Policy.* Rothman, D., and Wheeler, S., Eds. New York, N.Y.: Academic Press, 1981.

9. Stevens, R. *American Medicine and the Public Interest.* New Haven, Conn.: Yale University Press, 1971.

10. Hirschman, A. *Exit, Voice, and Loyalty: Responses to Decline in Firms, Organizations, and States.* Cambridge, Mass.: Harvard University Press, 1970.

11. Weber, M. *Essays in Sociology.* New York, N.Y.: Oxford University Press, 1946.

12. Gaffney, J., and Glandon, G. "The Physician's Use of the Hospital." *Health Care Management Review* 7(3):49-58, Summer 1982.

13. Steinwald, B. "Hospital-Based Physicians: Current Issues and Descriptive Evidence." *Health Care Financing Review* 2(1):63-75, Summer 1980.

14. Smith, H. "Two Lines of Authority: The Hospital's Dilemma." *Modern Hospital* 84(3):59-64, March 1955.

15. Pauly, M., and Redish, M. "The Not-for-Profit Hospital as a Physicians' Cooperative." *American Economic Review* 63(1):87-99, March 1973.

16. Harris, J. "The Internal Organization of Hospitals: Some Economic Implications." *Bell Journal of Economics* 8(2):467-82, Fall 1977.

17. Saltman, R., and Young, D. "The Hospital Power Equilibrium: An Alternative View of the Cost Containment Dilemma." *Journal of Health Politics, Policy, and Law* 6(3):391-418, Fall 1981.

18. Roemer, M., and Friedman, J. *Doctors in Hospitals: Medical Staff Organization and Hospital Performance.* Baltimore, Md.: Johns Hopkins Press, 1971.

19. Davis, K. *National Health Insurance: Benefits, Costs, and Consequences.* Washington, D.C.: Brookings Institution, 1975.

20. Bice, T. "Health Services Planning and Regulation." In *Introduction to Health Services,* Second Edition. Williams, S., and Torrens, P., Eds. New York, N.Y.: John Wiley and Sons, 1984.

21. Roemer, M. "Bed Supply and Hospital Utilization: A National Experiment." *Hospitals* 35(21):36, Nov. 1, 1961.

22. Pauly, M. *Doctors and Their Workshops: Economic Models of Physician Behavior.* Chicago, Ill.: University of Chicago Press, 1980.

23. Krause, E. *Power and Illness: The Political Sociology of Health and Medical Care.* New York, N.Y.: Elsevier North-Holland, Inc., 1977.

24. Brown, L. *Politics and Health Care Organization: HMOs as Federal Policy.* Washington, D.C.: Brookings Institution, 1983.

25. Goldbeck, W. "Health Care Coalitions." In *Health Care Cost Management: Private Sector Initiatives.* Fox, P., and others, Eds. Ann Arbor, Mich.: Health Administration Press, 1984.

26. Salkever, D., and Bice, T. "The Impact of Certification-of-Need Controls on Hospital Investment." *Millbank Memorial Fund Quarterly* 54(2):185-214, Spring 1976.

27. Ginzberg, E. "The Monetarization of Medical Care." *New England Journal of Medicine* 310(18):1162-5, May 3, 1984.

28. Ginzberg, E. "The Restructuring of U.S. Health Care." *Inquiry* 22(3):272-81, Fall 1985.

29. Enthoven, A. *Health Plan: The Only Practical Solution to the Soaring Cost of Medical Care.* Reading, Mass.: Addison-Wesley, 1980.

30. Donabedian, A. "The Epidemiology of Quality." *Inquiry* 22(3):282-92, Fall 1985.

31. Pfeffer, J., and Salancik, G. *The External Control of Organizations: A Resource Dependence Perspective.* New York, N.Y.: Harper and Row, 1978.

32. Havighurst, C. "The Changing Locus of Decision Making in the Health Care Sector." In *Health Policy in Transition: A Decade of Health Politics, Policy, and Law.* Durham, N.C.: Duke University Press, 1987.

33. Stevens, R. "A Poor Sort of Memory: Voluntary Hospitals and Government before the Depression." *Millbank Memorial Fund Quarterly/Health and Society* 60(4):551-84, Fall 1982.

34. Freidson, E. *Professional Powers. A Study of the Institutionalization of Formal Knowledge.* Chicago, Ill.: University of Chicago Press, 1986.

35. Hughes, E. *Men and Their Work.* New York, N.Y.: Free Press of Glencoe, 1958.

36. Wilensky, H. "The Professionalization of Everyone?" *American Journal of Sociology* 70(9):137-58, Sept. 1964.

37. Freidson, E. "Professions and the Occupational Principle." In *Medical Men and Their Work.* Chicago, Ill.: Aldine-Atherton, 1972.

38. Taylor, F. *The Principles of Scientific Management.* New York, N.Y.: Harper, 1947.

39. Edwards, R. *Contested Terrain. The Transformation of the Workplace in the Twentieth Century.* New York, N.Y.: Basic Books, Inc., 1979.

40. Haug, M. "Deprofessionalization: An Alternative Hypothesis for the Future." *Sociological Review Monograph* 20(12):195-211, Dec. 1973.

41. McKinlay, J., and Arches, J. "Towards the Proletarianization of Physicians." *International Journal of Health Services* 15(2):161-95, Spring 1985.

42. Haug, M. "Computer Technology and the Obsolescence of the Concept of Profession." In *Work and Technology.* Beverly Hills, Calif.: Sage Publications, 1977.

43. Abbott, A. *The System of Professions: An Essay on the Division of Labor.* Chicago, Ill.: University of Chicago Press, 1988.

44. Friss, L., and others. Working paper, 1987.

45. Simendinger, E., and Pasmore, W. "Developing Partnerships Between Physicians and Health-care Executives." *Hospital and Health Services Administration* 29(6):21-35, Nov.-Dec. 1984.

46. Ruelas, E., and Leatt, P. "The Roles of Physician-Executives in Hospitals: A Framework for Management Education." *Journal of Health Administration Education* 3(2, Pt 1):151-69, Spring 1985.

47. Glandon, G., and Morrisey, M. "Redefining the Hospital-Physician Relationship under Prospective Payment." *Inquiry* 23(2):166-75, Summer 1986.47.

48. Shortell, S. "The Medical Staff of the Future: Replanting the Garden." *Frontiers of Health Services Management* 1(3):3-48, Feb. 1985.

49. Mittman, B., and Siu, A. "Changing Provider Behavior: Applying Research on Outcomes and Effectiveness in Health Care." In *Improving Health Policies and Management.* Shortell, S., and Reinhardt, U., Eds. Ann Arbor, Mich.: Health Administration Press, 1992, pp. 195-226.

50. Shortell, S. "Hospital Medical Staff Organization: Structure, Process, and Outcome." *Hospital Administration* 19(1):96-107, Spring 1974.

51. Sullivan, R. "Physician Extenders, Protocols, and Quality Medical Care." *Bulletin of the New York Academy of Medicine* 52(1):125-38, Jan. 1976.

52. Hall, R. "Professionalization and Bureaucratization." *American Sociological Review* 33(2):92-104, Feb. 1968.

53. Freidson, E. "The Reorganization of the Medical Profession." *Medical Care Review* 42(1):11-35, Spring 1985.

54. Shortell, S. *Effective Hospital-Physician Relationships.* Ann Arbor, Mich.: Health Administration Press, 1991.

55. Kirkman-Liff, B., and Schneller, E. "The Resource Management Initiative in the English National Health Service." *Health Care Management Review* 17(2):59-70, Spring 1992.

56. Eisenberg, J. *Doctors' Decisions and the Cost of Medical Care.* Ann Arbor, Mich.: Health Administration Press, 1986.

57. Lemieux-Charles, L., and Leatt, P. "Hospital Physician Integration: Case Studies of Community Hospitals." *Health Services Management Research* 5(2):82-8, July 1992.

58. Fitzgerald, L. "Clinicians Late Management." *Health Services Management Research* 5(2):137-45, July 1992.

59. Wilke, R. "Practice Mobility among Young Physicians." *Medical Care* 29(10):977-88, Oct. 1991.

Eugene S. Schneller, PhD, is Professor, School of Health Administration and Policy, and Associate Dean, College of Business, Arizona State University, Tempe. Pamela Hood-Szivek, MHSA, is an independent researcher. Robert G. Hughes, PhD, is Director of Program Research, Robert Wood Johnson Foundation, Princeton, New Jersey.

Physician Executives and Integrated Health Care Systems

CHAPTER

3

by David J. Ottensmeyer, MD, FACPE,
and Howard L. Smith, PhD

T hirty years ago, Mary E.W. Goss, a research associate in the Department of Medicine at Cornell University Medical College, observed that physicians generally avoided almost any administrative activity.[1] The professional norms and values of medicine encouraged physicians, at that time, to emphasize medical practice, teaching, and research. However, similar to other professions, medicine has always relied on some physicians to fulfill the role of self-governance. Without such participation, a profession is susceptible to losing control of, or the ability to direct, professional activities. A decade later, several authorities observed that physicians were increasingly gaining access to governing boards,[2] to middle management positions outside of academic medical centers,[3] and to involvement in operating level management decisions.[4]

Now, three decades after Dr. Goss investigated the factors motivating some physicians to accept administrative positions, it is clear that effective physician leadership is crucial not only to physicians, but to health care as well.[5] In the midst of a crisis wrought by rising costs, the health care field is experiencing a public outcry. Reform of the health care system is widely demanded; some new approach to the financing of care seems inevitable. Restructuring is and has been under way for a decade in the form of managed care and integration of various components of the delivery system.

How will the medical profession and its new specialty of medical management (physician executives) respond to reform strategies supported by public consensus? The answer to that question is unclear. Confusion seems to grip the health care establishment (i.e., physicians, hospitals, and insurers), because they have been producing something they thought the public should want; increasingly that seems in doubt, at least in some critical details (i.e., cost, accessibility, and value).

An inability to accurately identify public desires is not unknown in our society or its economy. The automotive industry serves as a case in point. In 1978, General Motors possessed approximately 48.4 percent of the domestic automobile market. By 1987, its market share had fallen to 36 percent and was still falling. Foreign competitors had encroached on virtually every segment of the automotive market. These competitors methodically defined and filled specialty niches. General Motors' failure to understand what the consumer wanted provides important lessons on the role of strategic management and vision. General Motors did not establish a strategic planning function until 1979, well after the gasoline shortages in the early 1970s.[6] In many respects, General Motors relied on brute marketing strength and a system of local dealerships to stall the inevitable loss of market share. However, consumer demands prevailed. The Japanese and Germans manufactured higher quality, lower cost products that achieved better gas mileage and required less maintenance. Subsequently, American automotive manufacturers discovered competitors were entirely capable of redefining the business in which they were engaged.

The parallels to health care are instructive. Just as General Motors and other U.S. automotive producers were oblivious to the demands of the customer, there is reason to believe the health care establishment may have misled itself into thinking it knows what is best for medical consumers and purchasers. As the largest segment of the economy, providers seem to have assumed that the criticality of their services and the "brute force" of their industry was unassailable. In the same manner that General Motors, Ford, and Chrysler continued to implement superficial revisions in strategy despite a tremendously changed context, so too have health care providers been tinkering at the margin. Even with the proliferation of managed care and the emphasis on ambulatory services, the health care system remains inefficiently organized to deliver accessible, low-cost, and high-quality care. Despite the marginal tinkering, the fundamental delivery system has changed minimally in structure over the past 50 years, save in a few areas of the country. It remains organized around the mid-century model of fee-for-service, unstructured, and unmanaged delivery of care. The system is primarily driven by provider values rather than those of consumers of care.

In this style, the U.S. health care system has become essentially unaffordable. Without tax incentives and employment-based health insurance—both of which promise soon to decrease in value—the average health care consumer would face almost impossible choices. At the same time, the number of medically uninsured and underinsured continues to rise yearly. Moreover, the financial rationale of the health care system is disintegrating. Neither government, with its deficit, nor industry, with the challenge of foreign competition, can reasonably expect to continue supporting the economics inherent in the existing financing scheme. The health delivery system has declining productivity, unacceptable costs, and a deteriorating customer image. Most ominously, it is in the midst of a buyer revolt. The majority of Americans feel the health care system needs reform.[7]

This chapter will examine a response of the health care system (integration) that is now becoming evident and the role physician executives will play in the process. First, the rationale for integrated health care systems will be presented, focusing on causal factors for reform and on failures of the existing health care system to deliver constructive responses. This analysis identifies what effective responses are necessary and what leadership is necessary to formulate and implement these responses. Second, existing physician and hospital relationships will be examined to understand how they have evolved, and why they promise to be replaced by integrated health care systems. Third, the common denominators underlying successful integrated health care systems will be identified. Special emphasis is given to the importance of mutual trust among constituents as the essential glue holding the systems together. Fourth, the role of physician executives will be examined as key agents in managing and sustaining trust within integrated health care systems.

Reform of the Health Care System

Health care reform conceptually involves two themes. The first is equity and access for more than 35 million people who presently are uninsured or underinsured. The second is cost control in a system presently consuming nearly 14 percent of the gross national product and on the way to 20 percent within the decade. The first goal, equity, will drive up the cost of medical care, while the second is conceived to restrain costs. Equity is a political goal obtainable by legislation, albeit at an estimated additional cost of $60 to $120 billion a year. Control of costs is essential as a part of reform and is the conundrum of reform. It cannot be accomplished without reform of the delivery system. The present delivery system can no longer function around the paradigm of the past 50 years if costs are to be restrained. The only real proposal that exists for changing the delivery of health care is managed care. It has therefore been a ubiquitous feature of most reform proposals.

Health care reform will drive demand for managed care. Managed care is a process that imposes organizational structure, control, measurement, and accountability on the delivery of health care. It is designed to effect a balance in utilization of resources, cost containment, and quality management of delivery of care. Managed care employs the following three strategies:

- Alteration of financial incentives.

- Introduction of management control and oversight in the delivery of care.

- Use of information systems to facilitate administrative and clinical decisions.

The Rationale for Integrated Health Care Systems

Managed care is an integrational process; it drives the presently fragmented health care system toward consolidation and singular management. Integration of the fragmented components of the present health care system is essential if managed care is to employ the strategies noted above. Health care reform will create sweeping demand for managed care, which in turn will generate the need for integrated health care systems (IHCS). It is projected that, in the future, all care delivery will be either discounted or capitated.[8]

Today's health care system was built as a cottage industry of solo medical practice and independent community hospitals; it characteristically focused on patient care and was mostly oblivious to costs. The medical practitioner thought of finances around the simple notion of fee-for-service medicine, while hospitals capitalized on the undemanding economics of cost-based reimbursement. As long as government and employers willingly paid charges so generated, and philanthropy and cost-shifting covered the cost of indigent care, the health care establishment functioned satisfactorily. However, evolving sophistication in medical technology, proliferation of unfinanced government entitlements (e.g., Medicare and Medicaid), rising malpractice litigation, overbuilding of hospitals, shortages of primary care providers, and the disconcern of providers about cost ultimately combined to upset that system.

The overriding imperative in health care is control of costs. High-quality and accessible care is deliverable if adequate resources are available to fund them. The problem is that society can no longer fully fund all of its priorities. Trade-offs must be made. In the case of health care, society seems unwilling to tolerate the constantly rising and relatively exorbitant cost of the existing system. Although several models are available, it is likely that some form of prepaid, capitated arrangement will be the principal vehicle for reimbursement in the future. Where that has already occurred, the structure of health care quickly changed and its move to integration was dramatic.

Demands of Consumers

What do purchasers of health care want? The demands of purchasers (employers and the government) strike at the foundations of the present delivery system. Purchasers want some basic fairness in the allocation of the costs they must bear. This is especially true for employers, who have experienced yearly increases in the cost of health insurance they fund that far exceed the annual inflation rate of health care. They are well aware that the cost of unfunded care delivered by hospitals is shifted to them to cover the cost of indigent service as well as care for Medicare and Medicaid recipients. The unit cost of health care is incomprehensible to purchasers. They suspect that they are the victims of billing and coding systems designed to maximize revenue for providers. They want a rational and understandable pricing system that will motivate providers to be concerned about costs and quality of care. Purchasers and consumers want more information about health care services, including information about the quality and cost effectiveness of providers and the technology they use. Purchasers generally represent organizations and bureaucracies accustomed to taking risk on the basis of budgets, planning, and managed processes. They are suspicious of a system, such as health care, that is set up to function with open-ended, unstructured costs and that seems incapable of accurately projecting costs and contracting to deliver a defined service/product for a stated cost. Those same suspicions exist about the administrative infrastructure of the system, with its multiple fragmented parts, each with growing administrative costs that are passed on to the purchaser. Purchasers know that, despite the enormous costs they bear for health care, many of their constituents are not assured of care or are anxious about the availability of care if they become ill. Access to care remains a concern and a demand of purchasers.

The profile that emerges in figure 1, page 43, is a shift in how health care consumers think about their purchases of health care products and services. This shift is largely attributed to economic forces that have not been adequately resolved. In many respects, consumers have lost their innocence in thinking that quality of care is the most important priority; services should always be available on demand; they have limited responsibility for cost control or insurance; they must have a personal familiarity with a single physician; life should be maintained regardless of cost; and someone else

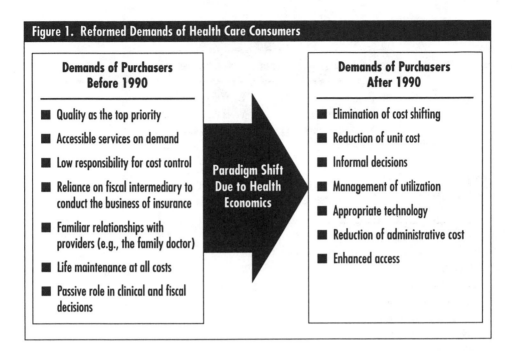

Figure 1. Reformed Demands of Health Care Consumers

Demands of Purchasers Before 1990	Demands of Purchasers After 1990
■ Quality as the top priority	■ Elimination of cost shifting
■ Accessible services on demand	■ Reduction of unit cost
■ Low responsibility for cost control	■ Informal decisions
■ Reliance on fiscal intermediary to conduct the business of insurance	■ Management of utilization
■ Familiar relationships with providers (e.g., the family doctor)	■ Appropriate technology
■ Life maintenance at all costs	■ Reduction of administrative cost
■ Passive role in clinical and fiscal decisions	■ Enhanced access

Paradigm Shift Due to Health Economics

will make fiscal and clinical decisions for them.

Responses of Providers

How are providers responding to the demands of health care consumers? The answer to this question is displayed in figure 2, page 44. The current response to the demands of purchasers varies according to the provider. Physicians are undergoing an affiliation frenzy. Should they link up with hospitals or health plans? Should they remain autonomous, or join another group? Physicians are pursuing technology ventures in order to offset revenue losses due to discounting and utilization controls of managed care. They are organizing into medical groups as a means for economic survival and for bargaining ability with institutions such as hospitals and health plans. The demands of health care consumers have forced many physicians to alter clinical behaviors to prevent losing fiscal ground. Unbundled procedure codes and coding creep are strategies that are adopted to counteract system controls. Unfortunately, most of these responses are ultimately designed to increase revenues rather than lower costs to purchasers. Thus, the responses of physicians tend not to be responsive to the demands of providers.

Hospitals are also altering their behaviors in light of consumer demands. They are in a scramble to establish the most lucrative affiliations with third-party payers who can channel patients to them. They expand into the outpatient care arena, a turf previously occupied by their medical staffs. This is a market share move that predictably damages relationships with physicians, a constituency of vital concern to hospitals. Development of hospital systems and formation of strategic alliances continue to occur, aimed at development of economies of scale and scope. Hospitals are also pursuing business

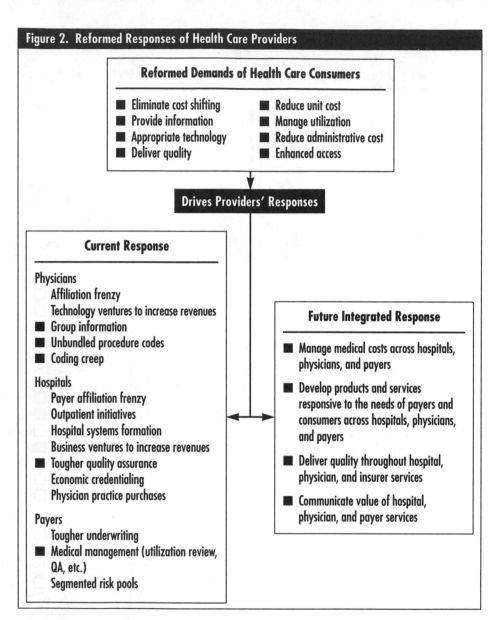

Figure 2. Reformed Responses of Health Care Providers

Reformed Demands of Health Care Consumers

- Eliminate cost shifting
- Provide information
- Appropriate technology
- Deliver quality
- Reduce unit cost
- Manage utilization
- Reduce administrative cost
- Enhanced access

Drives Providers' Responses

Current Response

Physicians
- Affiliation frenzy
- Technology ventures to increase revenues
- Group information
- Unbundled procedure codes
- Coding creep

Hospitals
- Payer affiliation frenzy
- Outpatient initiatives
- Hospital systems formation
- Business ventures to increase revenues
- Tougher quality assurance
- Economic credentialing
- Physician practice purchases

Payers
- Tougher underwriting
- Medical management (utilization review, QA, etc.)
- Segmented risk pools

Future Integrated Response

- Manage medical costs across hospitals, physicians, and payers
- Develop products and services responsive to the needs of payers and consumers across hospitals, physicians, and payers
- Deliver quality throughout hospital, physician, and insurer services
- Communicate value of hospital, physician, and payer services

ventures to increase revenues. They are establishing tougher quality assurance programs. Their medical staffs are subjected to closer review of care delivery and economic verification. In some instances, hospitals are purchasing physician practices to ensure retention of market share. As these illustrations underscore, hospitals are instigating many changes designed to enhance market share and improve profitability. However, the changes usually do not address the needs of providers, and they usually do not translate into lower costs for payers.

Like physicians and hospitals, third-party payers are under pressure to effect the same basic set of changes where they affect the system. They are implementing tougher underwriting to lower loss ratios and decrease risk. Medical review strategies have been significantly expanded by incorporating rigorous and systematic utilization review and quality assurance.

The overall result is, at best, an uncoordinated response to the demands of purchasers. There is little evidence of realistic market analysis to define the appropriate and constructive response. Predictably, the credible response would involve efforts aimed at delivery of cost-effective care, the development of products and services responsive to the needs of purchasers (e.g., managed care), measurement of quality, and communication of value. It is notable, however, that such strategies, even if accepted by providers, would be difficult to implement in a health care system constituted of segmented and uncoordinated provider units. The indicated strategies cut across the boundaries of the health care system (i.e., physicians, hospitals, other vendors, and payers). The need for coordination results in today's intense interest in integrated health care. It constitutes the rationale for the development of such systems.

Readiness of Consumers for a New System

The appeal of integrated health system to consumers is readily apparent in the western United States today. Consider an urban market in northern California, where the players include several not-for-profit community hospitals, two Catholic hospitals, a county hospital, a district hospital, a university hospital, three medium-sized group practices, and a mass of small medical partnerships and solo medical practitioners. This configuration is typical of health care for an urban area in the late 20th Century within the United States. Most services are delivered in cottage-industry style, with many vendors offering some subset of the various services needed by health care consumers. At first glance, this arrangement still seems the ideal service delivery configuration extant during the past 50 years. However, this is not the case; the market is in turmoil, profit margins of many hospitals are razor thin or absent, and physicians are angry and frustrated.

The market is not typical because there is an additional consideration that is critical in this illustration. Another competitor is present that delivers integrated services with concern for access, cost control, and quality. That competitor is Kaiser Permanente. This illustration offers a stark contrast between two competing philosophies of health care. One is the traditional fragmented health care model, and the other is an integrated system of health care delivery. How are they doing in competition? That should be the real test of two systems that are fundamentally different in orientation.

There are some interesting statistics pertinent to the community's health care. There is a decline for all traditional measurements of health care—patient visits to physicians, length of stay in hospitals, admissions to hospitals, and occupancy of hospitals. The statistics imply a disaster for the traditional system, because the statistics measure units of work that are charged out on a fee-for-service basis. The statistics are critical as indicators of performance in key profit centers in a volume-driven business where literally more medicine is better medicine—at least economically better medicine. In comparison, the statistics represent cost centers for Kaiser Permanente. Declining statistics of this type result in economic success for Kaiser Permanente. The comparison is even more noteworthy when other evidence comparing quality and outcomes in managed care systems is considered.[945] In age, sex, and severity-matched groupings, there is no significant difference between the two systems.

Consider a final comparison involving practice-related factors in the two systems. The number of non-Kaiser physicians in the community declined three percent between 1984 and 1987. The number of Kaiser Permanente physicians increased by 56 percent during that same period. Kaiser Permanente physicians have the highest starting income for primary medical practitioners in the area. They are heavily focused in primary and preventive care, rather than specialty care. They hire the majority of graduates of the primary care training programs in the area. The physicians at Kaiser Permanente have predictable work schedules and infrequent call or weekend schedules. They have a generous pension program that is noncontributory. Most significant, the value system, the management, the governance, and the agenda of the Kaiser organization are strongly influenced by physician involvement. That involvement occurs at every level of the organization, including executive management.

Is this simply a California phenomenon, the home of Kaiser Permanente and the HMO? The fact is that Kaiser has demonstrated its ability to be accepted in virtually any section of the country, including the southwest, the mountain states, the upper midwest, and the industrialized east. Moreover, it is not necessary to focus just on the phenomenon of Kaiser Permanente. Other integrated health care organizations have been highly successful over the past decade in their communities. Non-Kaiser Permanente examples can be seen in Albuquerque, New Mexico; Madison, Wisconsin; Detroit, Michigan; Minneapolis, Minnesota; rural central Wisconsin; rural Pennsylvania; Seattle, Washington; New Orleans, Louisiana; Boston, Massachusetts; and other locales.

Americans seem to be seeking a different kind of health care system. They are often finding it in the integrated health care system. The quest is expressed as a variety of complaints:

■ Costs are prohibitive.

■ I am baffled by it all.

■ I can't obtain services when I want them.

■ Medical center locations and doctor's office locations are inconvenient.

■ Billing and insurance forms are confusing, particularly in a hospital when I see many doctors.

■ Where do I go to for what?

■ I am tired of being shuttled from one office or institution to another.

■ Delays and repetitive paperwork are really annoying.

These are the needs that integrated health care systems seek to fill.

New Health Care Organizations

Physician Organizations

The structure of medical practice has changed over time. Solo practice gave way to partnerships and groups during the past 20 years. More recently, other varieties of physician-dominated organizations appeared in the form of preferred provider organizations, individual practice associations, physician-hospital organizations, and medical service organizations. The challenge now is to get individual physicians into organizations and then to integrate organizations with other vendors of care, such as hospitals.

An important focus of restructuring among health care institutions, including physician and hospital organizations, has been emphasis on building strategic alliances. The strategic alliance concept implies a loosely coordinated structure comprising member organizations.[16] Membership in the alliance is undertaken to counter intrusive competitive threats or to facilitate survival where regulations, reimbursement policies, or other environmental pressures confront the organization. As suggested in figure 3, below, strategic alliances for physician organizations have evolved out of solo practice and group arrangements. Joint ventures, medical service organizations, and physician hospital organizations are several of the alliances that result when physician groups pursue collaborative arrangements to improve their chances of overcoming adverse pressures, or to capitalize on potentially rewarding situations.

A fundamental feature of a strategic alliance, and of other organizational relationships throughout health care, is the ability to adapt as conditions change. Government reimbursement policy, strategic redirection by competitors, technological developments in medicine, managed care, and similar contextual changes suggest that, in the short term, organizations must be flexible and prepared to respond quickly to opportunities and constraints. A relatively static organization that changes little over time is not feasible. Thriving health care organizations now respond quickly to situations by alterations in internal operations, by internal reconfigurations, or through linkages with other organizations/providers.

Evidence of the trend toward more flexible organizations is apparent in at least two respects. First, as suggested in figure 3, strategic alliances are an intermediate stage in the evolution of physician organizations.[17] Predictably, physician organizations will be integral elements of IHCS. Physician organizations may seek to be or prefer to continue as autonomous corporations, but their ability to stand alone is diminishing. Second, there is growing evidence that many strategic alliances, joint ventures in particular,

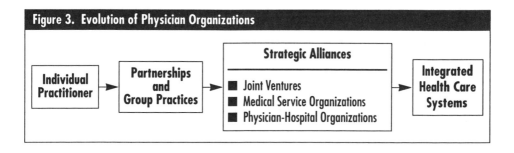

Figure 3. Evolution of Physician Organizations

| Individual Practitioner | → | Partnerships and Group Practices | → | **Strategic Alliances**
■ Joint Ventures
■ Medical Service Organizations
■ Physician-Hospital Organizations | → | Integrated Health Care Systems |

have not paid off for physician groups. Both legal developments and poor business planning are factors underlying pessimism about joint ventures.[18] Omnibus Budget Reconciliation Act (1989) restrictions on patient referrals played an important role in cooling interest in joint ventures. Additionally, physician groups and hospitals tended to blindly pursue many options that just did not make business sense.

Although strategic alliances may only amount to a temporary phase in the evolution of the health care system, they retain notable importance from the perspective of helping to sort out what does and does not work among providers. Joint ventures between physicians and hospitals facilitate sharing of different perspectives, even though the sharing process is often a painful one in terms of learning.[19] Hospitals and physicians develop a better understanding of what assets and liabilities the other party brings to the relationship. Furthermore, the ventures promote give-and-take, as partners recognize that compromises are often required to ensure longevity of the alliance and optimization of return.[20] Alliances are also beneficial in defining mutual areas for responsibility, as well as delineating where partners should temper efforts to exercise absolute control.[21]

The Shift to Integrated Systems

Three driving forces are stimulating the necessity for IHCS. First, integration is a means for enhancing market share. Physicians, hospitals, and insurance carriers are better able to present a single face to consumers (whether individuals or employers). Rather than using piecemeal efforts at bargaining and market segmentation, IHCS bundle services together and approach the marketplace with a single product. This can prevent affiliated physicians and hospitals from competing against each other or in a specific market served by both. Popular strategic alliances, such as joint ventures and management service organizations, may not avoid unintended competition with partners. The result is an ability to protect profitability. By controlling market share, the IHCS is better prepared to address health care reform initiatives because of economies of scale and risk sharing. An implicit assumption is that these attributes will contribute to improved responses by the IHCS to the needs of purchasers and payers.

A second driving force stimulating the need for IHCS is improved organizational efficiency. Admittedly, many health care systems that pursue the IHCS model still have some distance to go in achieving their goals. Nonetheless, vertical integration offers substantially more promise than diversification.[22] Diversification leaders in the health care field during the 1990s were those who acted as first movers (i.e., those who pursued the diversification option, differentiated services, or pursued related diversification options).[23] Vertical integration promises economies of scale, reduction of duplication, concentration of resources, specialization of management, and stability.[24]

The third force underlying IHCS is a response to consumer attitudes. The public is prepared for a new approach to health care that is less expensive, more adaptable, more accessible, and more accountable. In reality, physicians, hospitals, and insurers no longer enjoy the remarkable confidence of the public enjoyed only a few years ago. Reform is at hand. The IHCS model presents a means for enacting the new paradigm in thinking about health care delivery.[25]

The Shift of Physicians into Health Care Organizations

Restructuring and integration are far more difficult for the medical profession than for hospitals to accept. Physicians and organized medicine have historically worked hard to maintain a culture of autonomy. The medical profession itself worked to enforce professional socialization and legal mandates consistent with autonomy. It eschewed notions of public accountability, management, and consumer values, always favoring professional values.

A variety of models exist for bringing physicians into the integrated health care organization. Direct contracting, where hospitals function as employers to build seamless organizations is no longer uncommon. Examples include the Henry Ford Hospital in Detroit, and Main Line Health in Philadelphia.[26,27] The hospital-affiliated corporation relies on an arrangement designating as sole shareholder a physician who relates to both a hospital and a professional corporation. The physician shareholder serves as a hospital-employed medical director and president of the professional corporation and its board of directors. Alternatively, the hospital with a clinic-employed physician subsidiary has a hospital as the sole member or shareholder of a clinic. The physicians of the group are employees of the clinic, and the clinic is a division of the hospital. The Lovelace Medical Center in Albuquerque exemplifies this.

The physician-hospital organization uses a medical staff organization and a hospital organization that maintain ownership control of the integrated organization. It achieves control through service contracts with the hospital and the physician group. The Kaiser Permanente organization is a health plan that sells prepaid health care insurance to enrollees. It then has a hospital contract with the 501(c)(3) hospital component of Kaiser and has a professional service contract with the Permanente Medical Group, a professional corporation involved in the practice of medicine.

A hospital, as a solo member or shareholder, establishes a management service organization, which provides services to manage back office operations for physicians, including facilities acquisition, lease hold improvements, equipment acquisition, non-physician personnel, supplies, inventory, accounting, billing and collection, and general management. Examples of a related arrangement are the group practices that have been acquired by Phycor of Nashville, Tennessee. A final model for bringing physicians into the IHCS is the foundation model, consisting of a parent health care system operating a hospital, a physician foundation that houses the medical group, various for-profit organizations necessary as vendors of health care services, and usually some type of a charitable foundation, as exemplified by the Virginia Mason Clinic, Seattle.

The Challenges of Integration

Organizations thinking about these arrangements have a number of challenges, foremost among them being governance structure. The culture of the medical professional is not a culture of integration, nor does it readily understand governance beyond the ideal of collegial peer review. To succeed, strong physician leadership and management skills are necessary. Of equal importance as an obstacle to integration is the attitude of boards and hospital administrators whose paradigm of the health care organization is limited to the medical staff as a separate and independent volunteer entity. Integration means integration of everything, including control. That means power sharing and perhaps domination of the institution by the medical profession, which is central and essential to the success of the enterprise.

Such organizations moving toward the IHCS model must successfully balance utilization and quality requirements against professional and institutional values. Flexibility, decisiveness, and quickness are essential. The organization must be united in purpose. The internal politics of the medical staff, the administration, and the board must be harmonious.

Integration requires solutions for the crushing paperwork problems associated with today's health care. This includes the unnecessary duplication of medical records that can only be resolved by a single medical record. Integration at the clinical, administrative, and reimbursement levels requires the institution of computerized medical records and maximizing the quality of administrative records in order to deliver timely information for decision making. Administrative systems for managed care and insurance reporting must be managed. Management information systems capable of measuring cost of care and quality are essential for the integrated health care system. Unfortunately, the typical provider organization of today possesses virtually no computerized database (other than the billing system) describing what it is doing or providing the information needed for making decisions about cost, risk, and clinical practice.

Management information in the practice of medicine is at best nonstandard and at worst nonexistent. Physicians do not understand, know how to use, and trust clinical databases. Medical management information systems, including utilization and quality management programs, are still developmental. There is little agreement among clinicians about the standards or the protocols that should form the infrastructure of such medical management information systems.

Another overwhelming task in setting up an integrated health care system centers around physician compensation. Even experienced and long-existing group practices suffer frequent disagreements and unhappiness within professional ranks about the distribution of professional income. Agreement does not exist about the measurement of productivity either of physicians or from one specialty to another. It is imperative that IHCS organizations balance incentives against performance standards and that they assess the performance of individual physicians.

Finally, there must evolve a culture of customer responsiveness consistent with the creed of a service organization. The challenge is to combat impersonal service, to overcome the professional-centered value system of health care, to be involved in continuous quality improvement, and to add value—a function of cost and quality.

Common Characteristics of Integrated Health Care Systems

Because there are a variety of models, the IHCS is best described through a series of characteristics.

■ First and foremost, it is coordinated and managed.

Physicians are directly tied to the organization, either by employment or exclusive contracts.

Contracted or nongroup physicians usually work under the direction of an associated physician organization.

Single-specialty groups are often under contract as centers of excellence for the system, with sharply discounted fee schedules.

Primary care is a priority, and primary care foundations are sometimes involved to serve and retain a patient base.

There is a business-oriented culture capable of planning, marketing, finance, capital management, allocation of scarce resources, personnel management, and quality control.

Physicians are deeply involved in and committed to the organization and often control it; there are many physician executives present in its management.

IHCS work very well with managed care service lines, either through commercial carriers or with internally developed managed care services.

■ IHCS internalize their utilization and quality control systems, not waiting until an external agency challenges utilization of services or quality of delivered care. These activities are directed by health care professionals and often are led by physician executives.

■ IHCS are customer-driven and characteristically have diversified locations capable of placing primary care proximate to the consumer. They tend to offer economic, after hours, and seven-day service. They internalize systems that are patient-responsive, easing patient access in every way possible.

IHCS are devotees of the new agenda in total quality management and continuous quality improvement.

These characteristics add up to an organization where the agenda of the medical profession is integrated with that of other vendors of service. The IHCS promotes both vertical and horizontal integration of services. It is a distinct departure from the traditional system of multiple community hospitals with scores of physicians competing to peddle their professional wares. It is more than just sharing of facilities, personnel, and medical records. Here, organizational management works to create accountability, quality, and cost control. Management focus is on strategic goals and external pressures. The fundamental basis of such an operation is trust among all of the essential constituencies (i.e., board, management, medical staff, ancillary personnel, nursing, etc.). It is driven by the needs of health care consumers and those who pay for health care. It is not driven by the needs and goals of the professionals who work there. The recognized challenge is to work with payers and consumers to improve the health care delivery system. Competitive advantage consists of the ability to control costs, to increase access to care, and to improve the quality of care.

Trust Is Critical to Integration in Health Care

Integration of health care portends enormous change for all segments of the business. This is especially true for physicians and hospitals. No more can physicians withhold total commitment to the organization where they pursue their careers. No more can they have divided loyalties because they have attractive alternatives that allow them to take their practices elsewhere. Jumping ship will not be a ready option. With managed care, medical practices will not be nearly as portable as they were in the past. Progress and career development will be not so much a task of practice development as a challenge to become indispensable to the organization in which you work.

These changes may appear at first blush to represent good news to health care organizations, especially to embattled hospital administrators who have struggled for years with arrogant, fickle, and uncommitted medical staffs. Actually, there are distressing trade-offs for the hospital in these rosy prospects. The balance of power and control in the hospital at every level of the institution promises to change. Physicians, always important to the hospital, become more so. They become vital in new arenas, such as governance and management. Their professional skills are essential to new agendas, such as medical management, quality improvement, and the new paradigm of managing health.

To understand the transition in balance of power, it is essential to understand the problems facing health care organizations that now seek to vertically integrate services. Physicians are still the licensed professionals with the legal right and authority to use the dangerous, costly, and essential tools of health care delivery. Despite all the initiatives of regulatory bodies, managed care, and medical management, health care organizations remain dependent on physicians to enter into contracts with patients who want or need medical care. Thus, the evolution of the IHCS requires the willing cooperation of physicians. Predictably, physicians will be slow to commit themselves to institutions they do not trust. More important, they will reward and gravitate to those organizations where they discover cultures compatible with physician values.

In order to promote integration, health care organizations must address physician values, physician concerns about control, and the role of physicians in management. Uppermost to accomplishing that is the necessity of gaining the trust of physicians in the organization and its leadership. The quickest route to that end will be to convince physicians they will have sufficient control in the new organization to ensure survival of the things in medicine essential to them. These include authority and control of the clinical decision-making process and commitment to intellectual and scientific excellence, quality control, and their economic and security interests.

If physicians can or should have this prominence of role and authority in organizations, why have they resisted integration in the past? That is not difficult to answer. There was no compelling need to make such commitments; physicians could remain autonomous and do well. Today, however, they have far fewer options. Eventually, they will integrate because integrated organizations will have significant competitive advantage. Nevertheless, it is predictable that physicians will seek integration on their terms. That will probably mean integrated organizations where physician have meaningful influence in governance and management. To some extent, this is apparent today. Many of the most successful and most competitive health care organizations are physician-governed and physician-managed. Can it be done otherwise? Certainly, but at a price that is costly when that organization must compete with one otherwise blessed with a totally committed medical staff and a physician partnership that is facilitated by physician executives who establish and cultivate trust.

Is it worth all the trouble? Can the culture of physicians and hospitals be changed that dramatically? Time will tell, but some organizations and some physicians are already there. The indications are that they are doing well in the process, and they look like winners of the future. They commonly have incorporated physician executives as the agents of change.

The Role of Physician Executives in Integrated Health Care Systems

Trust and commitment are not characteristic features of the relationship of hospitals and physicians.[28] IHCS are better positioned to build trust among hospital boards (governance), management, and medical staff. IHCS emphasize mutual goals of the governing board, professional managers, and physicians. They balance professional values and institutional values. This is particularly pertinent in the area of total quality management. IHCS are positioned to act quickly and decisively in negotiations with purchasers. They develop the resources needed for management information systems that can link the needs of the purchaser with the capabilities of the delivery organization. IHCS can come to grips with the perpetually confounding problem of physician compensation. IHCS are attuned to customer responsiveness and systems ensuring quality responses.

All those and a host of other issues constitute a landscape of disagreement and suspicion that physicians and organizations must resolve if trust is to occur. Their resolution requires engagement of the key partners to integration at levels of understanding rarely realized in hospital settings of the past. The medical profession will need a skilled and understanding agent to lead it in the resolution of such issues. The physician executive is that agent. The hospital is also in need of a new agent—a new leader within its management ranks. An executive who, by nature, experience, and accomplishment, can acquire the trust of the medical staff. The obvious background for that agent is one combining the collegiality of the medical profession and the skills of a trained manager, i.e., a physician executive. This agent of the new health care organization needs an understanding of the compelling forces that will shape the new relationship between the medical staff and the medical delivery organization. Those are realities not well understood by many physicians.

■ The romantic "golden age of medicine" is past.[29]

■ "Private practice" is meaningless terminology.

■ Fee-for-service medicine will soon cease to exist.

■ The separate, independent, self-governing medical staff is anachronistic.

■ Clinical autonomy, not organizational autonomy, is the essential requirement for physicians.

- Competition will engage organizations rather than individuals.

- Management is the venue of action that shapes organizations.

- Medical management is an essential medical specialty that can directly influence patient care and the potential professional satisfaction of medical practice.

Those messages are strongly at odds with the existing culture of medicine. The question is, who can deliver that message?

The ability and acceptability of the physician executive as the leader and communicator to other physicians relates in no small way to identification with the medical culture. It is the pilot who commands the flying organization; the priestly imperative of the clerical hierarchy in religion. Physicians are more likely to follow the directives of a peer, particularly when their professional values have been addressed. The status of the medical degree, common language, experience, and acculturation create a credibility that is not easily earned by a nonphysician executive. The mystique of the medical profession is reinforced by the politics of professionalism: "You can't be in the guild if you haven't served the apprenticeship," "If you're not in, you can't lead," and the preferred style of influence is "leadership," not supervision or management! That reality creates an incapacitating barrier to nonphysician managers, whose true claim to competency is training and experience in management affairs.

Professional networks are another asset that derives from cultural membership in the profession. The physician draws on a professional network that powers itself by professional referral. The leverage of the political relationship of one physician to another in that influential network is a key ingredient in the physician executive's effectiveness as a change agent. In hospitals, they are often leaders in the informal organization that controls most hospital medical staff decisions. These are all factors that derive from professional membership in the medical culture and enhance the ability of physicians to manage health systems.

One would also expect to see the advancement of physicians to the management of professionals in the health care organization because of the primacy of the physician as leader of the medical team. Physicians are a logical choice for supervision of the professionally related operations of the health care business. In competition with administrators or other health professionals (nurses, technicians, etc.), physicians' historical position of authority and their scientific/legal role as licensed professionals affords them a strong advantage. Positions such as vice president of professional affairs are now filled by physicians, and they are beginning to extend their area of authority from medical staff-related operations to other professional services, such as nursing and ancillary services.

Presently, physicians retain a large residual reservoir of respect in society, despite their having suffered some loss of status and control in the recent past. That credibility is a distinct advantage to the health care organization in the competitive marketplace. Physicians are particularly well positioned in ambulatory care, which is an expanding area of health care.

In the strictly "doctor organization," such as a medical group, the imperative of the physician as the primary executive is most evident. Medical groups draw on an almost constant tradition of physician ownership, management, and control. Executive authority in most cases entails a favorable mix of professional competency, political savvy, strong leadership skills, competence in communication, and good networking within the medical group. The ownership of most doctor organizations by doctors makes this inevitable. However, the growing size and success of medical groups is evidence of the accomplishment of physician executives in the operation of this successful and competitive type of health care institution.

A distinct asset for the physician executive is a wealth of knowledge about the health care system derived from patient care processes. Their technological knowledge of the business from a hands-on perspective creates insights into the delivery process that are knowledgeable of patient-consumer needs. Comprehension of the consumer's tastes and preferences has been acquired through daily contact with patients. When physicians are trained in economics, systems, and finance, that knowledge can translate into cost-effective decisions that are arguable to other physicians. Because physicians have played the provider role, they understand the resources (goods and services) required to effect medical treatment. Very important, physicians are key in connecting quality of output to quantity of resources (input) used in the delivery of medical care. Where required to do so, they can gauge appropriate levels of productivity and thereby affect the cost-effectiveness of health care. Thus, medical experience is a decided asset in the management of the health care delivery process.

While they are qualified in many respects, there is still a reluctance on the part of some physicians to get involved in management or to respect their peers' desire to do so. For physicians, autonomy remains an important value. Doctors resist the notion of managing other professionals, looking upon management with suspicion and distrust. There is a suggested status differential, with administration appearing less prestigious and, sometimes, lower salaried. However, salaries are now becoming equivalent or greater on the average. There is the contention that "real doctors" practice medicine—a medical belief that draws frequent debate even within the councils of the American College of Physician Executives—i.e., "Does the medical director need to remain in practice to retain legitimacy in the eyes of other doctors?" Harking back to the original question, physicians may have the inclination to become executives, but they must be prepared to meet significant opposition within their own profession. Therefore, it is a hard choice for physicians to become managers.

By virtue of their medical training, physicians may have acquired several less obvious assets of value in management. Medical education emphasizes problem solving, decision making, and interpersonal skills. Physicians have been through a boot camp that drilled them in long hours, hard work, and high levels of stress. They have learned to examine the facts, analyze information, and arrive at timely decisions. They are taught to deal with crises and pressure-filled situations. Communication and people skills have been honed by the practice of medicine. By completion of a medical education, they have demonstrated that they are intelligent, highly motivated, and educable; they possess certain personality traits (perseverance, aggressiveness, competitiveness) that are most useful to the manager. The medical degree alone represents a substantial investment in human capital. The addition of training in management is a formidable preparation for a new genre of health care administrators.

On the other hand, medical training produces characteristics and attitudes that are antithetical to good management practice. Collegiality runs counter to the management notion of scalar authority in the organization. Physicians have been trained to work in one-to-one situations, where the doctor is dominant. They are excellent short-term diagnosticians, trained to make decisions based on data. Physicians function within the classical medical model—a scientific model in which, to arrive at a conclusion, data are required. If left to wonder, they are inclined to perform the infinite experiment, always asking, "Where are the data?" By contrast, managers often tend to deal with problems using limited data, trusting their reason, intuition, and experience. The two camps clash when the manager desires to act and the physician holds back, striving to be objective. The two professions are also different in their orientation to people and organizations, leadership and behavioral styles, and constraints of their working environments.

Lack of academic preparation for management is a clear shortcoming of most physician executive candidates. With only their medical education, physicians do not have adequate background or formal training to undertake executive responsibility in most organizations. Fortunately, they have come to recognize this, and many are now working to compensate for this lack of preparation. While the past training of many current physician executives has been experiential and on-the-job, physicians are now seeking postgraduate level education in management. A large number of physician administrators surveyed by Kindig and Lastiri[30] feel that formal graduate course work or advanced degrees are advisable (62.1 percent) or should be required (21.5 percent). Physicians are seeking continuing education through ACPE, the American College of Healthcare Executives, the American Hospital Association, the American Management Association, and the American Group Practice Association; through concentrated courses taught at universities such as Harvard Business School and Sloan School of Management at the Massachusetts Institute of Technology; and by returning to academia for graduate degrees in business or health administration. The Geisinger Foundation and the Lovelace Medical Center have presented a "mini-MBA program" in management to their physician leaders. The University of Wisconsin, Tulane University, and New York University have developed master of science degrees in administrative medicine organized for physicians. Physicians are seeking to rectify the deficit in their management training—an education that was formerly acquired only by mentorship or apprenticeship, self-teaching, and on-the-job experience.

As physician executives assume more management responsibility in the health care system, they will make a substantial contribution in addressing the needs of physicians who see the IHCS as an effective response to changes in health care. Those physicians will seek to maintain their professional arbitorship of quality of care, their clinical authority, and appropriate influence in organizational decisions. The independent self-governing medical staff is an ineffective vehicle to accomplish those goals. Physician executives are the managers to address those needs of the medical staff within the medical organization of the future.

Toward A Nation Served By IHCS

Over the past decade, physicians have assumed new roles in the management of health care organizations. Integration of the various services that make up the health care system has been occurring for several decades and is accelerating. The success of the IHCS concept requires effective decision making in an environment of synergy between both the medical and the management components of the institution. There is an evident need for an agent capable of spanning the disconnection that exists between the medical profession and the organization, an executive who can bridge the gap between the resource allocators and the deliverers of service. Getting control over health care expenditures and unifying the agenda of the health care organization are not likely to occur without the involvement of physicians. The public good will be well served by a blending of practice medicine and management of tomorrow's health care institution.

For the physician who is willing, who can work to acquire the management knowledge and skills, and who desires to be a manager, there is a place. As a manager, the physician has some unique attributes, skills, and experience to offer. Physician executives have demonstrated their ability to function in all types of positions and at all levels of organizations. Physician executives benefit from their practical knowledge of health care, certain legal realities, societal attitudes toward physicians, and the status of the profession. Physician executives can speak the language of patient care and of management, bringing a legitimate authority to health care to which neither nonphysician executives nor physicians without management training can aspire. As a specialist in management, the physician executive can serve the medical profession and the patient by sustaining the influence and authority of physicians within IHCS.

References

1. Goss, M. "Administration and the Physician." *American Journal of Public Health* 52(2):183-91, Feb. 1962.

2. Smith, R. "The Case for Physician Involvement in Governance and Management." *Hospital Medical Staff* 5(5):28-30, May 1976.

3. Fischer, D. "Commentaries on CHA Guidelines: Physician-Directors: A Logical Next Step." *Hospital Progress* 56(3):29,33,36, March 1975.

4. Lindner, J. "Point of View: Better Management, Not Just More Money: Physician Involvement." *Health Care Management Review* 2(3):47-50, Summer 1977.

5. Hillman, A., and others. "Managing the Medical-Industrial Complex." *New England Journal of Medicine* 315(8):511-3, Aug. 21, 1986.

6. Higgins, J., and Vincize, J. *Strategic Management.* New York, N.Y.: Drydan Press, 1989.

7. White, J. "Americans' Views on Healthcare and Rationing." *Health Progress* 72(1):14-5,32, Jan.-Feb. 1991.

8. Coile, R. "The New Medicine: Part I-"Medical Megatrends" for the 1990s." *Hospital Strategy Report* 2(3):1,4-7, Jan. 1990.

9. Retchin, S., and Brown, B. "Elderly Patients with Congestive Heart Failure under Prepaid Care." *American Journal of Medicine* 90(2):236-42, Feb. 1991.

10. Carlisle, D., and others. HMO vs Fee-for-Service Care of Older Persons with Acute Myocardial Infarction." *American Journal of Public Health* 82(12):1626-30, Dec. 1992.

11. Udvarhelyi, I., and others. "Comparison of the Quality of Ambulatory Care for Fee-for-Service and Prepaid Patients." *Annals of Internal Medicine* 115(5):394-400, Sept. 1, 1991.

12. Retchin, S., and Preston, J. "Effects of Cost Containment on the Care of Elderly Diabetics." *Archives of Internal Medicine* 151(11):2244-8, Nov. 1991.

13. Vernon, S., and others. "Quality of Care for Colorectal Cancer in Fee-for-Service and Health Maintenance Organization Practice." *Cancer* 69(10):2418-25, May 15, 1992.

14. Retchin, S., and others. How the Elderly Fare in HMOs: Outcomes from the Medicare Competition Demonstrations." *Health Services Research* 27(5):651-69, Dec. 1992.

15. Temkin-Greener, H., and Winchell, M. "Medicaid Beneficiaries under Managed Care: Provider Choice and Satisfaction." *Health Services Research* 26(4):509-29, Oct. 1991.

16. Zuckerman, H., and Kaluzny, A. "Strategic Alliances in Health Care: The Challenges of Cooperation." *Frontiers of Health Services Management* 7(3):3-23, Spring 1991.

17. Chenen, A. Hospital-Physician Joint Ventures: Beware of Hospitals Bearing Gifts." *Medical Staff Counselor* 5(4):67-9, Fall 1991.

18. Rosenfield, R., and others. "Health Care Joint Ventures." In Wolper, L., and Pena, J. (Eds.), *Health Care Administration*. Rockville, Md.: Aspen Publishing, 1987.

19. Reifsteck, S. "Physician/Hospital Bonding." *Medical Group Management Journal* 38(4):68,70,74-6, July/Aug. 1991.

20. Zismer, D., and others. "Successful Joint Ventures for Today's Competitive Health Care Marketplace." *Group Practice Journal* 37(5):27,30,35,38,40, Sept./Oct. 1988.

21. Korenchuk, K. "Once the Choice Is Made: A Close Look at the Joint Venture Option. Part 2." *Medical Group Management Journal* 38(4):24-8,30,33, July/Aug. 1991.

22. Fox, W. "Vertical Integration Strategies: More Promising than Diversification." *Health Care Management Review* 14(3):49-56, Summer 1989.

23. Shortell, S. "Diversification Strategy Benefits Innovative Leader." *Modern Healthcare* 20(10):38, March 12, 1990.

24. Brown, M., and McCool, B. "Health Care Systems: Predictions for the Future." *Health Care Management Review* 15(3):87-94, Summer 1990.

25. Barnett, A. "The Integration of Health Care as a Model for the Future." *Medical Group Management Journal* 38(4):16,18, July/Aug. 1991.

26. Johnsson, J. "Direct Contracting: Employers Look to Hospital-Physician Partnerships to Control Costs." *Hospitals* 66(4):56,58,60, Feb. 20, 1992.

27. Korenchuk, K. "Changing Concepts for Changing Times: Physician Employment Contracts Revisited." *Group Practice Journal* 40(6):10,12,14,16, Nov.-Dec. 1991.

28. Coile, R. *The New Medicine*. Rockville, Md.: Aspen Publications, 1990.

29. Burnham, J. "American Medicine's Golden Age. What Happened to It?" *Science* 215(19):1474-9, March 1982.

30. Kindig, D., and Lastiri, S. "Administrative Medicine: A New Specialty?" *Health Affairs* 5(4):146-56, Winter 1986.

David J. Ottensmeyer, MD, FACPE, is President and Chief Executive Officer, Lovelace Medical Foundation, Albuquerque, New Mexico. Howard L. Smith, PhD, is Associate Dean, Anderson Schools of Management, University of New Mexico, Albuquerque.

Why Physicians Move into Management

CHAPTER 4

by Michael B. Guthrie, MD, MBA, FACPE

W hy would a successful physician choose to leave the rewards and satisfactions of medical practice to take on the uncertainties and unfamiliarity of a management or executive position? Since that question was first asked in the 1988 edition of this book, a lot more physicians have chosen to make the transition.

A small group of pioneers, physicians in early management positions in group practices and some larger hospitals, came together in the mid-1970s to form the American Academy of Medical Directors. They were the first, 65-70 strong, who faced this question from their colleagues and others about their motivation in moving from medical practice into management. The American Academy of Medical Directors, and subsequently the American College of Physician Executives, has continued to grow, now numbering more than 9,000 active members. All of these physicians are in one way or another navigating the transformation from medical practice to an executive role in different health care organizations.

The need for physician executives continues to increase. The acceptance of physician executives is also growing. There is pressure for more physician involvement in executive decision making in a variety of medical environments—hospitals, health care systems, clinics and multispecialty group practices, IPAs, HMOs, PPOs, insurance companies, academic health centers, biotechnology firms, utilization management and review firms, and government. In addition, because businesses around the country are taking a more sophisticated and earnest approach in their negotiations for health care benefits, physician executives play an expanded role in the negotiations and communications between industrial buyers, third-party payers, and providers.

Finally, the political changes ahead for the health care system, including the variety of state-based health care reforms and the design of a federal health care system, demand the responsiveness of the balanced clinical and business orientation provided best by a physician executive.

Different Interests and Needs

The expectations of physician executives vary, depending on the role that they choose to play. The varieties of these roles, as mentioned here and elsewhere in this text, speak to and encourage a variety of different interests and motivations of physicians as they make the move into management. Physicians become executives not just because of a desire to better represent physicians to the hospital board or to better understand and manage clinical quality in their organizations. In addition, physicians are finding an expanding role in strategic planning, organizational change management, and championing continuous improvement in both clinical and nonclinical areas.

Understanding why physicians become managers has thus become increasingly relevant. Surveys show that nearly all hospitals of 200 or more beds have medical directors or are considering medical director positions. Data from other surveys show a steady increase in the number of hospitals interested in the medical director position. More physicians are also interested in new medical management positions related to non-medical staff affairs. Such positions are increasingly available in multispecialty group practices, clinics, and HMOs. With the rapid expansion of managed care over the past five years in most urban areas and the predicted continuing growth of alternative delivery systems under health care reform, the role of physician executives in prepaid and other managed care programs will continue to increase in importance and visibility.

Dissatisfaction with the Practice of Medicine?

Why does a physician make this remarkable career move into a managerial or executive position? Common sense, as well as theory, gives us some reasons, many of them confirmed by self-report survey data from physician executives around the country.

Taking physicians as a select segment of the population, it is fairly obvious that they are bright and well-motivated, successfully making it through the socialization and education processes to finally become a medical professional. These individuals generally show a high need for achievement, recognition, and challenge, as well an expectation for continuing rewards that go beyond pay and benefits. These implicit rewards come in the form of their understanding and appreciation for the significance of the tasks that they perform; their ability to operate with relative autonomy and control; their ability, and the frequent opportunity, to see their work completed from beginning to end; and the chance to get some direct feedback from the work that they perform for others. In addition, they have the continuing opportunity for advancement, social prestige, intellectual challenge, and employment of a variety of skills in their work.

For many physicians, however, medical practice turns out to be something of a disappointment. After a few years in a private clinical practice, many physicians find actual day-to-day practice offers scant opportunity for challenge and change, even though the rewards of patient care and contact continue. Many physicians at that point begin to look around for an opportunity to make a greater impact on the larger health care system as a whole.

Personal dissatisfaction can be expressed in a variety of ways. Some physicians seek advanced certification or subspecialty training. Many physicians look to outside activities in their communities. Some physicians advance through their subspecialty or local medical society organizations. Some physicians seek positions of leadership and authority in these professional organizations. Some physicians seek positions of leadership in the political structures of medical societies or medical associations.

In recent years, physicians have also become active in organizing alternative delivery systems, sometimes participating in entrepreneurial medical company development. For some physicians, the opportunity to influence political groups or government in a policy-making role has been a most challenging outlet.

Finally, many physicians with this experience consider moving into part-time or full-time executive positions in health care organizations, usually ones with which they have been previously associated.

Motivation: Results from the Literature

Two surveys conducted under the auspices of the American College of Physician Executives have reported on the reasons physicians opt for expanded management responsibilities. In 1986, the then American Academy of Medical Directors undertook a survey of physician executives, testing their reasons for moving from practice into management and analyzing their satisfaction with the results of this move. From the approximately one-thousand responses to that survey, a number of trends and distinctions were apparent.[1] In 1992, a random sample of 176 physician executives was reported, with similar results.[2]

Though the reasons for the change from practice to management are multiple and individual, there are common themes in these self-reports. In the 1986 survey, 97 percent of the respondents said desire for leadership was somewhat or very important as a motivation to become managers. Similarly, in the 1992 survey, 87 percent of those responding reported the single most important factor influencing them in choosing a management career was the perceived opportunity for leadership in a medical organization. Respondents in both surveys wanted to have an impact on many people and to be involved in health policy decisions. Desire for increased income or other financial considerations, such as fringe benefits, were important influences in less than a third of those responding in both surveys.

These same physician executives were asked to report their major goals when they made the change from practice to management. The goals reported in these surveys vary, but several were mentioned by most respondents in similar words. These physicians wanted to improve health services in their organization and to be a part of the new directions in health care. They also wanted to influence policy decisions for health care as a whole wherever possible. In addition, many physicians candidly reported that they wanted to search out more personal and professional satisfaction.

Given these desires, physicians who have become managers frequently get what they are looking for—leadership opportunities, impact on people, authority, challenge, and opportunities for professional growth. Seventy-nine percent of respondents in the 1992 survey stated a desire to have an impact on organizational policies governing medical care as a factor in their career decision to participate in management. Eighty-four percent of the respondents of the 1986 survey reported that they achieved opportunities for increased impact on people. Seventy percent in the same survey reported additional challenges in their work. Eighty-nine percent reported opportunities for leadership, 80 percent reported increases in authority, and 61 percent felt that they had achieved additional professional growth.

In the 1992 survey, an even larger proportion of those responding (69.8 percent) identified a need for more physician-centered direction in the management of medical organizations as a factor in their decisions to expand their management activities. Eighty-four percent of the respondents in the same survey found their physician executive roles very satisfying professionally.

One exception to the positive responses to these questions on satisfaction concerns reflection by physician executives on how much autonomy and control over their own working conditions they experienced after making the move to management. As one might anticipate, the transition from independence to interdependence in organizational life is a major hurdle. In the 1986 survey, 35 percent reported more autonomy and 38 percent reported less. Thirty-seven percent of respondents in the same survey reported more control over their daily lives, and 38 percent reported less.

Factors Influencing the Decision

What do physician executives report as the major influences on their career changes? The attractions of management itself are reported in the 1986 survey by 58 percent of the respondents as having been an important aspect of their willingness to make this change. In the 1992 sample, two other factors that conventional wisdom has suggested might be important in physician decisions to move away from clinical activities to administration were not significant to those respondents. Only a third of those responding to that survey gave weight to a desire to gain better control over their time as a factor in their expansion of management responsibilities. The number of respondents influenced significantly by the rise in cost of medical practice was even smaller, with 17 percent reporting it as an important factor. Still, nearly half (45 percent) of respondents did cite "quality of life" considerations, such as family time and stress levels, as important in their decisions to increase the percentage of time devoted to management.

In the 1986 survey, respondents indicated that their families gave some or a great deal of encouragement for this transition about 47 percent of the time and discouraged them only 13 percent of the time.

Contrary to conventional speculation, competition from other physicians was reported to have been of little or no influence in making the decision to move into management roles by 81 percent of the respondent physicians in 1986. However, boredom with medical practice was reported to have been a significant influence by 24 percent of these same respondents.

Given these influences and their goals for the change from practice to management, how do physician executives perceive the road by which they came to their management responsibilities? Responses from the 1992 survey show that service on medical staff committees or in medical staff governance and participation in practice management were much more highly valued than were experiences in medical society activities, nonmedical community organizations, or the military.

In the 1986 survey, respondents indicated that peers and colleagues in medical practice were generally encouraging of the physician to make the move into management (45 percent reported that they were somewhat or greatly encouraged by their peers), but there was more substantial encouragement from nonphysician colleagues in their health care organizations (65 percent of respondents indicated that they were somewhat or greatly encouraged by the nonphysicians in their peer groups).

Although burdened by the misconceptions of their medical colleagues (47 percent of respondents in the 1986 survey reported that they were seen as "administrators" by other physicians), physician executives still report positively on the authority and prestige they have achieved in the move to managerial positions.

Conclusions

Physicians move into management positions for many positive reasons, most of them having to do with their personal need for growth, achievement, and challenge rather than their fear of the negative pressures or demands of medical practice.

The positive reasons for interest in management that are cited most include the opportunity for impact on more people in their communities in a scope that is beyond that possible in private practice, a positive influence on policy-making decisions, and positive power in their organizations and in their communities. Additionally, the opportunity to redirect health care organizations in a more physician-centered direction and authority for decision making on a scale impossible for an individual physician are also positive reasons why physicians seek out increased management responsibilities.

Negative influences also exist that push physicians in the direction of management, including some dissatisfaction with the everyday aspects of medical practice, the physical demands, and the demands of patient care itself. These are not significant influences in either of the two surveys reported here.

Most physicians are encouraged by family and friends to make the change. Nonphysician colleagues seem to be more encouraging than peers. Most physician executives report that they are satisfied with the change, identify themselves now as managers or executives, and plan to remain in their management positions. When asked if they ever miss medical practice, most physicians clearly state that, although they enjoyed patient care, they have found that they can help more patients by being managers or executives than they would ever have been able to help as clinicians. Their roles are increasingly recognized as important for the future of the health care system, particularly in balancing the demands for high-quality patient care with the economic issues in our turbulent health care marketplace.

As these physician executives mature in their managerial roles and acquire greater self- and professional definition, they are functioning as role models for career decisions by other physicians facing the same personal issues and seeking additional challenge and impact. More and more physicians are electing to take on medical management positions as a professional option. As the medical management profession grows, it is also likely that physicians' interest will move—perhaps slowly, but definitely—to a more generalized view of management. While physicians can be expected to continue to play major management roles in the medical or patient care areas of organizations, they are also now taking on nonmedical management roles: in strategic planning and marketing, utilization management, quality improvement, and general operational management. Finally, physician executives are also functioning as CEOs of clinics, hospitals, and health care systems. Additionally, roles for physicians in entrepreneurial activities peripherally related to traditional health care management are expanding in the areas of biotechnology, medical informatics, medical supply distribution, and insurance functions.

Why do physicians move into management? When physician executives are asked these questions, they report that they are attracted by the challenges and opportunities that this new profession has offered and continues to offer in increasing variety.

References

1. Montgomery, K. "Today's Physician Manager: A New Breed." *Physician Executive* 12(10):14-7, Sept.-Oct. 1986.

2. Kimmey, J., and Haddock, C. "Physician Executives' Characteristics and Attitudes." *Physician Executive* 18(3):3-8, May-June 1992.

Other References

Guthrie, M., and others. "Productivity: How Much Does This Job Mean?" *Nursing Management* 15(2):16-20, Feb. 1985.

McCall, M., and Claire, J. "In Transit From Physician to Manager, Part I." *Physician Executive* 18(2):3-9, March/April 1992.

McCall, M., and Claire, J. "In Transit From Physician to Manager, Part II." *Physician Executive* 18(3):15-9, May/June 1992.

Michael B. Guthrie, MD, MBA, FACPE, is President and CEO, Health Dimensions, Inc., San Jose, Calif.

The Unique Contribution of the Physician Executive to Health Care Management

by David J. Ottensmeyer, MD, FACPE, and M.K. Key, PhD

CHAPTER 5

This chapter assesses whether the physician executive is truly a management asset to the health care organization. What attributes make the physician more or less valuable in managerial roles? Through a review of historical precedents, physician involvement in health care organizations, the current context of medical practice, and the unique socialization of the physician, we will examine the tenet that physicians possess distinct qualities and experience suiting them for management in the health care field.

History of Physician Involvement in Medical Organization and Health Care Management

Health care has always been labor intensive, characteristically a one-on-one relationship of the medical professional with the consumer of health care (patients). It remains, although rapidly consolidating, organized around that model, still constituted of hundreds of thousands of individual providers, institutions, and small vendors of care. It has been a fragmented business requiring rudimentary management infrastructures. Even in hospitals, where organizational size and complexity demanded the growth of a sophisticated management establishment, the medical staff continued as a largely undirected, separate, and independent professional group. The medical staff, a group essential to virtually all aspects of productivity in the hospital, was committed to "professionalism" and an associated resistance to the management process.

The early health care system was fragmented and functioned with little structure, planning, or coordination. The "doctor" side of the business was an enterprise of small business people and was carried out in the style of a cottage industry. Starr[1] describes medical practitioners as a profession derived from the European guild systems of past centuries. It derived from the English medical profession, which was caught up in the English class struggles of earlier centuries. As the American profession established itself, it too involved the quest of physicians to gain some level of qualitative social recognition alongside the established aristocracy. This effort continued during the colonization of the North American continent, when the roots of the present medical profession were transplanted from England.

The profession evolved into a "sovereign" profession—a term Starr uses to depict the social privilege, economic power, and political influence of the medical profession. Among the learned professions, medicine became the "profession among professions." It carefully and tightly controlled competition within its membership by control of the system of preparation (medical education), by restricting access with systems of licensure and credentialing, and by internally enforcing codes of ethics that upheld standards and controlled undesirable influences, such as overt competition. These normative influences were incorporated into the doctrine of "professionalism," which was strongly internalized by the rank and file membership. Professionalism focuses on concepts of self-governance and peer control by a collegial group, licensed and privileged because of its special body of knowledge.

Such professional sovereignty was ill-suited to management or oversight by nonpeers (sovereigns cannot be ruled by others). Indeed, it has been averse to any management at all. Manifestations of the historical resistance to management include idealization of the solo practitioner, the notion of an independent self-governing medical staff, private practice of medicine, and physician scorn of managed care. It rationalized the notion of "patient advocacy" and was fortified by a fierce commitment to fee-for-service reimbursement, which ensures control of the economic exchange at a very basic level within the system. Thus, the structure of the early health care system, the social positioning of the physician in society, and the professional structure of medicine did not lay a good foundation for development of management as a vocational concern of physicians.

In the first half of this century, the roles that did develop for physician executives were often token in nature or political in content. Characteristically, they were far removed from management policy or decisionmaking. The positions usually derived from an organizational need for technical, not management, expertise. Initially the nature of physician involvement in organizations included the following:

Bureaucrat.

Academic.

Technological supervisor or leader of a medical team.

Coordinator of a program.

Advisor to management.

Interface between line management and the medical staff.

■ Elder statesman.

■ Public relations spokesperson.

Physicians often filled the role of director in departments of public health, administering a *bureaucratic* subdivision of a jurisdiction's health operations. In this role, they depended on their professional expertise for legitimacy. The *academic* is personified in the chair of an academic department. The master/student pedagogical environment, as well as the Herr Professor/junior staff relationship depict the dynamic in that setting. In government organizations, such as the Centers for Disease Control, physicians similarly undertook the role of *technical supervisors* or *coordinators of programs*. The medical coordinator in a group practice is another example of a coordinator or facilitator of operations. *Advisors to management* are found in insurance companies and industrial organizations in a staff role. The military system frequently has a "staff surgeon" on the commander's staff. In the military, physicians assumed executive/command positions beginning in the early 20th Century, when separate organizations (hospitals, medical battalions, etc.) were formed as identifiable entities in the troop list.

The need for an interface agent between medical staff and line management was the genesis of the "medical director" or director of professional affairs position in hospitals. The position was frequently filled by an *elder statesman* who had credibility with the medical staff and possessed the political savvy and wisdom to avoid "rocking the boat." Finally, the *public relations spokesperson* was seen in the performances by Dr. Dennis O'Leary. His face became well known on evening television while former President Reagan was hospitalized at George Washington University Hospital in Washington, D.C., subsequent to the attempt on his life in 1981. Now chief executive officer of the Joint Commission on Accreditation of Healthcare Organizations (JCAHO). Dr. O'Leary was medical director at the hospital at that time.

These positions hold several things in common. Typically, physicians were hired for academic, professional, or scientific skills, not because they had management skills. Their promotion from mid- or entry-level positions to the ranks of manager/executives occurred from the need to oversee other physician-specialists/technicians and the professionally related operations of the organization. Their leadership was called upon to integrate other physicians into the organizational agenda. Some advanced to broader areas of authority, moving into line management, policy-making, or executive roles within the organization. Thus, the physician was typically hired as a technical specialist within management. Over time, some rose to main-line management jobs. Entry into this career progression usually occurred after a significant number of years of medical practice. It characteristically involved little prior academic preparation to undertake management responsibilities.

The technical or staff positions held by physicians tended to have little line or policy-making authority. In advisory positions, they did not constitute a threat to career managers—nor did they offer substantial experience in organizational affairs. They were intrinsically narrow in scope. When leadership was desired, the selected physicians were often trusted elder statesmen within the medical staff whose major qualifications were acceptance and trust by peers. They could be depended upon not to challenge management with their personal ambition within the management hierarchy. As a public relations person, the physician served as a diplomat, politician, figurehead, and "front man." This similarly did not challenge the authority of line management.

In hospitals, custom and regulation tended to exclude physicians from management or governance. In practice, both the medical staff and hospital administration espoused the concept of the separate and independent, self-governing medical staff. In that mode, the medical staff itself was suspicious of any physician who joined the

"Philistines" in administration. The '70s witnessed a growth of tension between medical staff and administration, with the formation of physicians' unions and work slowdowns. As recently as three decades ago, physicians were excluded from membership on hospital boards, in part due to the notion of conflict of interest.[2] During the 1940s and '50s, it was felt that doctors should not be involved in administration, management, and governance.[3] The '60s brought change. The 1968 Report of the Secretary's Advisory Committee on Hospital Effectiveness,[4] known as the Barr Report, recommended that physicians be involved in decision making and held accountable for decisions affecting costs of hospital care. Much of the writing of that era focused on strategies for physician involvement in decision making, to resolve conflicts among board, staff, and administration.[3,5] The position of medical director was the product of this strife. Physicians as a part of management took on the task of resolving hospital-medical staff conflicts, trying to replace conflict with cooperation.[6,7]

There were other factors that worked to reduce the number of physicians who devoted time to management of hospitals. While physicians had served as superintendents of hospitals in the late Nineteenth and early Twentieth Centuries, this practice declined over time. An American College of Healthcare Executives survey found that, in 1972, there were 813 physician hospital administrators; by 1978, there were only 92.[7] In part, this was attributable to a shortage of physicians. But, at the same time, a new "management professional"—e.g., one with a master's degree in hospital, business, or public health administration—began to populate the ranks of management in health care organizations. Concurrently, physician attitudes ("real doctors practice medicine") directed physicians into clinical practice and away from management endeavors. Those who were "unable to compete" or had grown "old and tired" were pictured as suitable for organizational affairs. In sum, many disincentives existed for physicians to become managers. They resulted from professional attitudes, prejudice, and economic and historical constraints, real or imagined.

Emergence of the Physician Executive

Despite the barriers and problems previously described, the 1980s found physicians moving into management at an accelerating pace. This decade produced more opportunity and greater need for physician executives because of the changes in health care. Cost containment required physician involvement, because they controlled both demand for and allocation of resources. In the face of increasing government regulation, successful financial management of hospitals became very complex, requiring cooperation and a more effective interface between doctors and administration. The advent of alternative health care organizations produced more need for management of the delivery process and more management opportunities.[8] The essence of managed health care is medical management: restructuring the delivery system itself by changing the behavior of physicians. This demands strong professional medical leadership and a management effort that differs from the management of past health care systems, which focused on facilities and services.

The recent increase in the physician supply has also produced more physicians interested in management. Those who are insufficiently challenged by the routine of clinical medicine or who desire a career change are pursuing management opportunities. This is not limited to senior physicians. Young physicians are now moving into management positions much earlier in their careers,[9] with more prior preparation and chance for on-the-job management education. The 20-year-old American College of Physician Executives (ACPE) has witnessed tremendous recent growth: total membership in January 1994 was 8,491.[10] In 1993, the average number of new membership applications was 152 per month.[10] Similarly, the American College of Healthcare Executives is targeting physician executives as one of its seven health care manager categories. Kindig and Lastiri found that physicians in administration constituted 3 percent of all MDs, or 13,500 physicians, in 1985. In 1992, the number had risen to 14,819 physicians. In their survey of 878 of these physicians, they found 33 percent working in hospitals, 24 percent in medical schools, 23 percent in government agencies, 5 percent in health care corporations, 4 percent in group practices/clinics and in industry, one percent in HMOs, and 8 percent in others.[11] In 1992, the American Medical Association reported that 14,819 physician listed their professional activity as "administration."[12] AMA data show that the number of physicians involved in administration has increased at an average rate of 9.0 percent each five years over the past 15 years. The age of physicians in administration is still tilted to seniority, with 52 percent being over age 55 and 22 percent being over age 56. These trends suggest that the number of physician administrators or executives will increase in the future.

Physician executives now occupy a variety of positions in health care and related organizations. Table 1, page 72, illustrates the logical niches for physicians in health care organizations. Possible management positions vary on a spectrum of involvement from the medical team leader, through the departmental supervisor, management staff support, and line manager, to, at the other extreme, the executive manager. These can be arrayed with increasing percentage of management time and decreasing amount of clinical time as the positions advance along the continuum. The positions are classified in the table as executive, line management, technical management, or staff support, with examples of each.

There is a difference between current roles for physicians and bureaucratic or technical positions seen prior to 1970. New positions for physicians entail more management and executive responsibilities. Management has been defined as both a discipline and a culture, which, through the responsible exercise of authority, organizes people and resources to achieve organizational and societal goals.[13] Executives are responsible for planning, staffing, directing, and controlling entire organizations.[14] ACPE survey data show that 1,029 of its members now hold senior executive positions in health care organizations.[15]

In conclusion, there are more opportunities now available for physicians with an interest in management, running the gamut from technical team leadership to top executive positions. The need for physician executives is increasing, and there are likely to be more candidates for these positions. Job descriptions are moving away from the administrative/technical/bureaucratic positions to genuinely executive-level roles. The question that remains to be answered is whether the physician brings any unique qualifications to the execution of those roles.

Table 1. Logical Niches for Physicians in Health Care Organizations

Organization	Niche
Group Practice	Executive Management[1] Line Management[2] Technical Management[3] Staff Support[4]
MeSH	Executive Management Staff Support
Independent Practice Association	Executive Management Staff Support
Managed Health Care Company	Executive Management Line or Technical Management of quality assurance, provider relations and contracting, utilization management Staff Support
Government/Military	Executive Management Technical Management Staff Support
Industrial	Technical Management Staff Support
Hospitals	Executive Management/Professional Interface Management of Professionals Management of Technology Management of Interdisciplinary Teams

1. "Executive Management" refers to leadership/policy roles (CEO, Chief Medical Officer).

2. "Line Management" roles include medical director and department chair (primary care, outpatient, and specialty departments), commissioners, and public health administrators.

3. "Technical Management" roles include department heads or specialties, such as radiology, pathology, and anesthesiology.

4. "Staff Support" includes occupational, industial, and insurance medicine; medical coordinator; and medical staff officer.

The Preparation of Physicians for Management Roles

There are some circumscribing legal consideration in the management of physicians in health care organizations. Medical practice acts vary from state to state, but they usually place a prohibition on corporations' employing or supervising physicians. In essence, only a physician is felt qualified to hire and supervise another physician in the practice of medicine. (HMO legislation may serve as an exception.) There are also limits of licensure that prevent other professionals and lay persons from engaging in the practice of medicine. Therefore those individuals cannot supervise physicians. State quality assurance/utilization review legislation may have a mandate requiring that programs of this nature be directed by physicians. Accreditation requirements from JCAHO include a standard that licensed physicians hold the majority of positions on hospital medical staff executive committees. Functionally organized departments of a hospital must be chaired or directed by board-certified or otherwise qualified physicians.[16] Thus, ready-made roles for the physician executive are "locked-in" by these stipulations.

The ability and acceptability of the physician as the manager of other physicians relates in no small way to identification with the medical culture. Physicians are more likely to follow the directives of peers, particularly when their own values have been addressed. The medical degree, common language, experience, and acculturation create a credibility that is not easily earned by a nonphysician executive. The mystique of the medical profession is reinforced by the politics of professionalism: "You can't be in the guild if you haven't served the apprenticeship"; "if you're not in, you can't lead." The preferred style of influence is "leadership" and pedagogy, not supervision or management. That reality creates an incapacitating barrier to nonphysician managers, whose true claim to competency is training and experience in administration.

As previously noted, the fragmented health care system in general and its physician component in particular are not comfortable with evolving requirements for more accountability. Health care evolved in favor of independence of providers, simple structure, professional norms, collegial relationships, and minimal accountability. Now there is intense concern in American society about the workability of that system. Demand for improved access, cost control, and accountability for performance and productivity is a primary social and political issue. The culture of the medical profession is ill suited for response to these concerns. Oriented to peer review of medical practice and professionalism, the accountability demanded affronts its notion of sovereignty and offends deeply held values of autonomy. The change required in mores and beliefs is enormously disruptive. It requires a cultural redefinition for physicians that is now a primary agenda concern for health care organizations and physicians. As organizations work to solve these problems, they are frequently turning to the physician manager to serve as the point person and change agent in the process. Among the array of health care executives and leaders available to tackle this task, the physician executive seems best prepared to deal with the uneasy profession.

Physician executives are well positioned to serve as professional supervisors. There are good historical precedents for the physician executive in that role. They include physician leadership/management in the academic medicine arena, physician directors of public health institutions, military command responsibilities, leadership functions on the medical treatment team, and the management success of physicians in group practices.

The physician who accepts management responsibilities brings attributes that serve the institution well. Status derived from medical education, the practice of medicine, medical acculturation, and membership in the medical clan affords a level of communication and trust difficult for those outside the profession to obtain. Physician executives predictably have excellent insight and instincts about medical politics, something of constant concern to the organization. Access to and understanding of the informal network of the medical staff are valuable tools available to the physician executive.

Physicians bring a number of additional strengths to the management team in the health care organization. A clinical view of nonclinical problems can be a valuable asset to management and can prevent embarrassing administrative "gaffs." The skill of management can be enhanced by the respect the physician may bring with the board, with health care consumers, and in the outside world. Physicians have a distinctly different perspective on the consumer's view of the institution derived from dealing one-on-one with patients at the bedside and in the consultation room.

The management of quality in health care has major aspects that can only be managed by physicians.[17] This is most obvious in attempts to understand the linkage between quality of output and the quantity of necessary resources (input). Moving to the management of medical delivery operations, the physician executive is essential in addressing quality of clinical care, clinical productivity, clinical cost effectiveness, physician performance evaluation, and professional reimbursement.

The growth of managed care and its predictable importance in the future leaves most health care organizations scrambling to catch up and adjust their organizational strategies. The challenge of managed care for the provider is to develop the ability to deliver care in a manner very different from the practices of the past. The task is to deliver all the necessary care to a defined population at a predetermined cost and a defined level of quality. That requires the ability to prospectively determine the amount of care needed, to cost the care, to set clinical and performance goals, to evaluate clinical performance, and to change the behavior of providers to attain desired goals. Those essentials dictate the presence of competent clinical managers who can lead the process at every step, especially at the tricky level of changing practice patterns of physicians. The physician executive is the *sine qua non* of that management exercise.

The health care industry has been consolidating for many years. That is accelerating; its scope is potentially the most fundamental reorganization of an American business witnessed since the end of the Nineteenth Century. It is evident in the hospital business with the formation of strategic alliances and heath care systems. Physicians are moving rapidly away from individual and small partnership practice of medicine into medical groups. In groups, physician executives lead and manage those institutions, many of which are now major corporations, with annual cash flows in the hundreds of millions of dollars. More recently, consolidation has lead to the formation of hospital-physician organizations, medical service organizations, and medical foundations designed to merge with hospitals and insurance carriers.

Consolidation of health care, sometimes called integrated health care, requires a fundamental rapprochement between physicians; hospitals; and, increasingly, insurance organizations. That was rarely accomplished in the past. Where it has occurred, it took long periods of growth and readjustment of culture—time no longer available in today's world of consolidation, managed care, and health care reform.

Despite overwhelming evidence that the future lies in smoothly running, integrated organizations, the medical profession and hospitals remain deeply distrustful of one another. New leadership is needed in both camps; leadership that can envision new relationships and the new opportunities that the integrated organization promises. For the medical profession, there is only one candidate for that role. The physician executive is best positioned to deal with the medical profession in this process. There is no more challenging problem for integration than this.

Even though physicians bring many talents and capabilities to their new roles in health care management, they have some deficiencies. Medical training produces certain results that are orthogonal to good management practice. Collegiality runs counter to the management notion of scaler authority in the organization. Several authors have described distinct differences between physician orientation and that of a manager.[18-22] For simplicity, table 2, page 76, presents the major characterizations of these differences. While most are self-explanatory, a few require further elaboration.

Physicians are trained to work in one-on-one situations where the doctor is dominant. They are excellent short-term diagnosticians, trained to make decisions on the basis of carefully collected data. Physicians function within the classical medical model—a scientific model in which, to arrive at a conclusion, data are required. If left to wonder, they are inclined to perform the infinite experiment, always asking "where are the data?" By contrast, managers often tend to deal with problems using limited data, trusting their reason, intuition, and experience. The two camps clash when the manager desires to act and the physician holds back, striving to be objective. The two professions are also different in their orientation to people and organizations, in leadership and behavioral styles, and in the constraints of their working environments.

Lack of academic preparation for management is a clear shortcoming of most physician executive candidates. With a medical education alone, physicians do not have adequate backgrounds or formal training in management disciplines. Fortunately, they have come to recognize this, and many are now working to compensate for their lack of preparation. While much of their past management training has been experiential and on-the-job, physicians are now seeking postgraduate education. The ACPE database shows 789 members with master's degrees in management, including 310 with MBAs.[23] A large number of physician administrators surveyed by Kindig and Lastiri[11] feel that formal graduate course work or advanced degrees are advisable (62.1 percent) or should be required (21.5 percent). Physicians are seeking continuing education through ACPE, the American College of Health Care Executives, the American Hospital Association, the American Management Association, and the American Group Practice Association; through concentrated courses taught at universities, such as Harvard Business School and Sloan School of Management at the Massachusetts Institute of Technology; and by returning to academia for graduate degrees in business or health administration. Particularly notable is the phenomenon of graduate level training in management available to physicians that can be accomplished in nonresident status while holding a full-time job. Examples are the programs at the University of Wisconsin, the Medical College of Wisconsin, the University of Colorado, and Tulane University. The Geisinger Foundation has presented a mini-MBA program in management for physicians in management at that institution.

Table 2. Traditional Characteristcis of Differences Between Physicians and Managers[15, 17, 18]	
A Physician:	**A Manager:**
Is autonomous; makes decisions alone.	Uses teamwork; is probably involved in line reporting.
Works one-to-one.	Works primarily in groups.
Is patient-oriented.	Is organization-oriented.
Is empathetic.	Is objective.
Is crisis-oriented.	Is a long-range planner.
Is quality-oriented.	Is cost-oriented.
Enjoys immediate tangible results.	Must often delay gratification and enjoy process.
Accustomed to controlled chaos.	Has a planned schedule, with more inherent flexiibility.
Sees people as material or objects.	Sees people as resources to be managed.
Is a doer.	Is a delegator; gets things done through others.
Reacts.	Proacts.
Is authoritarian in practice style;	Delegates authority; deals with antiauthoritarian as it pertains to people as equals— participative leadership style.
Has a specialist orientation.	Has a generalist orientation.
Is classical scientist.	Is a social scientist.
Is discipline-oriented.	Is socially oriented.

The Challenge of Managing the New Health Care Organization

Many forces are working to challenge the authority of physicians. Pressures confronting the profession include:

■ Corporatization of health care.

■ Paraprofessional and mid-level practitioners.

■ Managed health care.

■ Consumerism.

■ Demands for accountability in health care cost and quality.

■ Technology (data collection and management information systems, computer-based decision-making).

The health care organization is becoming the dominant factor in the health care business. Physicians still view these organization with suspicion and even disdain. But the balance of power is shifting toward the organization because of the importance of capital, management skills, marketing expertise, information technology, entrepreneurism, etc. Power, influence, and authority in the organization generally reside within management. To have an impact in organizations, a constituency (in this case, the medical profession) needs presence at the top. The historical position of the physician in a separate and independent medical staff creates a problem for both physicians and the new health care organization. There are problems in the traditional organization with two lines of authority, i.e., administrative and professional. The modern health care organization cannot tolerate the resulting struggle between administrative and medical staff thinking. That divided authority impairs the ability of the organization to act decisively in response to external change and challenge. Driven by the demand for efficiency and competitiveness, the effective organization must be capable of evaluating its environment, making decisions about indicated courses of action, and moving quickly to take the necessary action. With a high premium on decisiveness, the bipartite health care organization is inefficient. The independent, self-governing medical staff is a defective construct in that environment.

Physician executives offer a solution to the internal structural conflicts in health care organizations, as they serve to resolve these tensions. As physician executives compete within the ranks of management, some will logically rise into top executive positions. Some physicians have already done so. This promises to serve the medical profession by ensuring that physicians (in the management role) sustain the profession's authority in clinical decision-making and quality control of the health care product. The long-term implication is that the profession will tend to change in its relationship to the health care organization.

For the medical profession itself, one of the most compelling arguments favoring broader involvement of physicians in management is the profession's deteriorating control over patient care. As the medical profession moves into an era of surplus professional manpower and organized health care, the physician is becoming more and more circumscribed in authority and influence. If physicians desire to maintain control of health care by their profession, they can do so by moving to the helm of the new health care organization. This is potentially a rallying point within the profession in support of the physician executive. There is evidence that this strategy is becoming a reality. The AMA has granted delegate status to ACPE within its House of Delegates. ACPE and the American Board of Medical Management are working to gain recognition of medical management as a legitimate specialty for physicians.

Summary

Over the past decade, the importance of physicians in the management of health care organizations has become much more evident. The success of the organization requires effective decisionmaking in an environment of synergism between both the medical and the management components of the institution.[13,14] Getting control over health care expenditures is not likely to be accomplished without physician involvement. Public good will be well served by a blending of clinical practice and management concerns.

For the physician who is willing, who can work to acquire management knowledge and skills, and who desires to be a manager, there should be a place. As a manager, the physician has some unique attributes, skills, and experience to offer. Physician executives have demonstrated their ability to function in all types of positions and at all levels of organization. Physician executives benefit from their practical knowledge of health care, certain legal realities, societal attitudes toward physicians, and their status with the medical profession. Physician executives can speak the language of patient care and of management, bringing a "legitimate authority to health care to which neither nonphysician executives nor physicians without management training can aspire.[24] As a specialist in management, the physician executive can serve the medical profession and the patient by sustaining the influence and authority of physicians within the increasingly complex health care organization.

References

1. Starr, P. *The Social Transformation of American Medicine.* New York, N.Y.: Basic Books, 1982.

2. Smith, R. "The Case for Physician Involvement in Governance and Management." *Hospital Medical Staff* 5(5) :28-30, May 1976.

3. Schultz, R. "How to Get Doctors Involved in Governance, Management." *Hospital Medical Staff* 5(6):1-7, June 1976.

4 . U. S. Department of Health, Education and Welfare. *Report of the Secretary's Advisory Committee on Hospital Effectiveness.* Washington, D.C.: U. S. Government Printing Office, 1968.

5. Noie, N. "Doctors Move Beyond Medicine." *Hospitals* 50(7):69-72, April 1, 1976.

6. Morrisey, M., and Brooks, D. "Physician Influence in Hospitals: An Update." *Hospitals* 59(17):86-7,89, Sept. 1, 1985.

7. Friedman, E. "Physician-Administrator Making a Comeback." *Medical World News* 27(12):34-8,40-43, June 23, 1986.

8. Smith, H., and Piland, N. "The Physician Executive: A Survival Plan for Medicine." Unpublished manuscript, 1987.

9. Meller, G. "Management." *JAMA* 258(16):2301-3, Oct. 23, 1987.

10. Judy Rochell, Membership Director; American College of Physician Executives, Tampa, Fla. Personal communication, Jan. 31, 1994.

11. Kindig, D., and Lastiri, S. "Administrative Medicine: A New Medical Speciality." *Health Affairs* 5(4):146-56, Winter 1986.

12. American Medical Association, Department of Physician Data Services. *Physician Characteristics and Distribution in the U. S.* Chicago, Ill.: AMA, 1992, p. 18.

13. Fink, D., and Goldhar, J. "Management for Physicians: An Annotated Bibliography of Recent Literature." *Annals of Internal Medicine* 92(part 1):269-75, Feb. 1980.

14. Drucker, P. *Management: Tasks, Responsibilities, Practices.* New York, N.Y.: Harper and Row, 1973.

15. American College of Health Care Executives, Tampa, Fla. Membership survey, personal communication, Aug. 1993.

16. Joint Commission on Accreditation of Healthcare Organizations. *Accreditation Manual for Hospitals*, Vol. I. Oakbrook Terrace, Ill.: JCAHO, 1993.

17. Adams, O. "Getting Physicians Involved in Hospital Management, Trends." *Canadian Medical Association Journal* 134(2):157-9, Jan. 15, 1986.

18. Wallace, C. "Physicians Leaving Their Practices for Hospital Jobs." *Modern Healthcare* 17(10):40-1,44,48,55,57, May 8, 1987.

19. Meyers, T., and others. "An Approach to the Assessment of Learning Needs for Physician-Managers." *Journal of Health Administration Education* 4(4):629-43, Fall 1986.

20. Doyne, M. "Physicians as Managers." *Healthcare Forum Journal* 30(5):11-3, Sept./Oct. 1987.

21. Forkosh, D. "Good Doctors Aren't Always Good Managers." *Hospital Medical Staff* 11(5):2-5, May 1982.

22. Stearns, N., and Roberts, E. "Why Do Occupational Physicians Need to Be Better Managers?" *Journal of Occupational Medicine* 24(3):219-24, March 1982.

23. American College of Physician Executives. *1994 Membership Registry.* Tampa, Fla.: ACPE, 1994.

24. Hillman, A., and others. "Sounding Board: Managing the Medical-Industrial Complex." *New England Journal of Medicine* 315(8):511-3, Aug. 21, 1986.

David J. Ottensmeyer, MD, FACPE, is President and Chief Executive Officer of the Lovelace Institutes, Albuquerque, N.M. He has previously held positions as President of the Travelers Health Companies, Hartford, Conn.; Chief Medical Officer of EQUICOR, Nashville, Tenn.; President and Chief Executive Officer of Lovelace Medical Center and Foundation, Albuquerque, N.M., and President and Chief Executive Officer of the Marshfield Clinic, Marshfield, Wis. M.K. Key, PhD is a clinical community psychologist and Director of Research and Development of EQUICOR.

The Dual Role Dilemma

CHAPTER 6

by Michael E. Kurtz, MS

While physicians bring unique characteristics to the managerial role, they are also unique products of the culture of the medical profession. They have made major personal commitments to a profession and a career very early in life, and the professional culture they enter definitely shapes their values, beliefs, ideas, internal and external perceptions, behaviors, and personalities.

Physicians spend the most formative years of their professional lives almost exclusively in the company of other physicians (teachers, mentors, preceptors, etc.), and the professional values and norms of the world of medicine are strongly inculcated and reinforced on a daily basis. Also, for a physician to be successful in the clinical role and to achieve acceptance and recognition from the medical community, he or she must be willing to accept and demonstrate these values and norms; otherwise the physician will find him- or herself treated as an unacceptable member of the community and severely criticized. To be able to pass through the ranks, rites of passage, and hierarchy of the medical community, one must be willing to comply and behave in accordance with these norms and expectations.

The socialization process of the "becoming-physician" probably has more direct influence on behaviors exhibited later in practice than anything else. Upon examination, I have found that, although most physicians share similar values, have experienced similar initial training, and identify as a distinct professional group, the individual specialties of medicine provide further socialization, demand specialty identification, and develop unique behavioral characteristics within their subgroups.

When analyzed through a series of behavior-oriented assessments, each specialty is found to use behaviors that are unique and specific to it; i.e., most surgeons act and behave as other surgeons, most pediatricians act and behave as other pediatricians, etc. These behaviors (whether successful or unsuccessful in achieving the individual's goals) are reinforced by other members of the physician's primary identification group and are constantly rewarded and reinforced in the clinical setting.

In general, most physicians (i.e., all specialists) are oriented to certain behaviors and values in their clinical practices, and these behaviors are successful for them and most likely are needed if they are to achieve the desired outcomes and acceptance of colleagues and peers.

When the physician moves away from the clinical role and into the world of management, administration, and leadership, we find that he or she most often will continue to use these learned clinical behaviors, professional norms, and values. A negative result is seen when this occurs. While clinical behaviors are critical for success in the practitioner role, they tend to create conflict, resistance, and tension in the managerial role.

Through an ongoing study, a long list of differences between effective clinicians and effective managers has been defined. When factored to determine those that are most critical, a list of nine major differences emerges (see figure below).

Clinicians are *action oriented*. They are "doers" and hands-on oriented. They prefer to be directly involved in their work, and see themselves as the primary interacters in most situations (e.g., diagnostic workups, treatment, etc.). Managers, on the other hand, see their primary role as being in *planning and designing*. Managers work through a process that establishes goals and objectives and then facilitate the planning and designing of activities that will accomplish these goals. They are not "doers"—that role is delegated to staff. Once you become a "doer," you are a worker, not a manager. When clinicians actively participate in the work itself, they are most often seen as interfering in organization operations.

Clinicians feel most effective, and report feeling most comfortable and most successful, in *one-to-one* encounters and interactions. They prefer to deal with others on

Major Differences between Clinicians and Managers	
Clinicians	**Managers**
Doers	Planners, Designers
1:1 Interactions	1:N Interactions
Reactive Personalities	Proactive Personalities
Require Immediate Gratification	Accept Delayed Gratification
Deciders	Delegators
Value Autonomy	Value Collaboration
Independent	Participative
Patient Advocate	Organization Advocate
Identify with Profession	Identify with Organization

an individual basis—doctor/patient, doctor/nurse, doctor/family, doctor/doctor, etc. In a study of 800 physician executives, I found that they tended to be very selective in the groups they join. They preferred to be left alone and were somewhat detached, independent, and self-sufficient. They demonstrated low interest in being included by others (especially in social activities) and had little concern about prestige or what others thought. (This may be a result of the medical training process, which traditionally prepares physicians for solo practice and for orientation to the private doctor/patient relationship.)

This low inclusion behavior may prove to be successful for the medical practitioner, but it lowers effectiveness for the physician executive. The managerial role demands a high degree of *group interaction* in the organizational setting in order to accomplish effective decision making and problem solving and, where appropriate, to establish participative and collaborative team management. Approximately 73 percent of a manager's time is spent in meetings and group settings. Physicians find these situations (i.e., meetings) intolerable and perceive them as a waste of time.

Clinicians are trained as *reactive personalities*. They are inclined to wait for their clinical services to be needed and/or requested. The physician waits for the patient to present himself, or to be referred; the physician most often responds to a need already defined and/or in progress. To be effective in management, the individual must work from a *proactive stance*, which means that the manager must anticipate future needs and requirements and initiate and/or invent processes to address them.

Obtaining short-term and/or *immediate results/gratification* is reported as being extremely important to the physician, who desires to quickly see a result from taking an action or initiating an intervention and experiences frustration when this is not realized. Managers very seldom experience immediate results from their work. Because they most often work in planning and designing processes, anticipating future events, etc., they are forced to accept *delayed results/gratification* for the investment of their energies. A manager may not see the result of his or her work for months or even years (anyone who has been involved in a building project can easily understand this dynamic).

Physicians are trained to be independent problem solvers and perceive themselves to be the *deciders* in almost all medical/clinical decision situations. They see themselves as having the ultimate authority and responsibility, and they will almost always assume this role and display this behavior. While managers have the "right" of decision making and reserve the "right to veto," they will most often *delegate* decision making to their subordinates. As stated above, organization leaders *manage the process* of problem solving and decision making. To always be the deciders would place them in a position of being perceived as autocratic, authoritarian, and mistrusting of their subordinates. Also, it is important to recognize that, with the high degree of specialization and subspecialization that has evolved and developed in both the clinical and managerial fields, no one person can be expected to have all of the expertise and/or knowledge required for complex decision making. Multiple resources will always be required.

The perception of being the "decider" held by the physician is further reinforced by the clinician's *value of autonomy*. Physicians tend to see themselves as autonomous professionals whose responsibility is to their patients and their profession. They are the ones to determine their level of involvement and interaction, and they don't perceive themselves to be subordinate or subservient to others. They prefer to perform their roles independently and autonomously, only involving others as *they* determine. While this value of autonomy protects the clinician from being politically influenced, it can significantly interfere with his or her effectiveness in a leadership/managerial role. Managers cannot function autonomously by the very nature of their role and function. Managers value *collaboration* and integration. They see their primary function as being one of facilitating and supporting the merging of ideas through the collaboration or organizational functions and related personnel. The actions of any one part of the organization affect every other part of the organization. Therefore, shared information, integration of ideas and resources, and collaboration of team members with other managers are absolutely requisite in maximizing the larger whole (i.e., reaching the goals and objectives of the organization). All decision making and problem solving must be entered into with the orientation of what will be best for the greater good (of the organization) rather than of what will be best for the individual. The value of autonomy held by most physicians results in a fairly high degree of self-centeredness and is often perceived as selfishness by nonclinical members of the organization.

Concomitant with the value of autonomy is the *value of independence* held by the clinician. Physicians are trained to work independently, to make independent decisions, and to take independent responsibility for outcomes. They don't want to feel that they depend on others for the successes or the failures they experience. Research data demonstrate a very low need for inclusion of and involvement by others, a low need to participate with others in situations that don't directly affect them, and a relatively high need to take charge. Physicians enjoy making decisions and influencing others and resist allowing others to influence them. They don't want others (especially nonphysicians) to tell them what to do, and they consume a great deal of physical and psychological energy protecting this autonomy and independence.

Concomitant with the value of collaboration, managers strongly value *participation* and avoid independent behaviors and actions. To ensure quality and commitment in decision making and problem solving, managers recognize the need to involve others in the process. They see their role as one of facilitating and supporting the involvement and participation of others in order to obtain maximum synergism. An effective manager is a person who designs and plans an organizational system that creates a culture and environment that encourages and supports participation by all members of the organization and one that discourages independence and ivory tower decision making.

Another major difference between clinicians and managers is that the physician assumes the primary role of being an *advocate for the patient*. Physicians assume the responsibility of protecting patients from undue outside influence and interference. In many cases, the outside influence is defined as the organization and its management and administrative system. Clinicians are oriented to the concept that "if the patient needs something, one gets it for him or her." To be asked to do a cost-benefit analysis, or to be told that certain interventions or services are inappropriate, is unacceptable to clinicians and is seen as interfering with professional prerogatives and responsibilities.

While managers are not insensitive to patient needs and to an acceptable level of quality in patient care, they are required to function primarily as *advocates of organi-*

zations. The manager's role, function, and responsibility require that he or she work to enhance and build the organization as a whole and to maximize its efficiency, productivity, and assets. When working with others, managers do not represent themselves; they function as representatives and advocates of the organization. The manager will constantly be striving to ensure viability of the organization, and, therefore, decisions will be made that will be in the best interests of the larger whole rather than in the interests of individuals. Clinicians will often make decisions based on isolated, unique, and specific facts of a certain case that may appear (or be) inconsistent with decisions made in related cases. Managers, on the other hand, are expected to make decisions that are consistent with organization policy, values, and norms. This concept of consistency and predictability carries extreme weight in effective managerial behavior, otherwise the manager would be managing by exception to the rule, which would result in organizational chaos.

This difference in advocacy orientation is further exaggerated by the individual's identification with a professional group or organizational entity. Physicians identify with their *professional group* and, more specifically, with their specialization within the larger professional designation. When asked "who are you," a clinician will first respond that he or she is a physician and then further define this identity with his or her specialization. The next level of identification is most often as a member of a certain medical community or communities (e.g., XYZ Hospital medical staff, ABC Physicians, or several different hospital medical staffs within a community). The very last identification will be as a manager, administrator, or as a representative of a specific organization. The clinician identifies with the organization only insofar as it allows the practice of skills and demonstration of the clinician's expertise. Physicians do not relate to the concept of "employment" or "unemployment." They perceive themselves as being able to practice wherever and whenever they choose. Because of that orientation, the physician sees the organization as simply a place that provides the opportunity, facilities, and environment to "practice," and this place could actually be anywhere.

The manager is in quite a different situation; his or her identity is totally dependent on employment or unemployment by an organization. Therefore, the identification is with the organization and not the professional field. Without an organization to manage, the manager can no longer be identified as a manager. Managers derive satisfaction from the rewards given and by the value accorded by the organization, which, in turn, affords recognition and acceptance by the larger managerial community. When asked the same question, "Who are you?" the manager will respond that he or she is the chief executive officer or the manager/director of the computer sciences department of XYZ Health Center. The manager perceives him- or herself as "belonging" to the XYZ Health Center, and the organization provides, promotes, and dictates this identification. The manager's role and responsibility is to develop the organization and to protect its viability in the marketplace, which creates competitive behavior and further fosters the identification with "us." This feeling of "my country, right or wrong" is totally foreign to the clinician when translated to the organization context.

These differences between clinicians and managers are but a few in a long list of practical and philosophical differences, but they are the major ones and they tend to create the greatest degree of role conflict and dual role dilemma for the physician executive. It is important to recognize that each set of behaviors, practices, and skills is necessary for satisfactory performance in the specific role demand (i.e., clinician or manager), but the physician who chooses to enter into management and administration will most often find him- or herself straddling the chasm between the two.

Most physician executives feel that it is important to maintain a clinical involvement, and there is a strong argument for this. The clinician wishes to maintain, if not enhance, clinical skills and abilities, to learn and update knowledge and skills from participation and interaction with colleagues, and to continue identification with the medical community and specialty. The clinician has spent the major part of his or her adult life in this community and has developed almost an exclusive identity with it. To leave it and move into another "profession" and career path is a psychologically wrenching and threatening experience. It means turning one's back on the primary identification group, giving up membership in an exclusive and elite professional "club," and starting out on a new educational and professional road. This choice requires leaving an area of acquired personal and professional expertise and recognition that is very comfortable and highly rewarded and moving into a relatively uncomfortable area with little, if any, preparation. It demands leaving an area of recognized professional competence and moving into the role of neophyte, learner, and student. This shift, along with the basic negative attitudes and perceptions about managers held by most physicians, further feeds the role conflict and dual role dilemma for the clinician.

There is another identity issue that emerges for the physician executive. Along with the personal identity dilemma is the question of identification that is raised for the medical community and the organization membership. The physician can never rid him- or herself of the title of "Doctor" and will always be perceived as a physician by the organization's membership. The clinician will always be one of "them" in the eyes of nonphysician executives and staff, and, historically and through training and experience, "them" has always been an adversarial group. Therefore, the physician executive's allegiances, commitment, and dedication will always be questioned.

At the same time, the medical staff and/or community will not perceive its colleague as a member of the management and administrative staff, which has always been a "them" to that group. This is especially true if the physician executive is employed and paid by the organization and may lead to questioning and mistrust of communication and intent.

Some physicians and management experts will argue that it is impossible to maintain this dual role—that one cannot adequately and competently perform in one while practicing the other. The concern of becoming a "Jack of all trades, master of none" is a very real one and must be addressed by the professional community as well as the organization. With the strong movement to "professionalize" the role of physician executive taking place in the United States, it can be assumed that this role will require certification of competence and capability in the very near future and that this "certification" will require demonstration of education, training, skill development, and experience in managerial roles and responsibilities. No longer can the physician simply assume an organizational leadership or management role because he or she is a good clinician; these successful clinical skills and behaviors are being recognized as creating problems in the practice of management and administration.

A shift in thinking, philosophy, attitudes, and behavior must take place if the physician is to be seen as successful and as an asset to the organization.

I don't think that it must necessarily be an either/or question. Experience demonstrates that physician executives who are recognized as the most competent, capable, and successful have, through their own choices and the demands of their organizations, given up clinical involvement and have dedicated themselves to the professionalization of the physician executive role. They have not lost credibility with their medical colleagues because they have developed competence and expertise as managers. They are perceived as being sensitive to the needs and values of the medical community while being accorded credibility through the quality and fairness of their decisions and human relations skills. Their organizations tend to be large and complex, which requires full-time commitment and dedication to the managerial role. They also tend to be organizations that are physician-owned and/or physician-run, so that the entire medical staff is in some way involved in the management of the organization.

It is more a factor of the size and the complexity of the organization that will provide the answer. A 15-person medical group can't afford to have one of its physicians excluded from a clinical role, but a 60+-person group can't afford not to force the choice if it desires adequate and successful management.

I don't think that this dual role dilemma can be easily resolved for the physician executive. It will require some soul-searching, self-analysis, and the development of self-awareness for each individual. For the physician to be successful in the dual role requires that he or she thoroughly understand which hat is being worn at which time, be adequately prepared for each in order to obtain and maintain credibility, and make sure that people working for and with the physician executive understand which hat is being worn at any specific time.

It's also important for the physician executive to use this unique position to develop and enhance collaboration and integration of the medical and administrative staffs in the daily management and operations of the organization. Through this mechanism, the chasm of the dual roles and its concomitant frustration and conflict can be bridged.

Health care organizations are struggling with a rapidly changing economic, political, and social environment. Many are developing successful new businesses and service strategies, while others are suffering failure. It is predicted that 20-25 percent of currently operating hospitals will close within the next two to three years, and 30-40 percent of health care providers other than hospitals (e.g., clinics, group practices, HMOs, etc.) will initiate major organization restructuring, redesign, and redefinition, or be the targets of takeovers and mergers.

Upon reviewing more than 60 such situations, I found that, although various strategies are being tested, there has been one underlying theme that emerges: The activities of the most responsive and strongest health care organizations all, in some way, support the integration of their medical staffs into the operational management and leadership of the organization.

The traditional adversarial positioning of medicine and administration is being consciously challenged, and new roles and activities are being invented and designed that foster collaboration and cooperation. This new "partnership" may be the key to future viability, and many professional resources are being focused on the development of methods to assist in accomplishing this goal. The active involvement of the physician executive may be the single most critical element in this process.

The first step is to strengthen the formal medical staff organization. By-laws must be reviewed in light of current impacts from external sources, medical staff leadership must be enhanced and developed, and active participation in the organization by all members must be encouraged.

The next step is to provide training and education for the development of leadership and managerial skills of the medical staff and then to provide structured opportunities for actual integration with management staff through team and group development activities. Each group expresses unique characteristics and cherishes certain values and self-images that are usually misperceived and misunderstood by the other. This results in negative and adversarial perceptions and attitudes.

Upon examination, the two groups actually share many values, expectations, and goals, but there are major differences in how they are communicated and what methods are developed for their achievement. The development of a common language, a clearer communication system, joint planning and problem-solving activities, and joint education and training must be given priority if an integration effort is to be successful.

My experience and data strongly suggest that all health care organizations, from single-specialty groups to large comprehensive medical centers, need to first initiate an objective organizational assessment and analysis process to determine their current situations and states of integration. Second, a process of mutual goal setting and strategic planning must be established. Third, an integrated effort for planning and initiating activities that will lead to the desired change and/or objective must be developed.

An honest commitment to the development of collaboration and integration efforts by all parties may well be the key to survival. Assisting health care organizations in meeting this commitment is one of the primary roles and responsibilities of the physician executive and may be the most successful way to reduce the conflict and frustration of the dual role dilemma.

Michael Kurtz, MS, is an organizational psychologist and management consultant in Herndon, Virginia.

The Credibility of and Necessity for the Physician Executive

CHAPTER 7

by John M. Burns, MD, FACPE

Since the first edition of *New Leadership in Health Care Management: The Physician Executive* in 1988, two major events have occurred that add *necessity* to the discussion of the role of the physician executive:

■ The change in United States leadership to the Clinton Administration and to a White House committed to controlling health care costs.

■ The global business opportunities for many American multinational companies brought about by the collapse of the communist domination of Eastern Europe and the further expansion of European markets.

If American business is to compete successfully in a global economy, the costs of medical benefit plans and our nation's total health care costs must be managed. And management of health costs requires that the health care product be specified in terms of what is necessary and appropriate, not on the basis of what is covered under the benefit plan. The only constituency with the training and experience required to define health care on the basis of what should be done is the medical profession.

The credibility of the physician executive will be reviewed from the perspective of physician executives representing both purchasers and providers forming partnerships necessary to successfully manage health care costs. This approach can enhance our nation's competitiveness and allow us to take advantage of opportunities resulting from the world events cited above. These events expand the roles of the physician executive and make credibility and legitimacy even more critical foundations for health management leadership. Lurie *et al.* argue for physician involvement in health reform and make four proposals[1]:

■ Each physician should become a knowledgeable participant in the debate about health care reform.

- Physicians can help change unrealistic public expectations of the health care system that drive up health care costs.

- Health system reform cannot succeed in the long run unless the training of physicians is restructured; physicians need to learn about cost effectiveness and community-based approaches to common problems.

- Physicians can redefine the fundamental purposes of a health care system.

The most frightening aspect of current legislative efforts to reform the health care system is the single-minded emphasis on cost control. When cost controls (expenditure caps or global budget) are coupled with a new entitlement program to cover the uninsured and underinsured, they can only be a blueprint for health care rationing. One questions whether the Clinton Administration or members of the Congress have any understanding whatsoever of the practice of medicine. Little if anything is said about what should be done, what services should be delivered and paid for. Although lip service is given to preventive care services, it is primarily described as a new entitlement and then in only general terms. Reform "experts," economists, and pundits have readily accepted any number of health care buzzwords, but few if any of them have the knowledge or capability to specify health care on the basis of necessity, appropriateness, effectiveness, or efficiency. Publications such as the Report of the United States Preventive Services Task Force, entitled "Guide to Clinical Preventive Services,"[2] could serve as a basis for describing what should be done as opposed to what the new entitlement plan will cover.

Unlike automobile or life insurance programs, where increased access is not associated with a corresponding increase in automobile accidents or death rates, the creation of a medical benefit entitlement invariably creates demand that rises to the ceiling of benefits. The benefit design approach to cost control generally results in little other than cost and risk shifting. At no place in the reform proposals does the discussion involve a requirement that the health care product be specified through rigid practice standards when available or through practice guidelines and outcomes measurements.

The Clinton Task Force was completely devoid of physician membership. The only managers capable of describing the health care product on the basis of necessity and appropriateness were the people who actually practice medicine—physicians—and other appropriately credentialed health care professionals. True health system reform must require that the health care product or service be demonstrated to be necessary to improve or preserve health and be the most appropriate for an individual patient in cases where alternatives may be available. With the expansion of our global economy and the new administration's bent to reform the health care system, it is imperative that physicians be active participants in the reform process.

The Physician Executive

Physicians are entering the field of medical management in increasing numbers. Membership of the American College of Physician Executives in January 1994 stood at approximately 8,500. The American Board of Medical Management, established in 1990, now has certified more than 700 physicians in medical management. The challenge for those who aspire to the role of physician executive, in spite of impressive growth in the profession, is to demonstrate that the position is indeed legitimate. While there may be little argument from within the membership of the American College of Physician Executives as to the appropriateness of and critical need for this emerging profession, resistance to the physician executive by peers and subordinates and by the huge external world of "management" requires recognition of major barriers to acceptance and development of strategies to overcome them.

Credibility of the Medical Profession

Current medical literature, legislative activities in health care financing, business's involvement in health care purchasing and management, and media attention all focus on a disturbing characteristic of the health care system in general and of physicians in particular. There exists tremendous variability in the costs and quality of medical care system, in practice styles, in occupancy rates, and in outcomes. "Managed care" interventions, be they preadmission certification, second opinions for surgery, mandated outpatient surgery, or any of a number of cost-reducing techniques installed at the insistence largely of third-party payers, all validate the perception of purchaser and consumer alike that the system has been and is being "worked" by providers. And yet this very intrusion into the health care system adds to administrative and utilization costs that account for 26 percent or more of the total health care dollar.[3]

Regulatory solutions abound. The protestations of physicians and of organized medicine in this regard fall on deaf ears. In the business world (and perhaps government), it is perceived that the medical/health care system is completely out of control. Does the medical profession itself have credibility? The physician executive must be prepared to answer this question and discuss the issue if credibility is to be ensured for the profession. Aggregate and individual specific data should be available to the physician executive, who can answer medicine's critics by demonstrating that physician-driven standards of care, practice guidelines, the quality improvement process, and outcomes measurement can improve quality and reduce the costs of the current system dominated principally by nonphysicians.

As for the profession of physician executive, demonstrated leadership in the medical community itself is critical. Physician executives must have credibility among their peers. Respect, ownership, and judgment of competence by other physicians should be based on the physician executive's participation and demonstrated skills within the health care system. In addition, peer judgment of clinical or management competence should never be based on the practice affiliation or method of compensation of the physician being evaluated. Thus, **the first credibility characteristic of a physician executive:**

■ **Active participation and leadership within the medical community.**

The Role of Health Management in Establishing Medical Standards

A basic role of the physician executive, regardless of his or her position in the health care delivery system, is to participate in the process of establishing standards of health care. Standards of care, not measurement of norms, are needed. The medical profession must be held to these standards if credibility is to be regained or maintained. These standards will be based on defining care in terms of medical appropriateness and necessity. Diagnostic and therapeutic adventurism must be eliminated. The economic impact on providers of care, institutions and physicians alike, of a reimbursement system based on objective standards of medical appropriateness and necessity is formidable. Estimates of the amount of health care dollars spent on unnecessary care range from 20 to 40 percent.[4] The physician executive's personnel management skills and administrative expertise are certainly going to be tested as we move to a quality-based system from the current benefit design and cost control system.

Any number of "stakeholders" in the health care delivery system will be threatened by the proposal that objective standards for intervention or reimbursement be established. Only those who are willing to take leadership positions and face obstacles placed in the way of their efforts to establish objective standards should pretend to management positions.

Credibility implies that a "gap" does not exist. It implies that there is no disparity between what is said and the actual facts. One's professed motives are accepted as the true ones. Health care has been accepted by patients, providers, and buyers without question as to need or appropriateness. There exists now a characteristic of the health care system that needs attention. I refer specifically to the subject of variations in practice styles.

The medical system employs a number of explanations to justify variations in practice. Regardless of the explanation, however, reimbursement is almost always an issue central to the argument. "Doctor/patient relationship," "individual case," "usual and customary," "unique case," "protocol," "standard orders"—all these terms are used in the typically retrospective claims administration process where physician reimbursement is threatened or patient financial liability is an issue.

This same characteristic, variations in practice patterns for the medical profession, feeds the tort system and drives malpractice claims based on *post hoc-ergo proper hoc* outcome judgments. The same variability enablement that supports the reimbursement system absolutely encourages the malpractice claim.

The financial incentives attendant to the litigation process have encouraged the gathering of medical testimony (of course, in retrospect) to support the view that "something else could have been done" in cases where the medical care process has unintended results. The process has facilitated a new profession of expert witnesses. Prospectively established and communicated standards would reduce or eliminate the appropriateness of retrospectively based testimony as to what could have been done and require that malpractice be based on conformity to established standards. The physician executive representing the business or government purchaser of health care should work directly with the physician executive representing the provider (systems) to contractually describe the health care product so that "failure" to provide unnecessary care becomes a validation of quality. And the business physician executive will lead the purchasers' efforts to educate all beneficiaries as to what reasonable expectations should be and also to define care on the basis of necessity, not entitlement.

Thus, **the second characteristic of the physician executive**:

> ■ **The capability and willingness to participate in the establishment of standards of health care.**

Management Credibility

A massive amount of management literature exists. Management seminars abound and academic programs proliferate. Fueling all this is the phenomenon of emerging management specialties and subspecialties. A current challenge of some urgency is the need to specify the bank of knowledge that creates and defines the profession of physician executive. This second edition monograph you are reading is one component of a process aimed at clearly defining and improving this management specialty.

Basic training, skills, and experience in management are needed to construct the foundation of our profession. Certainly basic management training should be a requirement, and, with the increasing complexity of health care and health care systems, a formal training process would appear to be a must. In addition to experiencing and being exposed to the formal, didactic component of management training, the physician executive should broaden himself/herself through extensive reading of both general management and health care management literature. The classic efforts of Frederick Taylor, Alfred P. Sloan Jr., and George Siemens and the works of Douglas McGregor and Peter Drucker but skim the surface of a wealth of knowledge and ideas available in the literature.

Management is a discipline. Thus, **the third characteristic of the physician executive**:

> ■ **Training experience in the basics of management.**

The Credibility of the Physician Executive

Credibility is established through a process over time. It is not simply an event attendant to completion of a course or attainment of certification. Experience is acquired; credibility must be earned. The trained and experienced physician executive who is active in the medical community, engaged in the process of establishing objective standards of health care quality, and trained in management is positioned to earn credibility. That credibility will be established with superiors, peers, and subordinates; with the management profession; and throughout the health care industry. Business will only succeed through recognition of the necessity for and utilization of the physician executive.

The physician executive will gain the support of business. This support will come with business's recognition of the management skills of the physician, exhibited through leadership and willingness to set standards. Business needs and wants a partner in the management of health care. But that partnership requires credibility. The credibility of the physician executive rests on three prime characteristics: participation and leadership in the medical community, a capability and willingness to participate in the establishment of standards of care, and possession of training and experience (and accomplishments) in management.

References

1. Lurie, N., and others. "Now Is the Time: Physician Involvement in Health Care Reform." *Annals of Internal Medicine* 118(3):226-7, Feb. 1, 1993.

2. *Report of the U.S. Preventive Services Task Force. Guide to Clinical Preventive Services.* Baltimore, Md.: Williams and Wilkins, 1989.

3. Himmelstein, D., and Woolhandler, S. "Cost without Benefit: Administrative Waste in U.S. Health Care." *New England Journal of Medicine* 314(7):441-5, Feb. 13, 1986.

4. Brook, R., and Lohr, K. "Will We Need to Ration Effective Health Care?" *Issues in Science and Technology* 3(1):68-77, Fall 1986.

John M. Burns, MD, FACPE, is a health management consultant in St. Paul, Minnesota.

Key Management Skills for the Physician Executive

by Leland R. Kaiser, PhD

CHAPTER

8

This chapter is written for you, a physician executive employed in a modern health care organization. The chapter will help you reconceptualize your job and identify some of the key management skills you must master to be successful. The skills I describe are drawn from the current management literature and from my experience in working with physician executives. A bibliography is attached for further study.

Role of the Physician Executive

You are an interface professional. You work on the interface between the disciplines of medicine and management. Most of the problems in our contemporary health care system fall on this interface. A good example of an interface problem is the trade-off between cost and quality of medical care. This trade-off requires that both a medical and a management decision be made for each patient. You are qualified to make such decisions because you have expertise in both arenas and can simultaneously protect the patient's and the organization's welfare.

Your role and function will vary with the needs and interests of your employer. As a result of the wide range of job functions that physician executives perform, there is no uniform job description. In each new position, you must negotiate your role and function with your employer. You must match your interests and abilities to the job that needs to be done.

Advocating for both the patient and the organization places the physician executive in a value conflict situation. What is best for the patient is not always best for the organization. What is best for the organization is not always best for the community. What is best for the community is not always best for the federal government. A manager always faces conflicts of interest. The physician has the luxury of focusing only upon the needs of patients. You must take into account the interests of all the parties involved. Learning to think like a manager as well as a physician is one of your greatest challenges. You have mixed accountability, and often what makes one party happy with you will make another party angry with you. Good managers try to plan "win-win" games, but it is not always possible to do this in the real world of the physician executive.

Any manager is expected to promote the institution's philosophy and uphold its goals. You must be a team player and accept your role as a co-creator of your organization. You must be concerned not only with medical management problems, but also with the general welfare of your organization. This requires that you identify with organizational interests and problems that transcend your day-to-day functioning as a medical care administrator.

An alert physician executive will keep his or her organization well informed concerning new developments in medicine and patient care. This requires careful monitoring of the literature and attendance at medical meetings. You are expected to be an expert source for medical management, and other organizational managers will depend on your advice and direction.

The physician executive is expected to set the standard of excellence for physicians in the organization. You must play a leadership role in quality assurance and risk management. The medical staff should view you first as a doctor, then as a manager. The management team, by contrast, will view you first as a manager, then as a doctor. Because you live in both camps, from time to time you must engage in a little fancy footwork, convincing both doctors and managers that you are representing their respective interests.

Some physician executives continue to see patients; others do not. There is no simple rule to follow in this matter. The important thing is that you maintain clinical credibility with the other physicians in your organization. That is hard to do if you no longer see patients. Yet even if you continue to see patients, it will be difficult for you to maintain medical competence on a part-time practice basis and even harder to find enough hours in the day to also practice management. Most physician executives gradually move toward full-time management because of these twin pressures. Some physician executives want to keep a foot in both camps because they are not yet fully committed to the management role and want to keep their bases covered just in case they decide to return to full-time practice.

As a physician executive, you will be subjected to many organizational challenges and stresses. Being an interface professional is not easy work. Potential stresses include:

■ The time and effort it takes to stay current in two disciplines.

■ Dual identity as both a physician and a manager (this can lead to an identity conflict or a feeling you are neither).

■ Lack of role clarity in your organization.

■ Less hands-on satisfaction than you had as a pure clinician.

■ Trying to quickly learn the required new management skills.

■ Excessive work loads.

■ Being in the middle between the medical staff and management (conflict).

Having few professional peers to relate to (loneliness).

If you are successful in your organizational role, you will mediate, translate, integrate, and absorb shock. These situations are stress generating, and you must develop some good stress management skills if you hope to remain healthy in the job.

Of course, there are many benefits that go along with this exciting new profession:

Exploration of a new career.

Variety and change.

Identification with an organization (security and protection).

Exercise of power and control.

The challenge of mastering a new body of knowledge.

The pluses outweigh the minuses, but you must factor them both into the equation of overall job satisfaction. Learning to think like a manager represents one of the biggest challenges you will face. Characteristics of the mindset of a manager include:

■ Seeing the big picture.

Adopting organizational values and standards.

■ Engaging in objective analytical thinking.

Acting in the face of uncertainty.

Enjoying complexity.

■ Developing goals and objectives.

■ Translating goals and objectives into action plans.

Measuring organizational effectiveness.

■ Developing a distinctive style of leadership.

■ Assessing organizational effectiveness.

Though these skills are not antithetical to those of a physician, they are not usually well developed as a result of medical school education or clinical practice. Some physicians have a natural bent for management and have picked up some of the necessary skills. For other physicians, thinking like a manager is something that must be learned and practiced before proficiency is developed.

A physician gets direct positive reinforcement from patients. The physician is recognized and appreciated for what he or she does for them. A manager must depend upon vicarious reinforcement. He or she succeeds only through the efforts of others. Reward is second-hand at best. Often, good management goes unnoticed, and all you will receive are a lot of complaints if something goes wrong. People are unconscious of good management and are therefore unlikely to notice it when it occurs. If you want to feel good about yourself, you may have to pat yourself on the back for a job well done. Some physician executives miss the "good old days" when they were really appreciated by their patients.

It is important for the physician executive to develop a strong working relationship with the nursing manager. Both are clinician executives and working together can constitute a powerful force for change in the organization. After all, who can successfully oppose all the doctors and nurses in the organization? The nursing manager is working on the interface between nursing and management and must have many of the same skills and interests as the physician executive. They are major allies and should view each other as equals in the process of planning and delivering patient care.

Innovation is an important role for the physician executive. He or she should stimulate creative thinking in the organization and be a major force for new product development. Most physicians are trained to think conservatively, and innovation is often outside their interest and experience in providing patient care. An innovator is a risk taker and must be willing to make many mistakes in the process of developing successful business ventures. Although by temperament some physicians are entrepreneurs, few physicians have had experience stimulating innovation in organizational settings. Physician executives working in hospitals may wish to set aside some beds on a special research and development unit where new approaches to patient care can be tested and evaluated for cost, quality, and patient satisfaction. In some instances, the unit becomes a strategy for total organizational change as innovations developed there are accepted throughout the hospital by other caregivers. Patient-focused care is a good research and development project if the hospital has not already incorporated it into its philosophy and practice.

Managers spend more time communicating than engaging in any other management behavior. A primary role of the physician executive is to serve as a communication link between the medical staff and management. He or she must properly represent the perceptions of each to the other. Written and verbal communication, dyads, small groups, large groups, and public speaking all fall within his or her purview. The physician executive who is not an effective communicator might benefit from some further training in the communications department of a local college or university.

Ultimately, as the new kid on the block, you must make your own way in the organization. Your position as a physician executive will be what you make it. Your profession is new enough that health care organizations do not have a lot of preconceived notions about what you should do. You do not have to cut through a lot of history. You do have to become an architect of your future in the organization. If you are creative and quick to see how you can contribute, you will write your own ticket. If you wait to be asked, you may wait for a long time.

A major challenge may be resisting the avalanche of problems that beset you when you first arrive in the organization. We all have a tendency to react to whatever is demanding our attention. We have an inclination to do whatever we enjoy doing and are good at, whether or not it needs to be done. Discrimination is an important managerial skill. You must constantly ask yourself, "What most needs to be done in this organization at this time?" If you do not plan your work and your day, you will be swept away by trivia and will never have time to do the really important things. Your time is your most precious resource—learn to guard it carefully. There are too many good things to do and too few that will make any long-term difference for either your organization or your patients. Stand back and get perspective. Ask yourself, "Why am I doing this?"

Becoming a Professional Manager

You will achieve success by doing what you do best. Where you are the weakest, you will fail. The effective manager concentrates on what he does well and hires other people to do what he does poorly. Be sure to hire associates who are unlike you and do not share your weaknesses. Much of your career success depends on the match between who you are and where you are. Much also depends on your skill in surrounding yourself with competent subordinates. How well do you fit your current organizational space? What do you need from your organization to really do the job? If you designed the ideal job space for yourself, how would it look? A manager that is a failure in one organizational setting is often a success in another organization. Everything depends on fit. If the organization does not fit you—you are a misfit. You need a good fit between your personal profile and the map of your organizational environment. Here, self-knowledge is all important.

Where is your organization in its life cycle? Organizations, like people, have life cycles. Organizations are born, grow rapidly, reach maturity, and decline. It is more fun to manage an organization in its period of rapid growth than its decline. Many physician executives are being hired by relatively new health care organizations. This adds an element of excitement and optimism to the position. The downside is that many of these organizations are unstable, economically risky, and subject to disappearance. You may be forced to trade the security of maturity for the excitement of youth. Managing an organization in decline is a no-win situation. Remember, as a manager, your destiny is tied to the destiny of your organization. It pays to be a little choosey and not necessarily pick the job with the highest salary and greatest fringe benefits. It may not be around long enough for you to collect either.

Are your organization's values consistent with your values? Values are the lowest common denominator of action both in people and in organizations. You cannot be an effective manager if you do not agree with what your organization is doing. The best management is management by value. What are the corporate values of your organization? What are your personal and professional values as a physician executive? Are both sets of values consistent? If not, what do you need to do? Some organizations do not have a very clear sense of their values and need to go through a value clarification process.

Are you overtrained for your job? A professional manager feels best when he or she is challenged but not overwhelmed. Boredom is as difficult to live with as too much excitement. What is your optimal stimulus level as a manager? Do you feel a sense of accomplishment in your job and an opportunity to bring your full range of abilities into action?

Are you being adequately compensated for what you do? A physician executive should enjoy a high standard of living and a full return on the tremendous investment made in his or her career. You should compare your salary and benefits with other physician executives in comparable jobs. You may experience a decrease in income when you switch from fee-for-service, solo practice to an organizational salary. However, your expenses are less, you enjoy more free time, and the security is greater. As with everything in life, becoming a physician executive is a trade-off.

Did anyone precede you in your position? If so, you will inherit some organizational expectations created by the previous holder of your office. These may be good, bad, or, more likely, a mix. Talk to other people and try to recreate a picture of the world before you arrived. Decide what was right and wrong with that world and announce to the organization any needed changes you will be making. If you are going to make changes, the burden of proof is upon you.

Organizations always resist change. You may experience some of this resistance as you try to cut a new groove for your position. It also helps to know the history of your organization. Organizations are where they have been. Who were the founders? What were the major milestones in the development of the organization? By knowing the traditions and symbols of the organization, you enter its mythology and stand the best chance of helping in the transformation of the myth as the organization prepares to move into the future. The myth of the organization is its tap root and should always be taken seriously. Kill the tap root and the organization dies. Set yourself against the traditions of the organization and you will surely lose.

As a professional manager, you must build your knowledge base and remain open to new ideas. Every month you should peruse the leading management journals and read several of the best books on management. As we enter the turbulent information age in health care, new age managers will be practicing management by idea. Organizations that survive this "white water" period will be the "better idea" organizations. You will never be a better manager than your knowledge base permits. What you cannot think about, you cannot manage. There are few rules in management and little memory work. Management is primarily conceptual. A good manager is not a technician. He or she is a well-read thinker.

Because the role of physician executive is filled with ambiguity, it is important for you to project a strong self-concept. You must tell other people who you are and what you do. In some cases it is important to tell the organization what you do not do. It is tempting for an organization to load you up with things you should not be doing. You should be doing only what a person with your experience and dual training is qualified to do. If you are performing lower level tasks, the organization is wasting money and losing the unique contribution only you can make.

There are three big questions that any manager asks:

■ What should I be doing (values)?

■ How can I do that (knowledge)?

■ Who can do it (power)?

This is the equilateral triangle of management. A physician executive must manage values, knowledge, and power. Unless you are willing to become a power broker, your values and knowledge will not come to fruition. Organizations are political creatures.

Management decisions are often made on political grounds and fly in the face of both analysis and intellect. You must seek power in order to make a difference in your organization. You can only receive power from those who have power to bestow. For this reason, your relationship to the CEO and the board is critical. Without the support of those higher up in the power structure, you will not be effective and you will end up frustrated—able to see but not able to do.

Any professional manager depends on a network of colleagues to provide support and information. The physician executive needs such a reference group to avoid professional isolation. Begin cultivating professional contacts with other physician executives if you have not already done so. Stay in touch by phone and letter and arrange to meet at national and regional meetings of your professional societies.

Relationship with the Chief Executive Officer

Be certain the CEO supports you and your function in the organization. Work with the CEO to develop a clear job description and a location on the organizational chart that gives you a direct reporting line to the CEO. Obtain a commitment from the CEO for adequate budgetary and staff support. You should also request a three- to five-year employment contract after the first year or two of employment.

Work with the CEO to define your major goals and objectives for the fiscal year. Tie these goals to your budget and to your performance review. Make sure the CEO and you agree on organizational priorities and on your allocations of time and effort. Keep the CEO informed concerning your progress on goal achievement. If any unexpected events intrude on your projected work program, discuss them with the CEO and have him or her sign off on any changes in priorities. Your value to the CEO will depend primarily on the extent to which you keep your assigned organizational areas problem-free (do your job) and the degree to which you assist the CEO with his or her own perplexities (help the CEO with his or her job). It will pay you to spend some time every week worrying about the CEO's problems and suggesting possible solutions. Worry about what the boss is worried about, and you won't have to worry about the boss.

Request frequent feedback from the CEO and give the CEO frequent feedback. The most important part of your job is communication. If you want to enjoy a long and happy life in your organization, demonstrate consistent loyalty to the CEO and volunteer for jobs the CEO needs to have accomplished. Before long he or she will depend on your input every week.

Relationship to the Management Team

To be effective over the long haul, you must build a high level of trust with other members of the management team. Be certain that team members understand your role and function. Be certain they are satisfied with your performance. Always be prepared for organizational meetings and perform well in them. Performance in meetings is a major criterion used to evaluate any manager. Most of the work of an organization is done in meetings. From time to time, you will tire of meetings. Resist the temptation to bad mouth meetings. You will only lose ground with this or any other occasion of organizational criticism. Carry your share of the work load and always document your accomplishments with other team members. Encourage divergent opinions from the group, but avoid adversarial relationships with any team members. Aim for consensus decision making.

It is important for you to be available and approachable. Display company manners. Give frequent praise. Be a good listener. You need to be highly visible in the organization and to practice management by walking around.

Become a student of the organization's written policies and procedures. Play by the rules. If a rule needs to be changed, volunteer to study the rule and suggest a new policy better adapted to the changing health care environment. You win points on any management team by being predictable, open, fair, and loyal in your dealings with all team members. The time may come when your job tenure is decided by your team members. Avoid making enemies at any level of the organization. Remember, it takes a lot more effort to fight a war than to maintain the peace.

Because many changes are taking place on the interface between medicine and management, you should conduct frequent briefing meetings for team members. Organizations do not like surprises, and it is your job to see that none occur in your assigned areas. If you have important fears or doubts about what is happening in patient care, share your feelings with the group.

Relationship with the Medical Staff

One of your most important functions is maintaining positive relationships with other physicians. In hospitals and clinics, this usually takes the form of your interactions with the organized medical staff. Some physician executives believe the medical staff cannot be organized, and that simple fact alone is the root of most of their problems. It is not easy to organize doctors, yet that is your job.

Your transactions with doctors can take many forms. You may be involved in recruiting doctors for your organization. You may call on physicians in their private offices, offer practice management consultation, and act as a liaison to the hospital. Office-based physicians often welcome help with marketing and sale of their services. If the doctors do well, the hospital should also prosper. It is a "win-win" game. Often, physician executives develop orientation programs for new doctors joining the staff. The orientation program provides an excellent opportunity for you to explain the institution's culture and make organizational expectations clear to new physicians.

An important part of your role is to mobilize physician commitment to your organization's services. You may meet this challenge by initiating a medical staff development program that encourages physician input in organizational decision making and makes doctors part of the family. If you can develop a core leadership group as a result of your medical staff development program, you will find your job as a change agent much easier.

By providing financial and clinical outcome data to physicians, you can improve their performance. Prompt feedback motivates doctors to do a better job. If possible, medical education should be geared to problems documented in the performance reviews. As a physician executive, you must monitor physician practice patterns and estimate their impact on quality and cost outcomes. Sometimes it is a simple matter of keeping physician skills up to date. It may, however, come to dealing with the impaired physician or the physician who must be given reduced privileges. You will have to discipline physicians who are bad actors and coach failing physicians. In matters of discipline, you will work closely with the hospital attorney to protect the rights of all parties involved.

As a physician executive, you must set up an accountability framework for physicians and enforce the ethical and legal standards of your organization and your profession. This is never a pleasant task for a manager, but it is one that must be done. In these matters, the buck stops at your desk.

Part of your role as a physician executive is to teach other physicians to think like managers. You may need to hold some special educational sessions to explain all of the changes coming down the road that will affect doctors and hospitals. Physicians need help in learning to manage DRGs and admissions. Payer mix is an important variable in determining the hospital's economic survival. The physician is the major resource allocator in health care organizations and needs to understand his or her economic impact on the organization.

An important future role for physician executives will be developing new corporate structures that bring doctors and hospitals together as financial partners. No longer can doctors and hospitals compete with one another or choose to go their separate ways. They will hang together or hang separately. Physician/hospital organizations, IPAs, hospital-based group practices, integrated regional health care networks, primary care networks, hospital/community HMOs, direct contracting, and capitated managed care are only a few of the new corporate forms that may be needed in the reform and postreform periods of American health care. There is ample opportunity and incentive for creative experimentation by all health provider organizations.

Future health care will be dominated by computers and information networks. You need to view information systems as the new wave of medicine and management. How familiar are you with computers? Do you have hands-on skills? Now is a good time to begin experimenting with the new hardware and software being developed for physicians and hospitals. Does your hospital provide computerized literature searches for your physicians? Do you have a special shelf in you medical library devoted to books on computers and medicine? Are you using computers to help you with critical paths and clinical outcome measurements?

Product line management is a promising new way to plan and deliver health care in multispecialty group practices and hospitals. A production team composed of doctors, nurses, and other personnel plans the products for each specialty area in medicine. Market segments, packaging, distribution channels, volume, profit margins, and quality standards are determined for each specialty each year. Product performance is measured against production targets, and exceptions are noted and corrected. As a product manager, you can decide to position your products for cost, quality, service, or convenience. If you can position for all four, so much the better.

Service is becoming an important emphasis in health care. As a physician executive, you should help develop a customer service strategy for your institution. With extensive competitive bidding for contracts, cost and quality differentials will even out among providers and the emphasis will be on the user interface. Do you provide a good experience for the patient and family?

The dispirited physician is a phenomenon of our times. Many doctors are discouraged and have decided to leave the clinical practice of medicine. Early retirements and career changes are common. Part of your job is to maintain physician esprit de corps and do what you can to add hope and help to disheartened doctors who feel they have been sold down the river by society.

Competition among medical facilities will increase during the next few years until collaboration is finally recognized as the strategy of choice for health care in the United States. You must develop an effective plan for monitoring the competition and meeting it in the marketplace. What is your organization's distinctive competence? Can you develop centers of excellence? Where do you have the greatest depth in your medical and nursing staffs? Can you protect and extend your primary care base? Can you install more effective cost controls? Can you improve channels of distribution? How will the growth of managed care affect your profit margins? Are you ready for new methods of physician reimbursement? Does your governing board recognize the changing medical market?

An important role you have with the medical staff is that of change agent. You are paid to help doctors change the way they think. Each year, you should take a carefully selected group of doctors and managers on site visits to view innovative solutions to problems experienced in your institution. One site visit will change more physicians' minds than years of admonition and pleading. This means that you must maintain a list of innovation sites. This can be done by a careful search of the literature and by calling on your professional network of physician executives.

A routine but important job of the hospital-based physician executive is liaison with designated clinical, managerial, and governance committees. When appropriate, the physician executive should attempt to improve the functioning of these committees and their relationships with each another. If the hospital takes regular physician and nurse polls, the physician executive should be involved in the polling and the interpretation of results.

Joint ventures, mergers, consolidations, coalitions, and the formation of superboards represent important new arenas for physician executive involvement. These are complex organizational arrangements, and you should approach them with caution. A good business plan will avert many potential disasters. You should be able to read, understand, and evaluate business plans for any proposed organizational relationship. Consultants can help you in this area. Do not hesitate to use them. In the future, medical staffs will be more involved in these decisions. There will also be increased pluralism in all health provider organizations. Although the movement will be toward larger organizations, some doctors will continue as solo practitioners. Other physicians will join large multispecialty groups and regional integrated corporations that promise greater power and financial return.

Relationship with the Community

The mission of a medical care system is to improve the health status of the population it serves. Because the provision of disease care is only one element in the improvement of overall community health status, many physician executives will be extensively involved in community health outreach programs with schools, churches, business and industry, recreation departments, public health, welfare, housing, criminal justice, and transportation. The hospital will become a community health design center and an institution "without walls." Primary care will be decentralized to the neighborhood level. Attempts will be made to judge effectiveness of area medical care providers by measurable improvement in community health status. As medicine becomes population-based, accountability of doctors and hospitals can be determined and measured. Creating healthier communities is a new frontier for physician executives.

Relationship with Federal, State, and Local Government

A logical career progression for physicians is from clinician to physician executive to health policy analyst. Most of the health legislation in the United States is drafted by legislative aides who have never treated a patient or spent time managing a health care institution. That alone explains why much of our health legislation is so woefully inadequate. In the future, self-selected physician executives who have met the challenge of institutional management will go on to the policy arena. They will draw on their rich and diversified patient, organizational, and community experience to craft laws of the land. Of course, the political process in the legislatures will still operate, but it will be operating from an expert physician base.

Essential Professional Skills of the Physician Executive

As I indicated earlier, as a professional manager you will spend more time communicating than engaging in any other organizational behavior. Listening skills, personal observation skills, self-disclosure skills, and the ability to write and speak well are essential. You will communicate one-to-one, in small groups, in large groups, and on occasion before large audiences. Your ability to influence, motivate, and persuade others will determine much of your success in the organization. If you are a high-energy person, you can communicate your zest and vitality. If you are a serious, thoughtful person, you can communicate your solid grasp of problem situations. If you are a good listener, other people will seek you out to help them clarify their own thinking.

To win the confidence of your organization, you must avoid extremism. You will always be looking for the common denominator that will bring conflicting parties to resolution. You cannot afford to alienate a large part of the organization by adopting extreme positions. You are an organizational diplomat and must be able to see the validity of many points of view. Your constituents will promote conflicting ideologies and hold limiting assumptions. You must lend a friendly ear to both. You are a listening post for the organization and a mirror for those who want to see themselves through your eyes. If both liberal and conservative physicians respect you and view you as a friend, you are projecting the right image. Of course, you have your own opinions, but they should not get in the way of your managerial function as an interface professional—equally at home on either side of the fence.

A physician executive needs to be a high-energy person. On every side, you will be confronted by organizational inertia and physician passivity. Many of the battles you fight you will win because you can hold out longer than your opponents. View yourself as a spark plug. You are there to excite others to necessary action.

Your body/mind vehicle is the only tool you have as a manager. Physical and mental fitness are a precondition to organizational success. If you don't take care of yourself, you will be unable to care for the organization. Try to play a lead role in wellness programs and encourage others to conserve their health.

What theoretical perspective do you bring to your job? In my opinion, the systems perspective is the appropriate one for physician executives. You must be able to see connectedness and perceive interrelationships. Physician executives often work in complex health care organizations with multiple boards and overlapping jurisdictions. Vertical and horizontal integration, diversification, satellites, networking, joint ventures, and relationships with multiunit organizations are management realities that escape any unidimensional approach to management. You will benefit from readings in general systems theory and systems analysis.

As a physician executive, you are a change agent and must stimulate both organizational stability and organizational change. If you are prepared, you can capitalize on organizational crisis. Often, managers must wait until crisis occurs before they can motivate people to act. The good manager anticipates change and helps his organization manage it. The collective mindset of the organization is its ultimate limitation. An organization can change its future as quickly as it can change its mind. The effective physician executive is a futurist and a mind changer. New paradigm management has a quantum physics orientation. It stands in stark contrast to the Newtonian paradigm training of most physicians and managers. Quantum thinking embodies a relationship model of the universe. Newtonian thinking stresses autonomy and isolation. The physician executive must get doctors, nurses, managers, trustees, patients, and community members out of their boxes into a shared circle. The new paradigm universe is one fabric. Everything stands in relationship. Nothing stands alone. Physicians have been trained to stand alone. It is difficult for them to think organization, community, nation, or planet. Many community health and social agencies have the same problem. They think of themselves as separate and are more than willing to go to war to save their turf or budgets. As a result, most American communities are disintegrated, with huge gaps and overlaps in their services. Community health status suffers.

You need to develop your financial management skills. Everything in the organization reduces to economics. If you understand how the money flows in an organization, you understand most of the organization's dynamics. If you understand how physicians are reimbursed for their services, you can explain a lot of the variance in their practice patterns and professional behavior. You must be alert to the financial impact of all the decisions you make. Courses in cost accounting, pricing, taxes, financial management, budgeting, and investments will help you do a better job in your organization. As profit margins erode, you will become involved in downsizing, or resizing as it is often called. This may require taking beds out of service, dropping clinical services, letting employees go, and breaking relationships with managed care systems. In these instances, the required organizational decisions have both medical and managerial dimensions. Retrenchment management, as it is called, is not much fun, but it may be a necessary part of your job for the next few years.

In a rapidly changing market, your organization must decide each year what business it wants to be in. You should help your organization assess its strengths and weaknesses and reposition itself in the medical marketplace. The position your organization chooses to occupy will be translated into the type of doctors and nurses you recruit and the array of services you provide.

Effective managers create positive organizational climates and cultures of excellence. It is part of your job to clarify institutional values and convert these values into organizational behaviors. You should view yourself as a designer of the organization's culture. What kind of a medical care setting is required to ensure high-quality care and cost containment? What type of organizational climate turns physicians on and encourages physician teamwork? What does your organization really believe in, and what is it trying to accomplish? You must ask and help answer these questions.

As profit margins decline in your organization, you should be looking around for new revenue sources. An effective manager generates resources. New medical care products, new market segments, more effective marketing and sales programs, trendy packaging, optimization of existing product lines—these and other strategies will generate additional revenue. The health care field is moving toward integrated databases and data-based management. Hard facts will replace opinions as health organizations upgrade their management information systems. The physician executive needs data concerning the impact of physician practice patterns on the financial welfare of the organization. He or she can use these data to modify physician behavior. Without data, you must fly by the seat of your pants and outshout your opposition. You should update your knowledge about competing computer vendors and the information capability they provide. You should participate in the organization's decision to purchase a new computer system. Often, the information needs of the medical director are not taken into account in the buy decision. You should own your own personal computer and use it as a personal productivity tool. For better or worse, you will have to learn to manage with numbers.

Managed care is creating a major financial problem for many hospitals. You should view yourself as a managed care consultant and help the hospital select the plan that best fits its needs and financial survival. If you work for a managed care organization, you can use the same skills to design a better package for hospitals. Managed care is here to stay and is something you must understand. Most of the rules you have learned in fee-for-service, solo practice do not apply in this new arena. Capitated managed care will prove to be the supreme challenge for health provider organizations.

Each year, you should review the unmet health care needs in your community and determine if they represent a desirable new market for your organization. Unmet needs may be documented and made available to the public in written reports published by other organizations in your community, such as the public health department or a local planning agency. You may have to determine the unmet needs yourself by conducting neighborhood interviews, leading consumer focus groups, or talking to the various gatekeepers in the community, such as pastors or social workers. Many communities do not offer adequate wellness programs, and there is a growing interest in such programs. Consumer interest is a key factor in your marketing effort. Who wants and is willing to pay for a product that your organization can produce? The aging population represents a growing market segment. Industrial health services is a growing niche for many health care providers. By forecasting changes in your service area, you can often spot new product opportunities.

Changes in reimbursement policy and procedure are a constant problem for all health provider organizations. The physician executive needs to examine the impact of such changes on physician behavior, organizational response, cost and quality outcomes, and organizational repositioning in the marketplace. Reimbursement is perhaps the most important dimension to understand in the business dynamics of any health care organization. Reduced reimbursement often requires cost reduction and may lead to organizational retrenchment.

As a manager, you should be alert to signs of organizational decline. This may take many forms, including an eroding community economic base, new competitors on the scene, large industries moving out of the area, increasing obsolescence of your plant and equipment, growing ineffectiveness of your board of directors, deteriorating leadership of the CEO, aging medical staff, decreasing utilization of your services, declining market share, declining net worth, increasing morale problems, a talent exodus from the organization, increasing patient care incidents, increasing litigation, renewed interest in collecting bargaining, reduced quality and output, and increasing problems with third-party agencies. Organizations slowly slide into collapse if managers are not alert to the signs of decline and if they fail to engage in turnaround strategies. As a physician executive, you share responsibility for the welfare of your organization. You must alert other managers if you see signs of decline. Of course, the CEO and the board of trustees must also act. You cannot do it by yourself.

An important organizational skill for the physician executive is the ability to sell ideas and build people's enthusiasm for a better organization. You must be able to visualize a better organization and communicate that vision effectively to your fellow managers. The physician executive should be a visionary. Perhaps you should develop a think tank or futures group and get other people involved in your envisioning efforts. By creating images of possibility, the manager motivates others to excellence. Good management is high play and fun. Imagination is the key to a more abundant future for your organization.

Performance Outcomes for the Physician Executive

How do you know if you are doing your job? How will the organization measure your managerial effectiveness? Of course, your performance objectives will vary, depending on the kind of organization you are working for and the specifics of your job assignment.

The most important indicator for continued job tenure is usually how you get along with the CEO. If the CEO views you as a valuable resource and frequently consults you before making important decisions, you know you have arrived.

How popular are you with other members of the management team? Organizational satisfaction with your services is a valid indicator of your value to the organization. You can't do your job if other managers do not like and respect you. You will be evaluated on your technical expertise, interpersonal ability, and organizational participation.

Patient satisfaction is another indicator of your value to the organization. Although this is a difficult dimension to measure, you should be concerned with it. How can you increase the satisfaction of your customers? Satisfied patients tell their doctors and their friends and become repeat customers. When you manage customer satisfaction, you are managing the bottom line.

In general, the physician executive is expected to help the organization survive in the rapidly changing health care marketplace. Do you make a major contribution to the bottom line of your organization? If your organization is in the growth mode, you help it grow. If the organization is in a period of retrenchment, you help it resize. Have you been effective in your efforts to reduce costs? Whatever you do, it must be essential to the survival of the organization. If you are viewed as a luxury, your organization may not be able to afford you in a period of economic decline.

A physician executive can often help the organization expand its patient base by reaching into unserved markets. Who are potential buyers of your products who are not yet customers? A good working relationship with marketing and planning is essential in your attempt to find new patients. If you can convince "splitters" (doctors who admit patients to other hospitals) to admit more of their patients in your facility, you can greatly expand the patient base with very little additional effort. Sometimes, all that is needed is a word of encouragement or appreciation. It may be necessary, however, to buy new equipment, improve facilities, make changes in nursing, or fix production problems before you get more admissions from a splitter. It is usually easier to get more business from existing customers than to find new customers. You should carefully monitor the admitting behavior of each physician, note any changes, and act to improve the situation. Even if you are not hospital-based, you need to be actively involved in bringing more business into your organization. In a sense, you should view yourself as a professional sales person. You are selling your organization and its products to potential buyers. You may no longer be involved in manufacturing (the direct provision of patient care), but you should be involved in strategic planning, quality assurance, cost reduction, productivity improvement, marketing, sales, and advertising.

The physician executive knows he or she is doing the job if the quality of care in the organization is improving. You are a major control point for quality assurance, and, if quality deteriorates, it is your fault. You should also be involved in determining quality standards and in setting specifications for computer systems that monitor quality of care. Have you made a major contribution to the risk management program?

Problem solving and decision making are traditional management functions. What organizational problems have you solved in the past 12 months? Have you studied and improved the way your organization makes decisions? If you can streamline medical care decision making in your organization, you are accomplishing an important job function. This may require intensive work with the medical staff, redesign of staff committees, or the development of a new corporate structure for physicians.

Better management of patient care is also an outcome that should be traceable to you. Providing patient care is a production process, and you should view yourself as a production manager.

It is important that you periodically assess physician, nursing, and patient satisfaction with the production process. Are waiting times too long? Is there confusion regarding referrals? Are procedures inefficient? Is documentation of patient care inadequate?

Are the nursing units understaffed or overstaffed? Are admitting and discharge procedures quick and painless? You should diagram the flow of production in each patient care unit, with the times, procedures, and costs carefully noted. You may have to buy a stopwatch and do a little management engineering to determine if you have optimal production efficiencies. In our current reimbursement environment, a dollar saved is a dollar earned. Productivity improvement can offset eroding profit margins.

Another index of your performance is the quality of relationships you maintain with third parties. Do outside companies like to do business with your organization? In addition to being a physician, you must fulfill the roles of diplomat, negotiator, and public relations representative for your organization. It is important to maintain the right image and to facilitate working relationships with outside parties.

Physician satisfaction with your role in the organization and an absence of problems in your assigned areas of medical responsibility are important indicators that you are doing your job well. You are hired to solve problems, not create them. A well-organized and well-functioning group of physicians is a tribute to your capacity as a physician executive.

Are you successful in your attempts to recruit and retain physicians? If this is part of your job description, it is an outcome that should be measured. The right age and mix of the medical staff is important to the survival of your organization.

Innovation is an important organizational outcome and should be part of your performance appraisal. Have you developed new medical services and products for your organization? Have you increased the organization's service area? Have you developed profitable joint ventures? Have you designed an innovative new organizational structure for physicians working with your organization?

Is the community experiencing an improved community health status as the result of your work? This is a difficult performance objective to measure, but it is the reason your organization exists. Your attention to wellness and prevention services is an important step in reducing morbidity indices in your community.

Career Development

A physician executive must learn to manage his or her career. Your destiny depends on how well you function and progress in organizations. You need to develop a career strategy and plan that is reviewed and updated each year. You must know three things to be a good career planner:

- Where you are presently in your career.
- Your career destination.
- A plan for getting from here to there.

It may pay you to get some help from a career planner or to attend a career workshop. There is a large body of literature in this field, and you will benefit from some directed reading.

Don't stay in a bad organizational space. If the organization or the job does not fit you, get out! You will lose time and confidence fighting a losing battle. Remember, a good manager in a bad organizational space is a failure. Even if you can get by, you are losing opportunities to make valuable contributions to the field. Many physicians have never had occasion to resign or have never been fired. They feel that if they are having trouble, it must mean that something is wrong with them. That is a possibility. Another answer is that the fit between the job space and the physician executive is wrong. The only way to know for sure is for the physician executive to leave and seek greener pastures elsewhere.

Develop a professional network. Each time you attend a professional meeting, make contacts and collect business cards. You should have dozen or more peers with whom you regularly consult and share information. The best jobs come through professional networks. Often one of your peers has solved problems that stump you and, if asked, will be happy to share the solution with you.

Maintain a high visibility in your profession. You should be a member of the American College of Physician Executives. You should complete the Physician in Management Seminars offered by ACPE. You should attend the national meetings of ACPE. This builds a valuable network of contacts. If people do not know you, they can hardly help you.

Accept offices in national health organizations and serve on their committees. The practice is time-consuming, but it develops contacts and gives you valuable information not available to others in your profession. Remember, as a manager, you manage a knowledge base and you manage through the efforts of others. You have to stay in the mainstream to best serve your own interests and the interests of your organization.

Continue your formal and informal education. It may pay you to go for an MBA or an equivalent degree in management. The MD/MBA combination is a powerful vocational ticket. How much more education makes sense for you will depend on how many more years you plan to work as a physician executive.

Redesign your job. You can enrich your job and increase your satisfaction by adding new job elements that represent your special interests and abilities. Think about your ideal job space. If you could have it all, what would it be? Know what you need from your organization to be at your best.

Carefully analyze your successes and failures. Every manager learns from intelligent mistakes. Debrief your actions. Why did I win? Why did I lose? What will I do differently next time?

Good managers have a lot of experience and have made a lot of mistakes getting it. Unless you are willing to take risks and make mistakes, you will not learn. It is important that you work for an organization that will back you and take risks with you. No manager wants to be out on a limb.

Present papers at national meetings and contribute to the literature on physicians in management. As I indicated earlier, most management literature is not directed to your profession and is not easily adapted. If your writing skills are not up to par, work with a freelance writer. You will be the author, and the freelancer will prepare your manuscript for publication. A test of any professional is the degree to which he or she contributes to the literature of his or her profession.

Do not be afraid to file your credentials with one of the many professional search firms. You are worth to your organization what you are worth to other organizations. Determine your current market value and talk with the search firm concerning what you can do to make yourself even more attractive to other employers. Maintain an up-to-date personal resume and be certain that it has some recent additions to it.

You may want to develop your consulting skills both inside and outside your organization. Consultation is an important organizational development skill as well as a profession in its own right. What is there after being a physician executive—perhaps a consultant in physician management?

In general, it is good to be active in your community and to develop power bases outside your organization. You may wish to serve on the board of other community agencies and become active in community development. The more power and influence you have outside your organization, the more you have inside it.

Summary

As a physician executive, you are a key player on the management team. You are an interface professional spanning the disciplines of medicine and management. Your effectiveness in the organization depends on the appropriateness of your role definition and your possession of key management skills. This chapter has defined both of these. To further prepare yourself for success in your profession, consult the attached bibliography of current management literature. The bibliography is organized by topical area. Read in those areas where you will benefit most from further instruction. Although the selections are not written specifically for physician executives, you can easily adapt the material to your needs and interests. I have made no attempt to be exhaustive or necessarily representative of the vast literature available. I have instead included a few items in each topical area that I think will be of maximum benefit to you.

Bibliography

Career Planning

Bardwick, J. The Plateauing Trap. New York, N.Y.: AMACOM, 1986.

Davidson, J. Blow Your Own Horn. New York, N.Y.: AMACOM, 1987.

London, M., and Mone, E. Career Management and Survival in the Workplace. San Francisco, Calif.: Jossey-Bass, 1987.

Rein, I., and others. High Visibility. New York, N.Y.: Dodd, Mead & Company, 1987.

Brewi, J., and Brennan, A. Celebrate Mid-Life. New York, N.Y.: Crossroad, 1988.

Stockmyer, J., and Williams, R. Life Trek. Atlanta, Ga.: Humanics New Age, 1988.

Ferrucci, P. What We May Be. Worcester, Great Britain: Crucible, 1989.

Glouberman, D. Life Choices and Life Changes through Imagework. London, Great Britain: Unwin Paperbacks, 1990.

Belitz, J. *Success: Full Living*. Indianapolis, Ind.: Knowledge Systems, Inc., 1991.

Lewis, H. *A Question of Values*. New York, N.Y.: HarperSanFrancisco, 1991.

Morrisey, G. *Creating Your Future*. San Francisco, Calif.: Berrett-Koehler Publishers, 1992.

Boldt, L. *Zen and the Art of Making a Living*. New York, N.Y.: Arkana, 1993.

Woods, D., and Ormerod, S. *Networking*. San Diego, Calif.: Pfeiffer and Company, 1993.

Young-Sowers, M. *Spiritual Crisis*. Walpole, N. H.: Stillpoint Publishing, 1993.

Change

Martel, L. *Mastering Change: The Key to Business Success*. New York, N.Y.: Simon & Schuster, 1986.

Duhl, L. *The Social Entrepreneurship of Change*. New York, N.Y.: Pace University Press, 1990.

Beckhard, R., and Pritchard, W. *Changing the Essence*. San Francisco, Calif.: Jossey-Bass Publishers, 1992.

Cognitive Style

de Bono, E. *Six Think Hats*. Boston, Mass.: Little, Brown, 1985.

Sims, H., and others. *The Thinking Organization*. San Francisco, Calif.: Jossey-Bass, 1986.

Community

Schindler-Rainman, E., and Lippitt, R. *Building the Collaborative Community*. Riverside, Calif.: University of California Extension, 1980.

Bellah, R., and others. *The Good Society*. New York, N.Y.: Alfred A. Knopf, 1991.

Anderson, D., Ed. *The Loss of Virtue*. Great Britain: A National Review Book, 1992.

Etzioni, A. *The Spirit of Community*. New York, N.Y.: Crown Publishers, 1993.

Peck, M. *A World Waiting To Be Born*. New York, N.Y.: Bantam Books, 1993.

Competition

Porter, M. *Competitive Strategy*. New York, N.Y.: Free Press, 1980.

Sheldon, A., and Windham, S. *Competitive Strategy for Health Care Organizations*. Homewood, Ill.: Dow Jones-Irwin, 1984.

Porter, M. *Competitive Advantage*. New York, N.Y.: Free Press, 1985.

Kohn, A. *No Contest: The Case Against Competition*. Boston, Mass.: Houghton Mifflin, 1986.

Kelly, J. *How to Check Out Your Competition*. New York, N.Y.: John Wiley & Sons, 1987.

Computers and Electronic Networks

Boone, M. *Leadership and the Computer*. Rocklin, Calif.: Prima Publishing, 1991.

Sproull, L., and Kiesler, S. *Connections*. Cambridge, Mass.: MIT Press, 1992.

Rheingold, H. *The Virtual Community*. Reading, Mass.: Addison-Wesley Publishing Company, 1993.

Tapscott, D., and Caston, A. *Paradigm Shift*. New York, N.Y.: McGraw-Hill, 1993.

Creativity and Innovation

Burgelman, R., and Sayles, L. *Inside Corporate Innovation*. New York, N.Y.: Free Press, 1986.

Ray, M., and Myers, R. *Creativity in Business*. New York, N.Y.: Doubleday, 1986.

Albercht, K. *The Creative Corporation*. Homewood, Ill.: Dow Jones-Irwin, 1987.

Siler, T. *Breaking Through the Mind Barrier*. New York, N.Y.: A Touchstone Book, 1990.

de Bono, E. *I Am Right. You Are Wrong*. New York, N.Y.: Viking, 1991.

Fritz, R. *Creating*. New York, N.Y.: Fawcett Columbine, 1991.

Michalko, M. *Thinkertoys*. Berkeley, Calif.: Ten Speed Press, 1991.

Thompson, C. *What a Great Idea!* New York, N.Y.: HarperPerennial, 1992.

Futurism

Foss, L., and Rothenberg, K. *The Second Medical Revolution*. Boston, Mass.: New Science Library (Shambhala), 1987.

Nash, D. *Future Practice Alternatives in Medicine*. New York, N.Y.: Igaku-Shoin, 1987.

Hardison, O. *Disappearing through the Skylight*. New York, N.Y.: Viking, 1989.

Schorr, L. *Within Our Reach*. New York, N.Y.: Doubleday, 1989.

Boyett, J., and Conn, H. *Workplace 2000*. New York, N.Y.: A Plume Book, 1991.

Jamieson, D., and O'Mara, J. *Managing Workforce 2000*. San Francisco, Calif.: Jossey-Bass Publishers, 1991.

Schwartz, P. *The Art of the Long View*. New York, N.Y.: Doubleday/Currency, 1991.

Sinetar, M. *Developing a 21st Century Mind*. New York, N.Y.: Ballantine Books, 1991.

Land, G., and Jarman, B. *Breakpoint and Beyond*. New York, N.Y.: HarperBusiness, 1992.

Pelton, J. *Future View*. Boulder, Colo.: Johnson Printing, 1992.

Theobald, R. *Turning the Century*. Indianapolis, Ind.: Knowledge Systems, Inc., 1992.

Annison, M. *Managing the Whirlwind*. Englewood, Colo.: Medical Group Management Association, 1993.

Feuerstein, G., and Feuerstein, T. (Eds.) *Voices on the Threshold of Tomorrow.* Wheaton, Ill.: Quest Books, 1993.

Maynard, H., and Mehrtens, S. *The Fourth Wave.* San Francisco, Calif.: Berrett-Koehler Publishers, 1993.

General Management

Laureau, W. *Millennium Management.* Piscataway, N.J.: New Century Publishers, 1978.

Badawy, M. *Developing Managerial Skills in Engineers & Scientists.* New York, N.Y.: Van Nostrand, 1982.

Geigold, W. *Practical Management Skills for Engineers and Scientists.* Belmont, Calif.: Lifetime Learning Pubilcations, 1982.

Van Fleet, J. *The 22 Biggest Mistakes Managers Make.* New York, N.Y.: Parker Publishing, 1982.

Ginsburg, S. *Ropes for Management Success.* Englewood Cliffs, N.J.: Prentice-Hall, 1984.

Brown, W. *13 Fatal Errors Managers Make and How You Can Avoid Them.* New York, N.Y.: Berkley Books, 1985.

Clifford, D., and Cavanagh, R. *The Winning Performance.* New York, N.Y.: Bantam, 1985.

Harmon, F., and Jacobs, G. *The Vital Difference.* New York, N.Y.: AMACOM, 1985.

Hornstein, H. *Managerial Courage.* New York, N.Y.: John Wiley, 1986.

Smith, M. *Maxims of Management.* Piscataway, N.J.: New Century Publishers, 1986.

Young, A. *The Manager's Handbook.* New York, N.Y.: Crown, 1986.

Mitroff, I. *Business Not as Usual.* San Francisco, Calif.: Jossey-Bass, 1987.

Peters, T. *Thriving on Chaos.* New York, N.Y.: Knopf, 1987.

Primozic, K., and others. *Strategic Choices.* New York, N.Y.: McGraw- Hill, Inc., 1991.

Davidow, W., and Malone, M. *The Virtual Corporation.* New York, N.Y.: HarperCollins, 1992.

Quinn, J. *Intelligent Enterprise.* New York, N.Y.: Free Press, 1992.

Drucker, P. *Managing for the Future.* New York, N.Y.: Truman Talley Books, 1993.

Hammer, M., and Champy, J. *Reengineering the Corporation.* New York, N.Y.: HarperBusiness, 1993.

Wendt, H. *Global Embrace.* New York, N.Y.: HarperBusiness, 1993.

Wick, C., and Leon, L. *The Learning Edge.* New York, N.Y.: McGraw-Hill, 1993.

Health Behavior

Glanz, K., and others. (Eds.) *Health Behavior and Health Education: Theory and Practice.* San Francisco, Calif.: Jossey-Bass, 1990.

Health Care Management

Charns, M., and Schaefer, M. *Health Care Organizations: A Model for Management*. Englewood Cliffs, N.J.: Prentice-Hall, 1983.

Blair, J., and Fottler, M. *Challenges in Healthcare Management*. San Francisco, Calif.: Jossey-Bass, 1990.

Leebov, W., Scott, G. *Health Care Managers in Transition*. San Francisco, Calif.: Jossey-Bass, 1990.

Marszalek-Gaucher, E., and Coffey, R. *Transforming Healthcare Organizations*. San Francisco, Calif.: Jossey-Bass, 1990.

Healthy Company

Rosen, R. *The Healthy Company*. Los Angeles, Calif.: Jeremy P. Tarcher, Inc., 1991.

Leadership

Atchison, T. *Turning Health Care Leadership Around*. San Francisco, Calif.: Jossey-Bass, 1990.

Asay, L., and Maciariello, J. *Executive Leadership in Health Care*. San Francisco, Calif.: Jossey-Bass, 1991.

Mindell, A. *The Leader as a Martial Artist*. New York, N.Y.: HarperSanFrancisco, 1992.

Nanus, B. *Visionary Leadership*. San Francisco, Calif.: Jossey-Bass, 1992.

Ross, A. *Cornerstones of Leadership for Health Services Executives*. Ann Arbor, Mich.: Health Administration Press, 1992.

Wheatley, M. *Leadership and the New Science*. San Francisco, Calif.: Berrett-Koehler, 1992.

McFarland, L., and others. *21st Century Leadership*. New York, N.Y.: Leadership Press, 1993.

Terry, R. *Authentic Leadership*. San Francisco, Calif.: Jossey-Bass, 1993.

Management Succession

Gabarro, J. *The Dynamics of Taking Charge*. Cambridge, Mass.: Harvard Business School Press, 1987.

Managing Physicians

Valentine, S. *Physician Bonding*. Rockville, Md.: Aspen Publishers, 1990.

Shortell, S. *Effective Hospital-Physician Relationships*. Ann Arbor, Mich.: Health Administration Press, 1991.

Managing Professionals

Shapero, A. *Managing Professional People*. New York, N.Y.: Free Press, 1985.

Benveniste, G. *Professionalizing the Organization*. San Francisco, Calif.: Jossey-Bass, 1987.

Marketing

Coddington, D., and Moore, K. *Market-Driven Strategies in Health Care*. San Francisco, Calif: Jossey-Bass, 1987.

Fine, S. *Marketing the Public Sector*. New Brunswick, N.J.: Transaction Publishers, 1992.

Embley, L. *Doing Well While Doing Good*. Englewood Cliffs, N.J.: Prentice-Hall, 1993.

Medicine

Inlander, C., and others. *Medicine on Trial*. New York, N.Y.: Pantheon Books, 1988.

Bogdanich, W. *The Great White Lie*. New York, N.Y.: Simon & Schuster, 1991.

Cahalan, D. *An Ounce of Prevention*. San Francisco, Calif.: Jossey-Bass, 1991.

Smith, J. *Women and Doctors*. New York, N.Y.: Atlantic Monthly Press, 1992.

Negotiating

Fisher, R., and Ury, W. *Getting to Yes*. Boston, Mass.: Houghton Mifflin , 1981.

Jandt, F. *Win-Win Negotiating*. New York, N.Y.: John Wiley, 1985.

New Paradigm Management

Tart, C. *Open Mind, Discriminating Mind*. San Francisco, Calif.: Harper & Row, 1989.

Harman, W., and Hormann, J. *Creative Work*. Indianapolis, Ind.: Knowledge Systems, Inc., 1990.

Keck, L. *Sacred Eyes*. Indianapolis, Ind.: Knowledge Systems, Inc., 1992.

Renesch, J. *New Traditions in Business*. San Francisco, Calif.: Berrett-Koehler, 1992.

Shapiro, E., and Shapiro, D. *The Way Ahead*. Rockport, Mass.: Element, Inc., 1992.

Chappell, T. *The Soul of a Business*. New York, N.Y.: Bantam Books, 1993.

Coles, R. *The Call of Service*. Boston, Mass.: Houghton Mifflin Company, 1993.

Ray, M., and Rinzler, A. (Eds.) *The New Paradigm in Business*. New York, N.Y.: Jeremy Tarcher/Perigee, 1993.

Organizational Culture

Schneider, B. (Ed.) *Organizational Climate and Culture.* San Francisco, Calif.: Jossey-Bass, 1990.

Bolman, L., and Deal, T. *Reframing Organizations.* San Francisco, Calif.: Jossey Bass, 1991.

Frost, P., and others. (Eds.) *Reframing Organizational Culture.* Newbury Park, Calif.: Sage Publications, 1991.

Organizational Development

Weisbord, M. *Discovering Common Ground.* San Francisco, Calif.: Berrett-Koehler Publishers, 1992.

Organizational Politics

de Bono, E. *Tactics.* Boston, Mass.: Little Brown, 1984.

Yates, D. *The Politics of Management.* San Francisco, Calif: Jossey-Bass, 1985.

Block, P. *The Empowered Manager.* San Francisco, Calif.: Jossey-Bass, 1987.

Patient Care

Gerteis, M., and others. (Eds.) *Through the Patient's Eyes.* San Francisco, Calif.: Jossey-Bass, 1993.

People Skills

Greene, R. *How to Win With People.* New York, N.Y.: Hawthorn Books, 1969.

Stewart, D. *The Power of People Skills.* New York, N.Y.: John Wiley, 1986.

Performance Appraisal

Rausch, E. *Win-Win: Performance Management Appraisal.* New York, N.Y.: John Wiley, 1985.

Politics and Government

Barlett, D., and Steele, J. *America: What Went Wrong?* Kansas City, Mo.: Andrews and McMeel, 1992.

Greider, W. *Who Will Tell the People?* New York, N.Y.: Simon & Schuster, 1992.

Osborne, D., and Gaebler, T. *Reinventing Government.* Reading, Mass.: Addison-Wesley Publishing Company, 1992.

Marshall, W., and Schram, M. *Mandate for Change.* New York, N.Y.: Berkley Books, 1993.

Newman, K. *Declining Fortunes.* New York, N.Y.: Basic Books, 1993.

Productivity

Weisbord, M. *Productive Workplaces.* San Francisco, Calif.: Jossey-Bass, 1990.

Quality Improvement

Berwick, D., and others. *Curing Health Care*. San Francisco, Calif.: Jossey-Bass, 1991.

Leebov, W., and Ersoz, C. *The Health Care Manager's Guide to Continuous Quality Improvement*. Chicago, Ill.: American hospital Publishing, Inc., 1991.

Risk Taking

MacCrimmon, K., and Wehrung, D. *Taking Risks*. New York, N.Y.: Free Press, 1986.

Strategic Planning, Policy, and Management

Yavitz, B., and Newman, W. *Strategy in Action*. New York, N.Y.: Free Press, 1982.

Aaker, D. *Developing Business Strategies*. New York, N.Y.: John Wiley, 1984.

Cone, P., and others. *Strategic Resource Management*. Berrien Springs, Mich.: Andrews University Press, 1986.

Sawyer, G. *Designing Strategy*. New York, N.Y.: John Wiley, 1986.

Below, P., and others. *An Executive Guide to Strategic Planning*. San Francisco, Calif.: Jossey-Bass, 1987.

McGregor, E. *Strategic Management of Human Knowledge, Skills, and Abilities*. San Francisco, Calif.: Jossey-Bass, 1991.

Systems Management

Senge, P. *The Fifth Discipline*. New York, N.Y.: Doubleday, 1990.

Teamwork

Garfield, C. *Peak Performers*. New York, N.Y.: William Morrow, 1986.

Buchholz, S., and Roth, T. *Creating the High-Performance Team*. New York, N.Y.: John Wiley, 1987.

Transformational Management

Adams, J. *Transforming Work*. Alexandria, Va.: Miles River Press, 1984.

Kozmetsky, G. *Transformational Management*. Cambridge, Mass.: Ballinger, 1985.

Adams, J. *Transforming Leadership*. Alexandria, Va.: Miles River Press, 1986.

Tichy, N., and Devanna, M. *The Transformational Leader*. New York, N.Y.: John Wiley, 1986.

Leland R. Kaiser, PhD, is President of Kaiser and Associates, Brighton, Colorado.

Career Positioning

by Marilyn Moats Kennedy, MSJ

CHAPTER

9

O nce you've decided to pursue a career in management, career planning—as opposed to job hunting—becomes very important. Career planning is the process for deciding three things: what skills you want to use (presumably you've chosen your management skills); where you want to work (in the service of what values and types of organizations and where geographically); and, finally, how you will find the right organization and get hired there. Getting a job is never unimportant, but the real trick is getting a *series* of right jobs and thinking about those jobs as parts of a whole career plan, because the latter is the framework within which individual job choices are made.

What you want must be balanced against the demands of the marketplace. Career planning has changed dramatically since 1989, roughly the beginning of the recession. Because there will be no boom before 1995, most people will move more frequently from job to job and over a broader range of management jobs than in the past. There is more emphasis on transferable skills, especially people skills.

Age is an asset because most organizations have targeted flexible staffing, i.e., people will not expect to stay with an organization for life, and therefore the fifty- and sixtysomethings are highly desirable because they will stay 5 or 10 years at the most. Age discrimination now means rejecting the thirtysomethings for older, less permanent employees.

Locum tenens are now contingency workers and represent not a postretirement option but a permanent, if nomadic, life-style. Many physicians choose periods of practice interspersed with periods of management. These are generally younger, two-physician couples who are highly responsive to career-building opportunities wherever they occur. The hottest growth market in temporary employment is the temporary executive who comes into the organization, fixes a problem or problems, and then moves on. These are among the highest paid jobs emerging in medical management.

The most desirable manager is a player/coach who can inspire his or her direct reports to produce more and to find satisfaction in so doing. Evidence of leadership, the ability to get results by example as well as direction, is the most desirable quality a candidate can possess, recruiters tell us. Second, recruiters want people who have been through turnarounds, downsizings, or other organizational upheavals. As one hospital human resources manager said, "We have no time for virgins here." Third, health care and nonhealth care organizations are interested in people with entrepreneurial skills and zeal, however acquired. These ideas should be considered in positioning yourself as a candidate.

What is Positioning?

Positioning is the process of putting oneself in a particular relationship to a particular audience. For example, someone who positions himself or herself as a manager is signaling an audience to expect certain behavior. Someone who positions himself or herself as top management or potentially top management sends a different signal. The audience will make an independent evaluation but will be heavily influenced by your self-evaluation as expressed by the way you position yourself. Before you decide how to position yourself, you need to examine your managerial goals.

Goal Setting

Why did you choose management? Do you have an agenda of things you want to accomplish? Are you trying to "straighten out" some part of health care? Is this a preemptive strike, because you don't see anyone else where you are who is capable of management? You need to answer these questions in your own mind, because the answers are a prerequisite to positioning and career planning. They will influence your choice of an organization. Understand that you may change your mind again at any time, but saying, "I want to keep my options open," is not a choice; it's a refusal to commit.

What time frame have you set? Are you looking for the legendary fast track, a position to round out a career that began with clinical work, a way to maximize earnings now for a complete break in a few years? Each goal will require a different time frame.

Be aware that, at least until the turn of the century, you can expect the time it takes to move from organization to organization to be much longer than it was in the '80s. For example, if a medical director search took six months in the 1980s it can take as much as nine months to a year in this decade. This must be factored into planning, because too many people count on getting offers when jobs have been put on hold. You can't go wrong in assuming the decision-making process will be lengthy on both sides.

Finally, what are your plans for movement within management? Are you interested in top management, top medical management, or moving entirely out of medical management into the management of another function? Expect to be asked about this at serious interviews.

Targeting

Once you've answered these questions, you need to begin the process of targeting. Much has been written about organizational culture and its considerable impact on job and career success. Without repeating all of that, let's summarize and say that you will never be able to mold yourself to "fit" an organization. No surgical procedure known will accomplish that. Targeting is the task of finding an organization that will recognize your worth. In other words, if you have to sell yourself aggressively because there is no immediate recognition of mutual interest, you lose. Everyone must sell himself or herself in an interview, but a hard sell often foretells a bad fit. Do you and the organization share goals; values; and, most important, *approaches* to problem solving?

The targeting process always begins with you. What are your values? In what environment do you manage best? Are you pro- or anti-meetings? Do you want a large or a small organization? Are you a workaholic or someone with outside interests? These questions must be answered before you can target organizations and position yourself in the right way.

As you mentally construct your ideal organization, there are four factors to keep in mind. An organization might be ideal for you culturally and might easily recognize your worth, but it might be very bad for you because it has serious, unsolvable financial, structural, or marketing problems. Much of what you read about unhealthy organizations has to do with competitive positions. The organization's product or service is excellent but it's not competitive on either cost or satisfaction with others in the market.

There are certain general guidelines for healthy, desirable organizations, and these are especially important to people who want to move up rapidly:

■ Under $50 million in gross revenues. The most competitive organizations are small and can redirect their efforts quickly.

■ Fewer than 300 employees.

■ Growth rate of at least 15 percent per year for the past 2-3 years. A 20 percent growth rate during the recession, 1989 to the present, is excellent.

■ Not less than 5 and not more than 20 years old.

Of these factors, the growth rate is clearly most important. High growth creates jobs and bonuses. How does one subdivide and distribute nothing? In an organization growing at 20 percent a year, given normal turnover, virtually every employee below the CEO will have a chance to move up within two or three years. Contrast this with a shrinking organization. The work load will probably be greater in the latter, with little economic reward possible. Obviously, these criteria won't fit a hospital or group practice. However, growth of at least 10 percent per year, especially for a hospital, is important. A hospital that has a healthy census and expansionist designs (if realistic) is far more likely to provide opportunities for growth and advancement than one that has just announced its third layoff. The same is true of a growing multispecialty group versus one that is praying for several physicians to retire.

A hospital or group practice that has contingency plans for health care reform is a better choice than one with a "wait and see" attitude, especially because the shape of health care reform is unclear.

Deciding on Positioning within the Organization

For top management. If the CEO position is your goal, you will need to look for organizations in which some, or all, of the following conditions exist:

A CEO who is at least 20 years older than you or one who is nearing retirement. If you are in your late fifties or sixties, you're in luck, for two reasons. First, the most desirable quality any employee can have is that he or she won't stay with the organization forever. In fact, flexible staffing, from top to bottom, is at the top of every organization's wish list. Second, most start-up organizations deliberately hire older managers because the younger the company, the older the top management team, excluding founders, tends to be. There is more risk in these organizations, but your contribution will be generously rewarded as the business grows—assuming that it does.

If you're in your fifties, to become CEO you'll have to look for a fairly new or a troubled organization. In your forties, an organization with a 50-year-old CEO would be a poor choice. A 55- to 60-year-old CEO would be good. In your thirties, a 50-year-old CEO would be reasonable. A failing 45-year old CEO would not be good, because he or she will almost certainly be succeeded by someone 10 years older.

Besides the age of the present CEO, the ages of possible internal competitors need to be considered. If the rest of the top management team is much younger, the organization may already have done some succession planning, and one of those people may be in the process of being groomed to take over. A downturn in the organization's fortunes could eliminate this person, but that puts us in a turnaround situation again.

Consider the ambitions of competitors. It's not true that everyone who's a vice president wants to be CEO. Contented number twos are legion, although not one in 10 would own up to that. As the population puts more emphasis on life-style and quality of life, the competition for top spots decreases; it doesn't increase.

A typical scenario for an MD/CEO of a hospital would be to be hired as medical director by the CEO who's planning to retire, voluntarily or not, within three years. There may even be whispers of a golden parachute. The board has decided to "play in" a new person. The candidate most likely to be considered would be in his or her forties, with at least a few years as a medical department chair of a similarly sized hospital in a similar community, or vice president of medical affairs in a smaller hospital who could show an agenda for whatever the board perceives as its institution's future. He or she would be expected to play on the CEO's team, never once so much as suggesting that he or she was "in waiting." The board would be most interested in establishing that the candidate had good relationships with his or her current CEO. Any hint of rebellion or disagreement with the current employer will squelch the deal. The waiting period should be the time during which the candidate pursues an executive MBA from a top school.

The board of trustees/directors generally considers, although generally won't give the nod to, inside CEO candidates unless the organization is in trouble. In that case, an outsider will almost always be sought. If you're positioning yourself for CEO, no factor will be more important than being in a healthy organization, unless it's a turnaround situation and you literally are the physician applying the cure.

The worst strategy would be to go to an organization 20 years before you wanted to be CEO and attempt to bond yourself inextricably to the organization. This time frame is much too long for the current instability within the health care industry, indeed in U.S. industry in general. If you can't plot with some certainty a move into the top slot within five years, that organization probably can't meet your needs. It's somewhat ghoulish to peg your upward climb to the probability that someone will die or leave in the interim, but it's an excellent strategy.

Top Medical Management. If your goal is medical director or vice president of medical affairs, you'll have to target specifically the size and type of organization you want and whether you want to be a "first" or go in after someone has shaped the system. It's easier, with little management experience, to find an opportunity to be a "first." The organization doesn't really know what a medical director does, so you'll have time to develop the job. A job description that states "builds and maintains positive working relationships with physicians" is not really a description, it's a hope. Chairing a medical department at a hospital would be good experience for becoming a medical director, because the chair will face many of the problems of a medical director, but on a smaller scale.

If you want the top medical management spot in a company, you'll need to network for companies just starting to take benefits planning and case management seriously. Then you and top management will have to agree on a set of outcomes. You must have the power and authority to make a visible difference. If not, you'll be seen as extraneous and an ideal candidate for the next layoff.

Going into an existing position means that all normal job hunting rules apply. It becomes a question of carefully matching your level of management experience—and the problems you're best at solving—with the organization's needs. Caution: what your predecessor did—and how he or she did it—will influence the organization's expectations. Be wary of a situation in which the job description is being "rewritten." It means that your predecessor didn't do what was expected or did it badly. Organizations tend to react to mismanagement rather than act positively to encourage good management. They shop with a list of "never agains" rather than "must haves." You will need more leadership skills to follow a poor or disappointing performer. On the other hand, you will look much better with less effort, because your predecessor depressed the CEO's expectations.

Outside of medicine. Should you wish to work in a nonmedical environment, your positioning will again be different. You'll have to show the transferability of your management skills. That means you'll have to demonstrate the similarity between medical and nonmedical problems. We have watched many people make the transition in one jump by aggressively selling people skills and the concept of the generic manager—i.e., if you were good at managing people in one environment, you'd be equally good in another. They also used the "new perspective/new blood" argument. For example, serving as medical director of a 100-physician multispecialty clinic is necessarily a more difficult management task, with more personality problems involved, than managing any similar group of individual contributors.

Networking Nationally

Where do you find the right organization? You have to research this, and part of that will include networking. Nobody is likely to bare his or her organizational soul—warts and all—to a highly desirable manager—you. Without a national network, you might walk into any imaginable snake pit, moving your family thousands of miles only to find the situation untenable. Part of targeting is getting information on organizations that interest you long before any contact is initiated. If you don't keep ongoing files and regularly clip interesting stories from the business press about desirable organizations, you may find yourself wooed—and won—by a snake pit. This is true even if your strategy includes using search firms. It is not the recruiter's responsibility to reveal the client's problems. That's your homework.

It's not enough to be a star of the county or state medical society or well known in a specialty group. Management demands a network of managers, not practitioners. Certainly, for medical management, the American College of Physician Executives is an important group. A medical specialty group may provide second generation contacts—i.e., physicians who have access to the CEO—but is unlikely to have many CEO members, particularly of hospitals, HMOs, and companies. Business networks are vital outside medicine.

Networking requires planning and organization. It means putting and keeping one's name and interests before key contacts in a positive way. More often than for any other reason, people fail to reap the benefits of networking because they fail to follow up with contacts. No one can reasonably be expected to remember a person, regardless of competence or charisma, who is heard from once a year.

Job hunters need to be in touch with key contacts—e.g., those who hire for positions similar to those the job hunter is seeking and people who are often tapped for names of potential start—no less than once a month. No contact should languish for more than three months without some contact. If you're using search firms, they need regular contact, too. In this economic climate, monthly contact can cut months from a job search.

Pitfalls in the Career Planning Process

The saddest people we see are those who tried to short cut the career planning process, saying, "Forget goal setting. I will recognize the job I want when I see it." Wrong! The architecture underlying a job hunt is critical. Here are some of the traps to beware of:

■ Taking a job that does not represent a step forward toward your goal because you're "needed." This happens to physicians with depressing regularity because, by inclination and training, they respond to the needs of others. While medically sound, it's managerially bad practice. To be worth doing, the job must be the next step in a career, not a detour. Nothing dooms you with headhunters, always important job brokers, than one or more lateral moves. Don't let it be said about you, "He or she has two years' experience repeated five times." It's career death.

■ Kidding oneself about the importance of geography, the people environment, or the kind/type of organization. Did you assume that because the organization has a strong religious affiliation, it would be a less "political" environment? You didn't do your homework. People feel free to do anything when they're doing it in the name of the Almighty. If you love New York City, you may find Butte a bit dull and the natives slow to warm up. Knowing yourself and your family's emotional and geographic needs is very important.

■ Telling yourself that you're adaptable; you can stand anything for two years. Wrong! You may not survive three months. Two years in a hostile or uncongenial environment might be two lifetimes. If there's pain going in, nothing positive will come of the experience. You didn't like the medical director, and the CEO was no prize. Still, you signed on as vice president, medical affairs. This has disaster written all over it. Those people were on their best behavior. That was as good as it gets! You're in for it now.

■ Positioning yourself to work managerial miracles, because you were a medical miracle worker. "How bad can it be?" does not provide the frame, much less the picture. Never suggest that whatever problems they have would be nonproblems for you. Do you really have the managerial experience to assert that? Does anybody?

■ Agreeing to take a turnaround job unless you are getting paid to turn the place around. Any turnaround situation is high risk. If it's not also high reward, it's not the momentary loss that worries us. It's the fact that the people won't believe a miracle not paid for has truly occurred. Someone else will get the credit and how will you trade that up to your next job? Miracles cost much, much more than mere competence.

■ Positioning yourself on the fast track when you're actually there to ease burnout and into your retirement plan. They'll discover your real attitudes early on, as you unwittingly reveal your agenda—and you will. For example, maybe long-term planning is important to them, but you can't see the fine distinctions. That's because they don't affect your interests. You have no intention of being there that long!

■ Believing you're good at organizational politics because, as an attending, physicians and administrators liked you. Being "good with people," especially when you're already in a power position, is not the same as being good at managerial politics.

■ Positioning yourself as a manager and behaving as if you are still a clinician. This is a very common problem. Switching hats has to be a conscious effort. It's too easy to think like a physician when you ought to be thinking like a manager.

Finally, much of positioning is an ongoing process. It's not possible to decide now what you'll be doing in 20 years, even if you believe that's when you'll retire! Many people use retirement as a way to ease out of one career into another. It's important to reexamine your positioning at least every 18 months. That doesn't mean changing jobs at each career check point, but it does mean taking the time to reaffirm that what you are doing is a conscious choice, not something you've drifted into.

The big traps for physicians right now include going into organizations about to break apart from the stresses of rigidity. Always ask for examples of how the organization has approached problems in the past. Continuing to pay unproductive physicians rather than fight for present equity is an ostrich approach that bodes ill for anyone trying to manage the organization.

Avoid organizations that aren't actively doing worst case scenarios on health care reform. We don't know many that are. How many hospitals can imagine *not* being the linchpin of the health care delivery system and busily developing plans should that become the case?

Look for flexible thinkers top to bottom. A flexible CEO is nice, but flexible middle management makes a difference. Don't get into an organization that has hardened into a siege mentality and now looks to you to save it from years of poor planning or none at all.

Marilyn Moats Kennedy, MSJ, is Managing Partner, Career Strategies, Inc., Wilmette, Ill.

Managing Physicians in Organizations

by Howard L. Kirz, MD, MBA, FACPE

CHAPTER

10

The long-forgotten wag who first lamented that managing physicians was like "herding cats" would certainly have viewed the matter of this chapter with some skepticism, an oxymoron at best. In many ways, however, working with colleagues is at the very core of the work of physician executives in organizational settings. This chapter describes some of the major issues, some of the challenges, and some of the strategies for both successfully and happily fulfilling that work.

An Essential Value Conflict: Physicians in Organizations...Period!

One of the keys to working with physicians in any organizational setting is an empathy for and an understanding of the kinds of value conflicts a number of physicians face in all organizations these days. Articulating these conflicts, translating them into the context of professional values, and helping colleagues grapple with them are several hallmarks of the successful physician executive.

The first such conflict might simply be termed the "physician in organization" conflict or the Hobbsian conflict, named for Thomas Hobbs, who described the limits on individual freedom that occur as an inevitable part of membership in any society. Simply put, this conflict means that, to enjoy the benefits of membership in any given society, an individual gives up certain degrees of individual freedom and acquires in turn certain reciprocal rights and responsibilities. It may be one's individual right to drive drunk and blindfolded at 150 miles an hour somewhere on this globe, but not necessarily as a citizen of Washington and on the streets of Seattle.

The reciprocal to this limitation on individual freedoms in a society or an organization is the new right, and even a new responsibility, to be involved in developing the society's directions and norms, in other words to vote, to run for office, to lobby, to speak up, to participate as an enfranchised member of the society. The combination of these two phenomena, sometimes called the "social contract," describes the interdependent relationship between any individual and any society or, in our case, between

129

any individual physician and a health care organization.

For some physicians in organizations, this conflict is felt as undeserved organizational encroachment on the individual "autonomy" thought to be an inherent professional right. Starr and others described this conflict in the '80s as part of the gradual transformation of American medicine from a cottage industry largely comprising independent individuals to a vastly more complex and interdependent one peopled and powered by organizations.[1] In the '90s, particularly as health care reform creates even more complex organizations, this tension between individual professional rights and collective organizational rights has become part of the daily fare of most physicians and hence of most physician executives.

The limitations one experiences as a member of a defined medical organization and the reciprocal rights and responsibilities to help an organization define its norms and practice patterns are not necessarily obvious to individual physicians joining modern health care organizations. In fact, in some cases they're not even obvious to long-standing members of such organizations. And yet the two concepts, both the collective limitations and the needed contributions, are absolutely essential ingredients of the modern health care organization.

One of the first jobs of any physician manager in such a setting is therefore to help translate these general concepts into the specific professional milieu. To experience the numerous benefits of organizational life, not the least of which are a more certain flow of patients, an access to organizational services, and the use of the organizational franchise, individual physicians must accept both these limits and these responsibilities. It may for example be lawful and well within a physician's individual professional right to treat diabetics with coffee enemas somewhere on this globe, but not necessarily "on our enrollees," "in our hospital," or "as a member of our group practice."

As part of his or her daily work, the physician manager must be able to answer certain key questions that relate to these professional rights and limitations. What exactly are the benefits of professional membership or employment in this organization? What exactly are the limitations on professional autonomy to be expected as a member of this organization? Why? How can an individual physician participate in the development of group norms, practice expectations, practice guidelines, benefit packages, organizational strategies? What are the responsibilities of the individual physician for participating in such activities? Why? What are the expectations of individual physicians for doing other kinds of organizational work? Why? How are professional disputes resolved here? What are the rights of the individual physician in this process?

Although this "individual in the organization" conflict has its origin in the roots of civilized society, many physicians will first experience the conflict as a provider within one or another modern health care organizations. Helping colleagues understand these essential tradeoffs, dealing with the resultant tensions, and empathizing with the dilemma are thus key characteristics of the successful physician manager in any organizational setting.

More Values in Conflict: Kantian Versus Utilitarian Ethics

As if the foregoing weren't enough, a second major conflict for physicians in many health care organizations today involves the physician's obligations to an individual patient versus obligations to a served population. "Traditional" (at least post-World War II and post-third-party insurance) Twentieth Century medical ethics holds that the physician must do everything possible for the potential benefit of each individual patient, so-called Kantian ethics. Such ethics are relatively without conflict in a world of seemingly unlimited resources and uncontested medical truths. In such a world, the question of individual versus population outcomes can be viewed largely as a philosophical exercise or at least as one restricted to physicians practicing in "managed care" organizations.

In the '90s, however, the era of apparently unlimited resources has come to a grinding halt, and many more organizations have adopted the dual mission of providing high-quality health care within defined fiscal limits. Operating within such defined resources requires the organization and its physicians to continually seek the most cost-effective and care-effective strategies for achieving a given health outcome. It likewise requires difficult resource allocating decisions that often balance the health needs of one group of patients against the needs of the population as a whole.

Such organizational missions put practicing physicians in the unaccustomed position of simultaneously caring for individual patients while being guardians of the best use of organizational resources for the care of an entire population. Organizational policies, such as expectations for length of stay, indications for certain procedures, allocation of scarce capital, and the deployment of support personnel, all place the physician potentially at odds with traditional medical ethics. As national and local health reform initiatives create more organizations with these missions, a growing number of American physicians will find themselves grappling with such conflicts.

Besides these kinds of resource allocation conflicts, in recent years a number of previous medical "truths" have come under scrutiny through the emerging sciences of outcomes analysis and population-based research. How good is the evidence that the health of an individual mother or child is actually improved by the old truth that one C-section should always beget another? Does doing more hysterectomies really have a positive impact on the health of the population? If not, what are the indications and ethical requirements for recommending one to an individual patient? What about skull films in trauma? Do they add anything but cost to patient outcomes in minor head injuries? Does routine PSA screening improve the health status of men aged 50-75, or does it actually decrease it?

There are, of course, no easy answers to these ethical and scientific dilemmas, but it often falls to a physician manager to help colleagues deal with these conflicts in an organizational setting. This work typically includes regularly articulating the source of such conflicts in our limited resource world; actively involving physicians in organization-level decision making about such matters; translating abstract organizational policies into practical medical ones understandable at the level of departments and practices; helping colleagues find rational solutions for the care of their individual patients; and accepting personal responsibility for resolving these individual care dilemmas when absolutely necessary.

As managing the health of populations within available resources becomes increasingly the charge of American health care, the work of individual physician executives will increasingly include this kind of ethical and scientific conflict resolution. Such work, although difficult, carries with it the considerable reward of helping colleagues thrive professionally and emotionally in our dramatically changing health care environment.

Teaching the Organization's Mission and Values

While translating and helping resolve the two conflicts described above is now part of the daily fare of virtually all physician leaders, it is the regular teaching and inculcation of an organization's basic mission and core values that offers the most successful preventive approach to managing physicians in organizational settings. Such teaching is equally relevant whether at the level of the organization itself or at the level of an individual department or facility within it.

The mission of any health care organization or any subunit should answer three key questions: "Whom do we serve" (who are our customers?)? "Why" (for what purposes?)? "How" (with what range of products or services?)? Clarity about these questions allows physicians, nurses, managers, and other members of the health care team to come together around a sense of common purpose. It provides an answer to the basic workplace question: "What are we all doing here?" From the point of view of a physician executive, it also begins to lay the groundwork for a set of common professional expectations within the organizational context.

Defined values add greater detail to a mission by describing the most important beliefs of people working in the organization. Common examples might include the values of teamwork, cost effectiveness, defined levels of profit or growth, service quality to patients or enrollees, coordination between primary and secondary care, and active contribution to the community. Each of these explicitly stated values helps create a more consistent organizational culture and a clearer sense of appropriate behavior within the organization.

The physician executive has two important roles regarding mission and values. One is to teach, explain, and inculcate the overall organizational mission and its values to physicians who join it. Such teaching not only helps create a sense of shared purpose and of professional expectations in the organization, but also can go a long way toward helping avoid future conflicts.

A second role for physician managers at the department or facility level is to help local groups create a unique sense of mission and values within the overall organizational context. While the organizational level mission and values form a useful backdrop to this work, most clinicians are best able to identify with these abstract notions when they relate directly to their own practice settings. In this way, the abstract concept of customers can become "referring primary care and emergency physicians in our three county area," and the concept of product line becomes "operative orthopedics for the hand and back."

Teaching of an organization's overall mission and values and facilitation of a similar sense at the level of departments or facilities represent two important tasks for physician managers in organizational settings. Such group work is the essence of binding individual practicing physicians to a common organizational purpose and provides a critical baseline for managing physicians in any organizational setting.

The "Six Dimensions of Performance" (What Kinds of Physicians Do We Really Want?)

Not every physician should be in every type of health care organization. In fact, most physicians don't want to be in every type health care organization. And certainly most organizations don't want every physician. The needs of a staff-model HMO, a network of community physicians, a hospital-based specialty practice, an academic medical center, a multispecialty group practice, and a military treatment facility can differ dramatically. Carefully defining the physician characteristics that best fit a given organization's needs is an important step to the subsequent management of physicians within the setting.

In general, health care organizations seek practitioners with specific characteristics in six clusters of behavior—the "six dimensions of performance." Although organizations vary in their specific needs, some general observations can be made about each of the six dimensions, regardless of organizational setting.

- High technical and professional quality of care.

- High quality of patient service.

- High productivity.

- Commitment to appropriate use of health care resources.

- Effective peer and co-worker relationships.

- Contributions to the organization and community.

Technical Quality of Care

Knowledge of one's medical discipline and the technical ability to perform its clinical procedures are, of course, fundamental to the provision of excellent medical care. All physicians in an organization must possess technical and cognitive skills necessary for professional competence in their chosen specialty. In recent graduates, this is commonly demonstrated by the completion of the requisite residency, fellowship, or board certification. In the case of practicing physicians, a more detailed definition of appropriate procedural and cognitive skills required may be necessary. Credentialing and recredentialing processes are commonly used that detail these expected skills and competencies. As quality of care data systems become more sophisticated, organizations can increasingly define the desired technical quality in terms of procedure rates, complication rates, and direct patient outcomes. Every practitioner in an organization should be engaged in continuous self-education to maintain and upgrade these skills.

Quality of Service

The personal interaction between physician and patient to a great degree determines the level of satisfaction patients have with their health care and often with the organization itself. It is vital that patients find the "bedside manner" of their practitioners and support staff respectful, caring, and oriented to their needs. Although every member of the health care team affects a patient's perception of quality, it is the physician who can be most influential in both setting team norms and determining ultimate patient perception. Physicians should be expected to listen well and to clearly communicate their findings and plans to their patients. A number of organizations have developed detailed descriptions of the type of service behaviors they expect from their professional staffs. These expectations can include appointment and office wait times, patients' satisfaction with information received, explanations given, and even the physician's listening and respecting behaviors. A variety of organizational studies have demonstrated that patients and enrollees value quality of service at least as much as the technical quality of their care.

Practice Management Skills and Productivity

Modern health care organizations depend more and more on their ability to use every resource wisely. One measure of resource use is the output gained per unit of labor input—good old-fashioned productivity. In the purely fee-for-service world of the past, desired physician productivity could be fairly easily defined in terms of billings. With the onset of salaried physicians, capitation, and a variety of new organizational forms, definitions of expected physician productivity have become much more complex. Most definitions today, depending on the capabilities of the organization's encounter-tracking system, continue to include some measure of direct services provided—e.g., total billings, visits, procedures, relative value units, etc. Expected hours of work or total hours of patient availability (including call hours) are another common component. Panel sizes have become important in defining productivity expectations for primary care physicians.

Alongside such number counts, certain productivity-enhancing behaviors can also be defined. These include efficient scheduling practices, effective management of office staff, effective use of physician extenders, taking thorough responsibility for a defined population, and ensuring adequate backup or coverage for patients when unavailable.

Resource Utilization

Organizations today must be concerned about the most effective and appropriate use of all their health care dollars. Although physician labor costs represent only about 21 percent of total health care costs in the United States, physician behavior has a significant impact on other costs through styles of practice and through decisions about the use of other health care resources. With improved utilization- and quality-tracking systems, many organizations are attempting to describe desired physician utilization behavior with quantitative measures, such as average lengths of stay, costs per episode of care, referral rates, procedure rates, pharmacy costs, and overall utilization "profiles."

Because medical science is still so uncertain and because the sources of variation in most utilization data are vague, some organizations also define expected physician behaviors that will contribute to the most effective use of resources in any data milieu. These characteristics include a comfort with both the use and the limitations of such data, an interest in self-evaluation, a willingness to work with colleagues in the examination of utilization and quality data, and a commitment to the continuing search for best overall clinical strategies.

Peer and Co-Worker Relationships

An organization is, by definition, a complex interdependency of individuals working together to achieve a common purpose. Teamwork is critical to providing the very best and most efficient care. In all organizational settings, physicians must therefore be willing and able to work with a variety of others. These include departmental colleagues, referring and referral physicians, hospital and office nurses and support staff, and managers at a variety of levels. Physicians have a great impact on the workplace environment. Communication with peers and co-workers needs to be clear and respectful, and the ability to participate on and lead teams is frequently important.

Organizational/Community Contributions

Organizations are not composed of paper, steel, and brick alone. They require the continuous involvement of both groups and individuals in order to grow, thrive, and improve. For organizational physicians, this kind of involvement means more than just caring for one's patients and going home. It includes expectations for such activities as participation at medical staff and committee meetings, presentations at educational sessions and case reviews, involvement on quality improvement teams, working on clinical guidelines or organizational policies, and sometimes taking chairships or leadership positions. While the specific activity of individual physicians may vary with their interests and skills, a common expectation is that physicians will spend on the order of 10 percent of their time contributing in some way to the organization's growth and improvement.

In a like fashion, an organization exists within a geographic and professional community. Relationship to that community is important to the organization's success. Hence, physicians and other professional staff are frequently expected to participate in the community's activities. Local medical and specialty societies, charitable and political organizations, academic medical centers, schools, and sports teams are common examples. Some organizations desire professional publication, outside teaching, or research contributions from their professional staffs as well.

These six dimensions of performance form a basis for describing desired physician characteristics and for setting specific physician performance expectations in organizational settings. While organizations may vary in the exact characteristics they seek within each dimension, the overall template can be used in virtually any health care organization.

Carefully refining these specific professional expectations at a given organization usually involves the physician executive's doing group work with colleagues. This work can be done at both organizational and departmental levels. Few activities are as high yield. Simply getting colleagues together to begin to discuss common expectations has a strong effect on building the sense of group culture and organizational commitment. Detailed discussion of performance expectations helps clarify the sense of group direction and commonly reveals both existing and missing sources of data and support. Additional discussion generates understandable measures of performance. And finally, the definitions achieved through such work will prove invaluable in the subsequent steps of recruiting the right physicians to the organization; periodically reviewing physician performance, performance feedback, and coaching; and, when needed, managing marginal performance.

Recruiting and Selecting the Right Physicians at the Beginning

The initial "fit" between physician characteristics and organizational characteristics is one of the most important single determinants of subsequent physician satisfaction and performance. Developing and maintaining a recruiting process that ensures this fit is well worth the time.

Organizational recruiting begins with some prework, the most important aspect of which is a clear description of the kind of physician being sought. The "six dimensions" provide a useful template for such a description. Done in advance, this work can have a significant effect on the whole recruiting process.

Besides the six dimensions describing organizational expectations, the prework for recruiting should address issues related to the specific practice itself. This is sometimes called a "clinical job description." Common features in the clinical job description include the patient population served; common or special health conditions cared for; specific experience, skills, or certification needed; expectations regarding time commitment, work location, and schedule; hospital affiliation or privileges required; equipment, space, and personnel support available; contract, salary, benefits, and other financial arrangements; and the expected timeline for hiring. The next step in recruiting is what professional recruiters call "sourcing," i.e., generating an adequate pool of candidates. For most organizations, this is best viewed as an ongoing process rather than one triggered by an acute hiring need.

Examples of ongoing activities might include regular relationships with regional residency programs, local and national peer networking by professional staff, and periodic publications in professional journals. More acute sourcing strategies include advertising in selected professional journals, direct contacts with referred physicians, and the use of professional recruiters. "Cold calling," while common among securities salesmen and rug cleaners, has little place in professional recruiting.

Application forms should collect the basic information about experience, training, references, and other professional activities. The application process also provides some unique opportunities to explore questions about the possible fit between the candidate and the organization. Questions can be asked about virtually any of the six dimensions, about why this particular organization is of interest, and about previous experience in similar settings. Application materials and reference-checking can then be used to establish a first cut of candidates likely to thrive in the specific organizational setting.

With position requirements and organizational expectations in hand, a prescreening based on the application materials and reference checking can be accomplished, and an interview process can then be planned. The purpose of the interview is to accomplish three things: to elicit additional information from the candidate to help determine the fit, to provide the candidate with more information to help with his or her decision, and to begin the bridge to a potential long-term relationship. Good recruiting interviews are mutual exchanges in which both parties seek and learn information about the other. In conducting an interview, physician executives should explore how closely the values, philosophy, and goals of the individual match those of the organization. Good interviews likewise give candidates every opportunity to understand what joining this particular organization will mean to them. Ample time during the interview process should be made available to serve both needs.

When applications have been reviewed and interviews are completed, the selection process begins. Key questions are asked by the physician executive or selection committee. Are there ideal candidates who perfectly fit the organization's needs and expectations? Is the organization prepared to meet their needs and expectations? For candidates who, if not ideal, seem good fits overall, are the areas of risk or uncertainty acceptable? What should be done to minimize any of these uncertainties?

The physician executive can make a significant contribution to an organization's well-being by developing and managing a successful physician recruiting and selection process. Few decisions are as long-lasting as those about members of an organization's professional staff. A poor fit during this process rarely becomes a good one years later.

Orienting New Physicians

When expectations are clear and physicians are hired to fit those expectations, the orientation of new physicians to an organizational setting is a natural bridging process. If the first two steps are not completed well, physician orientation can easily become a conflict-ridden and frustrating activity.

The orientation of new physicians should follow closely on the heels of recruiting. Although the physician executive may not be personally appropriate to orient every new physician, he or she should ensure that the values and expectations discussed during recruiting are rediscussed during orientation, with additional specifics that address the particular practice setting.

In addition to the usual familiarization with people, forms, and places, physician orientation should include detailed information on clinical practice expectations. What quality measures are in use in this practice? How are clinical guidelines established here? What forums exist for involvement in developing these guidelines? How does the organization define and measure patient satisfaction? What are the exact productivity and practice management expectations here? What about expectations for work scheduling, case management, patient wait times, and utilization? What are the specific opportunities and expectations for the physician to contribute to the department, to the organization, and to the community?

A number of organizations use mentoring with a senior physician as a way to help new physicians acclimatize to organizational life. This technique is particularly useful during the first months in helping new physicians to interpret and deal with organizational norms for clinical practice. Many a recently hired physicians has found one timely bit of "how-I-really-do-it" advice worth reams of reading and days of touring.

Information for Periodic Performance Review

Health care organizations today often track large amounts of financial and utilization data for use in evaluating aspects of organizational performance. In addition, a number of organizations are developing improved means for measuring and tracking health care quality, including complication rates, clinical outcomes, and patient and enrollee satisfaction. Such systemic data can be invaluable for managing aspects of an organization's performance. To be truly useful in the management of individual physicians, it must be both accurate and interpretable to the physicians themselves. The role of a physician executive in this regard is to ensure that the organization's data systems meet these tests.

The conversion of aggregate data into usable information for individual performance management involves several steps. Accuracy of the separate data elements is an absolute requirement. No information system that relies on imprecise coding, incomplete capture of financial data, or inappropriate measures of quality can be reliably used for physician performance purposes. A second requirement is involvement of the organization's physicians directly in the design and formatting of data that will eventually be used in measuring their performance. This step, taken early in the evolution of such systems, not only will help develop data formats that feel and actually are understandable to clinicians, but also can go along way toward dispelling some of the mistrust that inevitably surrounds such systems. Physician managers who take the time to involve clinical colleagues at this early point can avoid much later confusion and conflict trying to interpret data that make little sense at the level of actual practice.

Finally, to be truly useful, this kind of aggregate data needs both a denominator and a comparator appropriate to the organizational setting. In other words, visits per week may be an interesting productivity widget, but visits per defined age-sex-health status-adjusted panel makes it interpretable in a managed care setting. Likewise, the presence of a predetermined comparator (or "benchmark") is what allows one to interpret performance in the light of some predefined organizational expectation.

Besides these systemic data systems, a variety of less quantitative information sources typically exist that can be useful in measuring other dimensions of physician performance. Examples include patient complaints and compliments, co-worker and colleague perceptions, quality assurance reports, PRO and malpractice cases, and the self-reporting of community and educational activities. Behavioral surveys are likewise in frequent use as a way to periodically gather information about peer and co-worker relationships and about service quality. The key with this kind of information, as with systemic data, is the accuracy, relevance, and interpretability of the data at the level of the individual practitioner.

Feedback and Coaching

Giving and receiving effective feedback is an essential part of the physician executive's skill set for managing professional colleagues. Research shows that, to be effective, feedback must be individual-specific, understandable, accurate, and made available in a timely, facilitative, nonjudgmental manner. Feedback in health care organizations can take one of three forms: systemic, intermittent personal, and periodic personal.

Systemic feedback consists simply of making available to individual practitioners financial and quantitative data produced by the organization's aggregate data systems on a regular basis. Common systemic feedback includes production reports, utilization rates, and regular measures of technical and service quality. As described above, the primary role of physician executives providing this kind of feedback is to ensure that the data are accurate, relevant, and interpretable at the level of the individual provider and that clinicians have been appropriately involved in their design and formatting.

Intermittent personal feedback consists of staying alert to episodic data, activities, and behavior within a department or an organization and seeking opportunities to provide timely and personal feedback based on it. The atmosphere of receptivity toward such feedback is significantly enhanced by the physician executive's own openness to receiving it. Intermittent personal feedback is most effective when it is behaviorally specific and when it relates observed behavior to that expected in the organization. In this way, feedback about an episode of loud public verbal abuse of a receptionist becomes less a debate about scheduling glitches and more a discussion of respectful relationships with co-workers.

Intermittent personal feedback can be especially useful when it focuses on the positive. When the physician executive catches a colleague "doing something right" and tells him or her about it, the effects can be extraordinary. Physicians, like other organizational staff, often feel a lack of appreciation for their contributions. Physicians respond quite well to a colleague's recognition of their work and also to understandable and behavioral specific observations that can help them do their jobs better. In the busy life of a physician executive, it may be difficult to remember this aspect of the job, but a few personal experiences have convinced many experienced physician leaders to spend the time needed to provide this important personal feedback to colleagues and co-workers.

Periodic personal feedback is typically part of a formal periodic performance review and is often part of the organization's annual review process for its professional staff. Such periodic reviews provide a regularly scheduled opportunity for face-to-face dialog between the physician executive and individual physicians.

Done perfunctorily or with a judgmental attitude, periodic performance review can easily become a source of dissatisfaction to the individual physician and a significant waste of time for the physician executive. On the other hand, physician managers who are open to reciprocal feedback and who use a facilitative and constructive approach can achieve excellent results.

The manner in which data are presented and discussed during periodic performance review significantly affects their reception. Facilitative, constructive feedback is descriptive. It provides a verbal picture, not a judgment. Instead of adjectives, opinions, and conclusions ("I guess you're just getting a little slower with age"), data are presented in clear, specific, and limited fashion ("On this report, your total visits are 15 percent lower than last year's"). Such an approach lends itself to mutual exploration and learning. Judgmental approaches impede the feedback process and inhibit learning by both parties.

Physician executives who use periodic personal feedback most effectively neither blame or judge; they simply provide the data clearly and make themselves available to help with the data's interpretation. The cause of various apparent performance variations is often not known to either party to the feedback until it is examined together. Mutual exploration of the available data without one-way analysis helps produce a neutral, open environment in which both parties can learn. Excessive interpretation by the physician manager, highly judgmental conclusions in any direction, and overreading the significance of minimal data are three common causes of failure of periodic feedback.

The notion of "coaching" captures the appropriate style for providing feedback to professional colleagues very well. Drucker has said that the essence of the coaching attitude is the simple question, "What can I do to help you be the best you can be?"[2] A coaching attitude acknowledges both the professional competence of the physician and the physician manager's appropriate role in jointly examining the data and in supporting any desired changes.

Performance Improvement and Managing Marginal Performance

Appropriate recruiting, clear definitions of expected behavior, accurate and interpretable information, effective feedback, and a coaching style are important tools in the armamentarium of managing physicians. Given most physicians' inherent intelligence and desire to do well, these tools are the most frequently used in helping colleagues succeed in the organizational environment.

Occasionally, however, these approaches fail, and physician behavior continues at a level and type that falls significantly below the organization's expectations. When such a problem occurs over time and is not corrected despite routine feedback and coaching, it may be termed "marginal performance." It is clearly one of the most difficult and emotion-laden management problems facing any physician executive.

Marginal performance, although rare, may occur in any of the six dimensions of physician performance. Although the frequency of each type of problem varies with organizational setting, the most common examples of marginal performance would include problems with peer and co-worker communications, patient satisfaction, technical quality of care, utilization of services, and productivity. In all health care settings, the behavioral consequences of substance abuse, depression, and physical illness can first appear as chronic performance problems.

A common approach to dealing with these significant performance discrepancies is the use of a "performance improvement planning" process. This approach begins with an explicit description of the desired behavior or outcome and a clear statement of the way in which actual behavior differs. It then moves to a mutual exploration of the possible causes of this discrepancy and a joint agreement on the actions to be taken by the two parties in resolving it.

Sometimes, obstacles are found that actually inhibit the physician's ability to perform as expected (e.g., inadequate office support). In these instances, the physician executive must frequently be willing to assist with the solution. Sometimes, educational or skill deficiencies surface that may require time or money to correct. Sometimes, the problem will be one of volition or lack of intent to change behavior.

Using a performance improvement approach, the next step is to negotiate a "contract" for change. What exact actions are expected? What supporting acts will be taken by the physician manager? How exactly will change be monitored? What will be the consequences of improvement? What exactly will be the consequences of failure to improve? When will the two parties next meet?

The components of a formal performance improvement process should always be captured in writing. This documentation must include a clear description of the expected behavior, data describing the discrepancy in actual behavior, dates and times of previous feedback, and all aspects of the "contract." The contract portion should include a description of the responsibilities of each party, the monitors, the dates of review, and the consequences of various results.

The need for a formal process is thankfully rare in dealing with professional colleagues. When needed, however, it can be essential to fair and measured management of significant performance discrepancies. In experienced hands, it can be expected that half or more of discrepancy problems will improve with such an approach. Continued monitoring and support for the change is often necessary.

When all else fails, the final option available to managing serious, unremitting performance deficiencies is use of the organization's process for involuntary adverse action. These processes, which vary by type of organization, are governance actions that unilaterally limit or terminate the relationship between the health care organization and the physician. Examples include contract termination, limitation or termination of privileges, termination of employment, limitation of work conditions, etc.

The use of such drastic measures depends in all but the most acute circumstances on the previously described foundation of data, feedback, coaching, and performance improvement. With an adequate foundation, adverse action can be effectively and fairly employed as a "fail-safe" in cases of unresolvable performance problems. Such actions are never pleasant or easy, but they must occasionally be taken in the best interests of patients, the organization, or the other professional staff.

Summary

Managing physicians is at the very heart of successful medical management in the organizational setting. Not only are physician behaviors essential to the provision of high-quality health care; they directly affect customer service perceptions, utilization rates and the cost of care, and the team and collaborative atmosphere essential for long-term success.

To develop an environment in which these things can occur with fellow physicians, the physician manager has many tools. Empathy for and assistance with the value conflicts experienced by many physicians in health care organizations is an important first ingredient. Facilitating, building, and teaching a sense of common purpose, mission, and values, at both organizational and subunit levels, is essential. Health care organizations and the physician executives within them need to clearly define what behaviors are expected of their professional staffs In at least six dimensions of performance. Armed with this clarity and clinical job descriptions, recruiting activities have a higher likelihood of finding physicians for whom the organizational environment will be a good professional and personal fit. Orientation procedures can further improve this sense of fit. Regular feedback of accurate and interpretable data and periodic review of performance with a positive, coaching style are strategies well suited to working with intelligent and highly motivated professional team members. Occasionally, when behaviors or outcomes fall below well-defined organizational expectations, a behavioral contracting model can be used to assist with marginal performance. Rarely, the fail-safe of adverse disciplinary action must be taken to protect patients and the organization.

Managing physicians is a complex, sometimes frustrating, and always important aspect of the role of physician executives. Done well, however, few activities can make so much positive difference to the well-being of the health care organization, its patients, and its professional staff.

References

1. Starr, P. *The Social Transformation of American Medicine.* New York, N.Y.: Basic Books, 1982.

2. Drucker, P. *Management: Tasks, Responsibilities, Practices.* New York, N.Y.: Harper & Row, 1973.

Other Reading

Allenbaugh, G. "Coaching...A Management Tool for a More Effective Work Performance." *Management Review* 72(5):21-6, May 1983.

Brennan, E. *Performance Management Workbook.* New York, N.Y.: Prentice Hall, 1989.

Mager, R., and Pipe, P. *Analyzing Performance Problems.* Belmont, Calif.: Fearon Pitman Publishers, Inc., 1970.

McGregor, D. "An Uneasy Look at Performance Appraisal." *Harvard Business Review*, May-June 1957, pp. 133-138, Reprint #72507.

Porter, L. *Giving and Receiving Feedback; It Will Never Be Easy, But It Can Be Better.* NTL Reading Book For Human Relations Training. Alexandria, Va.: National Training Laboratory Institute, 1982.

Scholtes, P., and others. *The Team Handbook.* Madison, Wis.: Joiner Associates, 1988.

Howard L. Kirz, MD, MBA, FACPE, is Executive Director, Northwest Center for Medical Management, Group Health Cooperative of Puget Sound, Seattle, Washington.

Physicians in Management: The Costs, Challenges, and Rewards

CHAPTER 11

by James E. Hartfield, MD, FACPE

arely does a blinding light from heaven suddenly surround the Chosen Physician as he or she trudges through evening rounds and a commanding voice proclaim, "I have created you to be CEO of St. Cedars General!" When such a promotion ultimately does occur, there is often more sublime serendipity than scholarly selection involved.

Until recent years, the designation of physicians as managers in medical complexes generally followed three criteria, professionally known as the "SAG factors"—Seniority, Accountability, and Gullibility. Within the scope of these salient features, little room for creative career design or targeting was possible. Given the unprogrammed and largely unprepared conscription of many physicians into early management roles, it is worth noting with pride the frequency with which these early, however "sagging," pioneers rose to the occasion. There is also competent support for the idea that good managers are born, not made, as the plethora of maximally degreed and minimally talented MBAs running loose in corporate ranks today attests.

This chapter seeks to summarize the preceding observations in this section and validate their accuracy with personal observations and experiences. While it is unlikely that any two physician executives would have duplicate management careers, some parallel insights may be useful for physicians entering this new specialty. The preceding introductory reviews of the current health care scene, with the evolving critical role of the physician executive as a major actor in this drama, provide an appropriate backdrop for the modern medical management stage. There is little tolerance of or excuse for relying on fate to plant a blooming medical executive in management's garden; today, dedicated preparation and targeted matching of skills to job are expected. The professional conflicts that have been faced over full- or part-time management, credibility without some clinical practice residual, compensation, etc. remain as points for discussion to be sure, but they are now largely recognized for what they always actually were—smoke screens to cover the personal insecurity involved in making a major career change.

This accusation deserves amplification. Many of us who entered management did so in a part-time arrangement because our organizations needed our continued professional participation. This is particularly true in small group practices, in staff model HMOs, and with hospital physicians. There is no magic number that automatically dictates full-time medical management commitment, whether that number indicates physicians, hospital beds, or health plan members. Clearly, the appropriate time for a full-time physician executive is when those defining jobs and hiring personnel for the organization decide it has arrived. Throughout the country and within the wide scope of management opportunities, the range of those organizational decisions is highly variable. The physician executive who finds him- or herself confronted with inappropriate part-time expectations by employers, credibility implications with peers, or inadequate compensation for his or her labors has three basic choices: first, work to convince the organization of the necessity for acceptable changes; second, reluctantly but resolutely accept the status quo; or third, move to a more satisfying position. For some, that last alternative has meant retreating to full-time clinical practice and leaving management altogether. Many others convince themselves that they are pursuing reasonable change within their organization while in reality they are settling for the second, more secure, option.

From the viewpoint of one who has traveled the management road through all of these options, some observations regarding physician management behavior seem justified. The essential foundation for all of these activities and observations is my deep and abiding respect and admiration for the profession of medicine. There have been many exciting developments along with alarming alterations in American medicine that demand persistence of concerned physicians to preserve the integrity and heritage of this proud vocation. The physician executive has the critical opportunity of being a profession conservationist while also being a leader and catalyst in the current medical evolution.

Observations Regarding Physicians and Management

Most physicians entering management are inadequately prepared for standard managerial techniques.

If there is any justification for adding business degrees after the MD, it would be to avoid the embarrassment many physician executives endure for having either basic ignorance of or deprecating attitudes toward "basics" in management, such as management by objectives, strategic planning, group dynamics, conflict resolution techniques, time management, etc. Even the most fundamental dynamic of how to utilize a good secretary or other support personnel effectively escapes many. It was not until I entered the corporate arena that I faced the start nakedness of an empty appointment schedule. In clinical practice my patients clamored for every 15 minutes—how could a waiting corporate world find my presence so undemanded? The luxury was short-lived fortunately, but it did provide a valuable lesson in time structuring for one whose schedule had always been regimented by rounds, conferences, nurses, and mothers. This cultural shock is equally severe in reverse for the academic physician, whose private office and classroom regimen is suddenly confronted with demands for heavier clinical schedules by the faculty practice plan.

Physicians resist management practices that they consider sophomoric forays into busy work—as many regard job objectives, policy writing, employee evaluations, and other things that were overlooked in standard medical school curricula. Whether this resistance reflects unfamiliarity or a valid assessment of present situations, it is uniformly a reflection of the physician's discomfort with management expectations.

The American College of Physician Executives was founded originally (then called the American Academy of Medical Directors) to address these educational deficits among physicians propelled into management. An honest appreciation of the essentials in management behavior is as needed as were the classes at Ft. Sam Houston in which those of us drafted into the medical corps were taught how to salute. We were at first extremely self-conscious; then we got the hang of it and even sort of enjoyed the activity, eventually accepting it as a tolerable part of military life and rank. Physician executives need to be cautious about having naive disregard for policies, traditions, buzz words, and personnel management. In the frequently alien world of management, MDs are the space invaders.

The skills required in good management often contradict the skills learned in good patient care.

Perhaps this observation explains much of the preceding paragraphs. Learning to move confidently and with dispatch through a crowded patient schedule or hospital rounds creates a self-assuredness and autonomy that is often foreign to business management. It is far safer to predict the results of treatment with penicillin or digitalis than to project the results of a marketing campaign or prosperity from a joint venture. Patient diseases are a piece of cake compared to corporate ailments.

Physicians are brainwashed from the first cadaver incision to the last residency prescription in the "scientific method" and the "proper" management of disease. With adequate clinical trials and experience, certain therapeutic regimens can be defined and results predicted, even expected. Organizational management is far less precise, and the effects of the most sincerely applied remedies are far less likely to be predestined. The confident demeanor and positive bedside manner that salvaged many despondent consumers of health care augur little more than false bravado in the board room. Conversely, the old reliable Kildarian technique of "leveling with the patient" about your frustrations and perplexities is generally regarded as the theatrics of an incompetent or ill-prepared executive by corporate observers.

On the other hand, among the most distasteful exposures experienced in many management arenas are the "standard" techniques of Covering Your Flank and Blame Shifting, which are generally absent in medical circles. Rather than conspire jointly to solve a problem, there is cautious avoidance of any association with potential failure, and an endless line of memos documenting every glitch or glimmer when escape from association is impossible. That is probably understandable when one's bonus depends on how the boss perceives one's performance.

As more physicians enter management, fewer will begin near the top of the organizational ladder. Even if those at the top are other physician executives, the culture is not, and will likely never be, the medical milieu of the examination room or operating suite.

While the experiences may often contradict, they need not conflict, and the agile physician executive will eventually learn to enjoy hopping among frying pans.

Physician executives tend to overestimate their management capabilities but underestimate their management value.

In Chapter 9, on career positioning, one of the pitfalls cited for aspiring physician executives is assuming that saving lives prepares the physician adequately for saving organizations. Such near omnipotence in the clinic is certainly commendable, but rarely does the opportunity arise to perform advanced CPR on the CEO. Although I occasionally suspected that my brilliant article published during medical school days on "Measuring Neurosecretory Material in the Pituitary of Sprague-Dawley Rats" could have had corporate application, I doubt that it was the highlight of my resume.

Frequently, I am asked to review the curriculum vitae of physicians who are interested in management positions. Most are faced with a common problem: they have published little or nothing related to management and have limited management experience. The unfortunate reality is that both are important, although the latter is more desirable. In spite of these customary deficits, the general physician expectation is to enter management at a senior level with an associated executive salary and benefit plan.

Often the disappointing reality surfaces during these resume reviews that in the drive to assume some medical management role of significance, the "medical" credential is subjugated. Experience, however, indicates that the MD degree remains the most powerful force in the entire resume. Physicians still enjoy an enviable mystique and respect, even among corporation executives. The awesome responsibility and basic intelligence credited to most physicians command respect, and care should be exercised to avoid clumsily allowing these assets to fade. Physicians should be experts in dealing with other physicians, defining appropriate clinical practices, establishing quality controls, etc., which were usually among the reasons for seeking a "medical director" in the first place. No one expects financial genius, marketing savvy, or computer literacy in physicians. If any of these are part of the physician manager's talent bank, they are frosting on the cake, but they will not adequately ice over a basic inability to monitor professional behavior or deal with an impaired colleague.

Physician executives tend to avoid conflict rather than manage it.

An unusual paradox hampers the effectiveness of many physicians, and it spills over into their management careers. There is a tendency to flee from personal confrontation rather than attempt to focus the energy involved in such conflicts into positive action. This reality has been a major factor in the professional disdain for peer review organizations and has played a major role in the current malpractice epidemic. Although many colleagues would vigorously deny such a milquetoast malady, this is a major fault in physician executives and reflects an honest interprofessional empathy that is discussed later. Most physicians would rather be challenged or disciplined by peers, regardless of the pain involved for both parties, and other nonphysician managers are delighted to relinquish this opportunity—they usually expect to be able to do just that. Physicians who are sincere and dedicated in clinical efforts simply do not want to believe otherwise of colleagues. Even the least productive and most aggravating associate is tolerated. In fact, the dances around confronting these individuals about commonly appreciated problems make *Swan Lake* pale by comparison. The business world, with its management hierarchy, titles, and status perks, excels in emphasizing the frailties of employees. It is no wonder that the recent runaway best sellers in management have been those that emphasize listening to employees, inclusion, praise, and other strange tactics taught in Psychology 101 in medical school. Perhaps we oversold the message to our students. Conflict usually means that people are alive and thinking, or at least reacting. Sure, it requires some digging to isolate a common framework of agreement for subsequent building or to displace emotional responses with constructive planning, but that is what should be expected when intelligent people address any issue. God spare us the robot mentality that prefers tranquil monotony over creative challenge.

Appropriate management requires as much concerted effort as direct medical care.

This observation is a corollary to the previous comments on overestimating management capabilities. After years of study, enduring the agonies of residency, mumbling through millions of phone conversations from patients, and surviving endless nights on call, it should certainly be a refreshing break to prop the old feet up on that huge desk and dictate to Miss Gorgeous. It's not that simple or pleasant. Begin with the realization that this is new turf, even if the new management responsibility is in an organization governed by physicians. Those who are being managed learn quickly to compartmentalize your efforts. The fact that you were an outstanding surgeon will only serve to reinforce those unspoken convictions that you should have stayed in the O.R. when the business begins to falter. Remember, those colleagues have likely not read this book and covertly believe that feet on desk and Miss Gorgeous routine. Medical management challenges are real. Addressing them appropriately will require intensive and extensive preparation. The "corporate culture" has a painfully real presence, whether in a major business, an academic setting, the military, a hospital, or a group practice. Before it can be massaged and remolded, if needed, it must be defined, and that may mean developing a perspective of organizational history—knowing local, state, or federal ordinance impacts, appraising key personalities, and assessing existing organizational commitments or anticipated alliances. For a professional who either had personal mastery over health care problems or could find readily available consultants or referral sources, the shift to dealing with amorphous possibilities or responsibility isolation can be quite uncomfortable. Remember the security derived by dusting off Harrison's or Nelson's or even *Current Therapy*? The books do not exist, nor are they ever likely to be written, that neatly index the management problems that crop up with surprising regularity. Most require the application of principles and concepts rather than pills and cutting and demand confident patience and thoughtful compromise.

The risks of failure for physicians entering management are greater than for their nonphysician counterparts.

In general, a conscientious physician who practices good medicine will be successful by almost any standard applied to success today. Even a sizable number of not-so-competent medical practitioners seem to enjoy considerable success. The same simply cannot be said for nonphysician managers throughout the broad spectrum of business endeavors. Endless possibilities exist in the corporate hierarchy to redefine the participation of marginal performers ranging from termination, demotion, or lateral (dead-end) transfer to side-track (safeguard) promotions or early retirement. To leave the security of a "sure thing" in medicine to opt for such management insecurity is undeniably risky, and on a much broader scale than for the nonphysician manager who never had it any better. The physician executive's risk is compounded by the extreme difficulty of reentry into full-time practice if the management golden opportunity begins to tarnish. A referral practice such as surgery or the medical subspecialties is almost beyond recapture, and the rapid progression of medical technology and pharmaceuticals quickly escapes any physician who must focus on other priorities.

In spite of the protests of "credibility maintenance" or "first love lost," the reluctance of many physicians to enter management on a full-time basis is rooted in the risk associated with leaving practice. While physicians are generally not regarded as being risk-averse, they are success-oriented (on behalf of their patients, they had better be). One should never underestimate the security concerns of the spouse as well.

I could almost set my watch by the regularity with which business colleagues ask, "Why did you decide to leave medicine?" Most of the time I am able to reply with some satisfyingly insipid remark. It is critically important that both we who are physicians entering management and those in the businesses we are joining recognize that physician executives are not "leaving medicine." We are merely changing specialties. My concern for the welfare of human beings has never abated. I have elected to transfer my efforts in support of those patients from the examining room to the board room, from prescribing therapy for specific diseases to developing pathways for fighting disease, from the practice of medicine to the preservation of medicine as an honorable profession for future colleagues and consumers.

Therein lies a further risk for the physician executive. To have significant influence in management, the physician executive must be capable. For the academic physician, it is understandably painful to fail an inadequately prepared medical student, yet the safeguarding of future patients is an overriding determinant. I have never been able to conjure comfort from any source when I had to terminate a physician executive. Of course, solid job performance must be expected from any manager, but can this colleague find a place of reentry, either to practice or other management? This decision will have major impact on the physician executive's family. The physician oversupply assumes new proportions when starting over at 55 years of age.

Perhaps this enhanced risk for physician executives is an argument for developing a management residency for the new specialty and forging a management career shortly following the academic years. I think not. While there are some attractive considerations, such as having an opportunity to gain experience, requiring lower starting salaries, and confronting less elaborate initial physician expectations, the time is not yet right for the physician community to afford leadership responsibilities to a colleague who has not "paid his dues." Roughly translated, for a physician executive that means "developed an appreciation for work in the trenches; demonstrated the ability to relate to patients and peers; and, in general, attained a position of credibility among a wide range of colleagues." This helps reduce the risks accepted by those being managed and currently goes a long way toward doing the same for the manager.

What Nonphysician Managers Think

Certainly these observations are not the only ones that could be or have been made regarding physicians as managers. They represent one physician's listing of impact assertions that need to be appreciated by those studying the field. A few years back, I was concerned about how nonphysician managers viewed the performances of physician executives under their direct supervision. Table 1, page 150, summarizes the responses from 31 nonphysician managers within the same company and with similar manager relationships. They were asked to identify the frequency with which some problems reported about physician executives were seen in the physician executive they directly supervised, and then to estimate by one to four checks the degree of job impact that problem produced for them. The replies are expressed as percentages of the choices given and the most commonly reported number of checks.

The most striking concern focused around time and task management, which is related in items A,E,F, and I and which had substantial job impact, as might be anticipated. The major shift from regimented appointment and O.R. schedules to personally directed time management seems difficult for many physicians.

For a profession in which talking to patients and families is a major time consumer, it is apparent that communication remains a problem (G). This charge is regularly leveled at physicians in general and has not been obviated by the transition into management. There is some reassurance in noting, however, that whatever and however the physician executive does, he does with conviction and confidence, regardless of how timely or well communicated (K).

Although this limited survey is far from definitive, a careful review of these responses is appropriate for all physicians in management. Given the high probability that no executive is perfect, the courage to expose imperfections is commendable. To discover them and then correct them is exemplary.

The Personal Bottom Line

She followed the rest of the preschoolers to the center of the stage and was immediately blinded by the harsh lights around the perimeter. Timidly glancing around, she noted one boy was screaming at the top of his lungs while another little girl was waving and smiling to the audience. One girl with long curls had wrapped her arms around a leg of the curtain puller—her face flushed with determination—and that little boy on the end had wet his pants. All of these seemed reasonable options at age three or four years when the time came for the first solo performance. Several decades later and after

Table 1. Problems Encountered with Physician Executives as Perceived by Their Nonphysician Supervisors in a Large Corporation				
Manager Problems	Rare	Frequency Average	Often	Job Impact
A. Inadequate appreciation of job tasks	30	40	30	!!!
B. Indecisiveness in dealing with staff physicians and other professionals	40	60		!
C. Inappropriate recognition of nonphysician manager's job requirements	40	60		!!
D. Reluctance to confront service problems	60	30	10	!
E. Inability to establish time and task priorities	10	60	30	!!!!
F. Inertia in task completion	30	40	30	!!
G. Failure to communicate effectively	15	70	15	!!
H. Inappropriate involvement in nonmedical areas	100			
I. Lack of relevant balance in addressing details	30	40	30	!!!
J. Inability to accept or respond to constructive criticism	70	15	15	!
K. Apparent insecurity or lack of personal confidence	100			

immeasurable trips to center stage, physicians who have been in some form of management need to appraise the health and stability of the only corporation over which they have ultimate control—themselves. This calculation of a "personal bottom line" should be done on a regular basis, not just when approaching retirement. It needs to begin with an honest realization of WHY. Why am I entering a new career phase? Why am I assuming the risks involved with such a move? Why do I presume to have the skills required? As indicated in Michael Guthrie's analysis in Chapter 4, most of us wanted leadership, challenge, influence, and involvement within the health care industry. So did you get what you want? Have you a prayer of ever fulfilling your ambitions?

It is unfortunately amusing that some of us are still on that preschool platform. Some are still clinging to security in the wings; others have moved bravely to center stage but are screaming about the injustices of our present situation (or are trying to be recognized by creating a disturbance); and others have soiled themselves so pitifully in public that they can neither advance nor retreat without pain or embarrassment. There will always be the upstagers who wave and smile at the crowd, but many of them keep doing only that long after the show has started, seemingly oblivious to the script or directors. Most of us will eventually start to sing or dance or recite, and while a few will be stars, most will be part of a chorus—performing as the essential, dependable, and indispensable backdrop for the panorama of modern medicine. Of course, that is all right, unless you wanted to be the star or unless you wanted to sing the aria or play the cadenza.

It is, in the final analysis, a matter of personal perspective—how the physician moving into management sees himself or herself. It is the standard of performance with which the physician can live, the degree of challenge he or she agrees to accept, and the end result with which he or she can be professionally proud and personally satisfied. There is a world of difference between cocky arrogance and quiet confidence. The world of medical management, just as the broad range of medical patients, is always looking for the latter and trying to avoid the former. While the chapters to follow are designed to provide the tools necessary to achieve management confidence, the appropriate and timely application of these techniques remains a personal challenge for physician executives. Your place on the stage is waiting.

James E. Hartfield, MD, FACPE, is Associate Vice President/Clinical Affairs, University of South Florida College of Medicine, Tampa.

The Content of Management

Economics and U.S. Health Care

by Hugh W. Long, MBA, PhD, JD

CHAPTER 12

A bsent resource scarcity, there is no inherent tension between economics and medicine. But once we are confronted with resource scarcity, medical decision-making must ultimately be tempered by economic reality.

By "resources," we mean anything directly consumed by human beings or used by human beings to produce something else directly consumed. General categories of resources are labor, energy, capital, raw materials, etc. The term "scarcity" does not mean that there is a shortage of any particular resource or even that we are running out of that resource. Rather, "scarcity" is a technical economic term:

If all of the economic units (individuals and organizations) in society answered the question, "How much of Resource X would you like to have if it were free?" we could add up all of their responses. If that grand total were a quantity of Resource X larger than the known supply of Resource X, then (and only then) would an economist describe Resource X as "scarce." The practical meaning of scarcity is that every economic unit cannot have as much of Resource X as it would like to have if Resource X were free. Almost all resources used for medical care and health care are scarce, primarily because these resources are exactly the same resources that are used to produce all other goods and services.

Once we are dealing with a scarce resource, the obvious decision that must be made for that resource is which economic unit or units must "make do" with less of the resource it or they would ideally desire. Deciding "who gets what" is also referred to as the "resource allocation decision." Allocating scarce resources is nothing more than the process, any process, that makes choices among competing alternative uses or users of the resource. From an economic perspective, the term "rationing" is simply a synonym for "allocating."[1]

Primitive societies answered the question of how to ration or allocate scarce resources by reliance on tradition, custom, taboo, or caste. Society simply had an order that was passed down from generation to generation and resource allocation occurred more or less automatically. Everybody knew who got what, and to what they were entitled, and anyone who challenged those traditions did so at great personal risk because of the threat that deviation posed to the continued orderly functioning of the society.

Modern industrialized society tends to abandon those original approaches and adopt new mechanisms. Two extremes among these new mechanisms are the "central planning model" and the so-called "free market or laissez-faire model."

In the central planning model, an individual or group of individuals with sufficient power and authority to impose and enforce decisions on others simply decide by fiat who gets what. For instance, Industry A gets 100 million tons of steel, Industry B gets 50 million tons of steel, Industry C doesn't get any steel but does get aluminum. Those are the allocations, plain and simple, with no room for argument by any of the affected industries. This type of central planning was typically associated with Eastern Bloc countries during the height of the Cold War, bringing to mind 5-year plans promulgated for the Soviet Union under Stalin.

In contrast to centrally planned allocation is the free market. For this method of allocating resources, we must invent something called money. Money's function is that of a common denominator that we use to exchange all types of resources among ourselves. In physical form, money can be whatever we want it to be. It can be large round stones lining the roads on the Yap Islands of the Caroline Group in the Pacific, or it can be rectangular pieces of paper with green and black ink on them in the United States.[2] Whatever money's form, all of us in the society agree, a social covenant if you would, that (1) we will each hold money, at least temporarily, as a store of value, and (2) we will swap money for resources.

Because we need and like to consume resources, and because money commands resources, it is self-evident that each of us prefers more money to less money. This prompts us always to be looking at how much money equates to a particular quantity of each resource. We want to know how much money we must give up to get a desired quantity of each resource, and/or how much money we can get if we part with a given amount of a resource we hold. That ratio, the quantity of money to the quantity of resource, is called the "price" of the resource. And our behavior is sensitive to that price.

If the price of a resource (the amount of money you have to give up to get the resource or that you receive for parting with the resource) is relatively high, people with money will tend to want less of that resource because they can use the money to command other resources. But people who already have the resource are willing to part with quite a lot of it, obtaining a good deal of money in exchange, increasing their capacity to command other resources. So the higher the price, the more people who do not have the resource do not want it and the more people who do have the resource want to get rid of it. Conversely, the lower the price, the more willing are those who do not have the resource to obtain it, and the less willing are those who have it to part with it.

So, in laissez-faire theory, all of the individual elements in the economy—individuals, organizations, money, and resources—interact in the "perfect market" of Adam Smith, in which large numbers of market participants, all on equal footing, exchange information, offer money for resources, offer resources for money, and haggle and negotiate in full "view" of all participants. After a while, says the theory, there will emerge for each resource a "market clearing equilibrium price" having the unique characteristic that at that particular price the total amount of the resource that those who have the resource are willing to part with is exactly equal to the total quantity of the resource that those who do not have it are willing to acquire (a.k.a., "supply equals demand"). All transactions, purchases and sales, then occur at this unique price, and we have de facto determined "who gets what," an allocation of scarce resources. We tend to associate this decision-making process with Western society, capitalistic countries like the United States, Canada, Western European nations, and Japan.

The reality, of course, is that neither of these economic models exists or has ever existed in pure form anywhere. At the height of the Cold War, one could find money and markets and prices and buy-and-sell transactions occurring in the Eastern Bloc. And in the United States, one can go to almost any state in the Union and find a small group of people, empowered by statute and regulation, sitting around making decisions such as Hospital A gets 100 beds, Hospital B gets 50 beds, and Hospital C doesn't get any beds but it can acquire a new $7 million imaging device.

When such decisions occur internally within a public-sector or private-sector system, they are part of what is called a "budgeting process." When the public sector imposes such decisions on the private sector systems, it's called "health planning." These latter decisions generally are made with no consideration whatsoever given to (1) the value of the services that might be provided in the presence or absence of beds; (2) the cost to patients, insurers, employers, or government of providing services from those facilities; or (c) the alternative benefits of using the resources elsewhere. In other words, market considerations are largely overwhelmed by fiat, by politics, by bureaucracy.

Health Care: A Major Force in a Service Economy

At first glance, health care regulation in the United States over the past three or four decades is a curious phenomenon. The biggest private-sector service industry is health care.[3] Indeed, health care is exceeded in size only by government. The service sector of the economy has grown much more rapidly than other sectors since World War II. Even in 1946, measured by employment, the United States was a service economy. Private-sector services alone provide the majority of all employment in the United States today. Total employment in manufacturing is only about 18 million people, about 13 percent of a total labor force of about 135 million.[4] Employment in service activities outside of government is about 70 million, about 4½ times the level of employment in manufacturing.[5] Of that 70 million, health care commands about 10 million, more than double employment in all construction and more than three times the employment in all of agriculture.[4]

Within the service sector, the major economic change besides growth has been deregulation. We have deregulated the airlines, deregulated trucking, deregulated communications (e.g., the AT&T break-up), and deregulated financial institutions. There is competition with the postal service (e.g., Federal Express), choice among many long-distance communications competitors, and discount brokerage firms. The basic thrust of the economy under all administrations from Lyndon Johnson's through George Bush's, whether Democrat or Republican, liberal or conservative, has been to deregulate service industries.

The single exception to deregulation, of course, has been health care. There is, in fact, more regulatory control of the health care industry today than at any previous time in our history. Health care has been treated differently from all other services primarily because of who pays for health care and how health care is paid for. The lion's share of health services is funded directly or indirectly by government, and, historically, government has not been a prudent buyer. Government, in turn, has looked at the skyrocketing costs and, rather than accept responsibility, complains that providers of care are "ripping us off." Government concludes that the only way to control costs is to regulate, to control, to punish the industry.

The Medicare End Stage Renal Disease (ESRD) program is a good example of why government views regulation as necessary.[6] While Medicare administers the program, it is "open" to all qualified beneficiaries, regardless of age.7 The program provides payment for maintenance dialysis and transplantation for patients with kidney failure.8 There are four types of ESRD patients: (1) dialysis patients, (2) transplant patients (those receiving a transplant during the current year), (3) functioning graft patients (those having a successful transplant in a previous year), and (4) failed graft patients (those whose transplanted organ from a previous year has failed during the current year).

The very existence of an entitlement program for ESRD is because renal failure is invariably fatal without treatment. Even today, if you are a 60-year-old citizen of the United Kingdom with kidney failure, and you seek care from the National Health Service (NHS), you will die if the NHS is your only recourse. The NHS does not provide maintenance dialysis to anyone over the age of 55 at the onset of kidney failure.[9] If you know about dialysis and can afford to pay for your own treatment, you can purchase it in the private sector, just as you could have in the United States prior to 1974.

Before 1974 in the United States, few households could afford the high price of dialysis. Because demand was price constrained, there was little economic motivation to provide dialysis capacity. This, in turn, limited motivation to make R&D investments to advance technology. Existing technology was bulky and dialysis processes relatively complex, with complications from treatment not uncommon. Dialysis was performed only in hospital outpatient departments in order to be close to inpatient back-up capabilities. Persons on dialysis tended to remain on the therapy, as many rudimentary problems with rejection of transplanted organs existed. Those few hospitals that offered dialysis service, and that could also afford to provide some uncompensated treatment, had death committees deciding who would receive care and live and who would be allowed to die. Such decisions were relatively easy when the choice was between a 65-year-old wino and an 18-year-old high school valedictorian. The decision was less easy when choosing between the valedictorian and a 24-year-old mother of three.

This was a dramatic example of the philosophical questions that can surround decisions for allocating scarce economic resources. Those decisions may be made explicitly or implicitly, but they will be made, and, as a result, some people will live and some will die. Traditionally, physicians have avoided being part of the resource allocation decision-making process at the system level, focusing only on applying all indicated resources on individual patients, case by case. To avoid being led toward bad system results, however, it would be better for physicians to participate in resource allocation decisions at all levels.[10,11]

It was against this background of case-by-case life and death decisions that the U.S. federal government established by statute the ESRD program, and directed the Medicare program to administer the new entitlement. The ESRD program began in 1974, paying 80 percent of the cost of maintenance dialysis after the first 90 days of treatment. More recently, it has also paid significant portions of the cost of transplantation procedures. Since 1983, the program has paid at various fixed rates for outpatient dialysis, depending on the setting. In 1973, when the ESRD program was being considered by Congress, the Congressional Budget Office estimated that the 1974 costs would be $75 million and that, by 1977, the cost would rise to $250 million. Projections also called for an ultimate stable-state beneficiary population of 90,000 persons. In actuality, the 1974 cost was triple the CBO estimate,[12] and cost has subsequently grown to about $8 billion annually (with a 1998 projection of nearly $11 billion), an annual compound growth rate exceeding 18 percent. The more than 200,000 current enrollment in the program is not only more than double the "stable-state" forecast, but is still growing at more than 5 percent per year.

The increase in entitlement spending for the ESRD population has often been cited in the media and by politicians as simply one more example of out-of-control health care costs and of irresponsible economic behavior on the part of health providers. In fact, while total expenditures for ESRD have grown 880 percent in real (adjusted for inflation) terms since the program's inception, the growth in the number of enrollees of 1,180 percent over the same period (12.9 percent per year compounded) has resulted in an absolute decline in the cost of the real resources consumed per program enrollee in every year since 1974. This average decline of 1¼ percent per year reflects gains in efficiency from spreading capacity costs over an increased quantity of service (economies of scale) and the effects of new knowledge and technology developed because economic rewards came into existence, enabling freestanding facilities and home-based dialysis to function efficiently and safely.

The rapid growth in ESRD beneficiaries, compared to overall U.S. population growth of about 1½ to 2 percent per year, reflects two phenomena: First, many of the enrollees currently in the program would have died in previous years in the absence of the program because of a lack of fiscal and physical access to care.[12] This is simply one example of supply creating its own demand, one of the classic "problems" of the health care industry. Health care in general, and medical care in particular, is a victim of its own success. Related to this is the rapid growth in enrollees who are older and sicker and for whom the prospects of survival were enhanced as the variety of treatment settings treatment modalities expanded.[13]

Second, out-migration from the entitlement population for reasons other than death has been much slower than forecast. This reflects the noneconomic fact that growth in our knowledge of the immune system has been slow despite the intense best efforts of well-funded researchers worldwide, and the economic fact that simple market mechanisms have been proscribed by the U.S. federal government with respect to human organs,[14] severely limiting the supply of transplantable kidneys, persons' signing the backs of their driver's licenses and executing living wills notwithstanding.

The economic reality is that generally, and regarding renal failure patients particularly, we're keeping more people alive on many fewer resources per person today than ever before. The bottom line result is that total expenditures continue to balloon each year.

It is impossible to give serious consideration to economics without also considering the other dimensions of the medical care process. The vast majority of the 200,000+ U.S. dialysis patients have as their major economic activity being dialyzed two or three times a week. Fewer than half of them are employed or employable. They are net consumers. Mental health problems are also prevalent in this group. And a number of enrollees have voluntarily withdrawn from the program after 10 or more years of enduring this unpleasant regimen.[15,16,17] Most of the people in the program, and certainly most of their families, are happy that they are still alive. From a purely economic perspective, however, they are not paying their way. An economist looks at the total bill of over $10 billion (combining Medicare, Medicaid, and self-pay deductibles and copayments) and wonders what would be the next best use of all that money, such as programs providing education, nutrition, drug/alcohol detoxification, and prenatal care for pregnant inner-city teenagers. Indeed, how much neonatal intensive care expense could be avoided if we focused $10 billion in that way?

These are the types of complex questions we must keep in mind as we describe the U.S. health care system and as we consider major modification of that system.

Overview of the U.S. Health Care System

Table 1, below, shows the growth in U.S. Gross Domestic Product (GDP) and in the U.S. health care sector measured by National Health Expenditures (NHE) from 1935 to 1993.[18] Table 2, page 161, shows various projections through the year 2000.[19] NHE in 1993 (estimated to be $910 billion) represented 14.2 percent of GDP; one out of every seven dollars was spent for health, or about $3,533 per capita. The United Kingdom, in

Year	GDP	Health Sector	Health as % of GDP	% Ratio for Health	Current Health $ per Capita	1987 Health $ per Capita
1935	$ 65.5	$ 2.5	3.8%	1 of 26	$ 19.6	$ 251.4
1945	212.2	9.0	4.2	1 of 24	64.3	706.1
1955	403.6	17.7	4.4	1 of 23	106.7	760.9
1965	702.7	41.6	5.9	1 of 17	214.1	1,105.7
1975	1,585.9	132.9	8.4	1 of 12	615.4	1,686.9
1985	4,038.7	422.6	10.5	1 of 9.6	1,772.0	2,031.8
1990	5,513.8	666.2	12.1	1 of 8.3	2,665.1	2,119.4
1991	5,722.9	738.2	12.9	1 of 7.7	2,922.1	2,379.4
1992 (P)	6,038.5	828.0	13.7	1 of 7.3	3,248.0	2,582.9
1993 (E)	6,395.9	910.0	14.2	1 of 7.0	3,532.7	2,809.4

Table 1. The Macroeconomics of U.S. Health Care

Table 2. Alternative Forecasts of National Health Expenditures Relative to the Economy (1994-2000)

HCFA (1992)

Year	GDP	△GDP	NHE	△NHE	NHE as % of GDP
1993	6396		910		14.2%
1994	6589	3.0%	1001	10.0%	15.2
1995	7069	7.3	ˉ102	10.1	15.6
1996	7521	6.4	1209	9.7	16.1
1997	8003	6.4	1326	9.7	16.6
1998	8515	6.4	1453	9.6	17.1
1999	9059	6.4	1591	9.5	17.6
2000	9639	6.4	1740	9.4	18.1

CBO (1993)

Year	GDP	△GDP	NHE	△NHE	NHE as % of GDP
1993	6396		910		14.2%
1994	6609	3.3%	998	9.7%	15.1
1995	6936	4.9	1089	9.1	15.7
1996	7270	4.8	1185	8.8	16.3
1997	7621	4.8	1288	8.7	16.9
1998	7971	4.6	1395	8.3	17.5
1999	8297	4.1	1510	8.2	18.2
2000	8630	4.0	1631	8.0	18.9

Clinton (1993)

Year	GDP	△GDP	NHE	△NHE	NHE as % of GDP
1993	6396		910		14.2%
1994	6616	3.4%	999	9.8%	15.1
1995	6950	5.1	1112	11.3	16.0
1996	7276	4.7	1237	11.2	17.0
1997	7640	5.0	1314	6.2	17.2
1998	7954	4.1	1376	4.7	17.3
1999	8264	3.9	1438	4.5	17.4
2000	8642	4.6	1495	4.0	17.3

Long (1994)

Year	GDP	△GDP	NHE	△NHE	NHE as % of GDP
1993	6396		910		14.2%
1884	6639	3.8%	1006	10.5%	15.1
1995	6891	3.8	1106	10.0	16.1
1996	7153	3.8	1211	9.5	16.9
1997	7425	3.8	1320	9.0	17.8
1998	7707	3.8	1432	8.5	18.6
1999	8000	3.8	1547	8.0	19.3
2000	8304	3.8	1663	7.5	20.0

comparison, spends approximately one-third this amount per capita, 70 percent of which is through its National Health Service. Although many health status indicators (e.g., life expectancy at birth) in the United Kingdom are somewhat below those of the United States, those same indicators in many North European countries and in Japan exceed the U.S. statistics. Yet Japan, for example, spends less than one-half the U.S. level per capita.[20] Further international comparisons appear in figure 1, below. The United States, however, does get things for its additional per capita outlays. Figure 2, page 163, presents a list of such items other than the usual health status indicators.

Figure 3, page 164, tracks U.S. NHE as a percentage of GDP annually since 1955. There have been three years since 1955 (1973, 1978, and 1984) when NHE declined as a proportion of GDP. Figure 4, page 164, shows, however, that health care has, during this period, never had a bad year. Thus, the occasional percentage declines can only be attributed to the fact that the rest of the economy had particularly good years (i.e., years in which growth was even better than the growth in the health sector) only three times in the past four decades.

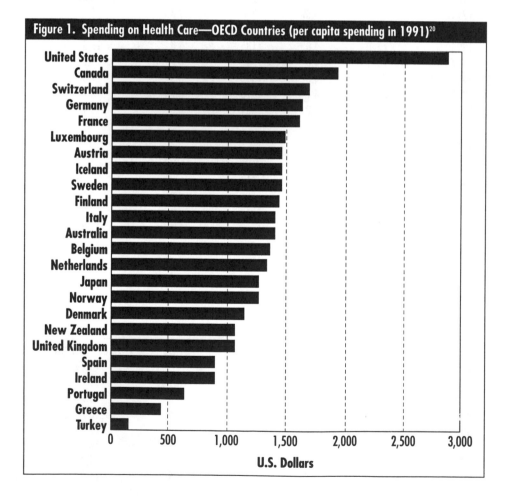

Figure 1. Spending on Health Care—OECD Countries (per capita spending in 1991)[20]

> **Figure 2. What the U.S. Gets for Its Extra* Per Capita Health Spending (a partial list)**
>
> ☐ High tech procedures become available sooner
> ■ Efficacious medications become available later
> ☐ More specialist physicians and non-physicians per capita
> ☐ More provider-level administration
> ■ Richer physicians, administrators, and other providers
> ☐ Substantial levels of amenity for patients
> ☐ Sufficient idle or excess capacity to eliminate the vast majority of queues, minimizing economic costs of lost productivity, travel, and pre-procedure morbidity, while maximizing convenience and personal choice
> ☐ A unique tort liability system
> ☐ Significant "defensive medicine" (defined as services that produce no measurable affirmative change in medical outcome, i.e., are unnecessary and/or redundant)
> ☐ "Good medicine" as probably philosophically intended by Hippocrates
> ■ A (too) large private insurance industry with its attendant administrative costs and arrays of choices
> ☐ Short (and ever-intensifying) hospital stays
> ☐ "Disquality" in primary care for medically indigent
> ☐ Medical responses to social problems that would be better addressed using non-medical responses (e.g., neonatal intensive care for teenagers' 500gm crack babies and emergency surgery for gunshot wounds from handguns rather than effective drug and handgun control, respectively)
>
> * Relative to other developed countries

And while overall growth in health care is impressive (about 10.9 percent per year compounded since 1953 and 11.2 percent per year compounded since 1975), it pales compared to Medicare expenditures. Since 1975, Medicare Part A (Hospital Insurance or HI) outlays have grown at an annual compound rate of 12.2 percent and Part B (Supplemental Medical Insurance or SMI) at more than 16 percent per year as shown in figure 5, page 165.

Table 3, page 165, presents the broad sources of the estimated $910 billion NHE figure for 1993. Just under half (46½ percent) of the $910 billion total came from all levels of government (federal, state, and local). Of government's $425 billion, the federal government accounted for about $292 billion, of which about $154 billion was for Medicare (table 4, page 165). Of that $154 billion, about $45 billion was spent on services delivered to beneficiaries who died within one year of receiving the services. In short, as much as 30 percent of all Medicare payments to providers, or about 5 percent of total national health care expenditures, are spent on services for Medicare beneficiaries in their last year of life.[21]

The second largest source of funding for health care came from private health insurance, which provided about 30 percent of the $910 billion total. Of that amount, about 85-90 percent represents monies paid by employers on behalf of their employees.[22] Payment by patients for medical expenses out of their own pockets is the third largest

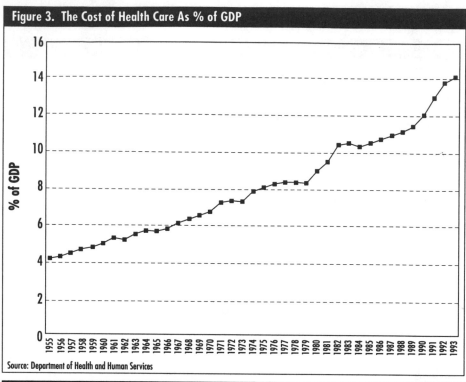

Figure 3. The Cost of Health Care As % of GDP

Source: Department of Health and Human Services

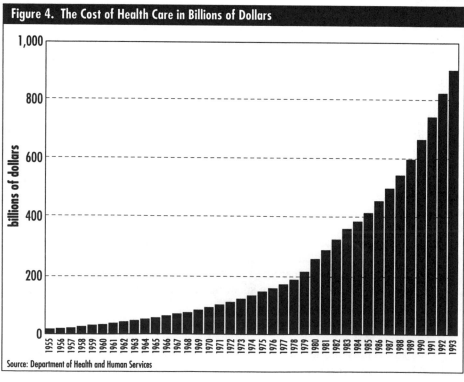

Figure 4. The Cost of Health Care in Billions of Dollars

Source: Department of Health and Human Services

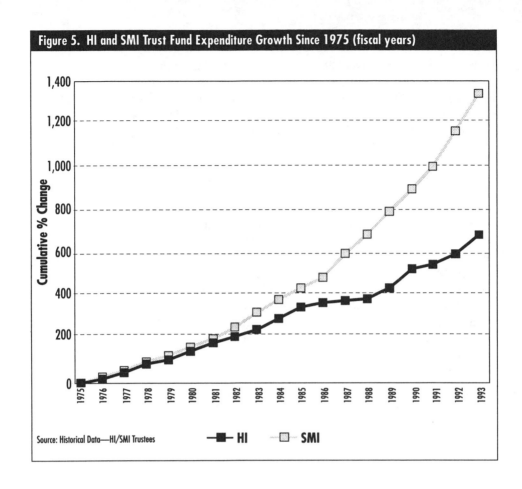

Figure 5. HI and SMI Trust Fund Expenditure Growth Since 1975 (fiscal years)

Cumulative % Change

Source: Historical Data—HI/SMI Trustees ▬■▬ HI ⋯□⋯ SMI

Table 3. U.S. Health Care Financing—1993(E)		
Source	**$ (billions)**	**%**
* Government	424.6	46.5
Private Insurance	275.7	30.3
Self-Pay	171.2	18.8
Other	38.9	4.3
	910.0	100.0
* Federal (68.8%)	292.2	32.1
State/Local (31.2%)	132.0	14.5

Table 4. Entitlement Program Outlays—1993(E)		
Program	**$ (billion)**	**% of NHE**
Medicare		
A	92.6	10.2
B	61.5	6.7
Total	**154.1**	**16.9**
Medicaid		
Federal	84.3	9.3
State	67.3	7.4
Total	**151.7**	**16.7**
Medicare & Medicaid	**305.8**	**33.6**

source, accounting for about 19 percent of the total. This includes payments for insurance deductibles, copayments, and noncovered expenses, as well as over-the-counter medications etc. Figure 6, below, shows how federal funding, private insurance, and out-of-pocket sources have changed dramatically since 1955. The "other" category in Table 3, accounting for 4 percent of the total, is largely a combination of (1) international transfer payments from other governments, (2) domestic philanthropy, and (3) corporate funding of on-premises care in the work place.

Table 5, page 167, shows how the $910 billion NHE was used. Hospitals commanded almost 40 percent of the total 1993 funds, with physicians having received 18½ percent of the total. Long-term care was the next largest category, followed by medication, and third-party (health insurance) cost. The latter is the difference between the premiums paid to private-sector insurance companies and the benefits disbursed (claims paid). The next lower tier includes dentists, followed by nonphysician professionals, such as podiatrists, midwives, and chiropractors. Following government public health delivery are medical durables (equipment), government research and development (private-sector R&D is imbedded in the other categories), construction, and home health.

In a very real sense, this itemization of sources and uses in tables 3 and 5 gives us a political roadmap. Major sources of funds will also be the sources of attempts to control expenditures. Government is clearly the number one controller or regulator, followed by private business through business coalitions, preferred-provider arrangements, and

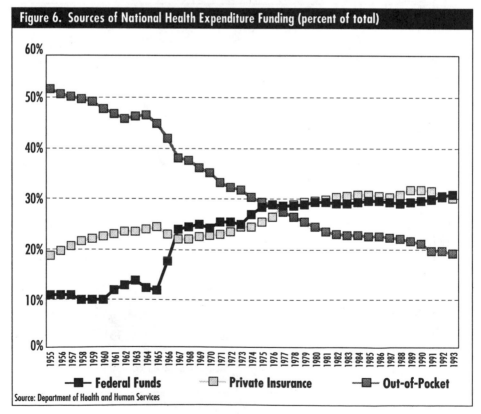

Figure 6. Sources of National Health Expenditure Funding (percent of total)

Source: Department of Health and Human Services

other managed care programs. Everyone's number one target has been hospitals, and as hospital costs have risen more slowly, physicians have become the next most significant target.

When one compares the economy in general with the health care sector, differences in performance are evident. As shown in table 6, below, health care has grown over the past four decades 40-45 percent more rapidly than the rest of the economy, both in real output and in inflation.[23] Only during 1973-74 and 1979-80 was the rate of inflation for the rest of the economy higher than for health care. The Reagan-Bush years brought a major reversal in inflation generally, but the "victory" largely reflected declining oil prices and certainly was in spite of medical care sector experience. While health inflation also declined, it dropped much less than inflation in other sectors, and, in 1993, the medical care inflation rate remained double that of the overall Consumer Price Index-Urban. From December 1992 to December 1993, health care inflation was 5.4 percent, compared to overall inflation of 2.7 percent.[24]

Every administration subsequent to Lyndon Johnson's and prior to Bill Clinton's considered health care costs (at least as embodied in the entitlement programs) as being out of control and requiring draconian measures to regain control. The post-Johnson Presidents viewed these costs as a major obstacle to their pursuing primary political agendas, liberal or conservative. Health care continues to take for itself a disproportionate share of the incremental dollar of tax revenue, in spite of the Nixon and Ford Economic Stabilization Program; Carter's pleas for cost control legislation; Reagan's Medicare initiatives via TEFRA, the Prospective Payment System using DRGs for hospitals, and the freezing of physicians' fees; or Bush's Physician Payment Reform of Medicare using RBRVS rate setting. These Presidents were continually constrained in promoting their favorite political agendas because new tax dollars were largely precommitted to the entitlement programs. It is little wonder that health care and its providers were consistently viewed as the "bad guys."

Table 5. U.S. Health Care Expenditures–1993(E)

Use	$ (billions)	%
Hospitals	361.5	39.7
Physicians	168.5	18.5
Long-Term Care	74.8	8.2
Medication	71.4	7.9
* Third-Party Cost	48.4	5.3
Dental	41.3	4.5
Other Professionals	45.2	5.0
Government Public Health	24.4	2.7
Medical Durables	14.0	1.5
Government R&D	15.8	1.7
Construction	11.8	1.3
Home Health	12.4	1.4
Other	20.5	2.3
	910.0	100.0
* Private Insurance	37.7	4.1
Public Programs		
Federal (Medicare, $2.7)	6.3	0.7
State/Local	3.6	0.4
Other	0.7	0.1

Table 6. Average Annual Compound Rates of Growth 1955–1993

Growth Rate	Entire U.S. Economy	Health Care Sector
Nominal	7.54	10.92
Inflation	4.42	6.42
Real	2.99	4.24

The more health competes for system resources, the more the system will push back against health care. As health care has grown from 4 percent of GDP 40 years ago to nearly quadruple that share now, so too has the political pressure to stop the growth. With projections, such as those in table 2, that health care will grow to at least 17 percent and perhaps 20 percent of GDP by the year 2000, political pressure will parallel that growth. Such pressure will also reflect the extent to which (1) access to care is expanded to those persons who currently experience limited access for fiscal reasons (e.g., no health insurance) and (2) broad-based taxes are used to finance such expanded access. Part of the major restructuring occurring in the health care sector today is in anticipation of these political pressures.

During the past half-century, the U. S. federal government stimulated both the supply of and the demand for health care services, increasing both physical and fiscal access, respectively. On the supply side, for example, the Hill-Burton program provided incentives to build and expand hospitals. Other federal subsidies encouraged medical schools to double the size of their faculties and, hence, their entering classes. Similar programs produced corresponding increases in allied health personnel, and the space program as well as private research and development produced an open-ended flow of new knowledge and technology that expanded what could be performed medically.

Public-sector stimulation of the demand side began with the 1954 tax act, the last significant reform of the tax system prior to that enacted in 1986. The 1954 legislation reversed an earlier IRS ruling and reaffirmed that certain employer-paid fringe benefits would not be taxable to the employee receiving them, while remaining deductible for the employer's income tax purposes as an ordinary cost of doing business.[25] Particular among these benefits was employer-provided health insurance. Thus, while an employer would be indifferent from the viewpoint of the cost after income taxes between spending a deductible dollar on wages and spending a deductible dollar on a health insurance policy for an employee,[26] employees were not indifferent. Between the end of World War II and 1954, labor unions had fought exceptionally hard in the courts and at the bargaining table to expand health benefits from covering only 600,000 workers in 1945 to 7 million prior to the 1954 tax legislation.[27] Thereafter, it became easy. Within a few years, virtually all labor union contracts in the United States contained significant health insurance provisions as the result of the 1954 statute, collective bargaining, and their spillover effects in a competitive labor market.

Today more than three-quarters of all citizens have some form of private health insurance, the vast majority of them as a result of policies purchased by their employers.[22] The importance of this tax-exemption mechanism for putting health insurance in place was shown in a study by the Employee Benefit Research Institute. Nationwide, nearly 20 percent of all workers having employer-provided coverage would choose not to have any health insurance at all were it not a part of their fringe benefits packages. Even more dramatic is the finding that more than 60 percent of workers earning $15,000 or less would choose not to retain coverage.[28] The tax-exemption mechanism is also important to government, in that, absent such tax code provisions, federal revenue would be $50-$80 billion higher per year, according to Congressional Budget Office estimates.

The second stage in the evolution of the U.S. national health insurance policy came in 1965, 11 years after the action on the income tax front. This second stage was the adoption of the Medicare and Medicaid programs. In concept, the 1954 tax subsidy had taken care of employed citizens and their dependents. The Medicare and Medicaid entitlement programs would now close the coverage gap for those not working, specifically the unemployed poor (Medicaid), and those who had stopped working because of retirement (Medicare). Today these programs cover approximately 65 million citizens.[29]

By the mid-to-late 1970s, the combination of the entitlement programs and private insurance along with other public-sector programs, including the FEHBP, IHS, CHAMPUS, VA, and the active-duty military, accounted for coverage of more than 90 percent of all Americans. This surge in public and private health insurance coverage from 1955 to 1975 placed tremendous purchasing power in the hands of consumers, and, not surprisingly, they exercised that power. As discussed below, the prevalence of "first-dollar coverage" in most such insurance gave consumers an unparalleled opportunity to spend someone else's money for their own benefit. Because few countervailing mechanisms existed to constrain that purchasing power, growth of the health care sector surged,

Table 7. U.S. Population by Health Insurance Source or Status*		
■ Employment-based—includes both public-sector (e.g., FEHBP and CHAMPUS) and private-sector insurance arranged (and, typically, paid for in whole or in part) by employers for employees and their dependents		145,250,000
■ Other private insurance (excluding Medicare supplements)		14,500,000
■ Medicare (net of dual Medicare/Medicaid)		31,500,000
■ Medicaid (includes dual Medicare/Medicaid)		33,000,000
Percentage of Income	**Number**	
Below 100%	20,250,000	
100% to 185%	7,750,000	
Above 185%	5,000,000	
■ VA/IHS/Other (only)		1,750,000
■ Uninsured		38,000,000
Percentage of Maximum "Poverty Income"	**Number**	
Below 100%	10,750,000	
100% to 185%	10,500,000	
Above 185%	16,750,000	
Total Population		**264,000,000**

* Estimates for 1995 extrapolated from historical data reported by the Health Care Financing Administration (HCFA), the Congressional Budget Office (CBO), the Current Population Survey (CPS), the Health Insurance Association of America (HIAA), and the Employee Benefits Research Institute (EBRI).

Table 8. Distribution of Approximately 2.5 Million People Losing Health Insurance (HI) Coverage Per Month in the United States (with mirror image events leading to gaining coverage)

23%	Lose **JOB**	(Take **JOB**)
22%	Change from **JOB** to *job*	(Change from *job* to **JOB**)
20%	Lose/drop nonemployment private HI	(Begin nonemployment private HI)
16%	Lose employment HI without change in job	(Gain employment HI without change in job)
11%	Take *job*/lose Medicaid	(Lose *job*/gain Medicaid)
8%	Other	
	Decrease in hours of employment	(Increase in hours of employment)
	Born to household without HI	(Born to household with HI)
	Divorces/survives spouse with HI	(Marries spouse with HI)
	Loses Medicaid by reaching majority or losing dependency	(Gains Medicare by meeting age or disability criteria)

JOB = Job with health insurance
job = Job without health insurance

creating a momentum that has continued, even as the percentage of the U.S. population with health insurance has declined to its current level of about 85-86 percent.

This decline in coverage left approximately 38 million citizens of the United States without health insurance (table 7, page 169). Characteristics of this group include the facts that the average duration of a spell without health insurance is less than six months, only one-sixth of the uninsured are without health insurance for periods exceeding two years (see table 8, above for a sense of why there is such a high turnover of uninsureds), and, of all the uninsured, one-sixth live in California, one-third are aged 21-24, one-eighth are in households with more than $50,000/year in income, and five-sixths are in households where at least the head of household is a part- or full-time employee.[30] Many of these working uninsured are in newly created jobs, and the most significant employment growth in the United States in recent years has been in the service sector. Service industries, unlike manufacturing and construction, do not have a tradition of trade unionism, collective bargaining, and relatively generous fringe benefit packages, and this sector tends to employ less skilled labor working at or near the minimum wage. Thus, nearly 85 percent of the working uninsured comprises persons earning only one-to-two times the minimum wage. A fringe benefit package that includes about $2/hour for health insurance is a relatively manageable 8-10 percent of a $20 to $25 per hour total employer labor cost in manufacturing and construction, but is prohibitively expensive relative to a $5 to $10 per hour total employer labor cost in small business and in the service sector.[31] It is easy to see why such employers are not enthusiastic about "employer mandates" that would raise labor costs 20-40 percent and wipe out profit margins four or five times over.

Figure 7, page 171, summarizes a variety of factors that have accounted for much of the real and inflationary growth in the U.S. health sector. While increased physical and fiscal access have been important,[32] a further contributor to real growth has been increasing intensity of care. Factors identified with increased intensity include an aging population, new technology and growing medical knowledge, economic incentives (especially in fee-for-service [FFS] and cost-based reimbursement [CBR] environments), "defensive" medicine, and regulation. Regulation represents intensity because compliance consumes real resources. There are forms to fill out, new computers, additional office employees, etc. Patients may never see the resources being consumed, but that alters neither their reality nor their cost.

Another contributor to "intensity" is idle or excess capacity, the cost of which is what we pay for avoiding queues, morbidity/lost productivity, and the loss of time that otherwise would be spent traveling and/or queuing.

The American Medical Association (AMA) estimates that between 5 and 10 percent of all health care expenditures are unnecessary, i.e., probably do no harm but also don't improve outcomes, even though they are the result of physicians' orders.[33] Estimates by consumer activists are two to three times those of the AMA. Some of these unneeded diagnostic and treatment procedures are in response to public expectations and demand. People hear about new studies and procedures in the lay press and run to their physicians saying, "I know you can fix it; I heard about it on TV or read about it in the newspaper." But, of course, should new or redundant procedures be omitted and there be an adverse outcome, those same people will find a trial lawyer and initiate a tort action. Hence, defensive medicine.

Beyond what actually causes real growth, the consumption of more resources, there are some things that are inflationary, things that make the dollar numbers larger without any change in what's real. By inflation we simply mean increases in prices without

---

Figure 7. Factors Contributing to Differential* Health Sector Growth (1955-1995)

REAL		INFLATIONARY
Access	**Intensity**	
Payment Programs	Aging Population	Payment Structure
■ Medicare & Medigap	FFS & CBR Payment	■ Nature of Insurance
■ Medicaid	Research----->Technology	■ Intensity---->Inflation
■ Fringe Benefit Packages	and Medical Knowledge	
▮ Unionization	"Defensive Medicine"	
▮ Income Tax Treatment	Regulation	
Hill-Burton	Excess Capacity	
Medical School Grants	<------------Licensure, Sub-Specialization, Unionization------------>	
<----------------------------Public Expectations--------------------------->		

*Relative to the overall economy

---

corresponding change in the actual quantity of resources being consumed. The very nature of the conventional payment structures of past decades not only increased intensity, but that intensity itself created inflation as discussed below. Licensure and subspecialization also contribute to both intensity and inflation through distortions of the labor market. In economic terms, licensure restricts supply and is a "barrier to entry." The limiting of competition to those having a particular license or credential allows those persons to receive higher compensation than would be available in a purely price-competitive market. "Quality" is but one reason there is resistance to allowing foreign medical graduates to practice medicine domestically.

The fact that intensity begets inflation can be described graphically (figure 8, below). The horizontal axis measures the dollar cost of resources that are consumed in producing health care. The value of the inputs is a nice, straight 45 degree line. This implicitly assumes that we have an efficient market for input resources, which is generally true in the United States. In the case of input resources, value would be the market price. Presumably, if one buys resources (say, to build an outpatient clinic) and then changes one's mind, those resources can be sold back into the marketplace for about the same price (net of transactions costs) and used for something else (say, to build a

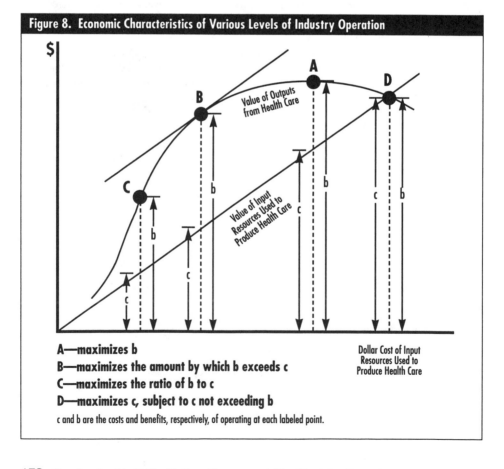

Figure 8. Economic Characteristics of Various Levels of Industry Operation

A—maximizes b
B—maximizes the amount by which b exceeds c
C—maximizes the ratio of b to c
D—maximizes c, subject to c not exceeding b

c and b are the costs and benefits, respectively, of operating at each labeled point.

Dollar Cost of Input Resources Used to Produce Health Care

retail store). Fundamentally, value is retained by the input resources. The output value is different. It reflects what society should be willing to pay for health care (which is not necessarily the same amount that is paid for that care). The difference between what you would be willing to pay and what you actually have to pay is what economists refer to as "consumers' surplus." For instance, you might be willing to pay $20,000 for a car, but if you negotiate a $16,000 price, you have obtained $4,000 of consumer's surplus and have a car that has a value of $20,000, even though you didn't have to pay that much. The curved line in figure 8 represents the value of the output. Its shape reflects the potential for consumer satiation. The more there is of a given output, the less valuable additional quantities become. For example, a rural community might be willing to pay a substantial bonus to get a primary care physician to locate there if there were no existing physician, and no bonus if there were already five such physicians already in practice there.

The four points, A, B, C, and D, in figure 8 depict value at various scales of activity. Point A labels the maximum value of aggregate output occurring at a fairly large level of input and output. Point B is where the value of the output exceeds the value of the input by the largest margin and reflects a somewhat smaller health care industry. Point C, a small industry, is where a maximum ratio between value and output value is attained. Point D is where costs are maximized, i.e., where the health care industry as a whole is at its largest without aggregate costs exceeding aggregate value.

Different constituencies or interest groups have very different preferences as to where they would like to see the health care industry function. Generally, physicians and most patients with insurance like Point A. Point A is consistent with the Hippocratic Oath; you do everything possible having affirmative benefit for each patient, and do no harm.

Point D reminds us that, in the desire to do all that is humanly possible, a physician needs to add an element of pragmatism. There is such a thing as doing a test too many times "just to be sure," in terms of patient discomfort and adverse side effects (e.g., increased risk of cancer caused by exposure to too many x-rays). Nonetheless, major economic forces continually press physicians and other providers outward toward Point D. Anyone supplying any input resource to the health care industry would prefer to sell the industry more rather than less of that resource. Whether it is medical supplies, I.V. solutions, labor, pharmaceuticals, high-tech diagnostic/therapeutic equipment, or office supplies, the more you buy, the happier the seller. Free samples of prescription drugs are simply one form of an invitation to move toward Point D.

Government has a bias toward Point C, not only because it lowers the scale of outlays and hence government's pro rata share of those outlays in a world where budget deficits are a political liability, but also because, as the point having maximum rate of return, politicians can fill their speeches with "efficiency in government" rhetoric, pointing with pride to each hard-earned tax dollar yielding the most health care "bang for the buck."

Unlike everyone else, economists like Point B,, where total net value-added is maximized. Beginning at the left side of figure 8 and moving past Point C, each time the health care industry buys $1 worth of resources, it produces an output that society should value at more than $1. Each time the investment is repeated, the amount of additional output value generated exceeds $1 by less and less. Eventually, when we arrive at Point B, a dollar's worth of additional input yields just a dollar's worth of output. This is the point at which marginal or incremental cost equals the marginal or incremental benefit of the output. (Note that the line tangent to the curve at Point B is parallel to the value-of-input line.) An economist would say this is the point at which to stop. If investment continues, each additional dollar's worth of resources will yield less than a dollar's worth of output.

Indeed, moving to the right of Point B is even worse than simply making an intrinsically bad investment. Because any additional input units must be bought in the market from their current owners who are at their own Point B, the potential health industry buyer must convince the current owner to part with such resources. The convincing is done with money. If the seller of the resource will forgo $1.01 of nonhealth output by parting with the resource, the health care sector must bid $1.01 for that additional unit of input resource, raising the marketing-clearing price from $1.00. The $1.01 received by the seller of the resource compensates that seller for the output that seller would have produced had the input cost only $1.00.

By offering $1.01 for a unit of resource, health care is telling the market that when the unit of resource is converted to health care, that health care will be valued by society at $1.01 or more. However, the additional value of health care realized is only $0.99 just to the right of Point B. Thus, health care has lied to the market. Bidding the resource price to $1.01 from $1.00 is, by definition, inflation, so we can see why such inflation is correctly characterized as a lie. Because the U.S. health care industry for 40 years has operated somewhere between Points A and B, where the incremental value produced is less than incremental value consumed, the industry has created much of its own differential inflation by lying to the market. The resource market is told that something is worth more than it actually is, and an inefficient allocation of resources results. We have forgone $1.01 worth of nonhealth output to get $0.99 worth of health care. Because moving to the right in figure 8 is associated with greater intensity of service, the phrase "intensity breeds inflation" clearly describes a major health sector phenomenon.

The Health Insurance Phenomenon (a.k.a. "The Moral Hazard")

For economists, the policy issue is how to move the health care industry back toward Point B. First, we must understand why any rational human being would be willing to spend one dollar on resources for only, say, 20 cents worth of additional benefit. There are two circumstances under which this could happen.

The first is when individual perception of value differs widely from a dispassionate, objective societal view. An example of this might be certain life and death situations. When resources are required within the next 24 to 48 hours to save a person, having the prospect of years of quality life remaining if death is deferred, the health care system just spends, regardless of the relationship between that spending and the hard economic benefits the spending may produce. Because such situations represent a very small proportion of total health care expenditures, and because society places high subjective value on saving such lives, such resource use is generally accepted.

The second circumstance when it is rational for a person to spend a dollar to get 20 cents worth of value is when that person is spending someone else's dollar. This circumstance has existed in most public and private health insurance programs. Typical health insurance has insulated care decision-makers, historically physicians, as well as patients from the cost of resources consumed to produce benefits.

Health insurance, as it has been structured, is far more than classical insurance, the purpose of which is to allow the insured to avoid the consequences of low probability catastrophic events, i.e., avoiding the risk of ruin. In one sense, U.S. health insurance has also taken on the characteristics of certain gambling games, e.g., lotteries. Imagine that you and nine other people get together to play a game. Each antes $125 a month, for a total of $15,000 a year for the 10 players. The house takes a 10 percent cut to pay for administrative costs, such as writing and enforcing the rules of the game, making actuarial predictions (calculating the odds of winning), and managing the game's payouts of winnings. A $13,500 grand prize is thus available. Now suppose you win the jackpot (by getting sick) and you have a shopping list of nine possible health care expenditures, each priced at $1,500 (such as emergency department visit, first day in hospital, surgery, etc., on down to a few days of home health care). Table 9, below, shows how you might rank order the nine items by their value to you (what you would be willing to spend of your own money to obtain each).

Now consider two different sets of rules governing winners of the game. If you receive the $13,500 in a lump sum cash distribution with no other rules, you will buy all of the items on the list that are worth as much or more to you than the $1,500 asking price. You will buy up to the point where one more dollar of expenditure produces one more dollar of benefit (rehabilitative therapy in our example). You will have climbed up on your output value curve to your personal "Point B." Once you have bought the five

Table 9. Health Care Shopping List*		
Service	**Cost**	**Benefit**
Emergency department visit and diagnostics	$ 1,500	$ 4,300
Initial hospitalization	1,500	3,450
Surgery	1,500	2,700
Hospital days (2-3)	1,500	2,050
Rehabilitative therapy	1,500	1,500
Hospital days (4-5)	1,500	1,050
One week of SNF/home health care	1,500	700
Hospital days (6-8)	1,500	450
Hospital days (9-12)	1,500	300
	$13,500	$16,500

* Assumes $13,500 can be spent in nine increments of $1,500 each.

things on the list to get to this point, that will leave $6,000 that you will apply to some nonhealth consumption, i.e., spending $6,000 for what you judge to be its highest and best use, e.g., taking a vacation to Hawaii.

Suppose, however, the rules of the game say that the prize is not $13,500 in cash but $13,500 in reimbursement for health purchases, and that any portion of the $13,500 not spent carries forward to the next game's grand prize. Now your decision should be to go ahead and buy all nine items on the list (because you can't touch any of the money not spent for these items). You are still happy, because you have the money you need for your health care and there is affirmative benefit from every item on the list. Your physician is happy because he or she got to practice "good medicine." The other nine people are not unhappy because, after all, they've had the peace of mind knowing that they were insured and might have "won." Health insurance premiums might go up a little next year, but that is next year, and, besides, your employer pays the premium. Your employer is not too unhappy because the premium is deductible for tax purposes and providing health insurance helps attract loyal employees. So all of us win. The only losers, unfortunately, are also all of us, because resources were consumed inefficiently and did not go to their highest and best use.

Strong empirical evidence exists that patient choices change, depending on source of funding. The RAND corporation conducted an 8-year study of patient sensitivity to price.[34] The study involved more than 4,000 people who were placed into 13 groups that differed according to health insurance mechanism but were matched with respect to demographic characteristics (e.g., age, income) and medical status (e.g., preexisting conditions). Twelve of the 13 groups had a maximum out-of-pocket exposure of $1,000 per family per year, but with each having a different deductible or copayment arrangement. One group, for instance, had a 25 percent copayment, and another had a 95 percent copayment (meaning they got 75 cents and 5 cents reimbursement for each dollar of the first $4,000 and $1,053 they spent, respectively). The thirteenth group had free care.

The results showed that the demand for health services is indeed price elastic (sensitive to price levels). For example, for every $2 of medical services (measured at billed charges) that the 95 percent copayment group consumed, the 25 percent copayment group consumed $3. They spent 50 percent more.[35]

The RAND study results suggest that people look at their own budgets and decide to forgo medical services they deem unnecessary so as not to incur large copayments and deductibles. But this might be penny-wise and pound-foolish, because they may have underlying illnesses that are not detected as early as they might have been, resulting in much larger expenses later on.

To address this concern, the RAND study continued to follow people for several years to see if they did, in fact, require larger quantities of medical care subsequently. In fact, there were no statistically significant differences between or among any of the 12 partial-pay groups with respect to mortality, morbidity, or expenditures for care. When these 12 groups were compared with the one group that paid nothing, distinctions related to income became evident. For higher income families, there were again no differences across the 13 groups. For families that were at or below the poverty level, however, those in the free-care group fared better than those in the other 12 groups.

For example, those who were poor and needed glasses nearly always got them in the free care group; poor individuals who had to pay for them often did not. And, if an individual was poor and hypertensive and in the free-care group, he or she was diagnosed and medicated much more frequently than an individual who was poor, hypertensive, and had to pay for care. There was even a slight increase in the actuarial life expectancy for the poor in the free group.[35]

In addition to the RAND study, Medicare statistics on hospital utilization also support the propositions that (1) the United States has been operating closer to Point A than to Point B in figure 8 and (2) that moving back toward Point B not only saves resources but can be accomplished without adversely affecting medical outcome. Subsequent to the initiation of the prospective pricing system in October 1983, there was a 20-30 percent decline in the average length of stay of Medicare beneficiaries, with no significant change in outcomes.[36]

The Medicare saving of the cost of an extra three or four days in the hospital is not a pure gain, of course. There is obviously a substitution of resources to provide alternative care outside of the hospital. That includes the opportunity cost to family members of having to provide some level of care or explicit out-of-pocket costs for providing skilled nursing or home care services. While 100 percent of the resources are not saved by shortening hospital stay, there is a significant saving nevertheless, and there has not been a significant change in morbidity or mortality statistics as a result of this dramatic reduction in hospital usage.[36]

Removing insurance's first-dollar-coverage insulation between the cost of resources consumed and the beneficiary of that resource use clearly works as a strategy for moving back from Point A toward Point B on figure 8. The federal government's attempts to apply this lesson to the Medicare program have been largely frustrated by the political clout of the American Association of Retired Persons, but private-sector business has been much more successful, generally constraining first-dollar coverage. Between 1981 and 1985, for example, the average deductible and copayment for U.S. employees quadrupled as employers successfully bargained with unions, offering benefit reductions in lieu of layoffs in a weak economy.[37]

The second major way to use economic incentives to shift health care resources from Point A toward Point B is to focus on the provider. Deductibles and copayments place on the patient the cost of resources initially consumed. An alternative involves making the provider bear the risk of greater-than-expected costs of all resources consumed by and for the patient without being able to pass any of these costs through to individual patients. Both prepaid care mechanisms and some rate regulation (e.g., Medicare's prospective pricing system) are examples of this approach. They place the provider at risk economically for actual resource consumption beyond average levels contemplated (or "budgeted") and incorporated in fixed rates set in advance for "packages" or "bundles" of many individual "line items" of care.

The generic problem with these approaches is that they tend to maintain the cost/benefit insulation at the level of the patient. They therefore create the potential for patient/provider conflicts of interests, and/or they cause "cost-shifting," "unbundling," and a variety of other provider system-gaming.

The U.S. Health Care System—Observations

As one surveys the U.S. health economy, a number of observations are in order: the U.S. population values physical access and convenience (meaning nearness, lack of queues), financing (meaning affordability—even if using someone else's money), quality (meaning the newest stuff, certainty of diagnosis, efficacious treatment, minimal discomfort, and absence of bad outcome), amenity (e.g., carpeted waiting areas with magazines and indirect lighting), and choice (meaning if I don't like provider A, providers B through Z are instant options).

Referring back to figure 2, page 163, among the differential things the United States buys are lots of high tech, idle capacity, choice, and amenity. As a society, the United States pays to have one MRI scanner for each 110,000 persons rather than to accept one for each 1,625,000 persons as does Canada. Scans in Canada are much cheaper than in the United States because there is no idle capacity to pay for. There is also in Canada a six-week wait for a nonemergency scan and typically an overnight trip to get to the scanner.[38] People don't queue for care in the United States unless they are poor.

As a society, the United States pays for the choices of coverage provided by more than 1,500 private insurance companies. Those choices cost more than $30 billion per year relative to Canada, where a single-payer system provides universal coverage but only a single benefit package and queues for more intensive or high-tech services. At the signing of the legislation establishing federally qualified health maintenance organizations (HMOs), President Nixon predicted a 90 percent enrollment of the U.S. population within a decade. Now, a quarter-century later, less than 20 percent of the population is enrolled, and IPA-model and point-of-service HMOs (the ones offering subscribers the greatest personal choice of provider) are growing in enrollment two to two-and-one-half times faster than traditional staff-, group-, and network-model HMO's.[39]

As a society, the United States pays for richer physicians. Median physician income in the United States is larger than average U.S. per capita income by a factor of five compared to Canada and Western Europe, where factors of three are typical.

As a society, the United States also pays for the technologically finest quality care in existence, as well as for defensive medicine and for tort liability awards.

All of this and more is what the United States buys, exacerbated by four decades of most of the population's having been addicted to tax-exempt, employer-provided health insurance, to being able to spend someone else's money via first-dollar coverage, and to expectations of government-paid health care post-retirement, even for the wealthy.

The U.S. health care system is rapidly evolving with market-like responses to (1) payers saying "enough," (2) the intrusion of "managed care" into a no-longer-sacrosanct physician domain, and (3) the continuing march of technology and knowledge to include the explosion of efforts to link interventions to outcomes and the grand potential of the Genome Project.

Aside from truly regional and teaching institutions, we are witnessing the shrinkage of the typical acute-care hospital of the 1950s to little more than a sophisticated way-station for local trauma cases. The areas within health care gaining market share are outpatient, ambulatory, and home health services. Adequate supplies of primary care physicians are forecast and an overabundance of specialists exists.

Mergers and consolidations of all types will dominate the health care industry for the remainder of the 1990s.

Although all of this was well on its way before the Clinton Administration provided the industry with added incentives to change, the economist continues to ponder Point B on figure 8, wondering whether the market or the *Federal Register* will ultimately define health care for the 21st Century.

References

1. Wilensky, G. "Making Decisions on Rationing." *Business and Health* 3(1):36, Nov. 1985.

2. Pine, A. "Fixed Assets, or Why a Loan in Yap is Hard to Roll Over." *Wall Street Journal*, March 29, 1984, 1,24.

3. U.S. Department of Commerce, Economics and Statistics Administration: Bureau of Economic Analysis. *Survey of Current Business*, Feb. 1994, Table 2.2 (p. 13); Bureau of the Census. *Statistical Abstract of the United States* 1993, Table 1326 (p.788).

4. Economic Report of the President, Feb. 1994, Tables B-33 and B-44, pp. 306-7, 318-9.

5. Economic Report of the President, Feb. 1994, Table B-44, pp. 318-9.

6. Much of the information in the discussion of the ESRD program that follows is taken from the *Green Book*, the document prepared annually by the staff of the Committee on Ways and Means of the U.S. House of Representatives to provide members of the Committee with an overview of various entitlement programs. Also see reference 29.

7. Specifically, qualified beneficiaries are those individuals who are (1) fully insured for old age and/or survivor benefits (even though not otherwise eligible to receive those benefits), (2) entitled to monthly social security benefits, or (3) are spouses or dependents of individuals described in (1) or (2). Approximately 7 percent of the population with ESRD is not eligible and is not covered by Medicare.

8. The benefits to ESRD patients derive from their enrollment in Parts A and B of Medicare, although Part B coverage requires the payment of monthly premiums for the protection.

9. Schwartz, W., and Aaron, H. "Rationing Hospital Care—Lessons from Britain." *New England Journal of Medicine* 310(1):52-6, Jan. 5, 1984.

10. Lister, J. "The Politics of Medicine in Britain and the United States." *New England Journal of Medicine* 315(3):168-74, July 17, 1986.

11. A prototypical example of explicit resource allocation decision making at the system level is provided by Oregon's experimental Medicaid program.

12. Rettig, R. "The Politics of Health Cost Containment: End-Stage Renal Disease." *Bulletin of the New York Academy of Medicine* 56(1):115-38, Jan.-Feb.1980.

13. A more general example of this phenomenon is given by the overall Medicare program. The average Medicare beneficiary is now about 75 years of age, has one or two chronic conditions that are eminently treatable and certainly not life-threatening, and a remaining actuarial life expectancy of about nine years. (Department of Labor, Bureau of Statistics, *Work Life Estimate effects of Race and Education*, Bulletin 2254, Feb. 1986.) Nine years hence, about one-third of this cohort is expected to be alive, but with three or four treatable chronic conditions and remaining life expectancy of five years. However, because of the growing efficacy and quality of care, the actuaries are likely to be wrong, and it may be that 40 percent will be alive and have a remaining life expectancy of six years. And so it goes.

14. National Organ Transplant Act, U.S. Code 42 § 274e, Prohibition of Organ Purchases, 1984.

15. Evans, R., and others. "The Quality if Life Patients with End-Stage Renal Disease." *New England Journal of Medicine* 312(9):553-9, Feb. 28, 1985.

16. Abram, H., and others. "Suicidal Behavior in Chronic Dialysis Patients." *American Journal of Psychiatry* 127(3):1199-204, March 1971.

17. McKegney, F., and Lange, P. "The Decisions to No Longer Live on Chronic Hemodialysis." American Journal of Psychiatry 128(9):267-74, Sept. 1971.

18. GDP is the standard measure of total economic activity in a nation. Generally, it measures all goods and services produced in a year in an economy, valued at their price to the final consumer. NHE components are shown in table 5, page 167.

19. The projections are an excellent example of the working interaction of politics and the numerical power of alternative assumptions. The Health Care Financing Administration (HCFA), prior to the 1992 election, forecast health care to be only 18 percent of the economy by 2000 if we made no changes in the system. This forecast was accomplished by assuming economywide growth in Gross Domestic Product or GDP (the denomination) of 6.4 percent per year compunded, a rate almost double actual recent experience, with some tapering off of growth in National Health Expenditures or NHE (the numerator). The Clinton Health Plan, when announced in September 1993, claimed to be able to hold NHE to only 17 percent of GDP by 2000, in spite of forecasting bullish overall economic growth, by using draconian regulatory controls on prices to cut NHE growth by about 60 percent to an unheard of 4 percent per year by 2000 (i.e., zero real growth after adjusting for expected inflation). The Congressional Budget Office (CBO) baseline, with which Clinton contrasted his plan, forecast NHE at 19 percent of GDP by 2000, using generally credible assumptions for both GDP and NHE growth, absent draconian measures. The sensitivity of all this to the assumptions made is shown by my 1994 projection, in which I assume a GDP growth rate between the actual growth during the Bush Administration and the Clinton projections and that NHE growth will slow by one-half of one percent *every* year through 2000. That produces a 20 percent NHE share of the economy, and would yield a 21 percent level if there were less slowdown in NHE growth.

20. Schieber, G., and others. "Health Spending, Delivery, and Outcomes in OECD Countries." *Health Affairs* 12(2):120-9, Summer 1993.

21. Emanuel, E., and Emanuel, L. "The Economics of Dying—The Illusion of Cost Savings at the End of Life." *New England Journal of Medicine* 330(8):540-4, Feb. 24, 1994.

22. Source Book of Health Insurance Data–1993, Health Insurance Association of America, Tables 1.1 and 4.4 and Figures 2.1 and 2.4, pp. 11, 14, 22, and 82.

23. Calculated by the author from data contained in Tables B-1, B-2, B-3, and B-59 (pages 268-73 and 335) of the Economic Report of the President, Feb. 1994, and from data on NHE provided by the Health Care Financing Administration, Department of Health and Human Services.

24. Economic Report of the President, Feb. 1993, Table B-63, p. 340.

25. U.S. Code 26 § 106, 1954.

26. In reality, employers are not indifferent, because employer-paid health insurance premiums are also exempt from payroll taxes of more than 15 percent, of which the employer pays half.

27. Starr, P. *The Social Transformation of American Medicine.* New York, N.Y.: Basic Books, Inc., 1982, pp. 312-3.

28. Employee Benefit Research Institute's simulation of private health insurance coverage with full taxation of employer contributions to health insurance, 1979.

29. U.S. Congress, House Committee on Ways and Means. *Background Material and Data on Programs within the Jurisdiction of the Committee on Ways and Means.* Committee print, 103rd Congress, Second Session, WMCP:103-27, July 15, 1994. Washington, D.C.: U.S. Government Printing Office, pp. 124, 798.

30. Employee Benefit Research Institute, Washington, D.C., "Sources of Health Insurance and Characteristics of the Uninsured: Analysis of the March 1993 Current Population Survey." Special Report Number 20/Issue Brief Number 145, Jan. 1994.

31. U.S. Department of Labor, Bureau of Labor Statistics. "Current Labor Statistics." *Monthly Labor Review* 117(6):94 Table 15 (p.79), June 1994, adjusted by author to include average cost of fringe benefits as reported by the U.S. Department of Commerce, Economics and Statistics Administration, Bureau of the Census: *Statistical Abstract of the United States 1993*, (Table 677, p. 430).

32. As noted above, subsidy programs to build hospitals and grants to increase health manpower output are supply-side stimulants that increase physical access to care. Entitlement programs and favorable tax treatment of insurance stimulate the demand side by enhancing fiscal access.

33. Davis, J. "Defensive Medicine and Medical Malpractice." U.S. Senate Hearing 98-1039, *Committee on Labor and Human Resources,* July 10, 1984.

34. Newhouse, J., and others. *Some Interim Results from a Controlled Trial of Loss-Sharing in Health Insurance.* Santa Monica, Calif.: RAND Corp., Jan. 1982.

35. Brook, R., and others. "Does Free Care Improve Adults' Health?: Results from a Randomized Controlled Trial." *New England Journal of Medicine* 309(23):1426-34, Dec. 8, 1983.

36. Tolchin, M. "22% Drop is Found in Length of Stay in Hospitals in U.S." *New York Times*, May 25, 1988, pp. 1,13.

37. Pear, R. "Companies Tackle Health Costs." *New York Times*, Mar. 3, 1985, p.F-11.

38. Long, H. "Health Care Resource Allocation: Canada, Mexico, and the United States." *Decisions in Imaging Economics* 5(3):29-33, Summer 1992

39. *Managed Care Digest*, "HMO" and "Update" Editions. Kansas City, Mo.: Marion Merrill Dow, Inc., 1987-1993.

Hugh W. Long, MBA, PhD, JD, is Associate Professor of Health Care Management, Department of Health Systems Management, Tulane University, New Orleans, Louisiana.

Cost/Quality Relationships: A Generic Model for Health Care

by Robert B. Klint, MD, MHA, FACPE, and Hugh W. Long, MBA, PhD, JD

CHAPTER 13

The U.S. health care system is undergoing an unprecedented period of change, precipitated by the interaction of major economic, social, political, and technological forces. The medical and managerial challenges wrought by these forces arrive, change, and disappear at a rapid pace. The health care sector, an incredibly complex aggregation of activities that has only recently begun to view itself as an industry, is often left in further confusion and inconsistency.

The introduction of rate-setting systems for hospitals and physicians, establishment of capitated rates, increased monopsony power of some health care purchasers, ongoing efforts to reduce federal spending, the growth of managed health care, and concepts such as managed competition and global budgeting (even as distorted in various health care reform initiatives), all tend to constrain the flow of dollars to each provider for each unit of services delivered. Rising public and professional expectations for realizing the benefits of expanding medical knowledge and technology, increasing provider operating expenses, rising capital needs, and unmet health care expectations for some population segments all increase demand for services and their attendant funding.

As these social, political, and economic forces vie for dominance, they do so in an environment characterized by an increasingly knowledgeable and assertive public, ever-increasing competition, growing provider networks and systems, the "corporatization" of health care, and continuing maldistribution of physicians, both geographically and by specialty. Questions of health care policy and social values have taken center stage in lay and professional press, on talk shows, and in political speeches, news conferences, and legislative proposals at all levels of government. There is broad public discussion of health care access, of divergent patterns of care and resource use, of the appropriateness of care for the terminally ill, and of the ethical and societal values at stake in all of these areas. There is increasing concern that "quality" will be compromised, even as that concept itself is altered and expanded beyond traditional boundaries. A new glossary has been developed; it includes "disquality," "undercare," "cost-quality tradeoffs," and "cost of poor quality."

The fundamental characteristics of our future health care system depend in large measure on decisions being made now by leaders in health care, government, labor, and business. The resource allocation and program decisions being made today by individual institutions, purchasers of health care, and designers of social and health care policy can be better formulated, implemented, and evaluated if we can develop a common framework and a common language that transcend the interests and viewpoints of particular constituencies.

This chapter presents a conceptual model for use by decision makers. The model is intended as a framework for discussing cost and quality, for allocating resources, for communicating between the many involved publics, and for clarifying some aspects of policy setting at both the institutional and the system levels. The chapter explores the nature of the cost/quality relationship and offers a model for describing and explaining the major external constraints within which resource allocation decisions are made.

Quality

Some have proposed that the health care industry has used "quality" as its "miracle weapon" in defending its march toward a greater share of the gross domestic product. Justification for the rising costs of care has been cloaked in a mysterious shroud understood only by medical professionals and health care managers.[1] Others have suggested that quality cannot even be defined; it is clearly recognizable only in its absence. "Disquality" was added to the glossary in 1986.[2] The quality (and cost) of measuring quality (of care) is viewed by many as questionable, even perilous.[3]

Still others have assumed that major components of quality can indeed be identified if not fully quantified. Brook and Williams found that quality is directly influenced by synergism between the technology of care and the art of care, as modified by genetics, patient behavior, public health, and error.[4] Donabedian suggests that we judge quality by the degree to which the care given is capable, on the average, of producing the greatest improvement in health care that science can achieve.[5] The definition adopted by the American Medical Association additionally incorporates the patient's emotional status, effective use of resources, the medical record, health promotion, and promptness.[6] Affordability and accessibility are elements[7]; so are availability and client satisfaction.[1,8] Risk should be minimized[9]; harm should be avoided.[10] Evaluating both the process for delivering care and the structure that facilitates that process are additional ways of dissolving the shroud.

Medical measures of outcome, such as mortality and morbidity, may be poor indicators of quality when the severity of the disease process itself precludes the desired outcome. In such circumstances, the patient's level of satisfaction with the process may become the principal measure of quality, an outcome yardstick that is highly dependent on the patient's initial expectations. Yet, as total quality management (TQM), which encompasses continuous quality improvement (CQI), continues to demonstrate its efficacy in the health care service industry, greater and greater emphasis is being placed on measuring and meeting (if not exceeding) the expectations of the customer.

Garvin has suggested five approaches to defining product quality. These approaches were described in the context of manufacturing, yet may have direct application to the health care industry.[11] The transcendent approach views quality as some indefinable and innate excellence; the product approach identifies a measurable and specific ingredient or attribute possessed by the product; the user-based approach incorporates the notion of client satisfaction; manufacturing-based definitions are concerned with process, conformity with standards, and control measure; and value-based approaches define quality in terms of costs, worth, and "affordable excellence."[11]

Garvin's categorization of multiple quality definitions can be applied to health care and appears to be useful in bringing some order to the diverse and conflicting definitions frequently encountered. Outcome measures such as Donabedian's "greatest improvement in health" are currently viewed as central to defining quality and seem analogous to the product-based approach suggested by Garvin. Presumably, no amount of amenity, courtesy, convenience, or availability can compensate for the avoidably poor outcome.

Refinements of quality definitions become increasingly important when outcomes in different provider settings are medically comparable. Such refinements may not assess outcome directly. They may be more indirect and more subjective, yet remain relevant ingredients in the evaluation process. These proxies for outcome include the processes by which care is delivered (a manufacturing set of definitions), the organizational structures and systems that support the process (also a manufacturing approach), and the patient's or purchaser's perception of the interaction (the user-based definitions).

Just as defining the quality of manufactured goods requires several approaches, so too does defining the quality of health care. Describing, defining, and measuring health care quality requires recognition of its multifaceted nature. Because no single approach is sufficient, both the definition and the systems used to monitor quality must encompass those major elements that individually represent input, process, and outcome. A quality assessment vector of eight major elements in that definition is described in the table on page 186.

Establishment of standards of care has been a major goal of the Joint Commission on Accreditation of Healthcare Organizations (JCAHO) and other accreditors, licensing bodies, peer review organizations, and professional associations. The prioritization and quantification of the component elements within the definitional matrix of the table on page 186 have been elusive. Rank ordering of clients' perceptions of quality by Ware and Snyder suggests that there is a considerable overlap in the importance of physicians' "curing" and "caring" characteristics and that a relatively high importance is placed on availability, continuity, and access.[12] Categories of desirable attributes of medical clinics have been ranked by administrators[12]; categories of physician actions by internists[13]; and characteristics of "good" hospitals by patients, medical staffs, and administrators.[8] A synthesis of physician characteristics revealed a high level of correlation between public and professional ranking of desirable and undesirable characteristics.[9]

Clearly, no universal or generally accepted ranking of the quality elements in the table on page 186 exists. However, we believe most clienteles or constituencies—patients, purchasers, physicians, nurses, administrators—would agree on a list of attributes such as these characterizing "good" quality care. We also believe that these same clienteles might well differ as to the rank ordering or relative importance of the elements in the table.[14] Further, we aver that different providers demonstrate varying amounts of the listed characteristics, as well as varying degrees of achievement relative to each element and that, ultimately, such provider achievements are measurable.

It is also important to realize that the notion of "quality" can be observed and perhaps measured from a variety of perspectives. For the purposes of this chapter, we identify three such perspectives:

Major Elements of a Health Care Quality Matrix

■ **Physician-Technical (input)**
Capabilities and characteristics of physicians as reflected by training, board certification, continuing education, liability history, medical records, and level of activity (numbers of procedures performed/diagnoses made).

■ **Hospital-Technical (input)**
Licenses, accreditation, and other official evaluations of institutional competence, such as JCAHO findings, university affiliation, currency of technology, nurse staffing ratios, level of activity (numbers of procedures performed), and liability history.

■ **Physician-Art (process)**
"Art of care" characteristics of physicians as reflected by peer review findings, rapport with patients, availability, and listening and instructing capacities.

■ **Hospital-Subjective (process)**
Hospital characteristics, including staff attitudes, service orientation, appearance, ambience, guest amenities, reputation, and empathy.

■ **Continuity of Care (process)**
The degree to which a comprehensive spectrum of health care services exists, including services such as education, preadmission planning, discharge planning, and follow-up care, as appropriate.

■ **Mortality (outcome)**
Patient outcomes resulting in death.

■ **Morbidity (outcome)**
Occurrence of complications or other outcomes that are less than ideal, including hospital-acquired infections, returns to operating rooms within 24 hours, repeated procedures, lengths of stay of more than two standard deviations above the mean, or, if discharged, delayed returns to work or readmissions for the same diagnoses.

■ **Customer Satisfaction (outcome)**
Evaluations (both subjective and objective) of the health care system's processes and outcomes by end-users, who include individuals, families, employers, and other purchasers. Key aspects for evaluation include illness and injury prevention, accessibility, and disease treatment.

- Individual—What is the quality of care received by a particular patient (either generally or in a specific episode of care)?

- Micro-Aggregate—What is the quality of care received by all patients of Doctor X? What is the quality of care received by all DRG 127 patients at Hospital Y?

- Macro-Aggregate—What is the quality of care for newborns nationally?

Cost

Associated with any output (good or service) of whatever quality are two types of costs. The first of these is the out-of-pocket quantity of cash required or credit incurred to command, directly or indirectly, the resources used to produce the output. The second type of costs comprises forgone opportunities, if any, to create additional wealth (cash flow), opportunities lost because of the very nature of the resources and the process employed to generate the output.

Out-of-pocket costs, while apparently a straightforward concept, are often difficult to identify in practice. For example, producers of output have a complex task of determining the relevant cost where:

- Significant fixed or capacity costs are spread over large quantities of output over varying lengths of time.

- It is very expensive to measure accurately the actual incremental or variable costs associated with each output among many.

- Use of resources is shared among many activities (e.g., overheads).

Allocation of costs among multiple time periods and/or multiple activities is necessarily subjective. Similarly, purchasers of output for others (e.g., employers' payments for health services for employees) may have a difficult time identifying their costs relative to an employee's illness when a fixed number of dollars not tied to current output has been paid into a risk pool, especially when future payments (premiums) are influenced by current resource consumption. It should also be noted that out-of-pocket costs necessarily include indirect costs, such as salaries of staff in the Health Care Financing Administration (HCFA) for the Medicare program, liability (malpractice) insurance premiums paid by health care providers, and the local HMO's advertising expenditures to gain market share. These are all real costs, even if distant from hands-on patient care.

Opportunity costs are no less complex, ranging from alternative uses of direct resources themselves, to the lost interest on prepaid premiums, to productivity forgone because of illness and absenteeism, to attendant tax revenues lost, and to marginally lower living standards reflecting excess mortality and morbidity.

The classical discussion of costs requires some modification to address the language of continuous quality improvement and statistical process control. Critical to that process is identification of the "costs of poor quality"[15] or "costs of nonconformance with standards."[16] These costs may be direct and out-of-pocket, e.g., salary dollars spent in reviewing medical records, costs of returning to the operating room because of complications, costs of hospital-acquired infections, and so forth. They also include some costs that are indirect and out-of-pocket, such as malpractice judgments, replacing lost patient items, and the expense of third-party utilization reviews. They may additionally include opportunity costs, such as those stemming from poor employee relations, the disgruntled customer, diminished productivity because of time spent on resolving problems, etc.

A critical message from TQM philosophy is that poor quality is identifiable; when identified, is largely measurable; and, when measured, is controllable. The costs of poor quality in the service sector may approach 30 percent of the total operating budgets of companies.[17]

Relationship of Quality to Cost[18]

Cost/Quality Viewpoint

The precise elements of a definition of quality, as well as the rank order of importance of those elements, may vary by clientele. It is equally true that costs differ by party. The opportunity cost to a physician of expending additional time with a patient or members of the patient's family is quite different from the direct cost to a hospital of the resources consumed in the carrying out of the doctor's orders occasioned by that extra time spent understanding the patient's needs. The cost to the hospital for those resources is quite different from what the hospital may receive from an external payer: billed charges, discounted charges, cost plus or minus, or a regulated rate such as a Medicare prospective payment using the DRG system, none of which is likely to match the actual premium plus deductibles and copayments paid by that patient or that patient's employer currently or in the past. RBRVS rates for physicians under Medicare bear no more relationship to real resource use in caring for a patient than do DRG rates for hospitals, even though both relate quite directly to real government costs.

Thus, it is necessary to specify not only a quality perspective (individual, micro-aggregate, macro-aggregate), but also a cost/quality viewpoint that must identify the clientele whose perspective is to be examined. The potential viewpoints include many divergent possibilities, such as patient, taxpayer, employer, Office of Management and Budget, HCFA, shareholder, not-for-profit hospital administrator, attending physician, patient's family, reviewer of outcomes or amounts of service, malpractice insurer, and more.

Cost/Quality Interactions

A number of generalizations that transcend both the quality perspective and the cost viewpoint can be made with respect to cost/quality relationships. For example, the maximalist school would suggest that additional quality will always result from additional resources dedicated to health care. Traditionally, many physicians have behaved in ways consistent with this view.[19] The hypothetical relationship is illustrated by Curve A in figure 1, page 189. At polar extreme would be the minimalist school, represented by some religious sects that believe no intervention is best and that any use of resources reduces quality of life and spirit. Curve B in figure 1 would represent such a position.

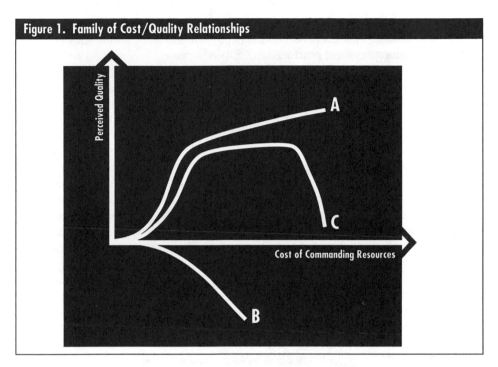

Figure 1. Family of Cost/Quality Relationships

Perceived Quality (vertical axis)

Cost of Commanding Resources (horizontal axis)

A

C

B

The optimalist school states that quality increases only to a finite maximum as more and more resources are applied, and declines thereafter (Curve C in figure 1). The extra laboratory test, the sixth stool guaiac, and the additional respiratory therapy treatment increase costs but may add little to the certainty of the diagnosis or to the likelihood of recovery. Their elimination may have no significant adverse effect on morbidity or mortality,[20,21] and their inclusion provides no salutary results. Indeed, quality ultimately declines because of iatrogenic outcomes, nosocomial events, or physical discomfort. Perceptions of quality may decrease because of psychological reactions to cost or to the environment in which diagnosis or treatment is administered. The family of cost/quality relationships must also embrace the spectrum of unnecessary surgery, improper prescriptions, and incorrect treatment, where the patient is compromised or harmed even as costs increase. It is in this broader context that we offer Curve C in figure 1.

The family of cost/quality relationships incorporates two types of quality-related costs: the cost of "feature" quality and the cost of poor quality.[22] Feature quality is defined as characteristics of a product or service that are desired by the customer. Examples in health care may include ambiance of waiting areas, extended hours of service, special meals for new families, or a parking garage. In general, they add to the expense of the service but tend to increase sales. Costs of poor quality, on the other hand, may be thought of as the expenses of not doing it right the first time. When identified and eliminated, these root causes of poor quality decrease the expense of production and increase quality.

Curve C conceptually incorporates elements of all of the relationships described above. We suggest that such a curve must ultimately describe all cost/quality relationships, regardless of viewpoint or perspective, particularly as public awareness of cost/quality relationships and provider competition increase.

For any cost viewpoint/quality perspective, resource allocation decisions are made that result in cost/quality combinations within the area under Curve C. These decisions are subject to two major constraints. The first constraint relates to quality and establishes a lower limit below which activity simply cannot consistently occur over the longer term without system failure (Line A in figure 2, page 191). Depending on viewpoint, this absolute floor is largely set by such activities, entities, or conditions as licensure, accreditation standards, the legal (tort) liability system, public accountability, reputation, utilization review mechanisms, union contracts and competitive labor markets, medical standards, the referral marketplace, morbidity and mortality outcomes, and ethics. It represents the product-based notion of acceptable outcomes. The position of the quality floor may be moved higher on the quality axis upon the initiative and at the discretion of decision makers having a particular perspective (e.g., physicians, managers, Congress, JCAHO).

The second major constraint is financial. From the economist's point of view, this constraint represents the point between the preservation and the consumption of capital. In a more immediate sense, it represents the crossover between solvency and insolvency (Line B in figure 2). Whatever the source of funds (fees, revenue, appropriations, gifts, grants, etc.) for a particular viewpoint, there is some level of cost so large that there is no possibility of its being covered by incoming funds. To incur costs beyond what can be covered guarantees system collapse within a funding/asset life cycle. Proponents of budget caps/global budgeting under "managed competition" would argue that inefficiencies in the current health care system are consuming payers' capital to a degree that will lead to the economic collapse of business, and that the solution is to fix Line B in place or even move it to the left, forcing inefficiencies out of the health care system.

Government rate regulation of some or all of the marketplace (e.g., Medicare's Prospective Payment System or RBRVS rate-setting for physicians, various state-level all-payer mechanisms, or the prospective rate-setting imbedded in several health reform proposals) defines the position of the solvency constraint along the cost axis. It is immediately apparent, of course, that centrally planned manipulation of this constraint in the name of "cost control" may simultaneously affect "quality control" by denying to the market (consumers) at least some higher levels of quality.

The area under that portion of the cost/quality curve above and to the left of the acceptable quality and solvency constraints represents all apparently feasible cost/quality combinations, which are re-depicted in figure 3, page 191. The cost/quality curve itself is the upper boundary of the area and corresponds to Garvin's notion of affordable excellence. It describes the maximum quality that can be achieved for a given expenditure of resources and the minimum cost at which a given level of quality can be realized. The curve further represents the maximum achievable cost/quality efficiency within each perspective and, as such, can be viewed as a process or technology constraint. As knowledge and technology expand, of course, we would naturally expect this boundary of "the possible" to shift upward and to the left, presenting an

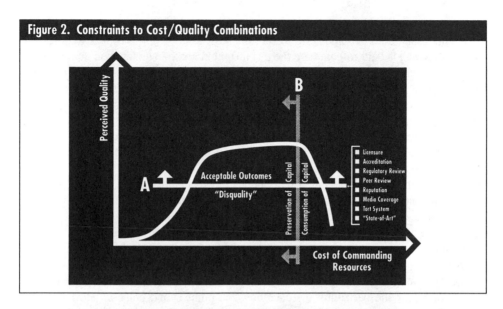

Figure 2. Constraints to Cost/Quality Combinations

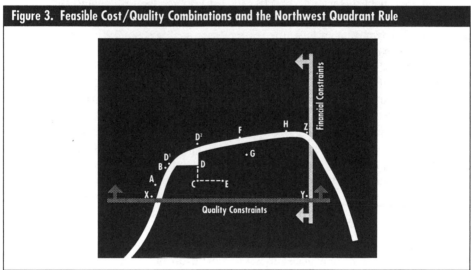

Figure 3. Feasible Cost/Quality Combinations and the Northwest Quadrant Rule

ever-moving cost/quality efficiency target. Any point within the area bounded by these three constraints (acceptable quality, solvency, and technology) represents less efficiency and less than achievable quality for the resources expended.

Cost/Quality Efficiency and Cost-Effectiveness

Regardless of cost viewpoint or quality perspective, a major goal for all decision makers is to make cost-effective choices. If each of the points labeled "A" through "H" in figure 3 represents a cost/quality combination within the feasible area XYZ, certain obvious guides for decision makers emerge. Primary among these is the "northwest quadrant rule." Any cost/quality combination to the left of or above a given combination (i.e., to the "northwest") is said to dominate the given combination. A combination due "west" of the given combination offers "identical" amounts of quality for less cost and is, therefore, obviously preferred; one due "north" of the given combination offers higher quality for identical cost and, likewise, dominates any choice between the two. Any combination both "north" and "west" of the given combination offers both higher quality and lower cost and hence dominates any comparison with the given combination. Thus, in figure 3, G is dominated by F; E by B, C, and D; C by B and D; and Z by F and H. D is inferior to any combination in the shaded area of figure 3 and is ultimately dominated by the D^1 to D^2 portion of the cost/quality curve that bounds the shaded area. Hence, only X, A, B, D^1, D^2, F, H, and all other points on the cost/quality curve to the left of H are undominated.

It is in this context that we can endorse the statements of some[23,24] that "quality costs no more" or that "quality is cheaper—doing it right the first time costs less." Quality improvement, system redesign, and quality planning focus on reducing the costs of nonconformance to standards, which are represented by the line of "undominated" points extending from A to H in figure 3. The maximum cost of nonconformance to standards is symbolized by the horizontal distance between point D and point D^1. Moving to any "undominated" point between D^1 and D^2 will cost less *and* improve quality. Only moving to D^2 improves quality without also saving money, while a move to D^1 maintains existing quality while maximizing savings. The costs of poor quality can *always* be reduced if the starting point is one such as D—one of cost/quality inefficiency.

Cost and quality are related, but that relationship is less than direct when functioning at points of cost/quality inefficiency. A direct relationship exists only when cost/quality efficiency is realized. Indeed, it is the set of efficient cost/quality combinations constituting the cost/quality curve that define that relationship. The characteristic shared by combinations X, A, B, D^1, D^2, F, H, and all other points on the cost/quality curve to the left of H (representing maximum attainable quality) is that no point on that boundary is dominated by any other. Each is "economically efficient" in cost/quality terms, and, collectively, they represent the efficient cost/quality frontier running from X through H.

Doubilet *et al.* have cautioned against misuse of the term "cost-effective," suggesting that its use be restricted to those instances where obtaining the additional health care benefit is worth the additional cost.[25] We cannot concur. In the context of our model, a cost-effective decision is any decision that moves the provider toward greater cost/quality efficiency, i.e., any northwest-moving choice. Problem-solving using the tools of CQI may be viewed as making northwest-moving choices (NWMC). Reduction of a cost of poor quality not only reduces expense to the customer, but also increases quality.

If hospital-acquired wound infections are reduced by a reallocation of existing resources (e.g., improved protocols derived from CQI programs), an NWMC direction is set, and cost-effectiveness is increased. There has been no cost/quality tradeoff. Ultimately, however, eliminating *all* hospital-acquired wound infections involves decisions that may mandate such tradeoffs. If the hospital has eliminated 99.5 percent of all such infections using standard protocols and procedures, it might be at point D^2 on figure 3. Point F might represent 99.9 percent elimination and point H 100 percent elimination of such infections, but each is attainable only with substantial additional cost to the hospital, which ultimately increases costs to patients or to other payers.

Once the technological boundary is reached and cost/quality efficiency is attained, the term "cost-effective" is no longer meaningful. Cost cannot be reduced without also reducing quality, and quality cannot be enhanced without incurring additional cost. There cannot be a meaningful cost/quality tradeoff unless cost/quality efficiency has already been achieved (through a series of cost-effective decisions); once these tradeoffs are required, cost effectiveness as a criterion must be supplemented by the judgments of the various clienteles who bear the resulting costs and enjoy the resulting benefits.[26]

As suggested above, increased public awareness of cost and quality considerations, combined with increased competition for market share within the health care sector, should ultimately force the system from the interior of the feasible region to the efficient frontier, as decision-makers follow the dictates of the northwest quadrant rule.

Cost/Quality Tradeoffs

What are ultimately more interesting, of course, are decisions that, once cost/quality efficiency has been achieved, involve moves to the northeast (should additional cost be borne to increase quality?) or to the southwest (should quality be lowered to reduce costs?)

Indeed, the entire concept of an efficient frontier having more than a single cost/quality combination gives lie to the mythology of "a single class of care." Market segmentation can easily be defined as targeting distinct cost/quality combinations, and the choice of *where* in a particular perspective one wants to be along the cost/quality frontier is a question of great economic and political significance.

Thurow[27] raised this question, suggesting a multitiered system reflecting the notion that, systemwide, patients will receive the quality they are capable of bargaining or paying for. An expansion of this notion is shown in figure 4, below. Note that this depiction

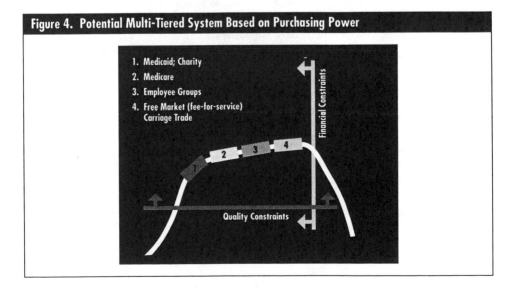

Figure 4. Potential Multi-Tiered System Based on Purchasing Power

1. Medicaid; Charity
2. Medicare
3. Employee Groups
4. Free Market (fee-for-service) Carriage Trade

Financial Constraints

Quality Constraints

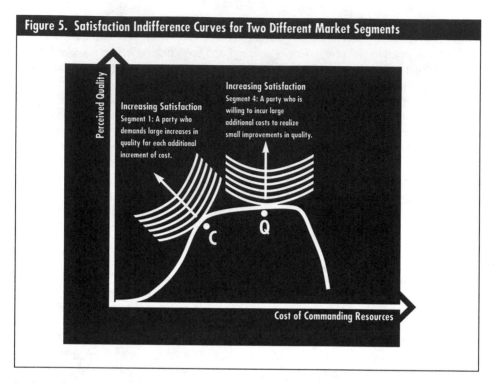

Figure 5. Satisfaction Indifference Curves for Two Different Market Segments

Perceived Quality

Increasing Satisfaction
Segment 1: A party who demands large increases in quality for each additional increment of cost.

Increasing Satisfaction
Segment 4: A party who is willing to incur large additional costs to realize small improvements in quality.

C

Q

Cost of Commanding Resources

is that of an economist looking at quality with a macro-aggregate perspective and at cost from a system viewpoint. It should *not* be interpreted to suggest that any *individual* provider entity would apply differential resources to patients based on expected payment from or on behalf of the patient.

Rather, individual providers may well be advised to choose a market niche that targets one of these market segments and to abandon the strategy of attempting to be all things to all patients. Economic reality suggests that it is only reasonable to concentrate on that portion of a market that will be satisfied on a reasonably consistent basis with a particular range of efficient cost/quality combinations.

Figure 5, above, depicts satisfaction indifference curves for two very different market segments. Segment 1 may represent the payment mechanisms society puts in place for the medically indigent. This societal perspective tends to be highly cost-adverse, constraining covered services, and is most "satisfied" at point C on the cost/quality curve. Providers choosing to serve this market must tailor their activities to the social, economic, and medical characteristics of this segment. Health care services provided through welfare programs are examples of this market segment.

By contrast, Segment 4 might reflect the "carriage trade," quality-seekers who are willing to pay for the search and who achieve maximum satisfaction at cost/quality combination Q. Some providers will undoubtedly choose to function in this market to the exclusion of others, reflecting the market's prestige as well as its economic attributes. Affluent residents of other countries who travel great distances to receive care are part of this market segment.

Conclusion

Many cost containment efforts in health care have been based on utilization review. The use of preadmission certification, second surgical opinions, and length-of-stay reviews largely applies the northwest quadrant rule, relying on an assumption that excessive resources are being consumed for a given quality level. The attention thus paid to cost may have been somewhat successful in controlling the rate of increase in health care costs, but questions about the resulting quality effects are being raised.[1,28,29,30,31] Quality of care is the single most important factor in deciding where to go for health care,[32] yet there is clear evidence that the health care system already has multiple tiers, which are distinguished by the relative importance different quality care elements are given and/or by external fiscal realities.[27]

Our conceptual model should serve as a useful tool in communicating these market realities to numerous publics. Figure 4, page 193 suggests that selected marketplace segments may be arrayed in different positions along the cost/quality efficiency frontier, based on the cost/quality trade-offs that have been made, either explicitly or implicitly. Policy makers at both institutional and national levels should be aware that all parties to the decision-making process may be forced to choose from among those segments as resources become more constrained.

For example, taken in isolation, the Medicaid reality may well be as shown in figure 6, below, where welfare or "social safety net" policy depresses the quality constraint and/or state-level constitutional requirements for balanced budgets shift the fiscal constraint to the left. The Oregon Medicaid experiment is an excellent example of these processes at work in an open, explicit way. Public hearings establish priorities among services and categories of case and the legislature chooses how far down the priority

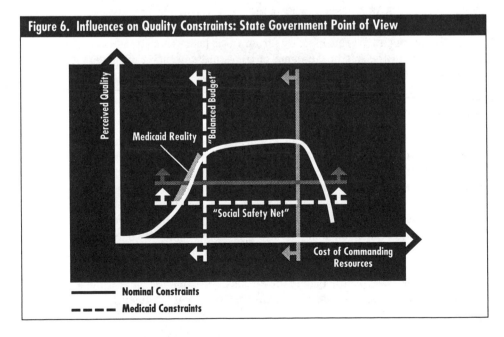

Figure 6. Influences on Quality Constraints: State Government Point of View

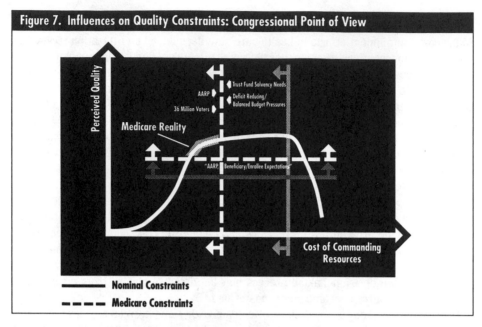

Figure 7. Influences on Quality Constraints: Congressional Point of View

Perceived Quality

Trust Fund Solvency Needs

AARP

Deficit Reducing/
Balanced Budget Pressures

36 Million Voters

Medicare Reality

"AARP, Beneficiary/Enrollee Expectations"

Cost of Commanding
Resources

——— Nominal Constraints

— — — Medicare Constraints

list it is willing to fund. This would contrast with figure 7, above, depicting Medicare reality. The American Association of Retired Persons (AARP) is possibly the most powerful political lobby in Washington. Its influence with both the Congress and the Executive Branch probably elevates the quality constraint by, for example, insisting that Medicare extend the range of covered services to include organ replacement. Simultaneously, AARP pushes against the fiscal constraint by opposing any policies that would limit access to care or drive providers from the market. This is mitigated by legislative or executive branch philosophy or fiscal policy that attempts to move the fiscal constraint to the left in the name of trust fund solvency and/or deficit reduction objectives that often override health policy.

Limitations and Directions for Further Research

By observing the effects of adding or withdrawing resources, one can estimate where a provider has been positioned along the cost/quality efficient frontier or within the feasible region at a previous time. Objective determination of a current cost/quality position is more difficult than *ex post* analysis unless there is a known historical "track." Even if absolute positions can reasonably be estimated, however, ascertaining position relative to the technological boundary (cost/quality efficient frontier) may be problematical. Not only is the shape and position of the entire boundary hard to estimate for a given provider, but, at best, the points on that boundary in our figures represent only central tendencies of distributions. These distributions often exhibit significant dispersion in both the cost and the quality dimensions, reflecting the natural range of disease processes and human response to them as well as to their treatment.

Nonetheless, applying this model at the micro-economic level, where expectations and values can be better assessed, can provide important input for provider positioning in the marketplace. While application at the macro-economic level suffers from the weaknesses of all generalizations, it should serve as a means of communicating with the numerous publics affected by public policy decisions.

Additional research into quantification and measurement of quality is needed. Finding agreement on the elements of quality and their relative importance will be important, at least within each clientele's viewpoint and at each level of focus. If quality is the manageable aspect of health care suggested by Ellwood[28] and if quality continues to appear as a major variable in employer health service purchasing, in provider marketing, and in public policy discussions, agreement on its component parts and on their relationships to cost will be critical, first, to achieving cost/quality efficient health care within our society and, second, to making open and well-informed choices on cost/quality trade-offs.

References

1. Reinhardt, U. "Quality of Care in Competitive Markets." *Business and Health* 3(8):7-9, July-Aug, 1986.

2. *Illinois PRO Objective Summary.* Peoria, Ill.: Mid-State Foundation for Medical Care, Inc., 1986.

3. Kassiner, J. "The Quality of Care and the Quality of Measuring It." *New England Journal of Medicine* 329 (17):1263-5, Oct. 21, 1993.

4. Brook, R., and Williams, K. "Quality of Health Care for the Disadvantaged." *Journal of Community Health* 1(2):132-56, Winter 1975.

5. Donabedian, A. "What is Quality?" Lecture, Center for Health Services and Policy Research, Northwestern University, Evanston, Ill., Oct. 6-7, 1986.

6. Billmeyer, D., and others. "Quality Care." *JAMA* 256(8):1032-4, Aug. 22-29, 1986.

7. Rose, J. "Americans Call for Affordable, Accessible, Quality Health Care." *American Family Physician* 33(4):97, April 1986.

8. Elbeik, M. "Perceptions of Hospital Care." *Health Management Forum* 7(1):70-8, Spring 1986.

9. Donabedian, A. *The Definition of Quality and Approaches to Its Assessment.* Ann Arbor, Mich.: Health Administration Press, 1980, pp. 8-64.

10. *The Genuine Work of Hippocrates*, translated from the Greek by Francis Adams. Baltimore, Md.: Williams and Wilkins, 1939.

11. Garvin, D. "What Does Product Quality Really Mean?" *Sloan Management Review* 26(1):25-43, Fall 1984.

12. Ware, J., and Snyder, M. "Dimensions of Patient Attitudes Regarding Doctors and Medical Services." *Medical Care* 13(8):669-82, Aug. 1975

13. Sanazaro, P., and Williamson, J. "A Classification of Physician Performance in Internal Medicine." *Journal of Medical Education* 43(3):389-97, Mar. 1968.

14. See, for example, our study of physician-executives' rankings of these elements across a variety of care scenarios: "Toward a Definition of Quality." *Physician Executive* 15(5):7-11, Sept.-Oct. 1989.

15. Juran, J., and Gryna, F. *Juran's Quality Control Handbook.* New York, N.Y.: McGraw-Hill, 1988, pp. 4,23.

16. Crosby, P. *Quality Is Free.* New York, N.Y.: Mentor Books, 1979.

17. Juran, J. *Total Quality Management.* Juran Institute, Inc., Wilton, Conn., 1990, pp. 1-29.

18. The elements of this model are based on a presentation by Professor Long to the faculty and students of the Hospital Administration Program in the School of Public Health at the University of Michigan in 1973. Thereafter, Professor Long used this model as part of his presentation in the "Physician in Management" seminars sponsored by the American Academy of Medical Directors (now the American College of Physician Executives) and originally funded by a grant from the Robert Wood Johnson Foundation.

19. Indeed, it is arguable that the Hippocratic Oath sets forth the value that every physician is obligated to do everything within his or her professional capacity that is of affirmative benefit to the patient (independent of the "cost" of "everything"—Hippocrates was silent on the use of cost/benefit analysis).

20. Neuhauser, D., and Lewicki, A. "What Do We Gain from the Sixth Stool Guaiac?" *New England Journal of Medicine* 293(5):226-8, July 31, 1975.

21. Zibrak, J., and others. "Effects of Reductions in Respiratory Therapy on Patient Outcome." *New England Journal of Medicine* 315(5):292-5, July 31, 1986.

22. Juran, J. *Planning for Quality.* Juran Institute, Inc., 1990, p. 5-5.

23. Winchell, J. "Reduced Costs Can Improve Care." *Health Care* 27(7):15-20, Oct. 1985.

24. McClure, W. "Buying Right: How to Do It." *Business and Health* 2(10):41-44, Oct. 1985.

25. Doubilet, P., and others. "Use and Misuse of the term 'Cost-Effective' in Medicine." *New England Journal of Medicine* 314(4):254-56, Jan 23, 1986.

26. Russell, L. "Balancing Cost and Quality: Methods of Evaluation." *Bulletin of the New York Academy of Medicine* 62(1):55-60, Jan.-Feb. 1986.

27. Thurow, L. "Medicine Versus Economics." *New England Journal of Medicine* 313(10):611-14, Sept. 5, 1985.

28. Ellwood, P., and Paul, B. "Commentary: But What about Quality?" *Health Affairs* 5(1):135-40, Spring 1986.

29. Rettig, P., and Paul, B. "Value, Not Just Costs, Need to Be Considered for Quality Managed Care." *Business and Health* 4(6):64, April 1987.

30. Jensen, J. "More Consumers Are Willing to Pay Higher Price for Quality Healthcare." *Modern Healthcare* 16(17):48-9, Aug. 15, 1986.

31. "Medicine: A Special Report: Declining Quality of Care for the Elderly is Hinted in New Studies, Which Blame Cuts in Medicare for the Situation." *Wall Street Journal* 210(37):1, Aug. 20, 1987.

32. "HMQ Survey: A Mandate of High-Quality Health Care." *Health Management Quarterly*, Fourth Quarter 1986, pages 3-6.

Robert B. Klint, MD, MHA, FACPE, is President & CEO of the Swedish American Health System, Rockford, Ill. Hugh W. Long, MBA, PhD, JD, is Associate Professor of Health Care Management, Department of Health Systems Management, Tulane University, New Orleans, Louisiana.

Medical Informatics and the Physician Executive

CHAPTER

14

by *Marshall DeG. Ruffin Jr., MD, MBA, FACPE*

Medical informatics shortly will be to physician executives what gasoline is to automobiles. Medical informatics is the systematic study, or science, of the identification, collection, storage, communication, retrieval, and analysis of data about medical care services to improve decisions made by physicians and managers of health care organizations. Medical informatics will be as important to physicians and medical managers as the rules of financial accounting are to auditors. The health care industry is close to a revolution in the ways it uses informatics technologies to manage patients and resources. This chapter will elucidate these trends and their significance for physician executives.

Medical information technologies, subsumed under medical informatics, will transform medical care services just as the same technologies have transformed the financial services and banking industries, the airline and travel industries, and military weapons systems. There is no subject matter more important for physician executives to grasp than medical informatics, because the single largest investment by health care organizations in the next 10 years will be in medical informatics technologies—transaction systems, decision support systems, and telecommunication networks to create the nervous systems of integrated health care systems.

Information processing technologies are increasingly important to help providers and their organizations measure outcomes for their patients and to compete for customers. Employer coalitions, regulatory agencies, and insurers are demanding measurable proof from providers that patients have acceptable clinical outcomes at competitive costs. And they are starting to take matters of data definition and data collection into their own hands through a number of related initiatives, all meant to define a standard database of clinical outcomes that all providers will be expected to collect. For instance, the employer coalition in Cleveland established a data set of several hundred indicators of hospital performance, and it expects that all hospitals that provide health care services to those employers' health care beneficiaries will collect those data. In Pennsylvania, the state legislature, several years ago, required that all hospitals collect the MedisGroups hospital inpatient data from all inpatient records of discharged patients. And the federal government, in the Health Care Financing Administration, has created the Uniform Clinical Data Set, which is meant to produce a common clinical database for all U.S. hospital patients insured by Medicare. In 1993, it is being implemented on a 10 percent sample of Medicare patients discharged from hospitals, more than 2,000,000 records in all. The Uniform Clinical Data Set requires, on average, about 90 minutes to abstract one chart. There are some 1,600 data elements that may be filled out on each patients, though the average is 300-400 per patient. The enormous expense of such laborious retrospective chart abstraction is offset by the value of having a standardized dataset with which the outcomes of care of hospitals can be compared.

As providers' incomes depend less on managing revenues from patients (by setting charges) and more on managing costs of care (because providers' prices are fixed by the competitive market or government fiat), information technologies will be increasingly important to them. Information technologies generally are for cost management. On a small scale, personal computers with word-processing software and printers reduce the cost of preparing text for printing. On a huge scale, worldwide networks of thousands of computers and printers make it affordable to send a package overnight almost anywhere in the world, to buy and sell securities, or get cash from a cash machine, anywhere, any time. They manage the intricate robotic assembly lines that manufacture computers, washing machines, and automobiles, reducing the costs of assembly. They manage the tabulation of the national census every 10 years, the calculation of millions of tax refunds each year, and the bank balances of millions of people every day, and they reduce the costs of producing laboratory tests and of monitoring patients' vital signs in hospitals.

Physicians and hospitals are joining forces in a rush to create PHOs (physician-hospital organizations) all across the nation. One reason for the aggregation into larger vertically integrated delivery systems is to agree on contracting strategies with payers, on information about patients they will share, and on telecommunication and decision support systems that may help them in contracting and cost management. It is important to recognize that telecommunications networks by which physicians obtain laboratory information about inpatients and radiology interpretations on line; enter orders for hospitalized patients; check the eligibility of patients for insurance coverage; communicate by electronic mail with utilization review organizations; send electronic mail consultations, with clinical data, from one physician to another; and access computer-based records of current and historical data about their patients that hospitals may have created are now available.

All these services become more valuable to both physicians and hospitals as they are used more. With greater use, there are more opportunities for electronic communication. Integration of providers into vertical health care delivery systems then permits the sharing of capital and agreement to standards for information and communication systems that make a community health care network possible. And the communication, transaction, and decision support systems that providers can share by joining a vertically integrated health care delivery system (IHCS) make joining that system much more appealing in the first place.

In the next several pages we will analyze market research performed for a vertically integrated health care delivery system in New Mexico. Presbyterian Healthcare Services surveyed benefits managers and directors of human resources for a number of large employers in Albuquerque and asked them what they wanted in the way of services from the health delivery network that they offer to their health care beneficiaries. In Albuquerque, there are four relatively mature health care delivery networks of organized and competing providers that contend for the health care business. One is based in the Lovelace Clinic and Hospital, a large HMO (more than 200,000 covered lives) that CIGNA now owns. The second is Presbyterian Healthcare Services, made up of several hospitals in Albuquerque, a large HMO, and several hundred closely affiliated physicians. The third is evolving from the University of New Mexico Medical Center, and the fourth is emerging out of St. Joseph's Hospital in Albuquerque.

When the benefits managers were asked to identify particularly desirable characteristics of a provider network that would strongly attract their business, they answered with six responses. In the following discussion, each response is listed and the informatics technologies required to accomplish the goals set out by the benefits managers are described.

A patient—by telephone or in person at a walk-in clinic, physician's office, ambulatory diagnostic center, or the hospital—can be quickly identified as an individual we have served before or as a brand new customer.

To identify an individual uniquely, and reliably, at any location of care requires a telecommunications network linking all locations of care to a master patient index. Summary demographic information would need to accompany the unique patient identifiers. In physicians' offices, urgent care centers, hospital wards, nursing homes, home health agencies, and pharmacies, among other locations where patients are treated within the delivery system, there must be computer equipment that can allow trained users to communicate over the network. An investment of millions of dollars is needed to establish a network that links hundreds of locations of care for thousands of patients. If the network has limited services, say giving users only access to simple demographic information about patients, it is unlikely that many target locations for the network, especially physicians' offices, will be willing to invest in equipment, software, and training to use the network. The network must offer a critical number of valuable services conveniently, or not enough people will use it to make it worth the investment.

The patient's lab tests and imaging results can be transported electronically as the patient is referred within the IHCS, thus eliminating the need for costly and inconvenient repetition of diagnostic tests.

In order to transport patients' lab tests and imaging results electronically within the integrated health care system, so that physicians without paper records of test results do not have to duplicate them, requires sophisticated informatics technologies. Laboratory, radiology, and pharmacy systems, along with patient care systems for hospitals, need interfaces to the network so that information produced by transaction systems flows onto the network and is available to providers who need them.

Fee-for-service indemnity insurance has paid providers to perform procedures, including diagnostic tests, and not paid them to invest in technologies to reduce redundancy in procedures performed. Managed competition and other methods for payment of organized groups of providers to care for populations of people over time under fixed budgets leads providers to invest in systems to reduce redundancy and to provide the most cost-effective, efficient, and effective health care services possible. Under capitation, the regional communications network linking all providers becomes strategically important and valuable in reducing costs. Previously, it was seen as an expense for which providers could not be reimbursed.

In this scenario, at a minimum the radiology reports of diagnostic imaging studies would be available to providers on the network as soon as they were transcribed. Ideally, the images themselves would be available over the network, so physicians could evaluate the images and the radiologists' interpretations of them in their offices, moments after they are performed. Images in electronic form never get lost, can be seen in more than one place at the same time, and do not need to be repeated, unless a physician wants to follow the temporal transformation of an image, such as a resolving pneumonia.

In order to send images promptly, the network needs to be faster than standard telephone lines. Leased telephone lines, integrated services digital network (ISDN), microwave, satellite, and the new broadband frame relay technologies (asynchronous transfer mode) make possible networks capable of sending high-resolution chest x-ray images in seconds, rather than the 12-15 minutes needed to transmit them over standard telephone lines. For transmission over the network, images need to be in digital form. Computer files need to be stored on large optical drives, or jukeboxes of drives, for effective retrieval. Laboratory results and radiology and pathology interpretations need to be stored in electronic form in their respective transaction systems in order for those pieces of information to be available over the telecommunications network. Even if the images and their text descriptions are captured and stored in digital format and those systems are available for inquiry over the network, there must be powerful personal computers, or workstations, with high-resolution monitors attached to the network and personnel trained to use them if the images are to be useful to anyone. There is a large investment in infrastructure required to make a network useful.

The same information can be viewed simultaneously by members of a quickly formed team of specialists functioning in separate locations but able to consult on the diagnosis and course of treatment for complex cases.

Patients do not like having to schedule appointments with subspecialists, wait days to weeks for consultations, and carry records and x-rays with them when they visit consultants. They want their physicians to talk about their care promptly, as they often do in large multispecialty group practices, where physicians share office space, medical records, diagnostic laboratories, diagnostic imaging centers, and film libraries. Ideally, patients would have physicians communicate immediately when one physician wants the opinion of another in selecting a diagnosis and a course of treatment. Telecommunications technology permits simultaneous consultation between physicians miles apart, and even the sharing of diagnostic images between them. This form of communication among physicians is an application of video teleconferencing, which is subsumed by the term telemedicine. Patients may be willing to wait days for a second opinion or a consultation, but the health care system that offers the most opportunities for teleconferencing between physicians may be the one that attracts the most subscribers. At least, that is what this survey suggests.

The Mayo Clinic has installed medical teleconferencing suites, which it calls telediagnostic rooms, in its satellite clinics in Scottsdale, Arizona, and Jacksonville, Florida, so that patients treated at those satellites can have the full power of the Mayo Clinic at their disposal. The telediagnostic rooms are used for telemedicine and administrative conferences between the satellites and the main clinic in Rochester, Minnesota. The Mayo Clinic did not install them with the expectation that it could cover their costs with billable services. It installed them to send a message to the communities of Scottsdale and Jacksonville that they had access to the full resources of the Mayo Clinic. In so doing, it helped distinguish Mayo physicians from other physicians practicing in the community who could not communicate directly with subspecialists in a world-renowned medical center.

Teleradiology and telepathology have proven their value in many studies. Teleradiology can reduce the time for a radiologist to overread an x-ray obtained, and initially interpreted, by a primary care physician or public health nurse in a remote primary clinic or an inner-city hospital. Telepathology permits general pathologists at small community hospitals to discuss unusual biopsy specimens with renowned subspecialist pathologists at major medical centers—to distinguish amelanotic melanomas from benign skin lesions and liposarcomas from lipomas for instance. In Albuquerque, the purchasers of care are saying that, all else being equal, the medical delivery network that uses advanced telecommunications to reduce the time patients must wait for physicians to confer and determine a diagnosis and a treatment is the medical delivery system they will select for their health care beneficiaries.

Documented quality outcomes demonstrate continuous improvement in all IHCS locations.

This is the most important requirement for health care delivery systems to address and satisfy. Purchasers of care, represented by coalitions of employers in many major urban areas, and individual employers represented by benefits consultants are demanding more data from providers about the outcomes of care for their patients. Purchasers of health care services know, now, that they must establish standards for the data collected by providers if they are to compare the results of one provider with those of others. That is why the Health Care Financing Administration has created the Uniform Clinical Data Set and has asked all professional review organizations to abstract a 10 percent sample of hospital records of Medicare beneficiaries with the UCDS. Similarly, Pennsylvania and Colorado have mandated that hospitals collect information on hospitalized patients using the MedisGroups system. A large coalition of major employers in Cleveland, Ohio, has mandated collection of data on inpatients by all hospitals and is using the results to compare the value of hospital care. Payers are contracting with hospitals using those data to establish fair comparisons of the performance of those hospitals.

There are many other examples. Most large insurers have been collecting and integrating claims data for years. They have just recently begun to use those databases to compare physicians' and hospitals outcomes of care. Blue Cross and Blue Shield of the National Capital Area has produced a sophisticated analytical system called ProFile that compares the risk-adjusted performance of physicians. They have used it to eliminate one-third of physicians in greater Washington from their new PPO products, which are predicted to have an enrollment of more than 500,000 health care beneficiaries of the federal government by the end of 1993. All payers are beginning to recognize that they cannot hope to control health care costs by contracting with all providers in a community, asking discounts from them, and then imposing burdensome, and expensive, regulatory utilization management functions on them. Aetna, Prudential, and many other insurers have begun to use their large databases of claims to identify physicians with "efficient" practice habits and to contract only with them, excluding others from their increasingly selective provider networks.

If providers cannot measure what they do for patients and cannot prove that their outcomes are as good as, or better than, those their competitors achieve, they will have to compete for patients on price. You cannot improve what you cannot measure. Providers need to invest in the same sorts of systematic, standardized data collection and analysis that payers and employers have invested in to improve the outcomes of their patients and to prove that their services are valuable for employers.

Systematic data collection about the services they provide, and about patient outcomes, cannot be accomplished without standardized outcomes surveys for all patients, standardized financial and clinical cost accounting systems, an enterprisewide relational database for health services and clinical research, and powerful decision support systems for ad hoc analysis of data collected for severity of illness and case mix. Of utmost importance is a standard data dictionary, standard definitions for services rendered and outcomes obtained and their costs, so that outcomes can be compared among health care facilities and providers. All too often, different hospitals use different patient satisfaction surveys, so satisfaction measurements cannot be compared. And different physicians use different functional status surveys for patients so that their functional status three months postoperatively cannot be compared.

The value of a shared relational database may not be immediately obvious, but it is enormous. With a single database, there is one data model and one data dictionary. If data about services received, and outcomes obtained, by patients of various providers can be stored reliably in one database, they can be analyzed in an infinite number of ways to identify trends in the outcomes of groups of patients that suggest better or worse than expected clinical care. This sort of shared database is the basic resource essential for continuous quality improvement and effective managed care contracting for payers. Without shared data about the processes and outcomes of care, providers have no means for systematic improvement of what they do. The Mayo Clinic faithfully maintained medical records on all its patients, cross-referenced by diagnoses and procedures. With that invaluable data resource, it became preeminent in the world for studying and publishing the results of services for patients. In the same way, the clinical database and computer-based patient record for a provider network will be its most important asset for continuous quality improvement and effective management of the care of defined populations of people over time and under a fixed budget.

New economic relationships formed by previously independent IHCS members have eliminated the incentives to provide care in any setting except one that is appropriate and cost-effective. Perverse incentives under capitation also have been resolved.

By this statement, customers are asking that the providers of care reassure them that neither too much nor too little care is delivered. How can such reassurances be given? One way, perhaps the only way, is to define proper practice by simple guidelines and then to measure the processes of care to determine whether or not care is generally practiced according to those guidelines. The purchasers of care are persuaded that financial incentives significantly affect the practice habits of physicians and the policies and staffing of hospitals. They want to know that care is managed according to rules defining optimal practice that are independent of the way care is financed, and the only way to do so is to measure the services received by patients, by diagnosis and treatment, and compare them to generally accepted guidelines for treatment. What proportion of children of a certain age should have received certain immunizations? What proportion of women of a certain age should have received screening mammograms? What is the expected number of days in hospital, and the expected number of physical therapy visits, for patients with a specific total hip replacement? The answers to those questions must be defined, and the data from a particular delivery system must be assessed to compare actual with expected frequencies of treatments.

This approach is a version of scientific process control, and it is characteristic of self-improving systems. The discipline to collect process and outcome data for all patients, and the informatics resources to store, retrieve, and analyze those data are indispensable to the delivery system that wants to answer questions such as these satisfactorily. To identify variations from expected patterns that may warrant attention, expert systems embedded in the database become important. We can now automate surveillance of millions of data elements from large delivery systems to identify trends that indicate possibly superior or inferior care and warrant closer scrutiny.

Employers seek out the IHCS for custom-designed benefit packages that fully satisfy their employees and are also affordable.

Mass customization—using computer technologies to produce a large variety of styles and colors for consumer goods, from food to clothing to automobiles—is a hallmark of modern manufacturing. We like this variety in our lives, but providers find similar variety in health care benefits the bane of their existence because of the enormous variation in benefits, deductibles, prior authorization requirements for procedures, and different provider networks with which they must deal. Computers and telecommunications can relieve some of the administrative burden that managed care has placed on physicians' offices, especially primary care physicians' offices. If physicians' offices can obtain electronically, and in real time, eligibility information, billing instructions, preauthorization for procedures, and current lists of physicians approved by each plan, and submit claims electronically, much of the paper work and staff time spent on telephone calls to insurers may be eliminated, saving the practices money.

To accomplish these electronic communications requires a wide-area network linking all physicians' offices and other locations of care to payers' information systems, to other physicians' offices, and to employers. The goal of extending the wide-area network linking providers to employers and insurers and utilization review firms as well is to make communication with these other firms much more efficient. The intrusions of third parties into the medical care process disrupt the work of physicians' offices and add to their administrative costs. Connecting those third parties electronically makes the communications easier and may reduce the operating costs of practices somewhat.

Notice that the word "affordable" is the first indication that cost is important to the benefits managers surveyed by Presbyterian Healthcare Services. All the other responses deal with quality and value. This confirms for me that measurable benefits are valued much higher than cost. If providers cannot measure the value of their services and prove that their care is adequate, all they have to compete on is price. But if they can prove that some of their important outcomes are superior, they may be able to earn a substantial premium from payers that want them in their networks.

This brings us to a key concept in understanding the importance of medical informatics for physician executives. Because accountability and responsibility for patients' outcomes is expected of providers by payers (employers and insurers), the information systems on which they will rely to manage effectively the care of defined populations of people over time will become the most important assets of their health care systems. In fact, the single most important asset of a health care delivery system, after the people caring for patients, is the computer-based patient record that the organization relies on for immediate patient care, cost control, and clinical quality improvement.

The three key categories of information technology that clinicians and managers will use to manage the care of their patients are transaction systems (clinical and administrative), communication systems, and decision support systems. Clinical transaction systems include patient care, nursing, laboratory, pharmacy, radiology, medical records, and appointment scheduling systems. Administrative systems include the most familiar information technologies in hospitals—batch-process accounts payable, accounts receivable, general ledger, cost-accounting, payroll, and materials management systems. Telecommunication systems include paging systems, links between terminals in hospitals and computers in separate buildings, telephone systems, enterprise networks linking all locations on the campus of a medical center, wide-area networks linking all computers of physicians and facilities in a metropolitan area, and the more state-of-the-art systems for telemedicine: video teleconferencing, teleradiology, and telepathology.

Decision support systems are the least familiar to health care organizations, because, until recently, they have not felt the need for them. They have been able to pass their costs along to payers and cost-shift from Medicare, Medicaid, and uninsured patients to those with generous insurance. Now, however, with managed competition emerging and payers more successful in sharing financial risk for the care of patients with providers, the importance of keeping an accurate database of all the services, diagnoses, procedures, and outcomes of their care has grown dramatically. With those data in relational databases, retrospective analysis to assess the processes of care leading to the best outcomes is relatively simple. Software has proliferated to help providers measure severity of illness and case mix of their patients and to risk-adjust the outcomes of patients that they want to study. Tumor, transplant, and trauma registries have been developed to keep track of patients requiring specialized treatment in these areas. Statistics and neural network packages and expert systems (relying on rule-based logic) help providers discover important trends in the masses of data they now collect.

Providers of medical care are aggregating into integrated systems for economic and technological reasons. Their customers increasingly are corporations demanding services (capitation, risk-sharing, outcomes management, continuous quality improvement, detailed data on outcomes) that individual physicians, hospitals, and single-specialty group practices simple cannot provide. Value-added services that integrated systems can offer to physicians, such as standardized office practice systems, access to applications over wide-area communications networks, and data analysis on their own patients from research databases, are increasingly important to them, because their costs of managing patients are going up as micromanagement by insurers and data collection requirements by a wide variety of agencies are increasing.

Among the most important value-added products or services that physicians' practices want are information and communication technologies, because these hold the promise of expediting patient care and reducing some of the inefficiencies of dealing with managed care firms. Hospital managers and trustees need to appreciate that hospitals represent more than inpatient beds; they represent stores of capital that their boards and managers must allocate to the technologies for organized care and the infrastructure of integrated health care systems. That infrastructure will be defined more in terms of information and telecommunication systems and less in terms of physical facilities. The hospital is becoming a necessary cost center in an integrated health care system, and the information and communication systems that the hospital may help to develop are becoming the principal strategic competitive assets of that integrated system of care.

Marshall DeG. Ruffin Jr., MD, MBA, FACPE, is Clinical Information Officer, INOVA Health Systems, Springfield, Virginia, and CEO, The Informatics Institute.

Marketing as a Necessary Function in Health Care Management: A Philosophical Approach

CHAPTER

15

by Eric N. Berkowitz, PhD

The changing competitive climate of health care during the past decade has led to greater sophistication in the management of medicine. One business function that has received greater attention in health care has been marketing, a traditional management tool.

The Evolution of Marketing

Common to many hospitals today is a director of marketing position. Yet, as late as 1976, fewer than 100 hospitals in the United States had marketing directors. While marketing is now more common, the marketing philosophy is not as well appreciated. Hospital and medical philosophy can be viewed as evolving to a marketing orientation over three phases.[1]

Phase 1—The Production Orientation. Through the 1970s, and for many hospitals today, the hospital has been a production-oriented institution. It might best be characterized by a mission statement such as: "We are a hospital providing high-quality medicine to the community. We must have physicians and nurses to provide it, just as we need administrators to keep the books." The focus of a hospital at this stage of its philosophical evolution is on the provision of "high quality." Providing high-quality services is the key force dominating all other hospital planning and strategy considerations.

Phase 2—The Sales Era. Of late, far more hospitals have moved to a second stage of philosophical evolution, sales. Hospitals have grown to recognize that there is competition for patients. Other hospitals, medical groups, and prepaid plans are but some of the providers striving to satisfy the medical needs of the community. At this point of organizational consciousness, the philosophical mission of the hospital could be paraphrased as: "We are a hospital providing a number of medical services to the market. We must have a first-rate public relations effort to encourage physicians in the community and patients to utilize our services to their fullest capacity." At this stage of evolution, the issue is one of capacity utilization. The goal is to fill beds. It is sales, not marketing, that is occurring at this point. The hospital develops an effective public relations effort to the community and provides staff breakfasts or orientations for the medical staff. All efforts are to stimulate demand to fill beds.

Phase 3—The Era of Marketing. While many hospitals have marketing directors, there are in fact few hospitals at this stage of philosophical evolution. It might best be described as: "We will assess the health care needs of the market and meet them." The focus of the organization is not on capacity to fill by attracting referrals. It is on attracting referrals through the provision of a needed service. In the third phase, the philosophical focus of the organization has shifted subtly, but importantly. Recall that, in the first phase (production), the organization's purpose was to provide medical care. In the second stage (sales), the organization develops strategies to fill beds. In the last phase of philosophical development (marketing), the organization exists to meet the health needs of the market, not as beds that are sold to the community. The health needs of the market determine the configuration of beds.

The Planning Process

To best understand the impact of a marketing philosophy on a hospital, it is important to consider the planning process undertaken by most health care groups. The typical hospital or group practice follows the nonmarketing planning approach described below.[2]

Nonmarketing Plan. Regardless of the industry, most organizations follow a similar planning sequence. Just a few words are usually dissimilar, which tends to make it appear that planning in one industry might be truly different from another. Consider the long-range planning process of a hospital. Figure 1, below, portrays the typical sequence in a nonmarketing planning approach. The first step is designating the mission. In most hospitals, the mission is global, such as, "Provide high-quality medicine to the community regardless of race, creed, religion, or ability to pay." The nonmarketing planning process really begins at the second step—specifying the strategy. Before discussing this stage, we will digress to consider the composition of those who define the hospital's strategy.

Most hospitals have long-range planning committees. Typically these committees are composed of a few members of the hospital board, the senior hospital administrator, and a department head or two. A few people are often more influential than others. These individuals might be termed the "hallway politicians." They are very effective at going door-to-door within the hospital, lining up votes for their programs or ideas.

Hallway politicians begin to exert their influence at the strategy stage. Strategy meetings are the crucial point at which the hospital must decide which two or three programs or areas will

Figure 1. Nonmarketing Planning Sequence

Mission/Goals

➡

Strategy

➡

Tactics

➡

Implementation

receive the attention and focus of management and, often, financial resources for the next few years. Several ideas are discussed at these sessions—starting a preferred provider organization (PPO), increasing the capacity of the laboratory to become one of regional stature, or building new facilities.

Within this scenario, a physician rises and proclaims his long-standing loyalty to the hospital. He notes that he has never admitted a patient to another facility. He may even cite his growing national stature as a futurist in the field of medicine. To him, the strategy for the future is clear, it is sports medicine (although any program can be substituted). It also happens that this physician is an orthopedic surgeon. Not everyone in the room may be as clear on this path for the future. Yet this physician had lined up his votes beforehand. The vote is 7 to 5 in favor of sports medicine. The hospital will commit its physical, financial, and personnel resources to establishing a sports medicine program in the ambulatory care wing of the hospital.

Tactics are the next stage of the planning process. This is when the hospital realizes there is no one in-house with expertise in sports medicine. A search firm is hired to scour the country for a director of sports medicine. A director is hired and conflict occurs. Any hospital has finite resources. New programs demand start-up dollars, and other departments find that their budget increase requests are put on hold. In many facilities, there is a space shortage. The appearance of a new program means that another department's space is reduced. Space and budget are two key sources of conflict in any hospital.

The fourth stage of the nonmarketing planning model is implementation. Before implementation occurs, however, an unsettling question suddenly arises among those in the administrative suites of most hospitals. "Where are the patients going to come from?" The hospital's public relations department is reminded that sports medicine is opening in 30 days, and a community open house is needed. The public relations director prints invitations and places an advertisement in the local newspaper announcing an open house for the new sports medicine program. The open house is held on a Sunday. Three people show up.

Four months later, the hospital finance committee meets to review the utilization of sports medicine relative to projections. It is discovered that sports medicine is not meeting expectations. Two explanations quickly surface. The first reason proposed for failure is simple. Public relations did a poor job, and there was not enough advertising. Occasionally, depending on the amount of capital invested and the size of the budget deficit, a second explanation is given. The director who was hired to run the program is not generating enough referrals. The question before the group is how to get rid of the director.

Both of these explanations are possible, but a third, competing explanation rarely is voiced. There is no need in the community for a sports medicine program. People who suffer sports-related injuries are satisfied with the treatment provided by their primary care physicians and by referrals to physical therapists. Physicians who treat sports-related injuries see no advantages in referrals to a program beyond what they are presently using. Alternatively, two or three sports medicine programs already exist in the area. The hospital's program is no different from (or better than) those of existing providers. The program will not make it.

Marketing-Based Planning. The alternative approach is one in which the impact of marketing can be seen. The two approaches are similar in many respects (figure 2, right). The first step is the same. Every organization, whether it is a hospital, a freestanding laboratory, or an automobile manufacturer, determines its own mission.

Figure 2. Marketing-Based Planning Sequence

The influence of marketing is felt in the second step. In the previous model, a group within the hospital determined strategies. In a market-based approach, the next step is to assess the needs of the market. This market could consist of physicians, patients, third-party payers, or corporations. Rather than deciding on an *a priori* basis to enter sports medicine, the purpose is to identify areas of need and to generate a significant competitive advantage over other providers. For example, in many areas, several endocrinology services are available for physician use. As the director looks for new opportunities, the question to pose to prospective referring physicians is, "What don't you like about the endocrinology group you now use?"

In a nonmarket-based planning model, the chief of endocrinology may act in the same way as the hallway politician described in the previous example. The chief may assume that he or she knows what the market needs or how it might want a service delivered. In a market-based example for sports medicine, a market-based approach might find that the incidence of injuries is not high, and sports medicine might be an area with little opportunity for establishing a differential advantage. The hospital might still decide to launch a program for other reasons, such as maintaining the loyalty of physicians for whom sports-related services must be produced. In this case, the marketing-based planning model might uncover little opportunity for sports medicine but a significant interest in the corporate community for an industrial medicine component with a strong toxicology program.

The third step in the market-based model is tactics. The assessment step would have defined the tactic, if the identified need (industrial medicine) matches the mission of the organization—high-quality medicine. In this case, an industrial medicine program would be consistent with the mission. Now the tactic is an internal challenge. Can the hospital put together an industrial medicine program that meets the market's expectations?

Figure 2 illustrates a second difference in the marketing model after the tactics stage. Before the hospital gets to full-scale implementation, the service must be pretested. Pretesting a service is more difficult than pretesting a product, where a company can make a prototype to test consumer reaction. Pretesting in a service industry entails pretesting the concept.

The provider meets with a group similar to the potential purchaser of the final service and in great detail describes how the service will be delivered, its price, and how the service can be accessed. The question to be proved with potential users is whether the described service is what they meant when they talked about laboratory outreach or industrial medicine and if they will buy it.

The foundation of this marketing-based planning approach is that the market, not the individuals internal to the organization, dictates the direction in which the organization will go. The marketing-based approach establishes the price of the service. In the "assessment of needs" and pretesting stages, the market must be measured in terms of how the market wants the service delivered. What location or hours are convenient for buyers?

The last stage of the marketing-based model is similar to the previous approach— implementation. Unlike the nonmarketing planning approach, there is less need for an open house to find the patients who might use the service. It is known at the implementation stage that the service is needed and that it has been configured the way the market wants in terms of delivery and price. The key remaining challenge is to inform the market that the service is available—to promote the service to the market.

In this conceptualization of the marketing-based planning approach, the definition of marketing becomes clearer. "Marketing is the process of identifying the market's need, of planning and developing a service to meet those needs, and of determining the best way to price, promote, and deliver the service." This definition contains the four components of marketing that are common to all organizations, whether they are for-profit or not-for-profit—product (service), price, promotion, and distribution. These four components, the basics for the tactics in any marketing plan, are referred to as the marketing mix and are described in greater detail at the end of this chapter.

Why Marketing Now?

Why is marketing an important issue among health care providers? Fifteen or 20 years ago, there was no need for a marketing orientation in a hospital or medical group. Until recently, in many communities, when a hospital service was offered, there was a need. In the past few years, however, more competitors have appeared in the marketplace. They have come from proprietary organizations, freestanding independents, and doctors' offices. Moreover, offering a new service can represent a significant investment in terms of expensive technology. Fifteen or 20 years ago, when a hospital or clinic offered a service that was not successful, the director or long-range planning committee summed up the failure as a "good learning experience." Fewer and fewer organizations can afford too many such learning experiences with today's financial and competitive realities.

Marketing-based planning does not guarantee success, even if surveys are reliable and pretesting is conducted. In the time intervening from conceptualization to final offering, conditions can change. Marketing cannot guarantee success, but it can reduce the probability of failure. The nonmarketing planning model places tremendous pressure on the director of the clinical laboratory to be an extremely accurate forecaster of market needs. Although many successes have undoubtedly been built on just this type of forecasting, most would agree that the probabilities of success are probably higher for creating a service that someone wants by first asking them what they prefer.

Risks of Marketing

The delineation of these two approaches to planning should reveal the potential advantages of a marketing approach. Fully understanding the differences between these two philosophies also reveals why marketing has been defined as advertising. Marketing is dangerous. Many professionals feel that, because they are professionals, they know what is best for the market. The professional does not want to hear the answer regarding the desired service or the way in which a service should be configured if this market preference goes against his or her view. It is safer to translate marketing as advertising. "Marketing" then becomes promoting the service the provider wants to offer. If the service fails to generate demand, marketing is at fault. The possibility that the service did not meet the market's preferences is not raised.

The difference between these two approaches to planning, coupled with the definition of marketing, should lead to an understanding of the differences between marketing and advertising. Marketing is not advertising, but advertising is one element of the marketing mix.

In health care, there is always an easy challenge to marketing. The needs assessment is done, and there is a clear understanding of how the market wants the service delivered, but the market's preference is counter to the professional's preference. The professional can always claim providing a service according to market preference would destroy the quality of care.

Consider this scenario. Twenty years ago, if a woman asked her obstetrician whether her spouse could be in the delivery room, the almost universal response was "no." Few lay people would argue with the reason given: It would destroy the quality of care of a routine delivery. Enough women desired this arrangement so that eventually some obstetricians met the need. Today if you visit a delivery room, the spouse and possibly siblings are present. Grandparents are occasionally allowed in, along with someone to run the video camera. In many communities, the only person missing is the obstetrician, who has been replaced by a nurse midwife. The lesson is clear. No organization has to bend to market demand provided that no competitor rises up to meet the need. In many hospitals today, volume has dropped dramatically, as more services can be provided in physicians' offices without the accompanying overhead charges. The risks for marketing are clear, but the costs of ignoring the market in today's competitive environment may be greater than most health care organizations can afford.

The Consumer Perspective

Inherent in the marketing-based planning process is the need for the organization to go outside to assess needs in the marketplace. Central to effective marketing is defining the product or service not from the provider's perspective but from the market's view. To more clearly address this issue, consider the decision on hospital selection.

When a patient is faced with hospitalization, the physician plays a major role in selecting the facility. The attending physician may have privileges at two or even three facilities where the technical capabilities are such that the procedure could be performed. The physician will indicate at which hospitals he or she has admitting privileges and ask the consumer if there is a preference. In this case, the consumer is making a purchasing decision.[3]

Figure 3, below, depicts the hospital selection decision from the consumer's perspective. The diagram has two components. One is labeled the primary product, the technology within the hospital and the medical expertise of the staff. The primary product is the portion of the service that must exist for the organization to even be considered a reasonable alternative. For example, if a hospital does not have the technology or staff to do liver transplantation, it lacks the primary product and would not be considered as a competitor.

The second component of figure 3 is labeled the offered dimension. This dimension represents the attributes that the consumer uses to judge the hospital in terms of service quality—attitude of the nursing staff, patient procedures, admitting process, and layout of facility. This aspect of marketing often troubles the health care professional. The primary product, the dimension most professionals view as the real "quality" aspect of the service, is taken for granted. Furthermore, the consumer is not judging on quality but instead on soft dimensions such as attitude, friendliness of staff, or waiting time in the emergency department. This perspective does not undermine the importance of quality. Rather, quality is not a source of a differential advantage but instead is the cost of entry for being a competitor.

In fact, the primary product component is important to the consumer in selecting between providers when the technical or expertise dimension can be observed or documented. The difficulty in health care is the specialty and even subspecialty nature of knowledge in areas such as internal medicine, endocrinology, nephrology, and clinical laboratory medicine. In most cases, only an internist can truly judge whether another internist is proficient in terms of primary product knowledge. The only individual capable of judging whether a clinical laboratory is truly high in terms of its primary product quality (its technology and staff expertise) may be the director of another clinical laboratory.

Figure 4, right, shows this same perspective in the selection of a clinical laboratory by a physician. As with consumers' selection of hospitals, many

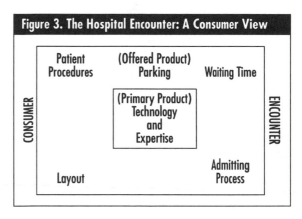

Figure 3. The Hospital Encounter: A Consumer View

CONSUMER / ENCOUNTER

Patient Procedures

(Offered Product) Parking

Waiting Time

(Primary Product) Technology and Expertise

Layout

Admitting Process

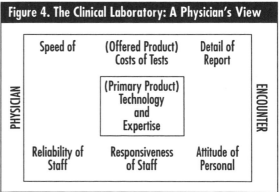

Figure 4. The Clinical Laboratory: A Physician's View

PHYSICIAN / ENCOUNTER

Speed of

(Offered Product) Costs of Tests

Detail of Report

(Primary Product) Technology and Expertise

Reliability of Staff

Responsiveness of Staff

Attitude of Personal

physicians can choose among several clinical laboratories. When physicians select one laboratory over another, they have purchased a product. This product has two dimensions: a primary and an offered component. Again, the primary product is technology and expertise. Yet the typical physician cannot differentiate among laboratories on this critical component. How do they differentiate among laboratories in deciding that one is better than another? The offered components of speed, cost, detail of report, reliability of pick-up, and drop-off service play the key roles. These dimensions can be observed and judged by the physician.

This discussion may lead one to question the importance of the primary product, medical expertise and technology, in health care marketing. Judgment of services on the offered product components does not mean that the expertise of the physicians is unimportant, but rather that most services exist within a reasonable range of primary product quality. In fact, one might describe the quality of medical care as a bell-shaped curve with the tail ends of the curve representing truly exceptional quality—either good or poor. Few providers operate on either end. The ability to perceive *real* differences on primary product quality for services within the middle range is difficult for consumers and physicians.

If one assumes a bell-shaped curve of medical quality, quality is less a point of difference. Quality becomes a given, the initial cost of entry to compete in the marketplace. In order to make the primary product a point of difference, the buyer must notice a difference. Because the challenge is difficult in health care, services are judged on the offered product components.

Strategies for Assessing the Market

To a large degree, the methodologies used to identify the market are technical details to which most physician managers need not avail themselves. Figure 5, page 219, however, does show the most common approaches used to gathering data. Each of these methodologies must be considered relative to the problem at hand and to the respective strengths of the methodology. There are four criteria listed within this figure on which these alternative data-gathering approaches can be considered. Prior to reviewing some of the details of this figure, however, it might be useful to also discuss one of the less well-known methodologies: focus groups. Basically, these are group discussions of 8 to 10 individuals that are led by a trained moderator. The moderator usually works from an interviewing guide that contains 8 to 10 questions. The interview process typically takes one and one half to two hours. The value of a focus group is often the synergy that is created with several people commenting on a particular area. For example, a focus group might be conducted among primary care physicians regarding the referral process in a particular area. Or a focus group among consumers who are new to an area might be conducted regarding how they establish a physician relationship. This method is useful in helping to define some dimensions or develop hypotheses for further investigation. This method, like those more common to market research, must be considered relative to some criteria.

Cost/economy—While self-explanatory, cost is an important consideration for any research project. Personal interviews are the highest in terms of cost. To a large degree, the cost of this approach is in hiring trained interviewers, the resultant travel, and interviewing time. A similar but more moderate cost is borne with telephone interviewers. While trained interviewers are needed for telephoning, the training is less rigorous than with personal interviewers. Telephone interviewers work off of a computer monitor that can prompt them regarding the questions, the sequencing of the interview, and any follow-up probes that are needed. Field interviewers cannot be so tightly controlled, so their initial training must be far more intensive. Of all the methodologies, mail surveys represent the lowest cost. Typically, this process requires postage out and back and the printing of forms. It is the low cost of the mail survey that makes this technique a common approach in many academic settings. However, for most health care marketing research, other factors limit the effectiveness of this methodology.

Focus group costs are derived in two areas—the moderator and participant compliance. To have a well-run focus group, a trained moderator is key. And participants in focus groups are often paid for their participation. The cost of this participation varies with the profile of those recruited to participate. Additionally, focus group discussions are taped, and there is a transcription cost for these materials.

Figure 5. Alternative Methodologies for Assessing the Market

Approach		Research Methodology		
Criteria	Personal Interview	Telephone Survey	Mail Survey	Focus Group
Economy	Most Expensive	Avoids Interviewer travel, relatively expensive. Trained interviewers needed.	Potentially lower costs. (if response rate sufficient)	Relatively expensive
Interviewer bias	High likelihood of bias. Trust. Appearance.	Less than personal interviewer. No face-to-face contact. Suspicion of phone call.	Interviewer bias eliminated. Anonymity provided.	Need trained moderator.
Flexibility	Most flexible. Responses can be probed. Assistance can be provided in completing forms. Observations can be made.	Cannot make observations. Probing possible to a degree.	Least flexible.	Very flexible.
Sampling and respondent cooperation	Most complete sample possible, with sufficient call back strategy.	Limited to people with telephone. No answers, refusals are common.	Mailing list nonresponse a major problem.	Need close selection.

* Reprinted from Hillestad, S., and Berkowitz, E. *Health Care Marketing Plans: From Strategy to Action.* Second Edition. Rockville, Md.: Aspen Press, 1991, p. 100.

Bias—For anyone conducting research, bias is an important concern. In personal interviews, the potential for bias is high. Often, one must be concerned about the social desirability of the respondent. A trained interviewer is a necessity to minimize the likelihood of bias by communicating some evaluation of the respondent's answers. As one can infer, interpersonal bias is still apparent with telephone interviews, but the lack of face-to-face contact minimizes the effects to some degree. Mail surveys have no interpersonal bias. The potential for bias does exist with regard to who responds to the survey. In order to assess this bias in a mail survey, it is useful to have characteristics of the group that is being surveyed. In this fashion, the demographics of the respondents can be compared to a broader profile to assess whether some group is underrepresented. The potential for bias is high with focus groups, because there is an interaction with multiple interviews at one time. Again, the importance of the trained interviewer becomes apparent. This person can often skillfully diffuse the social desirability factor that might color some participants' remarks.

Flexibility—Flexibility refers to the ability of a methodology to pursue various lines of inquiry as the data collection progresses. In this regard, one can see that mail surveys have little flexibility. Once the survey is developed and mailed, there is no way to adjust the questioning based on the respondents' answers. Focus groups and personal interviews allow the greatest degree of flexibility. As the respondent answers, the interviewer or moderator can probe to explore why the individual doesn't refer to a particular hospital, for example. Some limited flexibility exists for telephone interviewing, but the time constraints often found in telephone interviews limit flexibility to a great degree.

Sample—The most complete sample can be obtained with personal interviews. If there are key informants whose opinion must be obtained, the personal interview is often the best approach. The interviewer can do a number of call backs, prearrange a meeting, or even pay for the physician's time if the person's opinion is needed. The sample is often more limited in telephone interviews. Random digit dialing can get around an incomplete phone list, but another factor that greatly limits the sample is the cooperation of the respondent. It is very easy for an individual to terminate a telephone interview. In mail surveys, the problems are magnified. Mailings are restricted as a function of the quality of the list. And respondent cooperation is often difficult to achieve in significant percentages without using incentives. Even with the use of incentives, cooperation from professionals is often difficult to achieve. With focus groups, sample concerns often relate to representativeness, as the number of participants is often small, as noted previously. It is important to conduct multiple focus groups and to have an accurate profiling of who is being targeted.

Components of Marketing Strategy

In discussing the sequence of a marketing planning approach, the four components of strategy were identified as the service (product), the price, the location (place), and the promotion. These elements have been referred to as the four Ps of marketing. While space constraints do not allow significant discussion of any one element, the remainder of this chapter will highlight each "P."

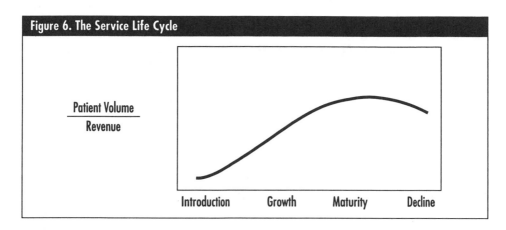

Figure 6. The Service Life Cycle

Patient Volume
————————
Revenue

Introduction   Growth   Maturity   Decline

Product. The essential element of any marketing program is a service that is desired by the market *and* configured in the manner that the market wants. The early testing stage for a service is critical, in that promoting a service not designed to market specifications may be a fast way to kill its demand. It is very difficult to restore a base of referrals if early physician experience with a service is negative.

In developing the marketing effort for any medical service, the concept of the product life cycle is useful. All services may be viewed as existing in one of four stages, depicted in figure 6, above. This graph shows a generalized life cycle. Time is represented on the x-axis and revenue or patient volume on the y-axis. Marketing objectives vary over the course of these stages.

In the first stage (introduction), a new service, such as an arthritis program, is introduced. The major marketing objective is to generate awareness. At this stage, promotion, particularly in the form of mass advertising, is important. Product quality is important in order that first-time referrers have a positive experience. In the early stages of a service's offering, it is also helpful to keep the number of alternatives within the program limited in order to help maintain product quality.

The second stage of the life cycle is growth. It is at this point that competitors enter the market. The key objective at this stage is to lock up the flow of referrals. For example, the arthritis program may sign capitation contracts with HMOs to be the treatment source for arthritis. Also, at this stage it is beneficial to offer additional varieties of the program to expand the market. For example, a specialized arthritis program for children might be considered as a way to expand market presence.

The third stage of the life cycle is maturity. As the curve indicates, demand is leveling off. The marketing objective at this point is maintenance. Any referrals lost at this stage cannot be replaced with new referrals. It is at this point that commitment must be made to develop new services to get back to the early stages of a life cycle.

Decline is the last stage of the life cycle. A service often declines for reasons beyond the control of the provider. Demographic changes have led to the decline of many hospitals' pediatric units. Technology has virtually eliminated polio wards. This stage is often the most difficult for an institution to address. It can be emotional. Often, it is hard to shut down a service on which a clinic built its early reputation. Services in the decline stage, however, tend to consume a disproportionate share of management time or financial resources. In medicine, declining services often cannot be closed down because of their link to the offering of other more profitable offerings. Yet the fiscal and personnel support of these declining services must be closely maintained.

Place. The place component of marketing is the distribution element. This comprises offered components, such as location and hours the service is offered. Location is often an important issue for specialty services that are offered in university settings or other large tertiary facilities. In this instance, access may be particularly difficult for the patient. The distribution strategy may entail having on-campus overnight accommodations; an out-of-town visitors' office; or, if possible, satellite offices.

For referral physicians, distribution is often defined as scheduling access. The primary product quality can be high, but the physician must be able to get a patient in to be seen. In an interesting distribution strategy, the Mayo Clinic is setting up a telecommunications satellite link with its three facilities. Similarly, the clinic's move to opening satellite facilities in Scottsdale, Arizona; Jacksonville, Florida; and Eau Claire, Wisconsin are all moves to enhance the distribution of the clinic's services. Physicians at locations distant from Rochester can talk to and see specialists at the main facility. This strategy is a great advantage in terms of access.

Within the concept of distribution is another factor that is important to marketing strategy. This is referred to as the channel of distribution. The channel of distribution can be defined as "the path a product takes as it moves from producer to end user." Figure 7, below, shows the traditional channel of distribution for a common consumer product. It moves from a manufacturer to a wholesaler to a retailer and, ultimately, to the end user (the consumer). In health care, one can view the channel of distribution as the path a patient makes moving through the levels of care to ultimate treatment. Figure 8, page 223, shows the several alternative channels of distribution with the consumer (patient) placed at the top. Figure 8(a) is the simplest channel, represented by primary care. In this instance, the consumer (patient) goes directly to the primary care physician. In more complicated channels, the patient gets referred to a specialist (b), to a hospital (c), or from there to a tertiary facility(d).

A central concern in marketing is control of the channel of distribution. There are two strategies to accomplish this goal. One is referred to as *push*, the other as *pull*. In a push strategy, the organization tries to control the channel by working through intermediaries. For example, in figure 8(c) the hospital administrator may try to develop loyalties with physicians or to build an attached medical office building for doctors to house their offices. In both these strategies, the hospital administrator is trying to work through intermediaries by facilitating or encouraging patient referrals. An alternative approach is a pull strategy. In this scenario, the hospital attempts to generate referrals by bypassing the traditional

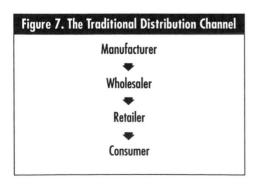

Figure 7. The Traditional Distribution Channel

Manufacturer

⬇

Wholesaler

⬇

Retailer

⬇

Consumer

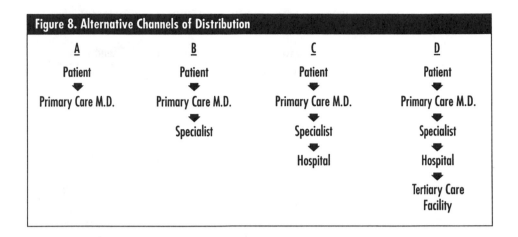

Figure 8. Alternative Channels of Distribution

A	B	C	D
Patient	Patient	Patient	Patient
⬇	⬇	⬇	⬇
Primary Care M.D.	Primary Care M.D.	Primary Care M.D.	Primary Care M.D.
	⬇	⬇	⬇
	Specialist	Specialist	Specialist
		⬇	⬇
		Hospital	Hospital
			⬇
			Tertiary Care Facility

referral sources (the primary care or specialty physicians) and promoting hospital services directly to the end user, the patient. In this case, the hospital may advertise its cardiology program as the Heart Institute or its obstetrics program as the Birthing Center. The goal is to have the patient either request the hospital with such a service or bypass doctors and seek care at the facility directly.

Price. The price component of medical services for many years was of little importance, because insurance coverage made it a nonissue. The appearance of large-scale contractual buyers, such as HMOs, however, has increased price consciousness. From a marketing perspective, there are two components to price. The floor component represents the internal cost of delivering the service and is determined through basic cost accounting. Marketing strategy, however, is concerned with the ceiling component, or the price the market is willing to pay. If the floor is higher than the ceiling, no amount of promotion can make the service acceptable to the market. It is the difference between the ceiling and the floor that represents the margin to the institution. An important aspect for early stage market research is determination of the ceiling price among insurers, HMOs, and consumers for a proposed service offering.

Promotion. While marketing is not sales, sales is a part of marketing. Promoting a service can be done through personal selling, advertising, and publicity. Historically, medical services have relied on publicity to get information on services to the public. Publicity consists of news stories on television and in the print media. This component is valuable for its appearance of credibility and because there is no direct cost for the time or space. The disadvantage of this method is lack of control. Mass advertising overcomes this disadvantage, although there is a sizable direct cost involved. Figure 9, page 224, shows the selection trade-offs for the various promotional media.

As health care has increasingly moved to a situation where providers are dealing with bulk buyers (corporations and managed care alternatives), marketing strategies with regard to promotion are focusing more on personal selling rather than advertising. Figure 10, page 224, shows some of the respective trade-offs in whether to use either personal selling or advertising. As can be seen, the more complex or technologically sophisticated the service, the greater the need for personal selling. The reason is (as is

Figure 9. Selection Tradeoffs With Alternative Media

	Cost of Placement	Selectivity	Message Quality	Lead Time
Newspapers	Relatively expensive.	Little selectivity except in major Metro areas. By zip code or region.	Poor photo reproduction. Person can spend time with message	Easy to obtain space with short notice.
Magazines	Relatively expensive.	Great selectivity by life-style, interest. Reasonably good selectivity by area (particularly metro).	Excellent photo reproduction. Person can spend time with message.	Often requires contracting for space for a month or more prior notice.
Direct Mail	Relatively inexpensive.	Excellent selectivity on criteria required by organization.	Excellent as function of dollars spent in printing.	Little required except to produce mail piece.
Radio	Inexpensive.	Reasonable selectivity.	Must be short, simple. Difficult to hold attention.	Little advance notice required to run a commercial.
Television	Expensive.	Reasonable—a function of time of day and show selected	Excellent for sight and sound. Relatively short messages required. Hard to hold attention.	Often requires substantial lead time with station for time.
Outdoor	Relatively inexpensive.	Little selectivity except by location of billboard	Requires short, simple messages.	Space availability often requires long lead time.

* Reprinted from: Steven G. Hillestad and Eric N. Berkowitz. *Health Care Marketing Plans: From Strategy to Action*, Dow Jones-Irwin, Homewood, Illinois, 1984, p.118.

Figure 10. Advertising vs. Personal Selling

SALES		ADVERTISING
High	Degree of Technical Sophistication	Low
Few	Number of Customers	Many
Push	Marketing Strategy	Pull
Complex	Size of DMU	Simple
Great	Degree of Risk	Little

true with many medical services) that there are subtleties or complicated aspects of the service that often require detailed explanation. Rarely can a sufficient level of detail be provided in an ad or in a brochure that a person will read and understand.

A second consideration in whether to use personal selling or advertising is the number of buyers in the market and their degree of concentration. The fewer the number of buyers and the more geographically concentrated, the greater the benefit of personal sales. For many specialty services or for contracts with companies, the actual number of contracts or referrers is relatively small. And most organizations attract such referrals or deal with companies in a relatively tightly defined geographic location. In these instances, personal selling is probably more beneficial. As previously discussed in the section on distribution, a push or pull strategy dictates whether there is greater emphasis on personal selling (push) or advertising (pull).

Another consideration is the number of individuals involved in the decision-making unit (DMU). The more people involved in the decision to contract with a particular provider or to use a particular facility or group for referrals, the higher the need for personal selling. A personal sales representative can then address the different concerns and issues that might be raised among a group of several decision makers. It is unlikely that one advertisement or one brochure can speak to the concerns of the health benefit officer of a company, the company medical director, the vice president of finance, and the union representative.

The degree of risk also affects whether one uses personal selling or advertising. The higher the degree of risk, the greater the need for personal selling to allay fears and to build trust with the buyer. The referral of a patient by a doctor always represents a real risk. To build such referrals, a personal sales effort is needed. For bulk buyers of health care, just as for corporations, the risk in signing a contract with a provider is great. In this regard, personal sales becomes a key part of the promotional strategy effort.

Prerequisites for Effective Marketing

Understandably, the transition to becoming a marketing-oriented organization has been difficult for many hospitals and medical groups.[4] Some get bogged down because they either do not understand or have not yet met four prerequisites for becoming marketing-oriented. These four prerequisites are illustrated in figure 11, below.

- ■ *Pressure to be marketing-oriented.* This first condition refers to a view that must be shared and accepted throughout the organization concerning the need for an improved marketing orientation. Not only must senior management feel pressure

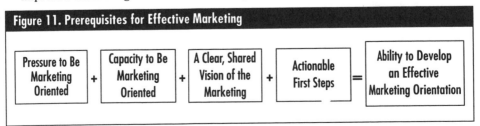

Figure 11. Prerequisites for Effective Marketing

Pressure to Be Marketing Oriented + Capacity to Be Marketing Oriented + A Clear, Shared Vision of the Marketing + Actionable First Steps = Ability to Develop an Effective Marketing Orientation

and want to become more marketing-oriented, but peer pressure must be strong throughout the organization to understand and respond to customer needs. In addition, information and reward systems must recognize the value of a customer orientation, and department or program marketing objectives and measurement systems must be tied to progress on this front.

■ *Capacity to be marketing-oriented.* This second component refers to the capabilities and depth of hospital management staff. The hospital must have enough staff members who are not only experienced and adequately trained, but also devoted to improving the hospital's marketing effort. To begin with, management and staff must be receptive to ideas on how to become more marketing-oriented. In addition to having appropriate people and management depth, and recognizing that significant time must be devoted to improving marketing efforts, an understanding must be developed as to how these efforts fit with other hospital priorities.

■ *A clear, shared vision of the market.* Many questions must be answered to develop an awareness and understanding of the marketplace. Who are the key customers and stakeholders? What are their needs? What changes must the hospital make to become marketing-oriented and to meet the needs of these core constituencies? How is this organization going to differentiate and distinguish itself from others?

■ *Actionable first steps.* Once the first three components are in place, the organization must develop an understanding of how daily marketing decisions and tasks must change. This effort requires a clear and complete set of written action plans and implementation programs. It also demands well-defined mechanisms to track progress and address minor difficulties in implementation before they become major ones.

Summary

Marketing has been presented not only as a functional dimension of management, but also as a philosophy to guide strategic planning. Advertising, in spite of common misperceptions, is only one dimension of a marketing strategy that begins with a needs assessment. The historical approach to developing health care services has been an inward process that results in looking for demand. In today's increasingly competitive marketplace, the goal is to identify a differential advantage for a service needed by a defined target group. The challenge for the health care organization is to use the marketing mix to meet the need.

References

1. Berkowitz, E. "Marketing: Its Meaning and Application in Rehabilitation Medicine" in *A Primer on Management for Rehabilitation Medicine.* Philadelphia, Pa.: Hanley Belfus, Inc., 1987, pp. 247-56.

2. Berkowitz, E. "Marketing the Clinical Laboratory: An External Perspective." *Clinical Laboratory Management Review* 1(3):133-45, May/June 1987.

3. Berkowitz, E., and Flexner, W. "The Market for Health Services: Is There A Nontraditional Consumer?" *Journal of Health Care Marketing* 1(1):25-34, Winter 1980-81, and Berkowitz, E. "Marketing the Hospital of the Future." *Proceedings,* 1981 Executive Symposium, University of Iowa, pp. 17-33.

4. Diamond, S., and Berkowitz, E. "Building a Marketing Orientation for Hospitals." Presentation at Academy for Health Care Marketing, American Marketing Association, March 1987.

Suggested Readings

Berkowitz, E., and others. *Marketing.* Homewood, Ill.: Richard D. Irwin Co., 1992, 4th ed.

Flexner, W., and others (Eds.). *Strategic Planning in Health Care Management.* Rockville, Md.: Aspen Systems, 1981.

George, W., and Compton, F. "How to Initiate a Marketing Perspective in a Health Services Organization." *Journal of Health Care Marketing* 5(1):29-37, Winter 1985.

Hillestad, S., and Berkowitz, E. *Health Care Marketing Plans from Strategy to Action.* Rockville, Md.: Aspen Systems, 1991.

Rathmell, J. *Marketing in the Service Sector.* Cambridge, Mass.: Winthrop Publishers, 1974.

Templeton, Jane Farley. *Focus Groups: A Guide for Advertsing and Marketing Professionals.* Chicago, Ill.: Probus Publishing Co., 1987.

Zallocco, R., and others. "Strategic Market Planning for Hospitals." *Journal of Health Care Marketing* 4(2):19-28, Spring 1984.

Eric N. Berkowitz, PhD, is Chairman and Professor, School of Management, University of Massachusetts, Amherst.

The Elements of Medical Quality Management

by *David B. Nash, MD, MBA,*
and Nelda E. Johnson, PharmD

CHAPTER 16

anaging medical quality in today's health care environment is a complex function that interrelates concerns not only about quality, but also about the costs and outcomes of health care interventions. New roles are emerging for physician executives to act as agents of change as more organizations undertake new quality improvement initiatives and establish priorities for measuring performance and assessing outcomes of care.

Seemingly endless demands for data on quality of care are arising from numerous sources—managed care organizations, regulatory agencies, and purchasers and consumers of health care. External organizations are increasingly asking doctors and hospitals to explain what they do and why they do it. Several forces are behind this drive to measure quality of care. After having attention focused primarily on cost reductions in 1980s, purchasers are now realizing the importance of obtaining health care services not only at a reasonable price but on the basis of quality as well. Now, the public and those who pay for medical care are interested in knowing whether they are getting a good value for their health care dollars. As a result, we are seeing an increasing number of health care contracts being awarded on the basis of both cost and quality measurements.

Physicians have long recognized that new approaches and applications to improving quality must be continually sought. But they have viewed traditional quality assessment efforts as intrusive and largely ineffectual. This opinion has developed primarily because these programs relied on case-by-case inspections of patients' medical records and used indicators and thresholds developed with little significant input from physicians. Thus, they are often seen as arbitrary measures subject to erroneous conclusions when used to assess the quality of care being provided. In addition, while this method of inspecting physician and hospital performance allows quality assurance staff to track problems and look for trends, it detects problems only after they have occurred and does little to prevent their recurrence. This traditional approach fails to recognize today's health care delivery as a series of interlinked processes requiring the coordinated efforts of many health care professionals. It also does not facilitate systematic analysis and subsequent improvement in patient outcomes.

Avedis Donabedian, often referred to as the founder of health care quality assurance, established a framework for assessing quality that stresses that quality can be measured not only in terms of the structure and process of care but also in terms of the outcomes of care.[1] Structure comprises the physical, human, and organizational properties of the setting in which care is provided. These properties include things such as equipment and the number of licensed doctors and nurses on staff. Process consists of the technical aspects of providing care and the procedures used to ensure that patients receive necessary care. For instance, adherence to widely accepted practices and regulatory requirements are process measures. Outcome encompasses those changes in patient health status that can be attributed to the medical care provided. Examples include mortality rates, adverse event rates, and changes in an individual's health-related well-being. While information about structure and processes of care provide valuable information and are related to the probability of obtaining good patient outcomes, they do not necessarily measure the quality of patient outcomes. In the past, health care regulatory agencies have concentrated on measuring the structure and process of care, with little attention given to outcomes.

Although there have been many attempts to define quality, there is no single comprehensive definition of medical quality, most likely because quality encompasses several different elements and aspects of care. Donabedian recently provided an in-depth review of the various aspects of medical quality.[2] Some of the quality components he described are effectiveness, efficiency, optimality, and acceptability of medical care. Two of the more familiar dimensions of medical quality are the technical aspects of care and the interpersonal aspects of care.[3] Technical quality relates to how well patients are diagnosed and clinically managed, while interpersonal quality depends on how well the patients' personal needs are met. Other descriptions of quality incorporate evaluations of patient preferences and considerations for the cost of care. Two such examples are:

■ "Quality is the degree to which the process of care increases the probability of outcomes desired by patients and decreases the probability of undesired outcomes, given the state of medical knowledge."[4]

■ "Quality health care consists of necessary medical processes that result in cure, significant measured improvement in the patient's condition, alleviation of pain or other desired outcomes, and provides real value for the dollars spent."[5]

Determining just which aspects of medical care should be used to measure quality has been the focus of intensive research efforts by health service researchers, the federal government, and regulatory bodies. Increased interest in this area has been spurred by research on wide variations in medical practice and the growing realization that traditional quality assurance methods have done little to ensure and improve quality and effectiveness of medical treatment.

The Joint Commission on Accreditation of Healthcare Organizations (JCAHO) has recently channeled its efforts into developing a new conceptual framework that will focus efforts on improving the results of health care. According to JCAHO, it is its intention to "make the improvement of patient outcomes an important and visible objective of the new accreditation process."[6]

In 1989, the federal government, under the auspices of the Public Health Service, created the Agency for Health Care Policy and Research (AHCPR). The charge for AHCPR is to enhance the quality, effectiveness, appropriateness, and access of health care.[7] With millions of dollars in federal funding for research, there is now a coordinated national effort focused on researching medical treatment effectiveness, clinical outcomes, new methodologies for improving quality of care, and development of clinical practice guidelines.

Numerous health services researchers have already contributed to the growing body of knowledge about ways to evaluate and improve the quality of medical care. Research and clinical practice evaluations in the following areas have led to new developments in the field of medical quality management.

- Use of continuous quality improvement techniques in health care.[8,9]

- Use of outcomes management to routinely and systematically measure the functioning and well-being of patients.[10]

- Role of the patient in assessing the outcomes of care.[11]

- Use of severity-of-illness measures to adjust for patient outcomes.[12]

- Degree of variation in clinical practice[13-16] and role of uncertainty in medical decisions.[17]

- Relationship between clinical practice variations and quality.[18]

- Role of nationally developed clinical practice guidelines.[19]

As new approaches to measuring and managing medical quality continue to evolve, it is likely that techniques will be drawn from several different sources and integrated in a comprehensive approach. The developing fields of continuous quality improvement, clinical practice guidelines, and outcomes management will provide a solid basis for creating successful quality management programs.[5]

Continuous Quality Improvement Theory

The theory of continuous quality improvement (CQI), or total quality management (TQM) as it is sometimes referred to in health care, has evolved from the manufacturing industry's experience with quality management. Industrial quality experts suggest that quality means "a continuous effort by all members of the organization to meet the needs and expectations of the customer."[20] Industrial quality management systems have adopted a number of CQI methods that increase the probability of successfully improving quality. Central to these methods is use of multidisciplinary teams to identify problems, data collection and analysis to understand and correct underlying root causes of problems, and reductions in unwanted complexity and variation in systems through the use of statistical process control theory. Total quality management creates an open climate that fosters self-motivation and cooperation, where everyone in the organization shares responsibility to improve quality. Attempts are made to break down barriers between departments and to improve communication throughout the organization and to drive out fear. CQI emphasizes that it is the processes themselves that should be the focus of quality improvement efforts, not individual workers. There is a belief that most workers are conscientious and are trying to do a good job, but that they face a multitude of system problems that can contribute to poor quality. By fully analyzing a process and understanding the root causes of variation, workers can develop and implement a successful plan to improve the process. CQI methods have been used successfully outside health care for a number of years and have resulted in significant improvements in the quality of products and services.

Evolution of CQI in Health Care

The application of continuous quality improvement techniques to health care has intrigued many health care providers and has been successful in a number of organizations. One of the initial success stories was the National Demonstration Project on Quality Improvement in Health Care.[9] In 1987, this ambitious one-year project matched 21 well-known health care organizations with experts in the field of industrial quality management. This nationwide experiment demonstrated that CQI techniques could be successfully used in the health care setting.

In the past few years, CQI has continued to gain considerable attention in health care, as is evidenced by the ever-increasing number of presentations at quality improvement conferences and articles in the literature. A nationwide survey conducted by the American Hospital Association in 1990 reported that 44 percent of all respondents had adopted CQI methods to some degree.[21] In 1992, it was noted that some 1,500 hospitals and health care organizations, including the Health Care Financing Administration, had been actively involved in using continuous quality improvement techniques.[22]

CQI techniques differ greatly from traditional quality assurance approaches. Traditional techniques tend to focus primarily on physician decisions, underemphasizing the effects that nonphysicians can have on health care processes.[20] In reality, decisions are only one source of variability in processes. A significant amount of variation may be attributed to other causes, such as unclear policies and procedures, defective equipment, or variations in the work of other health care professionals. A program that encompasses CQI acknowledges the importance of teamwork and offers physicians an opportunity to participate in improving the entire workflow process. Because CQI focuses on improving processes, it does not single out individual employees as "bad apples" and is associated with fewer negative connotations than traditional QA programs. CQI allows the people who are intimately involved in the process to make changes in the system, resulting in significant improvements in the overall level of quality.

Some of the key concepts of CQI are:

- Poor quality usually stems from complex processes or variation within a system and not from individuals' lack of knowledge or skills.

- Because most work is accomplished through process, the focus of CQI is on evaluating and improving processes, not on identifying individuals with bad behavior and trying to change them.

- Quality needs to be built into processes so that poor quality is prevented upstream, not measured by inspection at the end of the line.

- Quality can always be improved. Just meeting the minimum established thresholds for acceptability or compliance does not ensure high quality.

- Quality is based on a thorough understanding of the needs and expectations of customers, both internal and external.

- Decisions are based on facts and scientific measurements, not on presumptions or anecdotal evidence.

- Poor quality is costly and results from unwanted variations and complexity in processes.

Although there are a number of different CQI models used in health care, most models encompass the following general steps[9] to improve a process or fix a quality problem:

1. Clearly defined goals and objectives for the project are developed.

2. A multidisciplinary project team that knows the process is formed.

3. The team uses data to analyze a process and understand the key steps, variables, and root causes that contribute to quality problems.

4. A plan to improve the process is developed, implemented, and tested.

5. Data are collected and analyzed statistically to track the results of the improvement plan and to measure variation in the process.

Tools and Techniques of CQI

The cycle of continuously improving quality begins with the identification of priority areas for improvements and then moves on to data collection and analysis. The remaining steps are better known as the "Plan-Do-Check-Act" cycle. Throughout this cycle, cross-functional teams trained in CQI techniques use a variety of data-driven tools to analyze process-related problems, reduce variations in the process, and monitor improvements in the process. One of the key factors to success is the formation of a team with members who are intimately involved with the process being studied. If the team appropriately identifies the underlying root causes contributing to poor quality and makes the necessary changes, waste, rework, complexity, and the associated costs of poor quality can be reduced.[23]

Some of the tools that CQI teams use throughout the quality improvement cycle include[24]:

■ *Flowcharts* are developed by the team to describe the sequence of steps that occur in a process. They provide a point of common agreement on what the process entails and help the group to focus on areas of redundancy and rework.

Cause and effect diagrams are used to help identify and organize underlying root causes of problems or factors critical to the process.

Pareto charts (bar graphs) illustrate the frequency and impact of various problems in a process and help in the selection improvement efforts. The Pareto chart is an extension of the Pareto Principle, which states that the majority of problems within a process can be attributed to relatively few factors.

Histograms and scattergrams help to organize and characterize data and to look for relationships among variables.

Run charts are used to examine data for trends and patterns that occur over time.

Control charts help to monitor a process for statistical control. Upper and lower statistical control limits are established to define the standard deviation from the mean. Points falling outside the control limits represent special variations that are due to causes outside the usual process.

Two other techniques that have been used in health care to improve the quality and efficiency of care are benchmarking and clinical pathway development.

Benchmarking is used to compare the practices of an organization with the practices of leaders in the field. The goal is to identify and learn from the "best practices" and then to incorporate those practices into your own work.[25]

Clinical (or Critical) Pathways are used to define the optimal sequence of events and timing for certain medical interventions. They are usually developed through the collaborative efforts of health care professionals in hospitals to reduce length of stay, delays, and variation in care. They also help to improve communication among physicians, nurses, and other health care professionals.[26]

A quality management program will also incorporate several managerial components: quality planning, quality measurement and control, and quality improvement activities.[9,27] *Quality planning* involves developing a thorough understanding of the wants and needs of the customer and linking them to the day-to-day activities of the organization. The organizational culture should foster pride, joy, collaboration, and scientific thinking. *Quality measurement and control* involves developing measures to reduce unintended, unwanted, or costly variations in work processes. *Quality improvement* consists of efforts to continuously improve overall performance through cross-functional teams that collect, analyze, and act on data.[27,28]

As CQI efforts have become more widespread, some health care professionals have wondered whether these efforts will replace quality assurance departments altogether. In practice, CQI is often developed and implemented with the help of existing QA programs and personnel. QA staff often become a valuable resource for training and facilitating the work of cross-functional project teams. Other quality professionals may move into quality measurement and control functions within the organizational quality program. Each organization will likely develop its own approach within the context of its quality management program.

Barriers to CQI

Barriers to the implementation of CQI in the health care sector have been described in detail by Ziegenfuss.[29] Most of these barriers relate to systems within health care organizations, such as technological, structural, psychosocial, managerial, or cultural subsystems. Within these systems, a number of organizational barriers may arise because of the complex nature of health care work, inadequate personnel, power conflicts, or concerns for authority over quality improvement programs. One of the most frequently mentioned challenges is that of involving physicians in CQI activities. Reasons cited for this may include lack of time for or commitment to organizationwide activities.[9]

Additional barriers associated with planning, leading, and organizing for quality improvement activities may prove to be difficult to overcome, but the existence of organizational barriers to quality improvement activities needs to be recognized and addressed before quality improvement initiatives can be fully adopted in health care settings. Additional research and practice-related studies that help to explain how the different variables facilitate or hinder the adoption of CQI may help those interested in expanding their quality improvement initiatives.

The use of CQI techniques offers the health care executive a structured approach to managing and improving the process and outcomes of care.[27] It provides the tools necessary to reduce process variation, waste, inefficiencies, and complexity in health care processes. But, because CQI tends to focus on existing processes of care, it should be combined with an outcomes management program that focuses on the appropriateness and outcomes of various medical interventions.[30]

Practice Variations and Guidelines

There is significant interest in measuring patient outcomes to find out what works in medicine and what doesn't. Over the past 20 years, a growing body of research has demonstrated the existence of wide variations in clinical practices. Research conducted by Wennberg[13-15] revealed the significance of variations in the rate of different medical and surgical procedures within small geographic areas. These variations could not be explained by differences in patients' medical conditions and did not correspond to differences in health outcome, but were attributable to differences in physician practice styles.[15] This research has suggested that patients in some areas may receive unnecessary care, while others may not receive needed care.

Additional studies conducted by researchers at the RAND Corporation revealed that as much as one-third of medical care provided to patients may be unnecessary or of little benefit.[31,32] These results have raised questions as to the "best" or "most effective" treatment for some medical conditions and have contributed to concerns about the value and quality of medical interventions. Inappropriate care in the form of under- or overutilization of services for patients has indicated a great need to measure the appropriateness and outcomes of various medical interventions.[33]

As a result of these uncertainties, the federal government launched an ambitious effort to measure and improve the quality and effectiveness of medical care. In 1989, Congress supported a number of new health care research initiatives to study clinical outcomes, medical effectiveness, and clinical practice guidelines. The ultimate goal of this effort is to develop clinical practice guidelines for treatment of different clinical conditions. Clinical guidelines have been described as a tool for developing consensus among physicians about the most appropriate clinical practices.[34] Because variation and inappropriate care can occur when there is uncertainty and lack of consensus about appropriate indications for treatments,[13] well-researched guidelines should help physicians improve decision making, especially if they are continually updated as medical technology evolves.

Outcomes Management

A third component of a comprehensive quality management program would include the use of outcomes management techniques. Outcomes management combines the use of clinical practice guidelines with the results of outcomes research and focuses on finding out what works from patients' points of view. Outcomes management relies on the use of "standards and guidelines to assist physicians in selecting interventions; it routinely and systematically measures the functioning and well-being of patients; it pools clinical and outcome data on a massive scale; and it attempts to analyze and disseminate results from the segment of the database most appropriate to the concerns of each decision maker."[10] Outcome measures go beyond the traditional measures of morbidity and mortality and consider patient satisfaction with the care received, changes in patients' functional abilities, and health-related quality of life. Outcomes management reflects a trend toward measuring quality from patients' perspectives.

As previously described, health care consists of many different dimensions of quality. While the technical aspects of clinical quality may have been the primary focus of many quality assurance programs, there is now increased attention being given to the dimension of quality associated with interpersonal aspects of care. This dimension considers patient preferences for treatment options, patient-practitioner relationships, and the conveniences and courtesies of the medical service provided.[2] The attention given to this dimension of health care quality is becoming more evident as more managed care organizations begin to generate "report cards," with the results of patient ratings for satisfaction with physician office hours, waiting times, and friendliness of physicians and office staff.[35] As competition in health care increases, and as providers seek to attract patients to particular health care facilities, this dimension will likely gain more attention and be used to compare various health care programs.

Using patient satisfaction and outcomes as indicators of quality has led to questions about who should judge the quality of patient outcomes. Health economists would suggest that "the ultimate judge of quality and value of a product or service should be the consumer. Thus medical quality can be defined by the nature of the medical outcome as perceived by the patient."[36] It is expected that ongoing outcomes research will provide information about the care that best reflects the needs and wants of health care consumers. This is entirely consistent with the new emphasis on measuring quality from patients' perspectives and reflects the customer-driven focus of CQI. It has become apparent that it is no longer sufficient to measure quality by the traditional "assessment by inspection." Instead, quality must be built into health care processes, and outcomes of care must be measured in an ongoing fashion so that unwanted variation can be reduced and the overall quality of health care improved.

As leaders in health care, physician executives need to understand and address these issues if they are to participate in the debate on controlling costs and measuring quality. There is no doubt that quality can be improved by determining the best medical practices, adopting those practices, and continually measuring and improving the processes of care. The use of scientifically documented methods and tools to measure, analyze, and improve quality of care are already available and have been shown to be effective in the health care setting. We have entered an era of medical quality management that emphasizes the use of practice guidelines, embraces the concepts and techniques of continuous quality improvement, and incorporates new measures of patient health outcomes. The development of an integrated, comprehensive quality management program designed and run by clinicians will be the best approach to improving the quality of medical care.

References

1. Donabedian, A. "The Quality of Care: How Can it be Assessed?" *JAMA* 260(12):1743-8, Sept. 23-30, 1988.

2. Donabedian, A. "Defining and Measuring the Quality of Health Care." In *Assessing Quality Health Care: Perspectives for Clinicians.* Wenzel, R. (Ed.). Baltimore, Md.: Williams & Wilkins, 1992.

3. Nash, D., and Goldfield, N. "Information Needs of Purchasers." In *Providing Quality Care: The Challenge to Clinicians.* Nash, D., and Goldfield, N. (Eds.). Philadelphia, Pa.: American College of Physicians, 1989.

4. U.S. Congress, Office of Technology Assessment. *The Quality of Medical Care: Information for Consumers.* Washington, D.C.: U.S. Government Printing Office, June 1988 (OTA-H-386).

5. Nash, D. *Buying Value in Health Care.* Washington, D.C.: National Association of Manufacturers, 1992.

6. Roberts, J., and others. "The New Accreditation System: An Overview from the Joint Commission on Accreditation of Healthcare Organizations." In *Assessing Quality Health Care: Perspectives for Clinicians.* Wenzel, R. (Ed.). Baltimore, Md.: Williams & Wilkins, 1992.

7. Clinton, J. *Annotated Bibliography: Quality of Care Research.* Rockville, Md.: Agency for Health Care Policy and Research, Publication No. 92-0029, Sept. 1992.

8. Batalden, P., and Buchanan, E. "Industrial Models of Quality Improvement." In *Providing Quality Care: The Challenge to Clinicians*. Goldfield, N., and Nash, D. (Eds.). Philadelphia, Pa.: American College of Physicians, 1989.

9. Berwick, D., and others. *Curing Health Care: New Strategies for Quality Improvement*. San Francisco, Calif.: Jossey-Bass Publishers, 1990.

10. Ellwood, P. "Outcomes Management: A Technology of Patient Experiences." *New England Journal of Medicine* 318(23):1549-56, June 9, 1988.

11. Kaplan, S., and Ware, J. "The Patient's Role in Health Care and Quality Assessment" In *Providing Quality Care: The Challenge to Clinicians*, Nash, D., and Goldfield, N. (Eds.). Philadelphia, Pa.: American College of Physicians, 1989.

12. Iezzoni, L. "Measuring the Severity of Illness and Case Mix" In *Providing Quality Care: The Challenge to Clinicians*, Nash, D., and Goldfield, N. (Eds.). Philadelphia, Pa.: American College of Physicians, 1989.

13. Wennberg, J., and others. "Hospital Use and Mortality Among Medicare Beneficiaries in Boston and New Haven." *New England Journal of Medicine* 321(17):1168-73, Oct. 26, 1989.

14. Wennberg, J. "The Paradox of Appropriate Care." *JAMA* 258(18):2568-9, Nov. 13, 1987.

15. Wennberg, J. "Dealing with Medical Practice Variations: A Proposal for Action." *Health Affairs* 3(2):6-32, Summer 1984.

16. Chassin, M., and others. "Variations in the Use of Medical and Surgical Services by the Medicare Population." *New England Journal of Medicine* 314(5):285-90, Jan. 30, 1986.

17. Eddy, D. "Variations in Physician Practice: The Role of Uncertainty." *Health Affairs* 3(2):74-89, Summer 1984.

18. Roos, N., and Roos, L. "Small Area Variations, Practice Style, and Quality of Care." In *Assessing Quality Health Care: Perspectives for Clinicians*, Wenzel, R. (Ed). Baltimore, Md.: Williams & Wilkins, 1992.

19. Nash, D. "Practice Guidelines and Outcomes. Where Are We Headed?" *Archives of Pathology and Laboratory Medicine* 114(11):1122-5, Nov. 1990.

20. Laffel, G., and Blumenthal, D. "The Case for Using Industrial Quality Management Science in Health Care Organizations." *JAMA* 262(20):2869-73, Nov. 24, 1989.

21. "The Role of Hospital Leadership in the Continuous Improvement of Patient Care Quality." *Journal for Healthcare Quality* 14(5):8-14,22, Sept.-Oct. 1992.

22. Jencks, S., and Wilensky, G. "The Health Care Quality Improvement Initiative: A New Approach to Quality Assurance in Medicine." *JAMA* 268(7):900-3, Aug. 19, 1992.

23. Berwick, D. "Continuous Improvement as an Ideal in Health Care." *New England Journal of Medicine* 320(1):53-6, Jan. 5, 1989.

24. Plsek, P. "A Primer on Quality Improvement Tools." In *Curing Health Care: New Strategies for Quality Improvement*, Berwick, D., and others (Eds.). San Francisco, Calif.: Jossey-Bass Publishers, 1990.

25. O'Rourke, L.. "Benchmarking: A New Tool for Quality Improvement in Healthcare." *The Quality Letter for Healthcare Leaders* 4(7):1-9, Sept. 1992.

26. Coffey, R., and others. "An Introduction to Critical Paths." *Quality Management in Health Care* 1(1):45-54, Fall 1992.

27. Jennison, K. "Total Quality Management—Fad or Paradigmatic Shift?" In *Health Care Quality Management for the 21st Century*, Couch, J. (Ed.). Tampa, Fla.: American College of Physician Executives, 1991.

28. Berwick, D., "Controlling Variation in Health Care." *Medical Care* 29(12):1212-25, Dec. 1991.

29. Ziegenfuss, J. "Organizational Barriers to Quality Improvement in Medical and Healthcare Organizations." *American Journal of Medical Quality* 6(4):115-22, Winter 1991.

30. Reinertsen, J. "Outcomes Management and Continuous Quality Improvement: The Compass and the Rudder." *Quality Review Bulletin* 19(1):5-7, Jan. 1993.

31. Brook, R., and others. *Appropriateness of Acute Medical Care for the Elderly: An Analysis of the Literature*. Santa Monica, Calif.: RAND Corporation, 1989.

32. Merrick, N., and others. "Use of Carotid Endarterectomy in Five California Veterans Administration Medical Centers." *JAMA* 256(18):2531-5, Nov. 14, 1986.

33. Chassin, M., and others. "Does Inappropriate Use Explain Geographic Variations in the Use of Health Care Services?" *JAMA* 258(18):2533-7, Nov. 13, 1987.

34. Gottlieb, L. "Clinical Guidelines and Quality Management: A Match Made at HCHP." *Quality Connection* 1(4):3-5, May 1992.

35. Winslow, R. "Report Card on Quality and Efficiency of HMO's May Provide a Model for Others." *Wall Street Journal*, March 9, 1993, page B1.

36. Reinhardt, U. "The Importance of Quality in the Debate on National Health Policy." In *Health Care Quality Management for the 21st Century*. Couch, J. (Ed.). Tampa, Fla.: American College of Physician Executives, 1991.

David B. Nash, MD, MBA, is Director and Nelda E. Johnson, PharmD, is Project Director, Health Policy and Clinical Outcomes, Thomas Jefferson University Hospital, Philadelphia, Pa.

Maintaining Quality in a Cost-Conscious Environment

by David B. Nash, MD, MBA,
and Nelda E. Johnson, PharmD

CHAPTER 17

This chapter builds on elements of medical quality management discussed in Chapter 16 and provides information on different approaches to improving quality of care within the confines of cost containment activities.

The current push to provide evidence of the quality of care may stem, in part, from purchasers who seek reassurance that they are obtaining value for their health care dollars—that is, high quality at a reasonable price.[1] But this increased demand for quality comes at a time when purchasers are also demanding steep discounts and cost reductions. It is acknowledged that past attempts to hold down health care costs have not worked and have contributed to additional frustrations for both providers and purchasers of care.[2] This growing frustration over failed attempts to contain costs has been compounded by the lack of information about the quality and outcomes of various medical services.[3]

As noted recently by Fuchs,[4] future attempts to reduce health care costs will be painful, not only for providers but for consumers as well. Fuchs described three possible mechanisms to lower overall health care costs:

- Use fewer resources to produce the health care services.

- Reduce the number of services provided.

- Cut the prices paid to providers.

Obviously, none of these methods will be painless or without consequences for providers, but it is certainly in the best interests of physicians to take the lead and find ways in which health care services could be provided more efficiently, using fewer resources to get the best possible outcomes. This will be especially important as market forces continue to exert significant pressure and managed care organizations award contracts on the basis of cost and quality measures. Because competitive systems with negotiated prepaid rates are starting to replace traditional fee-for-service systems, physicians will need to evaluate areas of care where improvements in quality and cost can be obtained. This will require leadership, commitment, and support to achieve significant and beneficial results.

Ongoing concerns about cost containment activities have been evident since the introduction of the Medicare prospective payment system for hospitals in 1983. Over the years, numerous researchers have evaluated the relationship between cost and quality.[5,6] Because of this extensive research, we now know that the DRG-based prospective payment system did not automatically result in poorer quality of care for Medicare patients, even though it created strong incentives for hospitals to control costs.[7] In an analysis of discharge data from 656 hospitals, Fleming[8] found the relationship between cost and quality of hospital care to be complex and associated with a variety of factors, including the type of quality measures used, the type of patients from whom the measures were developed, and the characteristics of the hospitals. The relationship between cost and quality also depends on the level of quality already being provided.[8] There are some levels of quality where improvements can be achieved with significant cost savings. In some cases, just moving to a more cost-effective strategy of care can result in improved patient outcomes at a lower cost.

Physicians and payers are now realizing that, although cost considerations have been instrumental in raising awareness of quality issues, factors such as appropriateness, effectiveness, and outcomes can also affect the cost of medical care.[9] To understand where improvements can be made, it is essential to measure quality of care and target those areas where improvements will be most beneficial.

Although the most commonly reported quality measure appears to be hospital-reported, severity-adjusted mortality rates, several other measures of quality are available and appropriate to use as indicators. Traditional measures include morbidity, complication rates, and hospital readmission rates, while newer quality measures (often used to compare managed care plans) include immunization rates, improvements in patients' functional status after surgery, preventive health measures, and patient satisfaction with health care services.

A number of tools, such as continuous quality improvement and outcomes management, are already available to help physicians measure and improve quality of care. The use of patient outcome measures, such as functional status and patient satisfaction, can provide valuable information about the outcomes of care. While the use of patient satisfaction as a measure of quality may be difficult for some clinicians to accept, the literature shows that patient satisfaction affects both patient-physician relationships and, ultimately, patients' health status.[10] Patients can and do make sound decisions about their health care treatments, and many are interested in learning more about their treatment options. Physicians are well-advised to consider the design and use of patient satisfaction information, as it is routinely collected by departments of marketing, public relations, or quality assessment in hospitals and managed care organizations.

The use of continuous quality improvement techniques can help physicians examine health care processes and identify areas where inefficiencies or poor quality exist. There is a growing body of evidence to suggest that our health care system uses more resources than necessary to produce the services that it provides. In fact, after working with several health care organizations, industrial management experts have estimated that between 40 and 50 percent of health care dollars are wasted due to inefficiencies, complexity, variation, and duplicated efforts in health care processes.[2]

As we begin to understand that much of health care comprises a series of complex, interlinked processes, we will find that, by identifying and correcting flaws in the system, improvements in both quality and costs can be achieved. For instance, a lost laboratory test result or a delay in a patient admission due to inefficient processes in the system can be costly in terms of both patient care and money. One of the key tenets of continuous quality improvement theory is that "poor quality is costly." Using quality improvement techniques to reduce waste or inefficiencies in processes will usually more than pay back the initial time investment required to correct the underlying cause of the problem.

The availability of well-researched national clinical practice guidelines can help reduce inefficiencies related to practice variations by improving clinical decision making and reducing uncertainty in medical decisions. It has been shown that variations in practice patterns can contribute to higher health care costs, with little difference in patient outcomes. For instance, a study that compared the outcomes of patients admitted to two different institutions found that, on average, the length of stay was two days shorter for one hospital, but these patients experienced no significant differences in mortality or hospital readmission rates. The difference in length of stay was found to be attributable to local variation in practice style.[11] Finding out which practices result in optimal patient outcomes, with efficient use of resources, can help physicians provide high-quality care in a cost-effective manner.

Some hospitals and managed care organizations use sophisticated computer systems to improve access to clinical information and provide physicians with algorithms or locally developed practice parameters. At LDS Hospital, a member hospital of Intermountain Health Care located in Salt Lake City, an expert computer system offers physicians a variety of clinical algorithms and alerts for medications and laboratory test results.[12] This expert system can bring a clinical problem to the physician's attention, establish a hypothesis, and recommend action steps for the physician to consider.

A quality triad that incorporates the use of newer measures of health outcomes, continuous quality improvement techniques, and practice guidelines may allow physicians to replace time-consuming traditional quality assurance methods with those that measure and build quality improvement into the daily activities of clinical care. Reducing inefficiencies in the system and targeting processes for improvements will assist physicians in providing high-quality care while reducing costs. Although the direct connection between quality improvement and outcomes of care is uncertain at this time, the tools used in total quality management, such as self-evaluation, review of the processes of care, and reliance on data rather than on anecdotal information, can be useful in assessing and improving outcomes.

With the advent of sophisticated computer systems, physician leaders have an exciting opportunity to become involved with a new science that is developing—namely, the science of clinical evaluation. This new field is based on clinical evaluations of hospital-based or managed care clinical practices and can be used to identify areas for improvement. Facilitating the development of this new science is detailed information that is routinely available from administrative databases that merge financial information (such as LOS and use of resources by DRG) with clinical and severity-of-illness data. By combining these datasets, a powerful source of information can be generated. For example, detailed practice profiles of individual physicians can be produced and used to gauge their financial impact on the organization. In 1990, almost 51 percent of hospitals generated practice profiles for their medical staff members, but only 55 percent of those hospitals shared the data with their physicians.[13] This information should be used by medical staff leaders to track the use of resources and determine the most efficient clinical decision-making pathways on a DRG basis.[14]

Centers of clinical evaluation directed by physicians are now being established to formalize this approach and produce performance comparisons.[15] While this activity is still limited primarily to large academic medical centers, it can be expected to diffuse to smaller institutions soon. Typical activities performed at these centers for clinical evaluation include determining the appropriate use of resources, such as laboratory tests, pharmaceuticals, and radiology, and variations in outcomes and length of stay.

Initial areas targeted for clinical improvements should include those with significant practice variations or areas of uncertainty that result in differences in care or outcomes. These areas could be identified through a central planning or quality tracking program governed and led by a physician executive. Clinician leaders need to find out which clinical processes can be streamlined and standardized, with the goal of developing more consistent behavior among practitioners. Changing clinical practice patterns will not be an easy task and will require the use of appropriate and timely feedback to physicians.[16] A central resource group, with a physician leader to study practice patterns and oversee these activities, can help focus on issues of quality, outcomes, and cost-effectiveness.

Effectively managing quality improvement activities will involve having upper managers directly involved in planning an organized approach. Areas for quality improvements should be systematically identified, responsibilities clearly defined, and strategic plans and goals developed. Efforts should focus on areas with unacceptable outcomes or areas that offer a cost-effective opportunity for improvement. Some of the steps that physician leaders may use when undertaking these efforts include:

■ Using computerized databases to analyze practice patterns.

■ Identifying variables associated with poor outcomes.

■ Developing and using clinical guidelines for cost-effective practices.

■ Analyzing efficiency and outcomes of care.

■ Providing ongoing feedback to physicians through clinical quality reports.

In today's health care environment, quality must be measured and analyzed with regard to performance, patient satisfaction, and the cost-effectiveness of care. To show that value is being provided, health care providers will need to collect and report specific clinical quality data to purchasers and to the public. Measuring quality no longer means meeting minimum standards; it means striving for excellence and value in providing the care that best meets the needs of patients and consumers. Physician executives are already specializing in areas of quality management,[17] but the real challenge will be for physicians to lead the way in adopting new methodologies for quality measurement, identifying areas for improvement, and making the changes to improve quality, with resultant cost savings.

References

1. Nash, D. *Buying Value in Health Care.* Washington, D.C.: National Association of Manufacturers, 1992.

2. Berwick, D., and others. (Eds.) *Curing Health Care: New Strategies for Quality Improvement.* San Francisco, Calif.: Jossey-Bass Publishers, 1990.

3. Relman, A. "Assessment and Accountability, the Third Revolution in Medical Care." *New England Journal of Medicine* 319(18):1220-2, Nov. 3, 1988.

4. Fuchs, V. "No Pain, No Gain: Perspectives on Cost Containment." *JAMA* 269(5):631-3, Feb 3, 1993.

5. Scott, W., and Flood, A. "Cost and Quality of Hospital Care: A Review of the Literature." *Medical Care Review* 41(4):213-61, Winter 1984.

6. Flemming, S. "The Relationship between the Cost and Quality of Hospital Care: A Review of the Literature." *Medical Care Review* 47(4):487-502, Winter 1990.

7. Hsia, D., and Ahern, C. "Good Quality Care Increases Hospital Profits under Prospective Payment." *Health Care Financing Review* 13(3):17-26, Spring 1992.

8. Fleming, S. "The Relationship between Quality and Cost: Pure and Simple?" *Inquiry* 28(1):29-38, Spring 1991.

9. Nash, D., and Goldfield, N. "Information Needs of Purchasers" In *Providing Quality Care: The Challenge to Clinicians.* Nash, D., and Goldfield, N. (Eds.) Philadelphia, Pa.: American College of Physicians, 1989.

10 Kaplan, S., and Ware, J. "The Patient's Role in Health Care and Quality Assessment." In Nash, D., and Goldfield, N. (Eds.), *Providing Quality Care: The Challenge to Clinicians.* Philadelphia, Pa.: American College of Physicians, 1989.

11. Eagle, K., and others. "Variation in Intensive Care Unit Practices in Two Community Hospitals." *Medical Care* 29(12):1237-45, Dec. 1991.

12. Williamson, J. "Medical Quality Management Systems in Perspective." In *Health Care Quality Management for the 21st Century.* Couch, J. (Ed.) Tampa, Fla.: American College of Physician Executives, 1991.

13. Koska, M. "Physician Practices Go under the Microscope." *Hospitals* 64(4):32-7, Feb. 20, 1990.

14. Hughes, R., and Lee, D. "Using Data Describing Physician Inpatient Practice Patterns: Issues and Opportunities." *Health Care Management Review* 16(1):33-40, Winter 1991.

15. Nash, D. "Creating Centralized Clinical Evaluation Units." In *The Physician Leader's Guide,* Lord, J. (Ed.). Rockville, Md.: Bader and Associates, Inc., 1992.

16. Eagle, K., and others. "Length of Stay in the Intensive Care Unit: Effects of Practice Guidelines and Feedback." *JAMA* 264(8):992-7, Aug. 23-29, 1990.

17. Donabedian, A. "Specialization in Clinical Performance Monitoring: What It Is, and How to Achieve It." *Journal of Quality Assurance and Utilization Review* 5(4):114-20, Nov. 1990.

David B. Nash, MD, MBA, is Director and Nelda E. Johnson, PharmD, is Project Director, Health Policy and Clinical Outcomes, Thomas Jefferson University Hospital, Philadelphia, Pa.

Discipline and Commitment

CHAPTER 18

by Sandra L. Gill and Eric W. Springer, LLB

ealth care leaders are simultaneously facilitators of change and managers of professional standards. This requires knowledge, skills, and judgment in complex regulatory, organizational, and individual behavioral patterns. Physician executives are commonly called upon to address professional conduct within this complex work setting. This chapter provides guidelines for intervention regarding disruptive behavior, followed by principles for developing commitment.

Legal Perspectives

Health care managers are at risk for all professional activity that takes place under their jurisdiction, as an extension of legal duties placed upon the health care organization. Legal decisions have clearly established "that the hospital's legal responsibility for the quality of patient care embraces the quality of medical care as well, and that the hospital, therefore, has not only the right but the duty to establish and enforce standards of competence in physicians who practice in the hospital. The quality of care cannot be divorced and therefore the hospital must require that physicians, no less than hospital employees and visitors, meet reasonable standards of personal behavior in the hospital."[1]

Of special concern to many physician executives is the area of disruptive behavior. Disruptive behavior may include verbal abuse, physical abuse, sexual harassment, and political disruption.[2] For example, there continues to be widespread misconception that superior clinical expertise is sufficient to overlook or even forgive disruptive behavior. Thus, in many situations, excellent clinicians with chronically disruptive behavior have been tolerated.

Although concerns about workplace disruption and discrimination have long been a concern, recent media attention on sexual harassment has heightened leaders' concern with their substantial liability.[3] In addition to *quid pro quo* sexual harassment, a "hostile environment" is also an "actionable" violation under Title VII of the Civil Rights Act of 1964.[4] Health care leaders need to understand these requirements, develop and enforce policies, and act consistently within their institutional policies and bylaws.

Types of Disruptive Behavior

The disruptive practitioner is, by definition, unable to get along with others. He or she has a personal conviction that others—especially those in authority—are wrong, foolish, inept, or worse, which means that the disruptive practitioner always views him- or herself as right.[2] The need to be "right" often fuels a chronic pattern of finding fault with everything and everyone, especially individuals who are in a subordinate role or position.

Examples of disruptive conduct may include "sniping,"[5] in which part of the substantive comment is correct but is expressed in a mean-spirited fashion. Thus, the covert attempt to hurt, humiliate, or undermine others is couched in overt statements of which only a portion is correct. Frequently, these statements are thinly disguised as an "interest in better patient care."[6]

Other behaviors may include refusal to participate in medical staff and other departmental affairs, or doing so only on his or her own terms; rude and abusive treatment of others, including nurses, staff, visitors, and even patients, which he or she "justifies" by a busy schedule and unreasonable demands; nonconstructive criticism of physicians or hospital personnel or of the operation of the hospital; and even threats or physical assaults in the hospital, medical staff lounge, or parking lot. Unfortunately, these actions are often accompanied by a sense of active enjoyment in suing and threatening suit.[6]

It is important to differentiate the disruptive practitioner from one who is merely different—unorthodox opinions, unusual life-style, or different tastes. The organization must not discriminate against mere differences; rather, "it is only when personal idiosyncrasies, as expressed in words and deeds, begin to affect the ability of others to get their jobs done or impinge on their right to go about their business free of burdensome harassment, or when they begin to interfere even with the disruptive physician's ability to perform well professionally, that action is called for."[6]

Guidelines for Action

Common sense and social psychology support the need to act as soon as possible in the face of disruptive behavior.[7] While a single episode of disruptive behavior may not appear to be sufficiently serious to warrant action, time and time again it becomes clearer, upon investigation, that this is part of a larger pattern of behavior. In fact, some disruptive practitioners may argue that, regardless of past history, current behavior cannot be considered along with previous incidents. However, "no court has yet held that, by failing to take action at some particular point in a continuing course of disruptive conduct, the hospital has, in effect, waived earlier incidents and is therefore foreclosed from considering them in revoking an appointment."[8]

Initial documentation is essential in establishing a pattern of disruptive conduct over time, and should be specific. Suggested elements include date and time; impact or involvement on patients, if any, including the patient's name; circumstances that seem to have precipitated the event; factual, objective words describing the behavior in question; consequences as they relate to patient care and/or the operation of the care center; and a record of any action taken, including date, time, place, and names of those making the intervention.[9]

Intervention, however, is a delicate matter, so the initial intervention should accomplish two goals: provide a firm, professional gesture of helpfulness to the practitioner and make clear that continued behavior will result in more formal action to stop it.

Physician executives must prepare adequately for this intervention. A descriptive statement of the behavior, its impact on others, and related facts must be made. Leaders should expect a defensive reaction but should use firm but repetitive statements if necessary to make their point. An essential skill is learning to interrupt the disruptive practitioner in a firm but calm fashion to repeat that further behavior will not be tolerated. Various phrases should be rehearsed in advance, such as "...yes, and this violates our policy on professional conduct," or "...perhaps that is true, but it is not an excuse and this behavior will not be tolerated any further." Leaders should not underestimate the skill disruptive practitioners often possess in "turning the tables," creating a sense of sympathy for themselves, misstating events in their favor, and even threatening some kind of retaliation. Where retaliation is a strong possibility, the involvement of legal counsel at the outset may be useful.[10]

Of special note are situations in which the individual assigned the intervention is an economic competitor or has had a long-standing personal difference with the disruptive practitioner. In this case, another competent and appropriate leader should be found.

In the initial meeting, the disruptive practitioner should be informed that no further disruptive behavior will be tolerated. In some cases, a statement of apology from the disruptive individual to those harmed may be requested. Typically, a written letter follows the initial meeting, from the physician leader to the disruptive practitioner, affirming the agreement that the unacceptable behavior will stop. If it continues, progressive discipline should be invoked, rather than a series of ineffective oral or written warnings. Consistent with appropriate bylaws, fines and suspensions may be used, up to temporary and even permanent suspension from the medical staff. A continuing pattern of disruption, however, clearly requires the ongoing assistance of legal counsel so that the intervention is applied appropriately. Bylaws will vary regarding the requirement for a due process hearing, so leaders must be very well informed and prepared.

Because of the inherent distastefulness and tension regarding disruptive practitioners, many organizational leaders deny or displace appropriate intervention. This has the effect of conveying tacit approval of the behavior, which impedes long-term organizational stability. In many organizations, newly appointed and elected medical staff leaders are provided coaching and counseling in this matter, using case examples, role-playing, and videotape scenarios. Some health care organizations have intensive programs regarding sexual harassment for all employees and managers, in the context of new employee orientation, sensitivity training, and skill development. Numerous resources are available for contemporary physician leaders.[11] Specific skill training is strongly suggested, because this area of intervention is intrinsically unpleasant.

Developing Organizational Commitment

The overwhelming transitions occurring in the health care system heighten the need for medical staff commitment to organizations. While the social psychology of commitment is complex, two key leadership actions are especially effective.

A specific program for orientation of new physicians should be developed (see sample program below), including the organization's values, expectations for professional conduct, and sexual harassment policy. Within the context of new professional orientation, the physician leader can introduce these topics matter of factly, rather than as problem-oriented exceptions. Knowledge of organizational values can be a very powerful mechanism for developing esprit de corps, and for inducing self-correcting behavior within the care-giving team. Physicians often learn only the minimal resources of the

---

Sample Physician Orientation Program

Welcome   CEO, Board Chair, Vice President of Medical Affairs, Medical Staff President

Desired Outcomes for Medical Staff Members:

Increased Convenience Through Knowledge of System:
- Access to appropriate leaders and support staff   ■ Collaborative problem-solving

■ Coordinated Patient Care:
- Physician-hospital service coordination   ■ Continuous quality improvement

Satisfaction in Practice-Hospital Interactions

Key Health Care System Facts:

Leadership Roles and Team Members:
- Board   ■ Medical staff   ■ Executive team—administration, nursing

Mission and Professional Credo:
- Purpose   ■ Service commitment and area

Medical Staff Development and Support Services:
- Vision and planning process ■ Medical staff office   ■ Management service org./support services

Medical Staff Organization:
- Purpose   ■ Functions   ■ Structure
- Officers and leaders   ■ Bylaws   ■ Policies   ■ Your department
- Your responsibilities:
  - As a medical staff member
  - As privileged practitioner

■ Clinical Care Team:
- Nursing   ■ Hospital departments ■ CQI initiatives

Hospital-Office Practice Support Services and Liaison Program

■ Medical Staff Membership Manual

organization—parking, medical staff office location, and medical staff lounge. This expanded orientation program provides an opportunity for meaningful introduction to the chief executive officer, board members, senior management team, medical staff office professionals, key organizational values, quality improvement initiatives, leadership opportunities and resources for practice management, professional development, and even personal support for times of stress.

Specific skill building through sample cases and coaching should be provided to all new medical staff leaders and other physician executives. In the context of leadership skill development, the specific policy, protocol, and alternative approaches for intervention can be illustrated, discussed, and enacted within a supportive instructional context. Physicians often contribute their best judgment to these scenarios, providing an array of suggestions that can be reviewed in terms of current policy and legal precedent.

Summary

Dealing with the disruptive practitioner is an inevitable leadership task. Understanding that courts have consistently upheld appropriate leadership intervention may provide comfort, but clear policies and protocols will enhance leaders' skills. Guidelines for the initial meeting, the importance and content of documentation, and legal involvement for subsequent interventions have been noted. in addition, specific actions for developing organizational understanding and commitment to professional conduct have been described. Physician executives will need to maintain ongoing attention to this issue, because federal law and societal sensitivity will continue to affect professional conduct.

References

1. Horty, J. "The Disruptive Physician." *Hospital Law*, Dec. 1984, p. 1.

2. Horty, J."The Disruptive Physician." *Hospital Law*, June 1978, pp. 1-14.

3. Robinson, R., and others. "Sexual Harassment at Work: Issues and Answers for Health Care Administrators." *Hospital and Health Services Administration* 38(2):167-80, Summer 1993.

4. Equal Employment Opportunity Commission, "Guidelines on Discrimination because of Sex," 29 C.F.R. 1604.11 (July 1, 1992).

5. Bramson, R. *Coping with Difficult People.* New York, N.Y.: Ballantine Books, 1981.

6. Van Maanen, J., and Schein, E. "Breaking In: Socialization to Work," in *Handbook of Work, Organization and Society*, Dubin, R., editor. Chicago, Ill.: Rand McNally, 1976, pp. 67-138.

7. Springer, E., and Casale, H. "Hospitals and the Disruptive Health Care Practitioner—Is Inability to Work With Others Enough to Warrant Exclusion?" *Duquesne Law Review* 24(2):377-423, Winter 1985.

8. Horty, J. "Hospital Policy Regarding Disruptive Physician Conduct." *Action Kit for Hospital Law*, Feb. 1992, pp. 41-2.

9. Baxter, R., and Hermle, L. *Sexual Harassment in the Workplace*. New York, N.Y.: Executive Enterprises Publications Co., 1989.

10. Bureau of National Affairs. *Sexual Harassment: Employer Policies and Problems*. Washington, D.C.: The Bureau, 1987.

11. Sheehan, K., and others. "A Pilot Study of Medical School 'Abuse': Student Perceptions of Mistreatment and Misconduct in Medical School." *JAMA* 263(4):533-7, Jan. 26, 1990.

Sandra L. Gill is President of Performance Management Resources, Inc., a health care leadership development firm in Westmont, Ill. Eric W. Springer, LLB, is Principal with Horty, Springer, and Mattern, P.C., Pittsburgh, Pa., a firm specializing in hospital and health care law.

Alternatives for Group Behavior Problems and Group Decision Making

CHAPTER

19

by Sandra L. Gill

Apathy in the Group

Apathy may mean different things. If it means silence, a few techniques listed below may help stimulate group discussion. If it means a general depression or disinterest, another approach may be indicated. Often it reflects general fatigue or distraction, where using a different room or location may help stimulate new interest. Finally, apathy is often a symptom of a group where fear or anxiety exists, such as when individuals feel intimidated by a very strong personality or where a mean-spirited, critical individual humiliates others.

Overcoming the Silent Group

Groups may suppress or heighten individual behavior. Physicians have been identified as being more "introverted" than "extroverted" in terms of their personality profiles, according to the highly respected Myers-Briggs Type Indicator. Introverts prefer to think about things before verbalizing responses and process information within themselves. In contrast, extroverts typically "talk their thinking"—i.e., they verbalize their thoughts as they think about things. In a large group, introverts become more introverted, whereas they are much more verbal in small or one-on-one situations.

If individuals tend to "clam up" in a group, the following techniques may be helpful:

■ Start the discussion by asking folks to jot down their ideas, for about 1-5 minutes, before they are asked to talk about them. This silent brainstorming time usually provokes half a dozen responses per person, which they can then read from their notes or use to guide their responses with you. For example, you can say, "What occurred to you—what did you write down? I'd like for each of you to give me one idea, and I'll make a list of them."

■ In a variation commonly used in quality improvement work groups, the individual is asked to silently brainstorm his or her ideas for a few minutes, using a packet of cards or note sheets instead of a piece of paper. Then, the group leader asks each person to place his or her responses into common categories or into a flow chart or cause-effect diagram (figure 1, below).

The key technique is the act of writing *before* discussion occurs. It generates a larger number of ideas than we usually have when talking, and it provides a face-saving moment for more introverted individuals who prefer to think about their responses before they verbalize something.

Another technique is to ask each person to provide one comment, or to take his or her turn for one minute, as a way to get discussion going. In this setting, the comments of others are not permitted until each person has had a fair allotment of time. In most groups, we react to the first few comments and many individuals are not provided much time to offer opinions, unless they are very assertive.

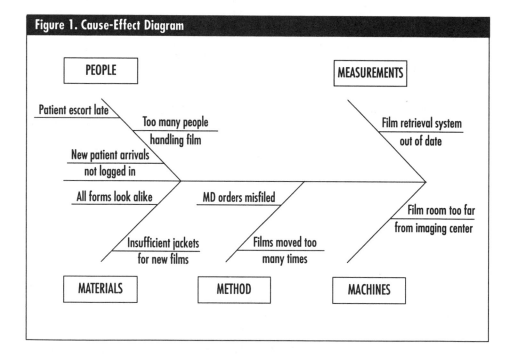

Figure 1. Cause-Effect Diagram

Dealing with the Disinterested, Depressed Group

If the group just doesn't seem to respond, and you feel a kind of sullen silence, it usually is advisable to stop and confront the situation. For example, you might use a little humor (if it's natural for you to do so) and say, "Well, your enthusiasm is underwhelming. Can someone tell me what the problem is? I'm not getting any sense of support for this issue." You will either open up a wellspring of response or get the same silent treatment. If the silent treatment continues, you might try a few other approaches. For example, you might ask folks to evaluate support for the issue on a 0-4 point scale, where the 0 means "no opinion," 1 is "strongly disagree," and 4 is "strongly agree." I recommend a silent ballot using a 3 x 5 card for this.

Dealing with Fear and Intimidation

Where the apathy reflects anxiety and people are quiet for fear of saying anything, the attacker simply must be confronted. This confrontation usually needs to be conducted with several of the key physicians, because those who attack others will usually reserve their most acute outrage for the individual who confronts their destructive behavior. Bramson provides specifically helpful advice on this situation.[1] The general rule of thumb is to confront difficult people with two or more individuals, because the one-to-one confrontation is either too risky or becomes misreported to others by the difficult person. Before such a confrontation, the group needs to come to a very clear agreement about possible sanctions to be imposed if even one more incident of such disruption should occur. It also has to be prepared to employ the sanctions when necessary.

In an episodic situation, where someone is unexpectedly nasty, one of the best techniques is assertive communication, where one calmly states what is and is not acceptable. For example, "Doctor Smith, I can appreciate your frustration, but yelling at me is simply not acceptable to me. I will talk to you in one hour so long as you remain calm with me. I will not participate in this discussion at this time. Thank you."

Another approach is to ask the group to critically evaluate the issue, and to specifically ask for *modifications that will improve* the issue at hand. This question usually provokes more interesting discussion. You must insist, however, that group members make specific comments to improve the matter, not just easy criticisms that do not provide any additional information.

Another approach is to change the venue, i.e., discuss the issue in another meeting, in another location or room, or at another time. As a last resort, you may ask for a motion to table the issue, or to refer it back to the subcommittee from which it came.

Developing Direction and Consensus among Diverse Professionals

This is an essential skill for group leaders, and it is a very demanding task. Several approaches may be helpful.

First, plan to set annual goals within the group. A group facilitation process (specifically, nominal group technique) is a powerful way to obtain individual opinions and aggregate them into group priorities. The nominal group technique was developed in 1975 to combine individual creativity with valuable group judgment and works extremely well when diverse individuals are trying to formulate a few key priorities. It is easier to see this group process than to describe it; a videotape illustrating the process is available.[2]

Another approach is use of "interest-based negotiation," as described by leaders in the Program on Negotiation at the Harvard Law School.[3-6] The essence of this process is a focus on fundamental, shared interests, combined with creative brainstorming to identify alternative "positions" or specific actions to optimize shared interests. A central leadership skill includes the ability to "actively listen" to colleagues, without getting absorbed in argumentation. For example, the leader may say, "If I understand correctly, you are concerned with...and you feel I have not paid attention to any of your previous comments to me." Active listening, in which you paraphrase in your own words both the substance and feeling you perceive in others, is an invaluable leadership skill and rapidly gets better with practice.[7]

Some groups have defined consensus voting to mean "almost total agreement" rather than the virtually impossible definition where everyone must agree. For example, consensus may be redefined to mean "all but three must agree." This allows for some individual opinions while allowing for much more than a simple majority. Most leaders learn the hard way that a simple majority vote is very thin ice on which to skate. Beware actions that only obtain a simple majority, because it most often melts away in the light of the next day.

Yet another technique for developing consensus is to back away from those areas where huge conflict exists and to start identifying smaller areas where there is agreement, to create a sense that agreement can be reached on things. As one leader moaned, "Our group couldn't agree to run out of a burning building together!" Fortunately, his hypothesis has not yet been tested!

Use of 3 x 5 cards will often identify the source of conflict in a group. With a very influential, vocal person, the group may appear to be in conflict when in fact, only one or two people support the vocal person. Using a 3 x 5 card to collect opinions in a face-saving way may identify the extent of agreement. Often, when provided this safe way to express opinions, individuals will express private support even though they will not publicly go against influential members of the group.

Identifying and Developing Leaders and Dealing with Informal Leaders

About the only way to identify leaders is to identify them! Clarification of the role and responsibility of leaders can be accomplished with short position descriptions, above what may be stated in the bylaws. Position descriptions usually include clear statements of important behaviors, clarity regarding accountability and authority, and performance review and evaluation. Prerequisite experience and skills should be included, and the frequency with which the role will be compensated should be mentioned. Specific compensation usually varies over time and is not included in the generic position description but is included in the letter of understanding to the leader from the board.

Groups should have position descriptions for each officer, board member, committee chair, and management role, at the least. Well-developed groups will have position descriptions for every member of the group.

Leadership development should be supported with a written plan of developmental experiences and education, tuition support, and regular retreats for leadership orientation and strategic planning. Some groups even provide new member orientation so that people who join the group are educated about the role of group leaders. New member orientation can go a long way to eliminate internal back-biting of current leaders.

Most groups have both the formal, elected or appointed leader and at least one or more informal leaders (such as the person who generates the greatest revenue, the group founder, or the strongest personality). Informal leaders will often engage in sabotage of the current formal leader as a way to preserve individual autonomy. Formal leaders need to learn assertiveness skills to confront this behavior. Humor can be especially helpful, if it comes naturally—sarcasm, however, may precipitate a more vengeful future attack. Formal leaders usually will talk one-to-one with informal leaders and solicit support. If this does not help, the group needs to make a decision to redefine consensus voting and move on. One of the oldest patterns among physician groups is the power of the individual to destroy forward progress by his or her singular vote against whatever the current proposal may be. Leaders need to have some specific mechanism to acknowledge disagreement and move on.

Integrating Needs of Physicians along Age Cohorts, Different Needs, Interests

One of the best ways to integrate different needs is to do an annual needs assessment, asking each physician to identify aspects of the practice that are most satisfying, areas in which he or she wants to provide leadership, and aspects in which strategic and operational attention is needed. This annual needs assessment becomes a source of baseline data the board uses to develop a strategic plan and annual operational goals.

Another approach is to have a board member, perhaps the president-elect/vice president, speak periodically to assess progress and satisfaction. I like the simple protocol shown below[8]:

■ Aspects that are excellent (continue these).

■ Aspects that we need to do more often (start doing).

■ Aspects that we need to stop (do less often).

This provides meaningful information, with an emphasis on positive features within the group. It is usually very gratifying for leaders to hear what is going well, because they won't unless they ask, in most settings!

In very large groups, the board may invite individuals from different age cohorts to sit as nonvoting members in board meetings and participate in group priority setting. Focus groups are another way to solicit concerns along age groups. Yet another method is the conscious identification of physicians across the age spectrum for committee assignments, so that a more representative committee composition and structure is established. Many times, we inadvertently overlook those who are different (younger, opposite gender) from the traditional leadership structure of the group.

Groups and Decision Making: Getting the Most out of Meetings[9]

Groups are distinguished by six characteristics, most notably described by Knowles and Knowles:[10]

■ A group requires a *definable membership*, i.e., members must know who belongs and who does not.

■ A group has a *consciousness* of itself as a single entity. Members of the group have a sense of identification with one another.

- A group has a sense of *shared* purpose, goals, or ideals.

- There must be *interdependence* among the group members. They must need one another to satisfy the group's goals.

- A group is distinguished by the *interaction* of its members, by the way they communicate, influence, and interact with one another.

- A group acts as a *single entity* rather than as a collection of individual actors.

Especially under conditions of conflict, many physicians withdraw from collective activity and act independently of their colleagues.[11] They have been described as "tough battlers" who single-mindedly pursue an individual goal. In the face of conflict, physicians often fight more aggressively or abandon public efforts to exert person-to-person influence. Thus, the physician executive is faced with individuals who only occasionally behave interdependently.

Types Of Groups
Knowing the varieties of groups is helpful in understanding a difficult situation as well as in knowing how to direct an effort that requires collective action.

Work Groups—The most obvious type of professional group is the work group. Work groups have been distinguished from other types of groups by their commitment to a primary task. Often, work groups are inhibited from task completion by unconscious, collusive behaviors, commonly referred to as "basic assumptions."[12] Because of basic assumptions, a group acts as if it had a purpose other than accomplishing its primary task. For example, a group may act as if it depends on someone inside the group (the leader, perhaps) or outside the group (the chief of staff, the hospital CEO, the board, or society) to complete its work. The group then engages in procrastination, scapegoating, and helplessness, acting as if it needs some additional power or force to achieve its goals.

A second type of basic assumption is "fight-flight." In this case, a group fails to accomplish its task because its members are preoccupied with fighting or avoiding some imagined force. For example, a group may create a scapegoat and spend the meeting time castigating the imagined scapegoat rather than designing effective strategies to achieve its goals.

A third kind of basic assumption is "pairing," where two of the group members pair to create a sense of hopefulness among the other group members that someone will absolve the group of its task.

Basic assumptions continually distract leaders from the primary task. They occur because group members prefer to create fantasies rather than face the often difficult realities of getting a job done. Fundamentally, basic assumptions serve to preserve the status quo. Specialists in basic assumption groups point out that all group leaders are susceptible to such tendencies and that recognizing one's own tendencies regarding basic assumptions can be helpful in preventing them from diverting attention from primary goals and tasks.[13] As Rioch states, "...in the mature work group, which is making a sophisticated use of the appropriate basic assumptions, the leader of the dependency group is dependable; the leader of the fight-flight group is courageous; and the leader of the pairing group is creative."[14] Thus, an awareness of basic assumptions in groups can enhance group productivity.

Reference Groups—Reference groups may be the result of formal or subjective decisions.[15] For example, the physician who is elected to the hospital governing board may perceive his or her role as representing the medical staff on the board rather than identifying with the governing board. The physician board member subjectively acts under the influence of the medical staff. In many cases, reference group membership does conflict with the goals of the actual group, and role clarification will be required.

Abstracted Groups—Abstracted group membership is important because it tends to establish expectations and behaviors for future group functioning. A group member may use a previous group experience as his or her role model for the current group. For example, an aggressive, combative role model from a previous hospital medical staff may be abstracted to the current medical staff, where conflict is normally smoothed over or avoided. The abstracted group model would violate current medical staff norms (expectations), and the group member would likely be perceived as a difficult colleague. Deviations from the current group's model of behavior may create discomfort or conflict within the group.

Hangover Groups—The term "hangover group" is used by Napier and Gershenfeld[15] to refer to the impact of unresolved conflicts and anxieties in previous groups on current groups. For example, growing up as the youngest child may have been a "sink or swim" situation in a large family with combative, aggressive, and stubborn fighting to get "one's own way." If this perception carries over into groups in adult life, usually at an unconscious level, the individual acts as if he or she is in the same situation. The difficulty with this, of course, is that group members make decisions on the basis of historical events and perceptions rather than current realities. Leaders are particularly inhibited in such situations, because members are not relating to current events that may be controlled.

Groups may be categorized in as many different ways as they have purposes. Groups are influenced heavily by members' past experiences, and effective group leaders must be sensitive to unconscious efforts among group members to act out previous experiences and assumptions. Leaders have a unique responsibility to provide clarification of the group purpose while at the same time not succumbing to group tendencies to become dependent on the leader for achievement of the group task.

Leadership For Group Development

There are numerous models of group development; indeed, different kinds of groups develop at different rates. Tuckman[16] provides a memorable conceptual model of group development derived from a variety of small group studies.

The first stage of Tuckman's model is called "forming." During this stage, the primary leadership task is to clarify purpose and task for the group. Leaders can expect to be challenged and tested during this stage, as group members attempt to discover and react to the task and to the ambiguity of achieving a goal effectively. Group members expect guidance and support from the leader in structuring this new situation and in achieving this first task of group development. Leaders can assist the group by providing a well-planned agenda, which includes attention to group discussion, brainstorming, and techniques for making decisions.

It is usually very helpful to start the first meeting with a brief overview of the purpose, time frame, available resources, constraints, and strategy for developing a working plan. Certainly, the leader should attend to careful introductions of each of the group members, including the reasons they were selected or appointed to the work group. The leader should also clarify his or her role and solicit reactions from the group regarding the leadership tasks needed to achieve the task. In the absence of such discussion, many erroneous assumptions are likely to be made and the possibility for group dependency on the leader is created. Group leaders need to be very clear about their own limits early in the development of groups. Most groups assume their leaders have much more time, energy, and resources than they actually do, and so come to be dependent on the leader.

It is especially important at this stage that the leader clarify shared values and interests to create an opportunity for group cohesion. In the absence of overtly discussed common values, small groups have a tendency to split into smaller cliques rather then function as a single entity. The group leader has to pay particular attention to this tendency and should reiterate at frequent intervals why it is important for the group to function as a single unit, preferably motivated by a common interest. In the absence of a common vision, a group can be expected to fragment and engage in conflicts.

Soon after the group's formation, the second stage of its development begins, which Tuckman calls "storming." The novelty of the new group wears off, and the reality of the task begins to create tensions. Often, the formal group leader is challenged in an overt or covert fashion. Members may disagree over how their work is to be done and over who should do what.

At this point, the leader's role shifts to that of a statesperson who facilitates problem-solving. The leader should acknowledge the conflicts and provide suggestions for a means to resolve the differences. Often, "active listening" is sufficient to displace the tension and redirect the group to productive discussions. However, the leader may also need to exert formal authority and make strong recommendations. General guidelines for this stage include the leader's attention to clarification and description of specifics, rather than making general judgments; a focus on changeable, doable ideas rather than fixed limitations and complaints about them; and a concern with the present situation and potential solutions rather than historical, unchangeable circumstances. It is at the second stage that many groups succumb to basic assumptions and attempt to move away from the group goal into more entertaining distractions (e.g., depending on the leader to make all decisions, solve all problems, etc.).

If the second stage is successfully developed, most groups move into establishing rules and protocols for getting their work done. This third stage is called "norming." Norms are expectations, most often unstated, that group members have of one another. Frequently, the norms of the group and those of its members are in conflict. Thus, clarifications of basic working procedures is a crucial task in group development.

Usually, groups determine quite readily what resources are needed and how to access them. In essence, the group must decide how to decide. However, this may not be so. Until a group determines its procedures for solving problems, a great potential for unnecessary conflict is ignored. Leaders who address these developmental issues early on will benefit from more functional behavior in later stages.

Tuckman describes groups as next moving into a more mature stage, i.e., "performing." Coordination of delegated assignments, frequent briefings and information exchanges, and achievement of closure on intermediate issues are of paramount concern here. Effective leaders attempt to anticipate group concerns by raising issues before they become crises, developing problem-solving methods, and providing group members recognition and support for jobs well done.

Group leadership is much more than task analysis, intuition, or social grace. A group leader must be sensitive to the needs of group members as individuals and as organizational representatives. Clarification of the group purpose, of individual roles within the group, and of decision-making alternatives and provision of recognition and professional support are ongoing tasks for group effectiveness. Leaders often draw upon various group members to provide appropriate contributions in each of these areas. It becomes the group's task to manage itself, where the leader facilitates and enhances the development of the group.

Decision-Making Guidelines for Group Leaders

Two of the most critical elements for effective group functioning are the leader's attention to agenda development and rehearsal in a variety of decision-making techniques.[17] Agenda planning and development can preclude numerous group dysfunctions. Armed with a variety of decision-making methods, group leaders can obtain decisions even when time and circumstance are less than optimal (figure 2, page 262).

Purpose/Outcome

Leaders have their greatest impact when they clarify the purpose and expected outcomes of the meeting in the first two minutes (when a quorum is present). The specific task of the group should be stated in terms of outcomes rather than beginning steps so that a shared vision and mindset for the group is formed. There are often many ways to achieve a task; the leader should focus more on results than on the methods for achieving them.

Date/Time/Place

While date, time, and place are often known, reiteration rarely hurts.

Number Of Participants

The size of the group has a dramatic impact on group functioning.[18] Essentially, any group larger than a dozen participants will require careful, assertive leadership to prevent dysfunctional cliques from forming and, potentially, subverting the group goal.

Seating Arrangements

Effective group leaders know that the stage is a crucial prop in the conduct of effective meetings and pay careful attention to seating arrangements. Most leaders intuitively

```
┌─────────────────────────────────────────────────────────────────┐
│ Figure 2. Meeting Planning Guide                                  │
├─────────────────────────────────────────────────────────────────┤
│ Purpose/Outcome: [Write down major result in verb-noun phrase]    │
│                                                                    │
│ Date/Time/Place:_____No. of Participants:_____     │
│                                                                    │
│ Seating Arrangements: [Alter seating to achieve key objectives]    │
│                                                                    │
│ Special Issues/Constraints: [Time, resources, politics, etc.]      │
│                                                                    │
│ Orientation to Participants: [How can they help you achieve        │
│ results?]                                                           │
│                                                                    │
│ Routine Information Items:   Est. time   Leader    Topic            │
│     Seating:                                                        │
│     A-V Needs:                                                      │
│                                                                    │
│ Action Items:              Est. time   Leader   Topic   1st, 2nd    │
│     Problem Solving:                                    Decision    │
│     Negotiation:                                        Mtd.        │
│                                                                    │
│ Outcomes/Results:                                                  │
│                                                                    │
│ Summary:                                                           │
│                                                                    │
│ Next Action Steps:                                                 │
│                                                                    │
│ Reminders:                                                         │
│                                                                    │
│ Evaluation of Meeting:                                             │
│     Results:                                                       │
│     Process:                                                       │
│ ─────────────────────────────────────────────────────────         │
│ © Sandra L. Gill.                                                  │
└─────────────────────────────────────────────────────────────────┘
```

know that round and rectangular tables facilitate group discussion. Theater seating enhances didactic presentations where group attention is focused toward the front. For many meetings, leaders may wish to start out with theater seating for briefings, announcements, short presentations, etc. Then, after a break, they may direct the group to rearrange tables and chairs for small group discussion, brainstorming, etc.

Special Issues/Constraints
Identify those special considerations and constraints that will affect your discussion.

Orientation to Participants
Group leaders should tell members how they can be helpful. For example, if the leader wants to present a series of quick announcements and doesn't want to be interrupted, members can be asked to withhold their questions until the end of the announcements. Asking members for helpful behavior provides a clear orientation and creates a constructive group norm.

Agenda Planning
For each item on a topical agenda, the speaker/leader should be identified. It is a

simple orientation to participants and listeners and helps cut down on potential disorganization. A time estimate for the topic discussion is a crucial addition. In the absence of time estimates, most speakers consume two to three times the amount of meeting time they would if given a time limit. How the time estimate is established depends on the nature of the group. Informal time estimates from participants are usually adequate. The leader may need to reduce original estimates to keep within the stated time of the overall meeting. I typically prefer that the group reduce time estimates so that the leader is not placed in an adversarial role with the group. Regardless of how time estimates are obtained and developed, they are critical to the timely completion of most meetings.

It is also extremely helpful to have a timekeeper at each meeting. Leaders are often engaged in the substance of discussion, and the presence of a collegial timekeeper makes a substantial contribution to the management of the meeting. A group member may volunteer to give each speaker several minutes' "warning" before time expires and to call time when it has expired. While this may sound strict or harsh, most groups quickly adopt this technique as a very effective mechanism for meeting management.

The agenda will identify both routine items and action items. Routine items would include brief announcements, noncontroversial reminders, etc. that require no group action beyond simple clarification. Action items require some kind of group decision making and need more strategic planning. Action items need to be prepared with a primary and a backup decision-making method so that if time expires and the group fails to make a decision with its preferred method, a backup decision-making technique has been identified to move the group through the roadblock.

Some action items will require creativity and brainstorming. Others will require more forceful negotiation and tradeoffs (figure 3, page 264). Effective group leaders must be clear about the kind of decision needed because these are two very different procedures.[19,20]

The next item is for the recording of meeting outcomes and results. This section provides an ongoing record of progress for the participants, especially if recorded during the course of the meeting on a flip chart or overhead transparency. Provided as a visual aid, it keeps group members focused on the topic; it also enables latecomers to enter discussions without referring to all previous discussions. Probably most helpful, it can provide a quick summary for meeting minute preparations. Some medical staffs have formulated actual memoranda with similar headings preprinted for the completion of departmental meeting minutes as required by the Joint Commission on Accreditation of Healthcare Organizations.

Summary, Next Action Steps, Reminders, and Meeting Evaluation are optional and very helpful considerations at the end of your meeting.

Recommendations

Use consensus to make or affirm simple decisions—it makes people feel good to occasionally "all agree."

Use majority rule to negotiate issues between factions, with "due process" structure; use estimates for aggregating judgments.

Figure 3. A Quick Summary on Decision-Making Methods

	Public Methods	Private Methods
YOU HAVE 3 BASIC CHOICES:		

Consensus	Voice vote
	Show of hands
	Other
	  "Vote with your feet, knuckles
	  win," signed memo or report
		Ballot card
		Closed chamber of panel

Majority Rule	Voice vote count Count of hands Thumbs up-down Other item selection or purchase etc.	Ballot card Forced choice Estimate submitted in writing, then tabulated
Minority Rule	Charisma "Marshall Law" Benevolent dictatorship or abdication of leaders Fiat/divide and rule Mob action	Covert divide and rule Character assassination and backbiting Coups and creating chaos

Use minority rule, i.e., exercise authority, in crisis situations and inform people of your decisions with requests for their cooperation because of the crisis.

Evaluation of Meeting

Most group leaders do not evaluate their meetings. However, should you choose to do so, it is recommended that you distinguish meeting results from the process dynamics of the session. Aggressive personalities, shy individuals, or people with high needs for control may artificially inflate or deflate evaluation results because they are dissatisfied with the process dynamics, even though they accept the results of a particular meeting. Interval scales, letter grades, or words may be used to elicit participant responses.

Summary

Decision making is the essence of an effective group. The precursor to effective decision making is agenda planning and strategy. Consideration of the meeting room; arrangement of tables, chairs, supplies, audiovisual aids, and participant orientation are important. Clarification of the purpose of the meeting and alternative strategies for making decisions are essential.

Developing responsible helpers, especially a timekeeper and a recorder/facilitator, from the decision-making group is important. Group leaders are then able to engage in substantive discussions without fear that the agenda will be abandoned.

The suggestions presented here have been summarized from more than a decade of experience with medical staffs and health care organizations. In the contemporary realm of health care leadership, management of groups and decisions is a basic survival skill. These basic guidelines are but a starting point.

An exceptionally wide range of literature is available to group leaders. The dynamics of small groups, meeting management, and decision-making protocols are widely published; videotapes, 35-mm films, and books-on-tape are also abundantly available for further skill development.

Productivity—Getting It and Keeping It

With the impact of RBRVS, the issue of group productivity has become even more crucial than in the past several years. Additional comparative information is routinely published each year by the American Medical Association in its *Socioeconomic Characteristics of Medical Practice* and *Physician Marketplace Statistics*.

Majority Versus Consensus Decision Making—Pluses, Minuses, and Techniques

Technically speaking, majority decision making refers to a simple majority. Experienced leaders know, however, that a simple majority almost always indicates a division within the group and is insufficient for effective implementation of whatever issue received the simple majority. Thus, the decision does not indicate successful implementation.

Consensus decision making technically means that all parties agree, i.e., a unanimous vote. Again, this term is frequently redefined to mean more than a simple majority. For example, a consensus may be defined as all in agreement except 10 percent of those voting, or a specific number in a defined group size.

Consensus decision making is excellent on major philosophical issues, mission statements, and major goals. It is often an exhilarating experience to have a highly professional group all agree—it is such a precious event! However, some research has shown that the norm of consensus might also create pressure on individuals to abandon their best judgment in order to remain a loyal member of the group.

One useful approach is to clearly define the meaning of either term—majority rule or consensus—in terms of how many group members must agree to reach a workable majority or consensus. This eliminates confusion on whether the decision has been achieved.

Meeting facilitators often identify agenda items requiring a vote or decision and then determine at least two ways for making that decision. For example, a compensation change may be decided first using parliamentary procedure, where a majority vote will carry the decision. If that majority is not achieved, a second option may be invoked, such as using a secret ballot where at least 80 percent of the voters must agree or the issue is tabled.

As a rule of thumb, I recommend using the most "face saving" approach, such as a 3 x 5 card to collect private ballots where a controversial vote may pit one partner against the other. Nonbinding straw votes or the use of a rating scale may also help advance controversial issues where a formal vote may result in polarization. Forcing people to make a decision may undermine their subsequent support for an issue.

Convincing Chiefs and Others of Value of Administration and Leadership

About the only approach I know to this most difficult issue is the use of a respected third party who endorses the leadership program. When someone has essentially made up his or her mind, further argumentation ("You're not being very open-minded on this" followed by "I've already been there and its just a waste of time") usually only polarizes the matter.

Negotiation principles suggest several useful phrases, such as "You may be right, and I am willing to take the risk to find out for myself." The point is to stop the endless "I'm right, you're wrong" approach and seek a higher ground where there is some agreement. For example, "I agree that the earlier program needed more fine-tuning, and I understand from the program director that many of the earlier criticisms have been addressed this time around." Using "I statements" instead of "you statements" ("You're just negative about everything") helps diffuse the argument. Sometimes a simple reply stops the argument cold, such as "Okay, I hear you," or "I guess time will tell." As the sage once said, "Stop trying to teach the pig to sing—it wastes your time and it annoys the pig." Some battles cannot be won.

Figure 4. Guidelines for Effective Committee Meetings

Write agenda with desired actions and time frames.
    Clarify credentialing procedures—15 minutes.
    Evaluate formulary alternatives—10 minutes.

Establish protocols for every meeting:
    Start on time; finish on time (shut the door).
    Select cochair and/or assistants:
        Time keeper
        Recorder/facilitator
    Use easels to track discussion.
    Move chairs to make small groups of 5-7 versus 10+.

Use a variety of decision-making methods:
    3 x 5 cards.
    Straw votes (nonbinding assessment) by show of hands, voice votes.
    Rank order (>10) most, least.
    Criteria list with 4-point scale.
    Parliamentary procedure.

Explicate the positives and ask others to help.

Schedule time for summary and next steps (responsibility chart).

Learn and practice brainstorming and negotiation[4]

Figure 5. Selected Trouble-Shooting Guide to Meeting Dynamics

PARTICIPANT PROBLEMS	POSSIBLE CAUSES	PREVENTION	ACTION Rx
Angry outbursts.	Person needs group or place to express deep feelings, concerns. Person may need security or control over outcomes; becomes provoked when meeting creates ambiguity.	Talk before meeting to solicit concerns and ventilate feelings, and reach agreement on behavior in meeting.	Use breaks, caucuses, or established guidelines for time and behavior management. Review *Coping with Difficult People* for additional steps.
People talking at same time or past each other.	Lack of listening skills or knowledge of meeting process or competing issues.	Develop and review discussion protocols with group; use round-robin speaking or writing to get all ideas out; assign person to help paraphrase or moderate discussion. Cite time limits for representative of key positions to make summary statements.	Invoke agreed upon rules for discussion. Ask moderator or recorder to restate previous issues. Cite sequence of speakers, and provide restatement of their concerns.
Person says or implies ideas are hopeless and dampens morale or enthusiasm.	Person may be "negative" or "complainer" with need to resist corrective actions or desire to block new approaches.	Meet with the person ahead of time to review his/her needs and views. Identify impact of negative behavior and ask for contributions. Be prepared to excuse person from meeting or otherwise control judgmental comments.	Set ground rules for separating creativity from evaluation comments; use silent writing to solicit evaluations. Ask people to identify "strength and modification to improve" vs. "weakness." Avoid commiseration or apology.
Many people talking about different issues at same time.	Lack of common agreement on decision-making and discussion protocols; conflict of ideas or leadership of meeting. Unclear outcome or goal of discussion.	Set up step-by-step design for meeting process; review agenda and meeting process with facilitator to assist with managing agenda process, if you are a content specialist.	State all agenda items in verb-noun outcome terms. Clarify each person's role in meeting before start. Clarify protocols for discussion. If it seems necessary, break up larger issue into subcomponents and focus on each part in some agreed upon order. Consider assigned task forces for simultaneous discussions and subsequent reports back to group as whole, for voting or action planning.

Figure 5. Selected Trouble-Shooting Guide to Meeting Dynamics (continued)

PARTICIPANT PROBLEMS	POSSIBLE CAUSES	PREVENTION	ACTION Rx
Dispute over major values, e.g., what's right, wrong.	Value conflict; need to be right; fear of unknown or lack of accurate information.	Identify some common values everyone holds, then work back to lower-level agreements or options. Use "shuttle diplomacy" to create common ground in more protected format than large or public meeting.	Appeal to common vision or common enemy to motivate sense of shared concerns. Agree to disagree and try to move on, with concerns appropriately noted. Use caucus or break to meet with principals or key representatives. Restate person's value to group to encourage search for solution. Consider use of outside facilitator or provide new insight.
"Broken record" repetitive discussion or adversarial positions.	People stuck on position vs. interests. Lack of perceived options. Emotional tie that is stronger than influence of new or different information.	Identification of interests vs. positions through brainstorming, scenario writing, personal discussions with friendly group.	Use Negotiation Model. Use brainstorming for set period, during which no evaluation is allowed. List options and use 3x5 cards for individuals to assign priorities or number values to their personal choices in a nonthreatening way.
Conversation dominator.	Feels he/she has more or better information on issues; feels need to be heard or need to be right.	Set up agenda with time estimates and identification of who talks when at outset of meeting. Meet with person ahead of time to review your methods for conducting meeting and managing discussion.	If necessary, interrupt person, thanking him/her for comments and asking others for discussion; be prepared to accurately restate person's comments along with agenda structure and participation rules you have set with group. Be prepared to identify sequence of speakers you will allow to make comments to give all time to speak

Figure 5. Selected Trouble-Shooting Guide to Meeting Dynamics (continued)

PARTICIPANT PROBLEMS	POSSIBLE CAUSES	PREVENTION	ACTION Rx
Person casts blame or incites others in meeting.	Person wants to deny his\her responsibility or role, transfer blame or views onto others; may want to divide group against itself. Or, person may feel defensive and unfairly treated in meeting.	Meet with parties ahead of time to have them focus on behaviors instead of attribution of motives and blame. Establish rules for interrupting or restating issues if they become accusative vs. descriptive.	Review rules and intent to interrupt or restate if accusations occur. Establish rule for managing questions, rebuttals, e.g., each party has time limit to make statements without interruptions to present full, descriptive case. Be prepared to restate each party's interests and concerns rather than positions.
Group not able to stay on time during the meeting.	Unclear assignment of available time and order of agenda; insufficient leadership authority or confusion over who's in charge; lack of clarity on what is action item and what is information only.	Assign time keeper and alert group to this ahead of meeting.	Review time estimates for each agenda item and role of time keeper. Ask group to determine priority among agenda items and decide what and how to attend to entire agenda.
Mountain-out-of-a-molehill sniping about minor point.	Commitment to personal needs beyond interest in group issues. Lack of experience in larger group.	Meet with person ahead of time to solicit views and ask for helpful meeting behavior.	Review protocol for productive meeting. Place issue in overall perspective. Ask to note and then set issue aside to achieve larger goals.
Lack of participation.	Anxiety; fear of being wrong or inappropriate. Lack of adequate information or experience; perceived status difference.	Brief members ahead of time; ask for specific input or help ahead of time. Review meeting format to reassure person.	Use round-robin recording or ballot cards to get input in systematic fashion. Break large group into 5-7 person groups, or into self-selected dyads for brief discussion periods. Ask for straw vote or show of hands on clearly stated options.

Figure 6. Summary of Parlimentary Procedures

To Do This:	You Say This	May You Interrupt Speaker?	Must You Be Seconded?	Is the Motion Debatable?	What Vote Is Required?
Adjourn the meeting	"I move that we adjourn"	No	Yes	No	Majority
Recess the meeting	"I move that we recess until..."	No	Yes	No	Majority
Complain about the noise, room temperature, etc.	"Point of privilege"	Yes	No	No	No vote
Suspend further consideration of something	"I move we table it"	No	Yes	No	Majority
End debate	"I move the previous question"	No	Yes	No	⅔ vote
Postpone consideration of something	"I move we postpone this matter until..."	No	Yes	Yes	Majority
Have something studied further	"I move we refer this matter to a committee"	No	Yes	Yes	Majority
Amend a motion	"I move that this motion be amended by..."	No	Yes	Yes	Majority
Introduce business (a primary motion)	"I move that..."	No	Yes	Yes	Majority
Object to procedure or to a personal affront	"Point of order"	Yes	No	No	No vote, chair decides
Request information	"Point of information"	Yes	No	No	No vote
Ask for a vote by actual count to verify a voice vote	"I call for a division of the house"	No	No	No	No vote
Object to considering some undiplomatic matter	"I object to consideration of this question"	Yes	No	No	⅔ vote
Take up a matter previously tabled	"I move to take from the table"	No	Yes	No	Majority
Reconsider something already disposed of	"I move we reconsider our action relative to..."	Yes	Yes	Yes	Majority
Consider something out of its scheduled order	"I move we suspend the rules and consider..."	No	Yes	No	⅔ vote
Vote on a ruling by the chair	"I appeal the chair's decision"	Yes	Yes	Yes	Majority

Source: Barbara Halsey, C.M.S.C., Medical Staff Coordinator, Salem Hospital, 1990, Salem, Oregon

Figure 7. Preparing Appropriate Medical Staff Minutes

Medical staff meeting minutes are considered legal documents, and need to be very carefully completed by the Department or Committee Chairperson. This is easily accomplished by attending to the points listed below:

DO:

- Remember that minutes are legal documents, not personal editorials.
- Dictate minutes as soon as possible, no longer than a week, after the meeting has occurred.
- Include department/committee name and meeting date.
- State if regular or special meeting; if special, record that proper notice was given.
- List all persons in attendance, specifying guests.
- List those absent, noting with or without excuse.
- Note that quorum was or was not present.
- Note when the meeting was called to order and by whom.
- Note reading and approval of previous minutes.
- Note actions taken, with clear wording of motions, resolutions, and results of votes.
- Note department/committee functions, including indicators, discussion, recommendations, and follow-up actions.
- Note time of adjournment.

DON'T:

- Include specific names of patients, names of voting members (unless requested), names of individuals making or seconding motions, who said what to whom, personal remarks, or other personal comments.
- Record how each member voted.
- Editorialize or otherwise include personal opinions about hospital matters.
- Use electronic recording devices or tape recorders.

Developing a Sense of Value, Stake in Our Future

Bramson describes one difficult personality type as the "negative," a person who has a very pessimistic attitude about life. His advice is to be prepared to go it alone, rather than trying to convince the "negative" of a positive value.[1]

Sometimes, before becoming a chronically negative person, we become overwhelmed by major changes and episodically apathetic or cynical. Cynics are usually not interested in the future, because they believe matters will only get worse.

Comparative information seems to be an especially powerful approach with physicians, and comparative revenue, volume, and outcome information may be most persuasive when physicians become overwhelmed in busy practices.

Another approach is to reach agreement on specific short-term goals, with intensive feedback, as the first few steps toward long-term goals.

Physicians in general have a problem-oriented focus and often fail to identify positive success. Specifically asking for positive comments may help break through the negative attitude.

References

1. Bramson, R. *Coping with Difficult People.* New York, N.Y.: Ballantine Books, 1981.

2. "Learning Nominal Group Technique: A Leader's Guide," #503. Minneapolis, Minn.: Brighton Books, 1993.

3. Fisher, R., and Ury, W. *Getting to Yes: Negotiating Agreement without Giving in.* New York, N.Y.: Penguin Books, 1983.

4. Fisher, R., and Brown, S. *Getting Together: Building a Relationship That Gets to Yes.* Boston, Mass.: Houghton, Mifflin Co., 1988.

5. Ury, W. *Getting Past No: Negotiating with Difficult People.* New York, N.Y.: Bantam Books, 1991.

6. Ury, W., and others. *Getting Disputes Resolved: Designing Systems to Cut the Costs of Conflict.* San Francisco, Calif.: Jossey-Bass, 1988.

7. Gordon, T. Leader Effectiveness Training. New York, N.Y.: Bantam Books, 1977.

8. Harrison, R. "Role Negotiation: A Tough-Minded Approach to Team Development." In *The Social Technology of Orientation Development,* Burke, W., and Hornstein, H., Eds. La Jolla, Calif.: University Associates, 1972, pp. 84-96.

9. Gill, S. "Groups and Decision Making: Getting the Most out of Meetings." In *New Leadership in Health Care Management: The Physician Executive, First Edition,* Curry, W., Editor. Tampa, Fla.: American College of Physician Executives, 1988.

10. Knowles, M. and Knowles, H. *Introduction to Group Dynamics.* New York, N.Y.: Cambridge Books, 1959. Revised edition, New York, N.Y.: Association Press, 1972.

11. Delbecq, A., and Gill, S. "Justice as a Prelude to Teamwork in Medical Centers." *Health Care Management Review* 10(1):45-51, Winter 1985.

12. Colman, A., and Bexton, W., editors. *Group Relations Reader.* Sausalito, Calif.: GREX, 1975.

13. Gill, S. "Guidelines for the Management of Temporary Task Force Teams." In *Managing Human Services.* Davis, Calif.: International Dialogue Press, 1977.

14. Rioch, M. "Group Relations: Rationale and Technique." *International Journal of Group Psychotherapy* 20(3):340-55, July 1970.

15. Napier, R., and Gershenfeld, M. *Groups, Theory, and Experience,* second edition. Boston, Mass.: Houghton Mifflin Co., 1981, pp. 47-92

16. Tuckman, B. "Developmental Sequence in Small Groups." *Psychological Bulletin* 63(6):384-99, June 1965.

17. Thompson, J., and Tuden, A. "Strategies, Structures, and Processes of Organizational Decisions." In *Comparative Studies in Administration.* Pittsburgh, Pa.: University of Pittsburgh Press, 1987, pp. 194-216.

18. Shull, F., and others. *Organizational Decision Making*. New York, N.Y.: McGraw-Hill Book Co., 1970, pp. 127-168.

19. Zander, A. *The Purposes of Groups and Organizations*. San Francisco, Calif.: Jossey-Bass Publications, Inc., 1985.

20. Janis, I., and Mann. L. *Decision Making: ʌ Psychological Analysis of Conflict, Choice, and Commitment*. New York, N.Y.: The Free Press, 1977.

Sandra L. Gill is President of Physician Management Resources, Inc., a health care leadership development firm in Westmont, Ill.

Communication as a Tool of Influence

by Barbara J. Linney, MA

CHAPTER 20

When humans are born, they influence their caretakers by screaming. Soon they learn smiling and cooing are helpful. Later, talking and, eventually, writing are added to the repertoire of skills. Listening well to another's concerns is the last skill to develop and is extremely important when influencing adults in the workplace. Good listening, speaking, body language, and writing skills are essential for the physician executive. The screaming must be left behind.

Lyons and Cejka say, "Moving into health care management means that physician executives must become expert communicators. Success depends not on how quickly diagnoses are made and treatments completed, but on how well the executive can hear what others are saying, validate concerns and feelings, build consensus, and bring people together. They must continually recall that organizations reward them not only for tangibles such as bottom-line results, but also for intangibles such as how a problem was resolved, how results were communicated, or how a decision was reached."[1]

Listening

If you want to influence people, you must first listen to them to find out what interests them, what their values are, what they want. People will more readily do what you want if they can also do or get something they want. Some common interests are money, recognition, and power. If you want me to make money for the company, I am more excited about doing it if I know I will get a bonus or if I will have a better chance of keeping my job, which gives me money to buy what I want—pay the mortgage, send a child to college, buy a car or a new piece of jewelry. People also want praise for a job well done. If they are making fairly high incomes, recognition is often more motivating than additional money. They also want a sense of power—the ability to persuade others, have their ideas listened to and taken seriously. You can only find out what is important to people by listening carefully.

"Empathic listening is...risky. It takes a great deal of security to go into a deep listening experience because you open yourself up to be influenced. You become vulnerable. It's a paradox, in a sense, because in order to have influence, you have to be influenced. That means you have to really understand."[2]

Listening is hard work. "While an average speech rate for many people is about 200 words per minute, most of us can think about four times that speed. With all that extra think time, the ineffective listener lets his mind wander. His brain takes excursions to review the events of yesterday, or plan tomorrow, or solve a business problem...or 'sleep.'"[3] You have to work to control your mind and make it concentrate on what is being said. If you are troubled by an impending malpractice suit, a divorce, or a child who is having problems, your capacity to listen will diminish drastically. You will need to be patient with yourself in those circumstances and perhaps tell the person, "I am a bit distracted; can you tell me that again."

Not listening can be expensive. "A sales manager for a large company asked his accounting department how he could charge off a $100,000 error caused by a dispatcher who routed a fleet of drivers to deliver building material to the wrong state. The dispatcher heard the city (Portland) but not the state (Maine). The result was eight trucks 3,000 miles off coast in Portland, Oregon.[4] ...[Y]ou can improve your listening if you have the desire, the interest, a high level of concentration, self-discipline and a positive attitude."[5]

If you decide you are willing to expend the energy to listen, here are some techniques that will help you listen so people will want to talk to you:

- Be quiet. You cannot listen if you are talking or if you are thinking hard about what you are going to say next. If you get very anxious about not knowing what to say when the person finishes, try putting all your energy into listening and then tell them, "I need to think about this. Can I get back with you in a while to talk more?"

- Use your body to let the person know you are there. Look at him or her. Don't let your eyes wander all over the room. Sit attentively but not tensely, not slouching or lying down. On the sofa watching TV or reading the paper are not good positions for listening. Neither is opening your mail in your office while someone tries to tell you something.

- Give an occasional "uh huh" or nod to let them know you are following their train of thought. If you are not following the conversation, ask them a question before you let them go on too long, and you are really lost.

- Ask nonjudgmental questions. "Can you say a little more? I'm not sure I understand. Will you try me again?" Don't ask, "Why on earth did you do that?" There is absolutely no decent answer to that question, and the person doing the asking is implying, "You are an idiot!" You may be right, but if you want communication to continue, you will have to discipline yourself not to say everything you think.

- Restate some of what the person has said. For example, "Let me see if I understand. You think Dr. X is showing up for his emergency department shift with alcohol on his breath."

■ Help with the expression of feelings—the speakers or yours. A bonding takes places when feelings are expressed. For example, Mary came home from a friend's house later than expected. Her mother asked where she had been. She explained that Janie's puppy had died and she had helped. "How did you do that?" her mother asked. "I helped her cry." Carl Rogers says, "When someone understands how it feels to be me, without wanting to analyze or judge me, then I can blossom and grow in that climate.[6]

You can guess about a feeling you think the person is having if it seems appropriate. For instance, "I can see why that would make you sad." They may reply, "I'm not sad, I'm angry." It doesn't matter if you are wrong. They will correct you, and you have gotten to a deeper level of communication when you find out how someone feels about a subject. They will feel a sense of relief and sometimes release when they identify the feeling.

In some situations, it is too risky to reveal feelings. You will be making a judgment call in each instance to see if the expression of feelings is appropriate. When they are expressed, people usually feel closer to each other.

When listening, our natural tendency is to give advice, judge, or tell how we have had a similar experience. When you do that, you have stopped listening and started talking about your own interests. It's not that these behaviors are never appropriate. We just have a tendency to do them too fast. If you ask a question for clarification or para-phrase what the speaker has said, you are still focusing on the speaker and helping him or her give you information. Listening for five minutes or longer without turning the conversation back to ourselves is quite a gift to a person and does much to enhance communication.

According to Covey, the strongest motivators are psychological. "If all the air were suddenly sucked out of the room you're in right now, what would happen to your inter-est in this book? You wouldn't care about the book; you wouldn't care about anything except getting air. Survival would be your only motivation.

"But now that you have air, it doesn't motivate you. This is one of the greatest insights in the field of human motivation: Satisfied needs do not motivate. It's only the unsatisfied need that motivates. Next to physical survival, the greatest need of a human being is psychological survival—to be understood, to be affirmed, to be validat-ed, to be appreciated.

"When you listen with empathy to another person, you give that person psychologi-cal air. And after that vital need is met, you can then focus on influencing or problem solving.

This need for psychological air impacts communication in every area of life."[7]

It is not easy to listen. We would all rather be the center of attention doing all the talking. This is not a terribly bad fact. It is just a fact. But if we do not learn to take turns, if we do not learn to listen, we will not have a chance of being heard.

Speaking

To influence people, at some point you need to ask for what you want. You may not always get it, but you have a much better chance if you ask for it clearly, describing in detail the behavior that you want. This is sometimes described as assertive communication. According to Baldwin, "Assertive communication is direct expression of one's feelings, preferences, needs, and opinions in a way that is neither threatening nor punishing to another person and that does not involve undue amounts of anxiety or fear for the person exhibiting the assertive behavior."[8]

For some people, the difficult demand of assertiveness is not being a bully who threatens to get what he or she wants. For others, the difficult part is asking for what he or she wants without undue amounts of anxiety. When you first start to change these patterns, you will feel uncomfortable. The threatening person will probably feel as if he or she is going to explode, and the fearful person will feel great anxiety, sometimes with the accompanying digestive disorders of nausea and diarrhea. It takes practice to become proficient and fairly at ease with new behavior.

It can be very difficult to say what you want. Perhaps you need to tell a co-worker about negative behavior that is disrupting the office. You need to be very specific—"I want you to stop sulking and making negative comments. You don't need to smile all day, but you need to look cheerful or neutral, not negative." As a physician executive, you may have to deliver unpleasant messages to other physicians—"I want you to stop yelling obscenities at nurses when things get hectic in the emergency department," or "We have had seven reports that you have prescribed the wrong drug. I want you to stop seeing patients."

You must speak clearly and be understood to influence. "I want you to love me more" or "I want you to pay more attention to me" is not specific enough. A clearer message is "I want to go out to dinner most every weekend and talk about things that matter to me—my work, your work, children. I want you to let me know you are listening by looking at me when I talk. I do not want you to insult me by saying something I did was stupid."

How you deliver the message is just as important as what you have to say. After you have listened and it is time to use your voice to influence others, use the following techniques:

■ Pronounce your words clearly. Enunciate. Don't mumble. You need to use whatever energy it takes to project your voice across to the other person. They should not have to strain to hear you. It is very annoying to try to have a conversation with someone you cannot hear or understand. But neither should you yell at them—that is just as offensive.

■ Don't talk too quickly or too slowly. Southerners sometimes have to speed up. Northerners sometimes have to slow down. Midwesterners usually have it about right.

■ Look at the other person. You don't have to stare at someone, but look at them at least 80 percent of the time. When you look at someone, you convey an air of confidence. You will be much more likely to get what you want.

■ Use average size words and fairly short sentences. If you sling a lot of jargon or large words that most people do not know, you alienate them. When you ask for something, you want your words to be easily understood. For example, "I want you to make notes in the chart within 48 hours after you see a patient"—not, "It's essential that everyone facilitate the record keeping."

■ Don't overuse big emotions, such as anger or tears. There are times when we are angry, and the other person must know it. They need to hear the loud voice and harsh words, but those times are rare. It's similar to the little boy who cried "wolf." If you are crying or angry in most of your exchanges, no one will listen or take you seriously. They will learn to tune you out or sometimes scream back at you.

Big emotions usually interfere with communication. The listener is often threatened, frightened, or repulsed by a show of uncontrolled emotion, and he or she cannot hear the words being spoken. The person raging or crying also cannot hear when the listener responds.

What can you do when emotions are raging? When you are the speaker: "Writing in [a] journal about people or situations that have evoked in us anger, anxiety, or a sense of defeat helps to stabilize our psychological situation and strengthen our ego. It helps us to 'get a handle' on our emotions without repressing them, and to get a look at the giant that threatens to swallow us. If we do this before we get into a discussion that might become highly emotional, the chances are good that we can express our feelings to the other person and not be consumed by them."[9]

When you are the listener: If you are feeling strong and collected, it is helpful if you can let the emotional person vent for a few moments. You might then respond, "I can see that you are angry and I'm not surprised. What can I do to help?" If you are not up to being in the presence of so much negative energy, you might say, "I'll be glad to talk about this when you are calmer."

■ Use good body language. How you say something and how you look when you say it are as important as what you say. What causes someone to understand you and respond well to you? Psychologist Albert Mehrabian did a study that suggests:

■ 7 percent of understanding depends on the words you use.

■ 38 percent depends on your tone of voice.

■ 55 percent depends on your nonverbal body language.[10]

Facial expression and voice communicate much more than you realize. A listener understands and interprets your message more through the tone of your voice and the look of your body than through your words. "No, I'm not angry!" said harshly conveys the message that you are angry. "I really love that!" said sarcastically implies that you don't like it at all. People complain about getting mixed signals when words, tone of voice, and body language send different messages. In that situation, they will believe the tone of your voice and the look on your face much more than the words you say.

Alexander claims people have a hard time accepting these facts. "The reality is that few people accept responsibility for anything more than their words. They have never learned that a harsh tone can deny the gentlest of words."[11] Most people refuse to believe it if they are the ones doing the talking, but they quickly believe it if someone else is doing the talking.

A positive voice is cheerful, satisfied, concerned, warm. A negative voice is sarcastic, scared, depressed, clipped, tense, too loud or soft. A positive face has a smile, occasional head nod, and eye contact. A negative face has a frown, smirk, or boring glare. A positive body is relaxed, leaning forward some, open arms. Negative body language is pointing, wandering eyes, picking at the body.[12]

Don't scream at someone to get what you want, and don't cry and beg. Ask in a calm, confident, firm voice. If you yell, the listener may scream back at you, perhaps becoming physically hostile. Other people will ignore you or tune you out. If you are crying, you appear weak, and you're not likely to be effective. Sit up straight. Look strong but not belligerent. Look directly at the person.

Most of the time, if you have listened well to the other person to find out what their needs are and have tried to meet them, and then have asked clearly for what you want, you will get it. More people than you think don't do those steps. But there are times when more is necessary—you must confront someone when the communication situation is more heated.

Confrontation

When you have an important confrontation coming up, prepare ahead of time. That is not cheating. Don't expect that you should be so brilliant that the right words will always come in an heated up conversation. In a freewriting style (not worrying about spelling, punctuation, or grammar), prepare by writing about the following topics:

■ Write out how angry you are. Also, find someone you trust to tell how angry you are, if you feel the need after writing.

"I can never find the charts I need because Jim keeps them in his office for weeks. I've asked him about it, and he says he'll change, but he doesn't. It causes me to be late finishing up. Yesterday, I missed a Little League game because I had not finished for the day. My son was disappointed and I was furious at Jim."

■ Write what you don't like and what you like.

"I don't like that I can never find the charts. They are always in Jim's office. What do I like about Jim? That's hard because I'm so irritated. He does bring in a lot of money to the clinic. Without him, I guess my overhead percentage would be greater.

■ Write what you want to happen.

"I want Jim to fill out the charts in two days."

■ Write the answer to the question, is there anything you can give to this person to negotiate and help him or her want to do what you want them to do?

"We can give you a clerical person to help you keep things organized." You might ask him what he wants. "If you do this for me, is there something I can do for you?"

What you want to give may not be what that person wants, so you have to ask to be sure. (When my children were little, I wanted my husband to spend time with them and let me do some things I wanted to do. His solution to the problem was to give me money to pay a baby sitter. I didn't want that all the time. I wanted him to spend some time with them. Then, when I came home from their being with him, I didn't have to deal with the emotional pay back that always seemed to be necessary when they had been left with a sitter.)

In some situations, you will not want to give the person an opportunity to say what he or she wants. For example, if you are dealing with an impaired physician, the deal you are presenting is not negotiable. "I want you to stop drinking, and the organization will pay for you to go to a rehab center."

■ Write what you will do if you do not get what you want. Find out who has what power. If there is nothing you can do, you may want to reconsider confronting the person. If you repeatedly bring up behavior that you want changed, but you can do nothing to make it happen, you may be perceived as whining and begging. You lose self-esteem, while getting nothing changed.

Consider what your options are. Can you fire this person? Are you willing to leave this relationship? Can you leave your job?

"If your charts are not up to date, I must bring it up with the medical director or the medical records committee."

Don't use a threat that is not realistic. "If you don't fill out the charts, I'll fine you $100,000."

You don't always have to use the power you have, but you need to figure out if you have it or not. When my children were little and misbehaving, I would sometimes go talk to a neighbor across the street. I'd come up with a plan and walk back in the house. The children would take one look at me and shape up. They could smell the power.

When you finish writing, you may choose not to confront. Perhaps you have gotten rid of all your frustration, perhaps you have decided the price is too high. But sometimes you will know you have to go through with the confrontation, because the cost of not doing it is too high.

If you decide to confront, you will use some of the information you have written, but maybe not all of it. If you have written about your anger, you may not need to express it. If you do express it, you can do it in a calm firm voice, not an explosive, tyrannical one. Ailes says, "...you'd be surprised how many people can't keep their emotions under control. This makes other people uncomfortable and reduces their ability to communicate effectively. Some people actually believe a wild display of temper makes them appear more important when in fact it always reduces their stature in others' eyes."[13]

Find a quiet place without distractions and ask the person for a certain amount of time (15 minutes, an hour, whatever you think it will take). In a calm firm voice:

Explain your view of the situation. Try to make "I" statements more than "you" statements. Instead of saying, "You are irresponsible," say, "I can't get my work done when I can't find the charts." Instead of saying, "You are a slob," say, "I get upset when clothes are lying on the floor."

Instead of saying, "'You never take me anywhere; you're always out with your friends,' attribute your feelings to yourself and use 'I' instead of 'you.' Say, 'I feel sad that we never go out anymore. I'd love it if we'd spend more time together.' 'I get depressed when I see you smoking and drinking.' Describe how their actions affect you instead of directly attacking them and putting them on the defensive."[14]

Say what you don't like and what you like if that seems appropriate. "You are a valuable member of this group. You are an excellent cardiologist."

Say what you want to happen. "People think you are having an affair with X. I don't know if it's true, but you have to stop acting in a manner that makes people suspect it. You are a good doctor and valuable to our organization, but we can't have this talk going on. It's disruptive."

Tell what you can offer to help the situation.

If all else fails, use the power you have. "It's been reported that you are screaming at nurses. When you scream at people, everyone's morale is lowered. The people watching a confrontation, as well as the people involved, get upset. I am frustrated because I have to listen to the complaints. Nurses are hard to get, and everyone must be treated with respect. This has to stop. The organization will pay for you to get some counseling. If it does not stop, you have to leave."

What Is Your Style for Dealing with Conflict?

If you tend to blow up, here are some tips that can help you stop.

Breathe—"The Tension Blow-Out Exercise: Take your breath in, hold it, and blow out all the air until your abdominal muscles contract. Then don't breathe for three seconds. Take the breath in, hold it, and repeat two more times until you've oxygenated yourself. It helps you control your temper so you won't antagonize the police officer, which can get you in trouble."[15]

Whisper.

■ Keep fingers open rather than clinching them.

Count to 10.

Lie down.

You have to want to change this behavior. If you get a kick out of having tantrums and watching people tremble, you won't change this behavior unless you stand to lose something, such as your job or a promotion.

If you avoid conflict, here are some tips that may help you get the courage you need.

- Breathe.

- Write out what you are going to say.

- Write out what will happen if you do nothing—My self-esteem will plummet, I may get hurt, organization will be hurt.

- Write out what might happen if you do something—The situation may change, I may love this person more, organization will keep good reputation.

Confront with a calm, firm voice, without attacking or avoiding the problem.

Writing

To influence in written communication, you must first get the document read. Writing needs to be a two-part process. First, you come up with some ideas without criticizing them at all. If you judge every word as you go, the creative part of you will get tired and stop sending messages. Just write down or dictate the words as they come to you. Once you have a draft of the document, become very critical when you edit. What will make people want to read what you have written?

- For starters, make it short. We may or may not be getting lazier, with shorter attention spans, but we are all definitely busy. Even the brightest executives want documents to be short, because they need to get through them in a hurry.

- Avoid needless repetition. Do not repeat the same word many times. The reader begins to hear the sing-song repetition of the word rather than your message. It is fine to use the same word over and over when you are generating thoughts. As a matter of fact, the subconscious seems to send us messages that way. Often, a first draft of a paper will have a word repeated 5 to 10 times, but you need to cut them later. Circle all the repeated words and try to eliminate most of them, unless you are repeating the word to emphasize its importance or changing the word would confuse the reader.

- Don't be redundant—writing the same idea a second time but using different words. Examples: end result, final conclusion, personal opinion, unexpected surprise. Always use fewer words rather than more words to express an idea. "In the event that" can simply be "If." "In view of the fact that" can be "Because." Elbow says, "Every word omitted keeps another reader with you."[16] It is especially important for physicians to use simple words and phrases whenever they can, because, so often, they must use the long technical words of their profession. Too many words of three or more syllables make for foggy, heavy reading. You usually are vocabulary experts from many years of rigorous academic training, but resist using all you know when you want to communicate with anyone other than a medical peer.

- Use nonsexist language. Avoid words that imply only a man or a woman could do the job. Instead of businessman, write business executive, manager, or business person. Instead of chairman, say chair or chairperson. When writing to a woman, use the title Ms. unless you know she would prefer Mrs. or Miss. Mr. indicates the person you are addressing is a man but explains nothing about his marital status. Ms. does the same for a woman. Instead of using the masculine pronoun (he, his, him) when referring to a group that includes both men and women, make the subject of the sentence plural and thus neutral. For example, write, "Workers must submit their travel expenses by Monday," rather than, "Every worker must submit his travel expenses by Monday." Sometimes, you will have to use the singular pronoun. When you do, write, he or she or he/she. Too many of these terms sound awkward, but it is no longer acceptable to use just he.

- Always choose precise words over vague words. Instead of "nice house" say "brick house." Instead of "circumstance" put "Hurricane Andrew." Use strong verbs rather than ones hidden in many words. "Decide" is stronger than "make a decision." "Buy" is better than "make a purchase." "Help" is clearer than "give assistance."

- Don't use jargon unless you are absolutely sure the listener understands it. Jargon, in its broadest definition, is any language that is hard to understand. Sometimes, it acts as a shield for those who don't have much to say. It can be specialized vocabulary that a particular group of people understand. Teenagers find a different set of words every two or three years that, ideally, will confuse their parents. Accountants, chemists, bankers, doctors, and others have their special terms that must be defined when they are working with the general public. Abbreviations that the listener does not understand are jargon. It's the writer's job to find out what the reader knows and doesn't know. When it comes to abbreviations, if you are in doubt, write it out.

Often jargon is phony, inflated, and uselessly complex language. A client told me once, "If I speak and write so others understand me, they will steal my job." The opposite is more often true—jargon interferes with communication and could cause you to lose your job. People get angry if you use difficult words without explaining their meaning. They put your memos in the trash and do not do what you have asked them to do.

Below, a passage from *Moby Dick* has lost its clarity and beauty because of jargon.[17]

The Original. "Call me Ishmael. Some years ago—never mind how long precisely—having little or no money in my purse and nothing in particular to interest me on shore, I thought I would sail about a little and see the water part of the world."

Jargon added. "You may identify me by the nomenclature of Ishmael. At a point in time several years previous to the current temporal zone—the precise number of which is extraneous information—devoid of sufficient monetary resources and lacking physical and/or psychical stimuli within the confines of my sphere of activity on land, I initiated several thought processes and concluded that I would commandeer a vessel of navigation with which to explore the aquatic component of this planet."

- Avoid trite phrases. Overworked expressions make a reader switch from paying attention to your message to being irritated that you are saying the same old thing.

"The bottom line," "the whole nine yards," and "l need your input" are phrases that need a few year's rest. If you can finish the following statements, they have probably been overused.

▎ Enclosed _____.

▎ We're sorry for any _____.

▎ It has come to our _____.

▎ Please call at your earliest _____.

▎ If you have additional questions, feel_____.

Try substituting some new words. Examples for the first two entries above[18]:

▎ Here is the information you asked for in your letter of June 5.

▎ Thanks for your patience with this delay.

■ Tone or manner of expression is as evident in the written word as it is in the spoken word. Business correspondence used to have a stuffy, legalistic tone. Now companies like a conversational, friendly tone that sounds as if a person, not a machine, wrote the letter. Pretend the reader is standing beside you. If you wouldn't say "per your request," to the person's face, don't write it in the letter.

Use a positive tone whenever possible. "Saying that someone is 'interested in details' conveys a more positive tone than saying the individual is a 'nitpicker.' The word economical is more positive than stingy or cheap."[19]

■ Finally, pay attention to how the words look on the page. Have enough white space on a page—areas where there are no words. Do you remember in the seventh grade when you started to read that larger geography book with more words on a page than you had in years before? You struggled through two columns of heavy words and then turned the page to find a picture that took up half the page. Weren't you happy, relieved? When we grow up, we pretend that we get over that thrill, but we don't. None of us wants to look at a page that is heavy and mostly black with words. If there are good top, bottom, and side margins, with spaces between paragraphs and perhaps a list in the middle with more white space around it, we are invited to read what is on the page rather than repelled by it.

I've given you several do's and don'ts, but what if you hate the whole writing process. Is there anything that would make you dread it less? The answer is writing more but in a different way. Write 10 minutes a day, 5 days a week on any subject that pops into your head. Use a kind of paper and pen that you like, or type it on a word processor if that's easier for you. (Whatever paper or instrument you decide to write on I'll now refer to as your journal.) Don't worry about spelling, punctuation, grammar, or anything that some English teacher told you to worry about. There is just one catch— you must start writing and not stop until the time is up. If you can't think of anything to write, just write, "I can't think of anything. I can't think of anything. This is one of the dumbest things I've ever done," but keep writing. Ideas will pop into your head if you keep writing that simply will not occur to you if you just sit and think.

If you were going to run in a 10K race on the weekend, you would need to do some daily running to get ready. The same is true for writing. You need to grease the machinery of your hand and brain to make it readily give you words when you need to write something.

If you decide to give this writing exercise a try, it will not only make the writing process easier but also can enhance your verbal communication skills. "Keeping a journal of our thoughts, experiences, insights, and learnings promotes mental clarity, exactness, and context...communicating on the deeper level of thoughts, feelings, and ideas...affects our ability to think clearly, to reason accurately, and to be understood effectively."[20]

Goldberg calls writing in a journal writing practice. "A friend once said that when she had a good black-and-white drawing that she was going to add color to, she always practiced first on a few drawings she didn't care about in order to warm up. This writing practice is also a warmup for anything else you might want to write. It is the bottom line, the most primitive, essential beginning of writing. The trust you learn in your own voice can be directed then into a business letter, a novel, a PhD dissertation, a play, a memoir. But it is something you must come back to again and again. Don't think, 'I got it! I know how to write. I trust my voice. I'm off to write the great American novel.' It's good to go off and write a novel, but don't stop doing writing practice. It is what keeps you in tune, like a dancer who does warmups before dancing or a runner who does stretches before running. Runners don't say, 'Oh, I ran yesterday, I'm limber.' Each day they warm up and stretch."[21]

If you have valuable skills, talents, and information, but you can't communicate them to others, all those valuable resources stay locked up inside you. Improving your listening, speaking, body language, and writing skills enables you to influence others by setting a good example and by sometimes convincingly persuading them to your point of view.

References

1. Lyons, M., and Cejka, S. "Getting a Firm Grip on the Realities for Physician Executives." *Physician Executive* 20(6):8-12, June 1994.

2. Covey, S. *The 7 Habits of Highly Effective People.* New York, N.Y.: Simon & Schuster, 1990, p. 243.

3. Swets, P. *The Art of Talking So That People Will Listen.* Englewood Cliffs, N.J.: Prentice-Hall, Inc., 1983, p. 42.

4. Bone, D. *The Business of Listening.* Los Altos, CA: Crisp Publications, 1988, p. 5.

5. Bone, D., *op. cit.* p. ii.

6. Goodman, G. *The Talk Book: The Intimate Science of Communicating in Close Relationships.* Emmaus, Pa.: Rodale Press, 1988, p. 41.

7. Covey, S., *op. cit.*, p. 241.

8. Baldwin, T. "Effects of Alternative Modeling Strategies on Outcomes of Interpersonal-Skills Training." *Journal of Applied Psychology* 77(2):147-54, 1992.

9. Sanford, J. *Between People: Communicating One-to-One.* New York, N.Y.: Paulist Press, 1982, p. 37.

10. Malandro, L., and Barker, L. *Nonverbal Communication.* Reading, Mass.: Addison-Wesley Publishing Co., 1983, p. 278.

11. Alexander, J. *Dare to Change.* New York, N.Y.: New American Library, 1984, p. 138.

12. Swets, P., *op. cit.*, p. 59.

13. Ailes, R., with Kraushar, J. *You Are the Message.* Homewood, Ill.: Dow Jones-Irwin, 1988, p. 60.

14. Glass, L. *Say It Right.* New York, N.Y.: G.P. Putnam's Sons, 1991, p. 207.

15. Glass, L., *op. cit.*, p. 187-8.

16. Elbow, P. *Writing without Teachers.* London: Oxford University Press, 1973, p. 41.

17. Hunter, V. Originally appeared in the *Brown Alumni Monthly*, Feb. 1981. Taken from Kolin, P., *op. cit.*

18. Nelson, J. *Write to the Point! How to Sharpen Your Business Writing Skills*, 3rd Edition. New York, N.Y.: American Management Association.

19. Kolin, P. *Successful Writing at Work.* Lexington, Mass.: D. C. Heath and Company, 1986, p.13.

20. Covey, S., *op. cit.*, p. 296.

21. Goldberg, N. *Writing Down the Bones.* Boston, Mass.: Shambala, 1986, p. 13.

Also Consulted

Sarnoff, D. *Make the Most of Your Best, A Complete Program for Presenting Yourself and Your Ideas with Confidence and Authority.* Garden City, N.Y.: Doubleday and Company, Inc., 1981.

Barbara J. Linney, MA, is Director of Career Development, American College of Physician Executives, Tampa, Florida.

Hiring and Firing

by Marilyn Moats Kennedy, MSJ

CHAPTER 21

The most profound changes in employment practices and goals have occurred since 1989. The white-collar recession eliminated all trust between employers and employees and stretched loyalty to the thickness of a fiber optic. Hiring became riskier as each side sought to say what the other wanted to hear. Candidates felt no moral dilemma in suggesting they'd stay forever while mentally planning to move on within a year to 18 months or whenever a better opportunity surfaced. Organizations did the same and quietly, in the name of flexible staffing, selected candidates who'd be up or out in three years.

With fewer perceived job opportunities, employees fought to keep the ones they had. The changed organizational climate made adversarial relationships rather than cooperative ones the norm. Hiring and firing must be seen against a far less trusting, more fearful background.

Is any decision riskier than hiring someone? Think of the potential problems. You might hire the wrong person. Later, that person might not agree he or she was wrong for the job. When firing is the only answer, the victim might sue. How do you make informed choices? It's a question of establishing and then following a step-by-step procedure to reduce the risks of making the wrong choice.

Checklist of Job Specifications

Before you fill out a job requisition, place an employment advertisement, or call a recruiter, you need to consider the following:

■ What is the salary range for the job? Have I checked to see if it matches current offers from other organizations? (Do not assume that the recession has lowered salaries. It hasn't. It has decreased annual increases to employees.) Can I buy the package of skills I need for that amount? If you try to hire someone for less than market because you assume there are lots of unemployed people who will work cheap, you'll find that the outstanding candidates won't consider the job and the poor ones will refuse to be discouraged. The latter realize you'll have to settle for one of them unless you raise the ante. The most desirable candidates know that they bring value to the organization and will hold out for the upper end of market.

Be wary of anyone willing to take a decrease. That person has a very weak ego, is tragically flawed, or is stupid. He or she will not be magically healed by getting an offer from you.

What does the job require in terms of education, experience, technical/special expertise, interpersonal skills, and managerial or supervisory skills? What's your minimum in each area? When you hire physicians, don't forget that 50 percent of all the physicians now practicing—and the nurses, technicians, etc.—graduated in the lower 50 percent of their classes. What exactly does it prove, ten years out, to have graduated in the top 10 percent unless the person is in research? Don't get trapped in the past.

Don't worry if someone has been laid off or moved around during the past five years. Many of the most competent, energetic, and overall desirable candidates have. Focus on accomplishments. How did they make a difference? Did the organization prosper when the candidate was there or suffer less than comparable organizations?

How much training are you willing—more important, able—to give the new hire? How much training or orientation will others provide? How much specialized training, if any, is necessary before the new hire becomes fully productive? This issue is often the beginning of the end with a new employee. Unless you can answer these questions with a specific number of hours, you're not ready to begin a search. Don't underestimate the break-in time. It's probably going to be twice as long as you'd like—or anticipated.

Are set working hours crucial? Does the person form a link in a chain such that his or her hours must be set? This can be very important in recruiting. For instance, a desirable physician or insurance clerk might be available at odd hours. Is 8 to 5 really crucial?

Could the job be shared or done by a contract worker? Does the person really need to be a full-time employee with benefits? By 1995, 50 percent of all professional workers will be contract workers because top management's number one goal is flexible staffing.

What is the work flow of the job? Will there be frantically busy times bordered by lulls? Are there periods of extraordinary stress? Don't kid yourself—much less a candidate—about this. Painting the picture a bit blacker than your view of reality means that the new hire will feel he or she is doing well when things aren't quite as hectic as you said they would be.

How much information on policies/procedures will this person need to store mentally? The more that must be stored, the longer the break-in period. Some people work best from written instructions. Do you have most policies and procedures in writing for easy access?

- Do co-workers have any preconceptions about the kind of person who should be hired? Are these preconceptions important? If they are not addressed, could co-workers create political problems within the organization? A clinic we know decided that the way to reduce nursing turnover was to hire only "mature" nurses. These nurses, when confronting younger physicians, did not hesitate to indicate that they had more practical knowledge than the physicians. Sometimes they did, but the resulting political warfare was destructive.

- Is there enough work for a full-time person, or could this be a half-time or two-thirds time job? If hiring the wrong person into a job is terrible, boring an outstanding hire is even worse. There should be 60 hours work in a forty-hour-per-week job. Most organizations have already told everyone that 45-50 hours, not 40, is *expected*. Estimate the work load accordingly.

- What are your priorities for this person? Do you have a clear idea of what is crucial to success and satisfaction in the job?

Once you have your job specification, you're ready to write a job description—or revise an existing one. It's important not to view a written job description as more than a fence around turf. That is, a job description must be a living, changing document—a map to the territory, not a prison. Most organizations can't revise job descriptions as quickly as jobs change. This is particularly true in health care. Consequently, hiring a new person must be preceded by a look at the job.

What are important are the outcomes the person must achieve. Describe the outcomes you expect from the job, the means the person has to work with, and the limitations he or she will have to work within. Do *not* write a series of tasks and call it a job description. You will be evaluating the person on how well he or she achieved outcomes, so that's what should be in the job description. Distribute job descriptions and then solicit resumes. Don't solicit resumes before you can produce the outcomes you're looking for. Your time is too valuable to be tied up screening resumes, and only you should screen them. That means *preventing* inappropriate candidates from applying, not mechanically screening them out later. Time is money!

Don't fall in the trap of, "I need to see what's out there." You don't. Think in straight lines. You won't miss anyone by focusing only on those who fit your specifications.

Reviewing Resumes

The best sources of candidates are current employees, your opposite number at another health care provider, the personnel department, or recruiters. The names you get will be prescreened. Solicit the people for resumes, or try to determine each individual's willingness to change jobs. If you can't get good candidates from these sources, use help wanted advertisements. Ads will pose more screening problems and produce fewer stars than any other method. The cost of a want ad is cheap compared to the cost of processing and responding to candidates. (Only an organization with no ethics or style would not respond to each candidate. A form letter is acceptable.) Blind want ads should not be used, because they signal the good people in the market that you have something to hide or are behaving unethically, e.g., someone is in the job you propose to fill and you don't want the employee to know he or she is on the way out.

The best way to choose interview candidates is to make three piles of resumes: 1) to be interviewed, 2) definite no's, and 3) maybe's. After the first pass, review the "maybe's" until you have put each one in either of the other two piles. Finally, go through the people you'd like to interview and pick 6 to 10. If there are only 5, so much the better. Give the rest of the resumes to the person who is sending out rejection letters. Why not keep all the rest in case your first few choices don't pan out? Because if you didn't like them the first time around, you're kidding yourself if you think they'll look better later. If they do, you've succumbed to panic or to unseemly haste in filling the job.

Interviewing

Once you're ready to interview, schedule as many as you can in one day. It isn't true that the first person or the last person to be interviewed has the best shot at the job. If you see people serially, it's easier to make comparisons than if they are strung out, one a day, for weeks.

There are two types of interviews:

- **Initial.** This is usually done by the personnel department or a recruiter. It screens out people whose resumes are all right but who, when interviewed, turn out to be unqualified. This interview also verifies data on the resume or application and seeks to ascertain the applicant's interest in the job. All this can be wrapped into the next step if there are few candidates and no personnel department. Initial interviews can be done by telephone. In fact, most initial interviews and first evaluation interviews are done by telephone because it's so much less costly than bringing candidates on site.

- **Evaluation.** This is a thorough oral review of the candidate's qualifications. By talking one-on-one with a candidate, the interviewer can decide if he or she is a "possible" or an "improbable." The meeting usually lasts a minimum of 60 minutes. The average is about two hours. Obviously, at any point the applicant may cut the interview off. The interviewer needs to be very careful so the applicant doesn't decide he or she wasn't given a fair shake and is a victim of discrimination.

There are four parts to an effective evaluation interview.

- **Rapport building.** This includes about two minutes of general discussion designed to help the candidate catch his or her breath and relax a bit. Caution: This chitchat is where lawyers tell us people make illegal statements. Confine yourself, as Henry Higgins told Eliza, "to the weather and the state of everybody's health."

- **Q&A.** This is the body of the interview and includes all the questions that will verify or amplify information on the resume. It also includes a concise description of the job, the results to be achieved, its sociopolitical context, a breakdown of percentages of time to be spent on different tasks, and some information about the style of the organization—how it does things.

The applicant should participate freely with any questions he or she has. If the applicant doesn't ask the right questions, answer the ones he or she should have asked. "When was my predecessor promoted?" "What is the career path for this job?" "Describe a typical day." "What personal qualities, other than skills/experience, are important to success in this job?" Note: When you interview for a job always ask these questions.

■ **Applicant response.** At some time during the interview, you must give the applicant a chance to tell you why you should hire him or her. You can ask, "Do you have anything you'd like us to know about you?" or "Is there anything you want to highlight about your work?" or you might simply stop talking. The applicant can introduce any topic he or she feels is important. It is the applicant's responsibility to sell you at this point.

■ **Close.** This is the time when you tell the applicant when he or she will hear from you. Explain that you are interviewing several candidates. Don't say "I was impressed with your background" unless you were. Within two weeks, you need to contact each candidate again and give him or her a status report. Useful questions to ask in the close are if the applicant feels he or she understands the style and culture of your organization or department. Don't get into discussion of why the candidate won't be considered. You could slip here and say something you'd regret. Friendly, neutral interest is best.

Others may also do evaluation interviews. It's common for candidates to have as many as seven interviews with different people or, as is more common in health care, a group interview.

Group interviews, an interesting form of torture because they torture both candidate and interviewers, must be managed carefully. Before you bring in a candidate, he or she must be briefed on the group process. Say, "It's very important that you give equal eye contact to everyone at the table. They'll all be involved in the decision." More good candidates are lost because they alienate people while trying to burn a laser-like hole into people they believe will make the decision, thus alienating everyone else, than for any other reason.

Warn candidates that the group will undoubtedly ask questions you've already asked. Suggest that the applicant simply repeat the original answer.

You control the seating at the group interview. Instead of sitting next to the candidate, which means you'd be giving him or her no positive eye contact, sit across from the candidate. Put the more difficult people on either side of the candidate so he or she won't have eye contact with them. Arrange the seating by putting name labels on file folders in which you've put the candidate's resume.

Tips for Successful Interviewing

■ Prepare questions in advance and try them on the employees you're happiest with.

If these paragons can't answer them satisfactorily—or they react unfavorably—change the questions. Remember that questions reflect your values and style and give clues to the organizational culture. Do the ones you've prepared convey the message you want to give?

Take careful notes, even if it slows the interview.

Avoid curiosity questions that may be illegal. Questions about marital status or children are two such questions. "Have you ever been tested for AIDS?" is in a legal gray area. Don't ask it.

Focus on the why and how. "Why have you decided to apply here?" not "Why did you decide to become a physician, nurse, secretary, etc.?" "What influenced you to seek this kind of position with us?" "Were you referred to us?" "Do you know us by reputation?"

If you don't understand an applicant's answer or if the answer isn't complete, rephrase your question and come at it again. Let an important topic drop because you've run out of questions and you may have to interview a second time.

Listen intently to the applicant's answers, not only the content but also the phrasing.

If you feel you need more information, reinterview. Do this even if it means flying the candidate in again. The cost is cheap compared to hiring the wrong person.

The Selection Process

Go through your serious candidates and rate each on a scale of one to 10 points using the following criteria:

Skills/experience for the job.

Fit with the organization, including personality/style.

Your gut response to the candidate, as in like/dislike. Yes, it's legal to like some people more than others.

Input from others—every interviewer should rate candidates on the same scale.

■ Probable longevity in the job, if that's important.

Other important factors.

Add up the points and decide if the total reflects your overall gut response. It is almost always fatal to hire someone you're not keen on but who seems to be a perfect fit, or to hire someone with a string of job failures who "needs a chance." Charity begins at home—and ought to stay there.

Offers and Contracts

All offers of employment should be in writing. An oral offer may bind you negatively, i.e., the candidate may say you offered the job when you were really only questioning availability. If you're offering a contract, here are the elements it will need to contain:

Crystal clear details of your compensation package, including all perks. Don't assume anything. Spell out the fringe benefits, especially nontaxable ones, such as medical, life, disability, dental, optical, and legal insurance; expense account; and stock options, as applicable.

Terms of agreement. How long does the contract run? What are the results you expect the person to achieve? Can he or she be fired at will, with or without cause, or does he or she have some job security? The grounds for termination should be spelled out, as well as what the termination package will be. How much severance will be given? If a contract can be broken for cause, the possible causes on both sides should be spelled out. It is almost impossible to hire good people without a generous severance package and outplacement assistance.

References. Specify what information the organization will report in a reference check.

■ Noncompete agreements. If the new hire leaves the organization, can he or she work for a competitor?

Confidential information. The courts are likely to uphold an employee's duty not to divulge confidential information, but you must specify in the contract exactly what is confidential.

Attorney's fees. If either party has to sue under the contract, the winner of the suit gets money plus attorney's fees. This promotes great reasonableness.

Location of work unit. Where will the employee be based? Can you reassign to a distant unit, or must this be negotiated?

Successor provision. What happens if the organization is sold or merged? Does the person's contract go to the next owner? Can the employee exercise a severance clause if he or she doesn't want to be "sold?" In uncertain times, such clauses are very important to desirable candidates.

Orientation

Your offer is accepted and now it's time to play the new person in. Here's the best approach:

Day One. Plan to spend almost the entire day with the new hire if he or she is your direct report. Even though the person has recently been through the interviewing process, go over the job description in detail. See that the employee meets everyone in the immediate work unit. If you have coffee breaks, invite others to join the two of you. Provide a tour and begin explaining policies and procedures.

Day Two. Ask for questions that the person may have after the first day. Assign three to four hours of substantive work. Then meet for a mini-appraisal. How did things go? More questions.

Day Three. Arrange for the new hire to meet with all those with whom he or she will interact to get a feel for those individuals' expectations. Ask for feedback on these meetings.

Day Four. Lunch with top management (depending on the level of the new hire) or with your boss if it's a lower level hire. Go over the telephone directory and explain who does what. How are supplies requisitioned?

Day Five. Spend an hour or so with the new hire talking about the job as a whole. Beginning on day six, he or she will be doing it all, with you available but not standing by. Emphasize how important it is to ask questions now.

Here's the rule: The more time you spend up front with the individual—and we know five days is excruciatingly long—the less time you will spend later. You are buying your way out of a mess of retraining three months from now. If you abdicate the training function, the people you least admire in the work unit will fill the void. They'll "orient" the new person in ways it will take you months to change. Protect your investment.

Early Warning Signals

Just when you thought everything was under control (by the way, why did you think that?), your gut begins to tell you that your new hire isn't going to work out. Your instinct is to batter the messenger and deny the message. As Rosie said in "The African Queen," "Human nature is what we're put here to rise above." So it is in management.

The first whisper that all is not well should be leapt on pronto. Call in the new hire and say, "Joe, I understand there are some problems in OB/GYN." This a neutral opener and gives Joe a chance to say anything he wants to. The worst response, from your point of view, would be for Joe to assert that there are no problems. If he were aware of them, they might be easier to solve.

Use the grapevine. Most people haven't the sense of urgency or the courage to complain directly about someone's performance when that person has only been there a few weeks or months. This is a problem because the person is still new enough to be changed. If the vine is picking up a lot of negatives, you should listen. Begin taking notes. Start asking the sources of the rumors if they're true. Don't wait until someone comes to you with a formal complaint.

Meet with the person once a week and explain what problems you're seeing or hearing about. Don't ask the person if he or she did, or failed to do, something. Instead, say, "This is how we need it done. Can you do it?" It's better to ask this question too often than not often enough. If the person says, "No, I can't or won't do it that way," you've just been handed a resignation. You won't like it particularly, but it beats having to fire someone.

Termination

There are any number of valid reasons to fire an employee, but it's rare that skills failure is the only one. The reasons that cause most terminations include inability to work well within a team framework; inability to adjust to the organization's style (with physicians this may be entrepreneurial zeal); or inflexibility, i.e., "I am medically state-of-the-art, and I must do it my way."

It is much better for the organization and the individual if you handle the termination in the following way. We assume here that you've been going over the person's performance defects, whether technical or interpersonal, so that there's little chance of his or her being surprised when you initiate the warning/suspension process. Surprised people tend to sue. Don't surprise anyone. Likewise, "Things may not work out around here" is an observation apropos of nothing, not a warning.

Step One

Verbal warning. At the person's work station you say, "You are not seeing the appropriate number of patients. This is what you need to do," or "Five patient complaints per week about your care are too many. You must deliver and maintain a service that does not generate more than one complaint a month. You must satisfy the patients such that they respond favorably on our satisfaction surveys."

Then you ask the same fateful question: "Can you do this?" If the person says, "No, I can't," you are two-thirds of the way to a resignation. Stating that he or she can't perform the job means that the person has little choice but to leave.

Step Two

Two written warnings, accepted and signed by the employee. Why two? Because it's more than one. There is no set standard, but five written warnings takes the teeth out of the warning process. Warnings begin to look like traffic tickets.

You should insist that the individual sign the warning. Understand that this doesn't mean he or she *agrees* with the warning, only that he or she has read it. If the person doesn't understand that is what his or her signature means, explain it. If the employee still refuses to sign, get a witness that the warning was indeed presented.

Step Three

Termination. Because firing is the organizational equivalent of taking someone off life support, death to follow, there is a tremendous, natural reluctance to fire. This is doubly true if the employee's problem is interpersonal rather than technical. The solution is to make a decision and implement it as quickly as possible.

The alternative to firing is to keep someone who isn't performing until he or she voluntarily leaves. This is unwise and damaging to the organization. It reduces productivity in the immediate work area and reduces the willingness of co-workers to live within the organization's culture and rules. It weakens management's control and destroys any semblance of leadership image.

From a legal perspective, if you keep an unsatisfactory employee for several years and don't use the performance appraisal system to institute corrective procedures, and that employee also happens to be over 40, you may involve the organization in a lawsuit that any lawyer would be glad to take before a jury.

Tips on Firing Humanely

■ Fire at the end of the day. Is there anything worse than "forgotten but not gone?" The longer the dearly departed hangs around, the longer it takes others to get back to work. If you're firing a physician, using a locum tenens is preferable to keeping the person on until someone is hired. Arrange for coverage in advance with someone outside the organization unless you want the grapevine to light up.

■ Call the person into your office and explain the terms of departure. It's cruel to make someone ask how his or her organizational life will come out. Your explanation should include when the employee is to leave, how much severance pay will be provided, and what kind of references can be expected. Allow the employee to resign if that's possible.

■ Detail what other support, if any, the organization will provide. Outplacement? Counseling? Don't offer the employee a chance to use the organization's facilities. It's embarrassing for the employee and has a negative effect on general productivity.

■ Don't imply that there is any possibility of reconciliation. This is FINAL. Don't talk about "things not working out as either of us expected." The other person may believe that he or she isn't being dismissed, just warned.

■ Ask the employee to clean out his or her work space and turn over work in process to a specific person. Only in the most extreme case should a security guard accompany the employee back to his or her office. It's done in corporate America but it's still a bad, unnecessarily humiliating practice.

■ Thank the employee for his or her contribution. Wish the person well. Do not say you are sorry to see him or her go unless it's true. Why add hypocrisy to the stew?

The major engine for firing humanely—even when you feel like announcing the departure with champagne all around—is the effect anything but the most humane treatment will have on survivors in the organization. They are watching, and they are your most important constituency.

Finally, did you learn anything about the selection process from the firing? Did you learn anything about your biases for or against certain kinds of people? Ultimately, the lessons of each firing should be reflected in the hiring of future employees.

Reaching for the Stars: Effective Recruiting

by David R. Kirschman and Jennifer R. Grebenschikoff

CHAPTER

22

No manager can go long without being exposed to the recruitment process. This includes the physician manager charged with identifying practitioners for a department or service area, with bringing new practitioners into the community, or with recruiting a physician to serve in a managerial role in the organization. Indeed, physicians serving in senior medical manager positions such as medical director will almost certainly have an ongoing role in recruitment. They may be asked to develop and manage entire recruitment programs or to participate as advisors in recruitment efforts.

In either case, physician executives must be capable of making the recruitment process work for their organizations. In recent years, the demand for high-quality physician executives and physician practitioners has exceeded the supply. Consequently, it behooves those who would recruit to do everything possible to analyze their needs thoroughly, plan well, and follow through properly. If you hope to recruit the best available talent in the marketplace, you must do all you can to be effective recruiters. Good managers should reach for the stars in the profession; they should not be satisfied with the merely acceptable candidate. Stars exist in the medical profession and can be recruited. This includes clinical stars in all specialty areas, as well as physician executive stars, who carry clinical excellence forward into the managerial arena.

In this chapter, we provide a framework for a successful internal recruitment program that will allow you to locate and recruit stars to your organization. Because physician executives are mostly responsible for the recruitment of physicians, our comments are directed to this professional group. However, good recruitment practices work well with any professional group. These comments will be helpful whenever you become involved in recruiting, at any level.

Preparation

The key to the success of any management process is thoughtful and complete preparation. This is certainly true of recruitment. Aside from the benefit of better candidates and hence better employees, effective planning also saves your organization money and other resources. While luck certainly plays a part in successful recruiting, more often success is characterized by hard work. Attention to the details of a search is very important and should be considered when you begin the planning phase of a recruitment effort. The following key questions should be addressed in detail as the planning process is initiated:

1. Who has the responsibility and authority to conduct the recruitment effort? Whose advice will be sought? Who will make the final decision?

2. For each position, do you have a clearly defined job description or statement of professional expectations? Do you have agreement by all key managers?

3. What individuals or groups will be included in the planning stage and will provide input to guide recruitment efforts? Who will be involved with interviewing and selection?

4. Have sufficient funds been authorized to support recruiting activities? Is there agreement about the compensation package to be offered? Have you considered the opportunity costs for any delays that may occur? Are you prepared to make a decision?

5. What are the realistic time frames for this recruitment effort? Does everyone understand the time necessary for such an undertaking?

6. Has sufficient staff been assigned to assist with local coordination? Is everyone in agreement?

These questions all pertain to the details of the recruitment process and the potential problems of completion that may arise. Each question should be considered and answered before you begin to market a position and seek candidates.

Assign a Search Committee

The first step in preparing to recruit for a professional position should be assignment of responsibility for the recruitment to a specific group, a search committee. This group must have a clear charge from the organization's leadership as to the extent of its authority and duties. If it is to review candidates and make recommendations only, it should understand that role. On the other hand, if it is to make the final decision and selection, that authority should be understood and should guide its activities.

We always recommend smaller committees for the obvious reason: too many participants make a timely decision difficult. While the committee should not be too large, it should include representatives of the key groups affected by hiring a new person. In the case of a physician to be recruited for a hospital department management position, the committee should include a key administrative person (with the authority to make a decision for administration), a physician from the department or from general medical staff, and the senior physician executive or a designate. If expectations are for this new chief to develop an expanded program or a new service, someone representing the planning committee should also be included. Additional members of the committee can be assigned as politically necessary. Having more than seven members on a search committee is unnecessary and will inhibit decision making. A group as small as three members is reasonable if constituencies agree to the representation of committee members.

Successful committee work is judged by the recruitment of a satisfactory candidate and by satisfaction of those affected by the recruitment that it was a thoughtful and appropriate choice. Therefore, even the small search group should take steps to include a wide range of representatives in the interviewing process, to ask for reactions and recommendations, and to see that a consensus is reached. In any case, we recommend involvement only of members of the search committee in the final selection decision.

Develop Recruitment Objectives
The first meeting of the committee should include a review of its charge and agreement on objectives. A search committee is usually ad hoc and expected to do its duty and disband. Therefore, one objective should relate to the time frame in which a final decision will be made by the committee. There should be some expectation about when the new person will be on board and working. Once that time is established, the group can work backward to the current time to plan its schedule. Without some recognition of the realities of timing, the committee might never meet its goals.

Another important objective of the committee is agreement about the credentials and traits of the person to be recruited. The committee should decide what is absolutely required and what is preferred in the candidate of choice. Requirements should include, for example, board certification, minimum years of certain experience, and personality type. Preferences might include such variables as training locations, specific experience, and a management degree. The group should understand the difference between preferences and requirements and be prepared to consider candidates who have the basic requirements for the position, even if they do not meet preconceived notions of exactly what background he or she should possess. More often than not, the originally stated criteria change when the committee is faced with a different, but acceptable, alternative candidate. This is especially true in situations in which candidates are difficult to identify and to recruit to your location.

Another objective might be ensuring that candidates have the opportunity for exposure to a wide range of people and viewpoints during interviews. Objectives having been established, the committee can move to the process steps necessary to conduct a search for candidates and recruit the best for further consideration.

Establish a Budget
The committee should be aware of any financial constraints it has in meeting its objectives. The committee should be aware if money is no object and the person to be recruited is so important that any reasonable cost will be acceptable.

More often, however, the committee will face at least some restrictions. The methods and amount of advertising of the position will, for example, be influenced by the funds available for such activity. Whether or not the committee will engage the services of a search firm is also a financial consideration that should be addressed. A good understanding of the resources available to administer the search will be of significant value as the committee begins to chart its strategy.

The details of the compensation and relocation package to be offered to the candidate of choice should be defined early. Compensation may be a sensitive issue; you may have to be somewhat vague in terms of a specific salary, but a range should be defined. Knowledge of what can be paid to entice prospects will be necessary as the committee decides the level of experience it will target in its recruitment efforts. An entry level compensation package will define the level of experience that can realistically be expected. There is little value in expending resources in recruiting candidates you are unprepared to compensate.

Other financial information, such as the benefits to be provided and special perquisites, should be known initially to help sell the position. Relocation expense reimbursement for the new employee, family, and possessions are reasonable expenses of recruitment and should be recognized as the search begins to avoid any problems at negotiation time. Also reasonable are expenses for the candidate and spouse to visit for interviews. They should be included in the budget.

Valuing a Candidate's Worth

Both you and the candidate you select for the position will be interested in the compensation package to be offered. The candidate will want to be sure that his or her services are being fairly and adequately paid for. You will want to be sure that it matches, but does not greatly exceed, the market value for the position. One thing to point out to candidates is the net economic benefit relative to other opportunities and relative to their current positions and locations. In order to do that, the cost of living where the organization is located should be compared with the cost of living where the candidate currently resides or is considering another offer. Sometimes the difference is sufficient to justify a 5-10 percent differential in competing situations. It is rare, however, that an organization can disregard local compensation practices and the national marketplace when recruiting.

Compensation averages throughout the industry are reported in a variety of surveys conducted periodically. The American College of Physician Executives conducts periodic surveys of its membership, and the Physician Executive Management Center (PEMC) conducts biannual surveys of the health care industry to learn about trends in physician executive compensation. The Medical Group Management Association, PEMC, and a variety of other organizations conduct annual surveys to learn about physician practitioner compensation. The salaries or total compensation amounts reported in these surveys should be used as guidelines in determining the value of the candidate you will be recruiting. It is often helpful to compare the results of more than one survey in arriving at your position's value.

Develop a Job Description

Whether the position is newly created or has been in existence for several years, the organization should have a written description of its duties. This document assists in developing consensus among search committee members and other organizational decision makers about the job being offered. You do not want the committee at odds about the duties of the position once interviews begin. Any areas of disagreement must be negotiated prior to the visit.

There are any number of formats to follow when developing a job description. We suggest it be succinct in language, broad in scope. The description should include several objectives of the position—why it was created and what the incumbent's role is in the organization. Additionally, the job description should include a brief reference to each of the key departments or areas of responsibility for the position.

This somewhat abbreviated description should be used to inform potential candidates about the position. It provides a flavor for the position, but does not suggest a rigid, no alternative position. In the event you are looking for a senior manager, a physician executive for an important new service, you should certainly be flexible. The ideal candidate will likely not have skills in every area connected with the position, so some of the duties may have to be delegated or reassigned. On the other hand, the new physician executive may have skills and interests to expand the job beyond what was originally conceived. Therefore, we suggest that the job description used in recruiting be general rather than specific, enabling rather than restrictive.

Summary of Preparation

The activities mentioned previously should be taken by any organization planning to initiate a search to recruit a key manager. These issues are important whether you plan to conduct the search portion of the process internally or contract with a consulting firm to provide assistance. You should be fully prepared to address the many matters that can arise during the recruitment process. To be unprepared sends a message to the marketplace, and specifically to a candidate, that the situation is uncertain and may involve greater risks than are evident on the surface. Once proper preparatory steps have been taken, you are ready to begin the next phase, searching for candidates.

Searching for the Stars

Recruitment is the business of enticement. The goal is to woo someone to a position. There are basically two kinds of candidates; voluntary and involuntary. The former are candidates who are actively in the job market. They answer ads and can be available with very short lead times. Involuntary candidates are more difficult. They are not looking for jobs and are probably happy where they are. They have to be attracted to new positions. That is where your recruitment process takes over!

Two factors make the difference between success and failure in recruitment—timing and attitude. The average "shelf life" of an attractive candidate is about 60 days. Someone will reach the candidate in that period, or the candidate will reach someone on his or her own. The candidate has absolutely no reason to delay a decision, because he or she doesn't even know that your organization is interested in filling a position. One week can lose a good candidate.

Attitude is of equal importance in influencing a candidate. When you are interviewing or otherwise expressing an interest in hiring a candidate, your attitude should be one of accommodating the needs of the candidate. It is not enough to rearrange schedules and make room for interviewing the candidate. In every possible way, the candidate must feel wanted, even pampered if possible. All arrangements should be taken care of by your organization. Otherwise, the candidate, through lack of familiarity with your organization and location, may make travel or lodging arrangements that are unsuitable. Remember, the purpose of the recruitment process, including the interview, is to interest the candidate in your organization.

It is useful to view the recruitment process as a three-stage approach to the acquisition of employees: sourcing, recruiting, and closing. The first two stages involve locating prospects and convincing the best of them to at least visit the organization to be interviewed. The two objectives of the interview are to discover whether the candidate is attractive enough for your organization and to sell the candidate on the opportunity. A problem inherent in interviewing is that these two objectives are mutually exclusive tasks. What most of us do is spend the biggest part of our time trying to learn whether the candidate is acceptable, and little on trying to sell the candidate on the opportunity that the organization and the position represent.

Sourcing

Sourcing is all about coming up with an attractive candidate. It is the process of casting a wide net so that the largest possible pool of candidates is available for choice. Calling a friend and asking for a recommendation is a good example of sourcing. The goal is to cast a net wide enough that, after a winnowing process, at least a couple of fish remain. When you seek practitioners, the source with the highest probability of success tends to be colleagues. A call to 10 colleagues for recommendations of candidates in the specialty in which recruitment is intended should provide at least one qualified candidate.

Next in order of probability when searching for practitioners are existing physicians on your organization's staff. Of course, this advice has to be tempered by knowledge of the physicians' biases, but frequently the best candidates come from recommendations from those most closely associated with the environment into which the candidate is to be recruited. Professional recruiters frequently will use only this technique with a fair amount of success.

Medical training programs near the organization can also be a source of candidates for staff physicians. But don't write a letter—call. A letter to the residency program will be posted on a bulletin board along with all the other letters that have been sent requesting residents, and rarely will you receive a response. A personal call to the department chair for recommendations will usually elicit good ones. The chair is often anxious to place his or her best candidates.

National meetings of specialty societies can also be an excellent source of candidates. A substantial amount of recruiting occurs at these meetings outside of the sessions. Physicians currently employed by the organization are likely to attend the meetings and may be willing to interview candidates. In this case, a note on the bulletin board can attract some good candidates.

State medical associations are another possible source. Most of them have listings of people who would like to move. The technique is low cost, even if the results are somewhat unpredictable.

Advertising as a sourcing technique is high cost and low return, low yield. It may generate a lot of responses, but there is no screening mechanism. Anybody who chooses can respond. It isn't the cost of the advertising that's so high; it's the time and costs in screening the responses. It's the professional job hunters who routinely answer ads. The satisfied candidates aren't overtly looking for a new position, so the advertising pages don't normally attract them. Of course, some organizations may be forced to advertise for political or legal reasons. In any case, expectations of results should not be high.

Recruiters are also high cost. They require low time involvement on the organization's part and can be high yield. They can also be merely high cost. Whether a recruiter is worthwhile has a lot to do with its caliber. In choosing a recruiter, carefully check references. Networking with other managers can be especially productive at identifying a list of firms.

Direct mail is also high cost and takes some special talents to be performed well, but its big advantage is that it's targeted. Lists that have only those persons who meet the basic criteria for the position to be filled can be purchased from organizations such as the American Medical Association. In addition, screening before the list is purchased will ensure that the only potential responses are those in which the organization is interested.

Direct mail is not a high-response technique. Generally, the response rate is about one percent. Including a prepaid postcard or a toll-free telephone number for reply may help, but a one percent response is typical. More important, if list selection has been done appropriately and prescreening has been performed, the responses come from persons who match the criteria for the position to be filled.

If the organization enjoys a dominant position in the community, there is a high probability of success in recruiting locally. The approach has many advantages. Relocation time is reduced, and there is greater knowledge of the person being recruited. The military, government agencies, the U.S. Public Health Service, and the Veterans Administration may also be good sources of candidates. There are about 14,000 physicians in these organizations, and about 20 percent of them will leave each year. Lists are hard to obtain, but they are worthwhile places to look for candidates.

Preinterview Stage

The interview stage should be approached with the same care and planning that has characterized other segments of the recruiting process. After the list of interested candidates has been developed, an in-depth telephone conversation should be conducted with each candidate before interview invitations are extended. There are four key issues that need to be answered:

■ Why is the candidate interested in the position?

■ Why is the candidate worth spending time and money on?

■ What is it about the candidate that would make the organization want to extend an offer?

■ What will it take to get the candidate to accept the position?

In the initial telephone conversation, questions should be asked about the candidate's present earnings and earnings expectations. When the time comes for an offer, this information is invaluable. The questions also are asked at a neutral point, and the answers amount to little more than background information. When they are asked at the end of an interview, room for maneuverability is lost.

References

References should always be checked by telephone, not in writing. Few references will be willing to be candid in writing. Also, references should be checked in advance of interviews so that all interviewers are better prepared and will know what weaknesses and what strengths to look for. Start with three references. If you have three clean references, stop. Negative references require a decision: to look further or to end consideration of this candidate. If you feel the candidate is worth the effort and may not have deserved a bad report, contact several more references until you are comfortable with the candidate.

We recommend that the calls be tape recorded so that the caller's concentration can be on the conversation and not on notes. Of course, the reference must be told that the conversation will be taped. If your request to tape the conversation is rejected, then don't, but take good notes.

The health care field is unique when it comes to references. It is the only field in which references will tell you anything. If the right questions are asked, almost any important information can be learned from references in this field. There is a caution, however, if the reference is bad. Any information that you receive that reflects poorly on a candidate must be retained in strictest confidence. However, you should make the most of this situation and learn as much as you can about a prospective candidate.

Preparation for Interviews

Thorough preparation improves the chances of interviewing success. There are a number of issues that should be addressed as you consider interviewing.

Search Coordination. There are many matters that must be addressed when arranging the interview. There are broad policy decisions that are usually made by your search group, implementation decisions (by a member of the search committee), and day-to-day follow-up decisions. We recommend that your organization designate two people to be responsible for search coordination.

- Manager—For overall implementation of the direction provided by the search committee, you should assign a senior manager. This manager will direct the flow of arrangements for the interviews. Additionally, the manager should contact candidates personally prior to the visit to ensure that all their needs will be addressed during the visit.

  The manager should be authorized to make day-to-day process decisions to facilitate the search. Also, the manager should be reasonably accessible to candidates to answer any questions and be willing to devote a significant amount of time to recruitment.

■ Coordinator—You should have a day-to-day contact person who will be involved with the details and logistics of the candidates' visits. This person should be pleasant to work with, flexible, and attuned to handling the many details of a recruitment process. The coordinator will work with candidates and your organization's staff for scheduling and will prepare for interviews, meals, lodging, and local transportation. After initial arrangements have been made, the coordinator should continue involvement to verify the schedule and confirm arrangements with all parties prior to the interviews.

The person for this position can be the organization's recruiter, someone from personnel who is accustomed to recruiting arrangements, or an assistant or secretary who has the experience to represent the organization well.

Planning for the Visit. Arrangements for a candidate's visit to your community should not be difficult. Because you are familiar with the area and its resources, arrangements for the visit are best coordinated by staff of your organization. You know the best and most reliable sources of hotels, dining, transportation, and other details of having a visitor in your town. You should guide the process.

■ Transportation—You have two options when making plans to bring a candidate to your community; you make the arrangements, or you have the candidate take care of it. While your taking the responsibility for all scheduling and purchase of tickets is a nice touch and is often appreciated by interviewees, it can be difficult if the candidate needs to make last-minute changes. We recommend that the candidate make arrangements to travel to your area and that you ensure timely reimbursement for any expenses.

Once the candidate reaches your community, you should make all of the arrangements to have him or her transported from place to place, such as from the airport to hotel, to meals, etc. If it is convenient and appropriate, having someone from your organization meet the candidates when they arrive at the airport is the best option. It demonstrates your level of interest and also allows for informal discussions to begin. Use of a rental automobile is another option; in this case, always provide written directions and a map to various contact points. Goings and comings should not be stressful exercises; your goal should be to make it easy and comfortable for the physician and for you.

■ Lodging—For visits requiring an overnight stay, you should make arrangements for a place for the physician to stay. This should be a good quality hotel or motel in reasonable proximity to the organization. It need not be a four-star palace, but it should be a place where a guest will be comfortable with the accommodations and that has services available for travelers, such as room service. If practical, you might make arrangements for the expenses to be billed directly to the organization.

- Meals—For the most part, you should make plans for all meals during the time the candidate is in town. Meals are an excellent time for your staff to meet and talk with the candidate on a less formal basis and should be used to maximum advantage. You may wish, however, to allow the candidates to eat lunch by themselves since that will give them some free time to relax and prepare for the rest of the day. When making arrangements for these meals, it is not necessary to use the highest priced restaurant in town. Rather, a comfortable place with good food and an atmosphere conducive to conversation is recommended.

Planning the Interviews. The interview has two purposes: your evaluation of a candidate's abilities, and his or her evaluation of your organization as an acceptable place to work. You should prepare for the interviews carefully by considering the people you want involved, the physical setting for interviews, and the content of the discussions. The interview is the most important part of the whole recruitment process, and you should be well prepared.

- Interviewers—The number of people to be involved in first interviews should be limited to a select group of decision makers and providers of information. First interviews might include the candidate's prospective supervisor, the organization's CEO, representatives of the medical staff, key administrative personnel, and a representative of the governing body. Obviously, those chosen should have a future relationship with the position being filled.

We recommend against large group interviews, because they often create too formal of an environment and more of a board examination than an opportunity to exchange views and learn about each other. Rather, we suggest interviews be arranged in small groups for most participants, such as two or three physicians from the staff in one group, a trustee and a top administrator as another group, etc. This allows for an easier flow of conversation and gives a friendlier feeling in the discussions. For those not experienced with interviewing, it will help the 45-60 minutes go more smoothly.

Individual interviews are often appropriate for the CEO, the potential supervisor, and perhaps one or two key physicians from the staff. Schedule these sparingly, but as necessary to accommodate the information exchange appropriate for initial interviews.

Remember, the intent of the first interview sessions is to evaluate the acceptability of the candidate and to promote your organization to the candidate. Refrain from scheduling a large number of people to interview the candidates; it adds little to the decision. You should have faith in your search committee to make an appropriate screening decision. This is not the time for all bases to be covered and everyone to become involved with interviewing. The second and any subsequent interviews allow added time for all other parties to be consulted about a hiring decision.

- Interview Scheduling and Preparation—Once dates have been established for the candidate's visit, you should prepare to ask the right questions and provide the right information. One of the ways to be able to make the most of the visit is to plan a strategy for the entire time the candidate is in the area.

Each person or group that meets with the candidate should have a specific area to cover. It should be their job to discuss a defined area regarding the physician's credentials, the proposed position, your organization, or the community. This emphasis can be easily coordinated by the chair of the search committee as you plan for the visit. Most important, it avoids a situation in which every interview session covers the same ground and asks the same questions of the candidate.

If possible, begin the day of interviews with a strong, well-informed person who will be able to present the organization in a positive light. The candidate's first impression of an organization should be the strongest one.

Schedule interviews with a 5-10 minute break for the candidate every hour. Give yourself some room for late arrivals or meetings that run longer than expected and perhaps have a backup interviewer to fill in an unexpected open time slot.

The last person to interview the candidate should also be a strong person who represents the organization well. The last interview of the day is the time for you to ask the candidate about continuing interest in your organization. It is also a time to describe the steps your organization will take as it moves toward a hiring decision and to give the candidate an initial impression of how well he or she was received by your organization.

- Evaluation of Results—Subsequent to the candidate's visit and interviews, you will gather reactions to his or her candidacy. Unless the search committee will be meeting immediately following the date of the interview, and all interviewers will be present, some sort of an evaluation form should be used. We suggest use of a one-page form that is distributed to the interviewers prior to the interviews for completion and returned immediately following the interviews.

The evaluation form should include several criteria that help to measure the credentials of each candidate. Typically, these criteria include the candidate's ability to communicate ideas well and his or her understanding of the organization's environment. Also, it should include an answer to the two key questions each interviewer should address: "Can he or she do the job?" and "Can I work with him or her?" Indeed, getting the answers to these two questions should be the focus of the interviews.

Conducting the Interviews

The ability of your organization to present itself in the best possible light ultimately depends on your personnel. Candidates for a position will certainly be concerned about financial viability, organizational stability, and physical facilities. However, the decision to join an organization is more often made on the basis of perceptions of the people they will be working with and for and their vision for the future.

We suggest that you prepare your employees and staff for interview sessions. Consider the overall image you would like to project to the candidate, and plan the interviews and related activities around this objective. An image as a highly professional, well-run organization with a strong interest in developing human potential will always impress candidates. To actually be that organization is even more impressive.

Communicate the status of the search to your staff and enlist their support before the visit. All persons who come in contact with a candidate should, at least, understand the rationale for the position and understand why a search is occurring. This information can be presented in writing, at routine staff meetings, or both. Having a variety of staff members aware of a candidate's visit and greeting him or her by name is an excellent way to welcome a candidate to your organization.

Prepare a final itinerary to be provided to the candidate prior to or at the beginning of the interview day. Include the full name and title or position of all interviewers so that the candidate can mentally prepare his or her interview day.

A copy of the itinerary should also be provided to those involved with the interview to avoid any confusion about session times. Also, it is a good way to remind the staff of their obligations for interviewing and perhaps encourage any final preparation that is necessary.

If at all possible, schedule all interviews at one location, with the coordinator designated to help keep the process moving. Reminding participants of time schedules (and people waiting) is important to ensure that everyone has a chance to interview without a rush at the end of the day.

The interview location should be reasonably decorated and have comfortable chairs, controlled temperature, and the ready availability of a restroom. A small conference room is ideal, especially if it has coffee, sodas, and fruit available for the interview participants. The interviews should be protected from loud noises and interruption to facilitate communication.

A tour of your facility is normally a good idea, regardless of your organization's size and complexity. Most people who are serious about a position will be very interested in seeing the physical plant, treatment areas, office areas, and other areas of the facility. This may be their future home, and they will have an interest in seeing it for themselves. Any tour should include discussions of any planned new building or renovations that will affect the facility and its future.

Make every attempt to have someone greet the candidate when he or she arrives at your facility. A personal welcome will help the candidate feel comfortable with the people in your organization. The best person to greet the candidate is the search manager, who will have been (ideally) in contact with the candidate prior to the visit. This sets the stage for a personal, friendly visit for the candidate.

Remind those who will be actively involved in the interviewing sessions about potential discriminatory issues. While most personnel professionals are aware of the issues to be avoided in interviews, others often have little experience in this area. Ideally, you will not unlawfully discriminate when making this employment decision, but you also do not want to be perceived as violating the law in the interview sessions.

Basically, you should not ask questions that concern non-job-related issues. The intent of the interview is to determine whether the candidate can do the job and, if so, whether you can work with him or her. Questions concerning age, religion, or national origin will probably not come up in most conversations, but interviewers should remember to not initiate discussion of such topics. Other potential discriminatory areas include disabilities, gender, race, marital status, number or age of children, and future plans regarding children.

Questions for candidates generally fall into three types: open-ended, allowing for a wide range of potential responses; specific, eliciting an objective fact or opinion; and filler, those with no discernable expectation. When an open-ended question is posed, the interviewer should expect to hear a fairly broad response and perhaps some unique or unusual opinions. Sometimes, open-ended questions allow the interviewer to learn a lot about style and priorities of the candidate. However, it is also true that, while these questions can often be interesting, they may not be particularly effective at gathering specific answers to questions of interest to the search committee.

We suggest that an interview be structured to include a mix of open-ended questions and specific fact-finding questions. While you will have an interest in candidates' overall perceptions of the health care industry, you should also address issues related to their experience and credentials to do the job you have in mind.

If time permits, interviewers should make an attempt to interject some personal level of discussion, perhaps to identify common interests or answer questions about the area. The interviewee should also be open to answering questions about professional and personal concerns. Remember, the idea is to recruit the candidates at the same time you evaluate them for your position.

As we mentioned previously, the final contact of the day with the candidate should be by a key participant in the search process. At that time, the candidate should be told of the next steps that will occur (other candidates to be interviewed, search committee to meet, etc.). If it is clear that the interviews went well, this information should be shared with the candidate. Indeed, he or she should be encouraged to share reactions and you should arrive at agreement that all parties continue to be interested.

Second Interviews and Selection

As soon as possible following the last of the first interviews, your organization should take steps to make a decision about candidates, initiate second interviews, and prepare for selection of a final candidate to whom you will make a job offer. Assuming the process has gone well and you have at least one viable candidate, this is the time to move quickly to gain consensus in your organization and closure. Long delays for any reason at this stage of the search can cause you to lose your best candidate to another organization.

Committee Deliberations. The search committee should meet to discuss all candidates under consideration and consider the next steps to be taken. It should review individual comments and evaluations for each candidate and attempt to agree on the first and second choices. If at all possible, the committee should select only one candidate to return for a second interview.

If a consensus cannot be reached, and there is serious question about making a decision favorable to any candidate, it may be time to consider additional candidates. While it may be painful to start over with additional first interviews, it is preferable to hiring the wrong person.

Second Interview Preparations. Your organization now selects the top candidate and asks him or her to return for a second visit. This is a time for your organization to expose the candidate to areas and people in the organization that were previously not covered. You will presumably be ready to make an offer if everything goes well, so you should ensure that all issues have been addressed and that all people pertinent to the decision have had an opportunity to meet with the candidate.

The second interview should last two days (and sometimes longer) to allow time for meetings, tours, social events, etc. In order to accommodate a larger number of people during the visit, you might consider scheduling a number of group meetings or a breakfast or lunch buffet where there is an opportunity for a number of people to meet the candidate in an informal, nonstructured environment. Key meetings with the CEO or the person who will be discussing the terms of an offer (assuming one is made) should be scheduled for this purpose toward the end of the visit.

Spouse and Family Arrangements. The second visit is normally the time to introduce the candidate's spouse to the area and organization. While the candidate presumably has a positive view of the position and has talked with his or her family, actual exposure of the spouse to your organization is extremely important. The family must feel welcomed and understand the resources available should it move to the community. The best way to recruit a spouse (and family) is to involve local spouses in the process. At a minimum, they can be involved in regular meal functions and, at best, can participate in a tour of the area or spend some individual time to talk about the area and its style of living.

We recommend that someone from your organization contact the spouse directly to discuss the visit and learn about any special interests. The areas of interest (schools, sports, arts, clubs, etc.) should be the cornerstone of the spouse's visit and plans should be made to expose the spouse to any and all resources for areas of interest during the visit. Perhaps a spouse or person from the organization's staff has a similar interest and can be scheduled to meet. The important thing to keep in mind is that people will normally relocate only if they can envision living happily in the area. Their professional and personal interests must be met, as well as those of their families, for a successful conclusion to occur.

If the spouse has a separate career and is interested in job opportunities in the area, you should find a way to include someone on the spouse's itinerary who can intelligently discuss that option. Arranging for the spouse to meet with a person from the community in the same line of work would be a good way for the spouse to gather job information and assess the possibilities of living in your community.

Conclusion

The future of health care delivery will be replete with change. Much of it will include adding or replacing staff to meet changing needs of the marketplace. Physician executives, like other managers, will be active participants in identifying and selecting new personnel. They should be prepared to be effective and efficient recruiters. They should also be willing to devote meaningful time and effort to the process. That way they will be able to reach for the stars, recruit the stars, and enable them to continue to shine.

David R. Kirschman is President and Jennifer R. Grebenschikoff is Vice President of Physician Executive Management Center, a firm in Tampa, Fla., that specializes in the recruitment of physician executives.

The Physician Executive and the Law

*by Miles J. Zaremski
and David B. Goodman*

CHAPTER 23

Historically, a hospital had only the responsibility to provide room and board for patients, facilities for operations, and attendants to assist physicians in patient care. Because attending physicians were not employees of the hospital, liability for injury resulting from a physician's negligent patient care did not pass through to the hospital; only the physician who caused the injury bore responsibility. Consequently, legal issues concerning health care institution management were relatively simple. Those days are past.

Today, hospitals and other health care institutions find themselves the dominant force in administering patient care within their respective facilities. The judicial system, reacting accordingly, now places a great deal of legal responsibility on the health care institution itself for the quality of overall patient care. A hospital's ultimate responsibility for quality of care, combined with the litigious nature of American society, makes it imperative that the physician executive be aware of some of the more common legal issues that a health care institution may confront.

Legal issues a hospital is most likely to confront include liability to a patient for negligent injury and liability to a health professional for granting or withholding medical staff privileges. The ever deepening sea of legislation and regulations associated with reimbursement from state and federal governments exposes hospitals and physicians to additional sources of both civil and criminal liability. Because institutional responsibility includes the use of reasonable care in selecting, retaining, and monitoring medical staff, a close look will be taken at the Health Care Quality Improvement Act, a federal law that mandates centralized reporting of potentially substandard medical conduct.

As exposure to civil liability increases, a hospital must undertake effective risk management techniques that require the maintenance of firm control over the quality of health care administered within its walls. However, an institution that holds the reins too tightly may face a legal doctrine mandating that only licensed persons, not corporations, be allowed to practice medicine. This places the institution in an awkward position. The fulcrum that determines what constitutes the "practice" of medicine is control.

Thus, while a hospital is responsible for overall patient care and must exercise firm control to maintain high-quality care, an overzealous hospital administrator may expose the institution to the charge of unlawfully practicing medicine.

Enhanced hospital responsibility for patient care means that an institution must continually review and evaluate the quality of care rendered by its staff. The predictable result is that some practitioners will have privileges denied or terminated. Because a physician's livelihood often depends on hospital privileges, the denial or termination of such privileges may have dire financial consequences on the physician's ability to maintain or develop a practice. Therefore, a conflict may develop between the hospital's interest in firm internal control and careful screening and the practitioner's interest in broad freedom to practice his or her profession. The result may be a lawsuit with the allegation that denial or termination of staff privileges constitutes an unlawful restraint of trade that violates antitrust laws.

Hospital mergers are already a familiar part of the health care landscape, as are integrated health care delivery networks. Hospital mergers and the formation of integrated health care delivery networks will likely continue to be routine, pushed on by both economic imperative and health care reform. Yet, both mergers and the formation of integrated networks pose potential antitrust concerns and raise, for the hospital and the physician executive, the specter of civil liability and costly litigation. As a consequence, the restructuring of health care delivery networks currently under way presents antitrust issues that must be addressed by hospitals and physician alike.

When all else fails and a lawsuit commences, the physician executive should be familiar with rules that govern a plaintiff's right to discover data generated by the institution, such as peer review records and risk management documents. Moreover, careful attention must be given to document retention policies and preservation of records. Otherwise, hospitals and physicians run the risk of liability for spoliation of evidence and statutory violations in conjunction with the litigation in which the subject documents were sought.

Hospital Liability for Negligence

Upon initiation of treatment or admission of a patient into a hospital, a duty arises requiring the rendering of patient care services that meet the legally required standard of care determined by reference to hospital bylaws, regulations, and JCAHO standards. When a hospital or other health care facility breaches this standard of care, liability may result pursuant to two primary legal doctrines: respondeat superior (vicarious liability) and corporate negligence.

Historically, hospitals were not responsible for the negligent acts of physicians using their facilities. In fact, at one time, hospitals enjoyed an absolute immunity from tort liability, at least in part on the basis of the perception that hospitals functioned as charitable organizations.[1] Hospitals were, in effect, administrative shells providing the framework within which doctors practiced. While a hospital could be liable if it failed to provide an adequate environment, the facility was not directly responsible, nor could it be held directly accountable, for the quality of care itself. However, the days of hospital tort immunity are gone. Hospitals are no longer perceived to be "charitable organizations," but, rather, as highly sophisticated corporations competing in the health care market for revenue.[13] As a consequence, hospitals have, to an increasing degree, been held accountable for the care and treatment rendered within their walls.[13]

Respondeat Superior (Vicarious Liability)

Under general rules of agency law, an employer may be liable for the acts or omissions of an employee who committed them while acting within the scope of employment. This doctrine, known as *respondeat superior* (let the master answer), means that a health care facility may be held indirectly accountable for the negligence of its employees. Thus, although a hospital may have breached no direct duty to a patient, if someone within the hospital's control, such as a physician on the hospital's payroll, is responsible for patient injury, the hospital will be held accountable. Physicians, too, may be held accountable for the acts of those under their "control or supervision" under *respondeat superior*.[4] Liability under *respondeat superior* is generally determined on the basis of the claimed principal's right to control the negligent actor.[4] In passing on whether a physician should be held vicariously accountable for the acts of operating room personnel (hospital employees), it has been recognized that, often times, such personnel are not truly under the control of the surgeon but are akin to the highly sophisticated equipment furnished by the hospital. They are hired and trained by the hospital, and the hospital is generally accountable.[4]

The only wrinkle in the above analysis is that, traditionally, physicians with staff privileges, other than residents and interns, have not been treated by the courts as hospital employees. In order to maintain physician control over patient care, courts historically precluded physicians from dividing their responsibility and accountability between patient and employer. Thus, historically, the hospital was treated as the administrative shell within which physicians, as independent contractors and not as hospital employees, were allowed to practice. However, the times have changed and hospitals, to an increasing degree, are accountable for the actions within their walls. In fact, one of the proposals contained in President Clinton's Health Care Security Act provides for the creation of demonstration projects to examine the effect of enterprise liability on health care delivery.[5] Specifically, health plans participating in the demonstration project would assume full responsibility for medical malpractice claims arising from the provision or nonprovision of health care services under the plan.

While hospitals have often escaped liability for the negligence of physicians acting as independent contractors, certain individuals, such as residents, nurses, or full-time salaried physicians, are undeniably hospital employees for whom the rule of *respondeat superior* will apply. However, a second legal doctrine, the borrowed servant doctrine, sometimes serves to protect the hospital from liability, even for the negligence of its direct employees. If a hospital's actual right to direct and control the activities of an employee is delegated to an independent staff physician, such as when a surgeon instructs a nurse in the details of a specific act, the doctor, rather than the hospital, may be liable for the negligence of that employee. The doctrine of *respondeat superior* still applies, but, in this instance, the independent contractor is deemed to have borrowed the employee from the hospital and, therefore, is treated as the employer.

Additionally, a hospital's liability may be predicated on a third rule of agency law known as either ostensible or apparent agency. If an independent contractor holds him- or herself out as, or is reasonably perceived to be, a facility's employee, and a patient relies on that perception to his or her detriment, the hospital will be judicially precluded from denying the agency relationship. In such circumstances, the hospital will be treated as the employer, even when the physician is, in fact, an independent contractor.[2,3,6-10]

As hospitals engage in ever more expansive advertising campaigns and market themselves to the public as health care providers, they open themselves to vicarious liability for the acts or omissions of "ostensible" agents.[1-3] Courts have demonstrated a receptivity to hospital liability predicated upon principles of "ostensible agency" on the basis that the modern hospital is held out as a business offering and rendering health care services.[1-3] In other words, hospitals have held themselves out to the public as more than structures in which the patient's chosen physician renders services. Rather, hospitals are perceived to be providers of care, with physicians acting under their aegis, and as such are significantly more likely to be held to be "guarantors" of the quality of care rendered by physicians on their staffs under principles of ostensible agency.[1-3]

In general, except in cases in which a patient is drawn to a hospital to obtain care from a physician of his or her choosing, patients are solicited by hospitals for the quality of care offered by the institution itself and are drawn by the institution's reputation. This is notwithstanding the fact that hospitals may contract with physicians as independent contractors. Ostensible agency is premised, in part, on the idea that appearances may speak louder than words and may foil a hospital's ability to insulate itself from liability for the conduct of those physicians, regardless of the individual contractual relationships between health care provider and hospital.

For example, in *Kashishian v. Port*, the Wisconsin Supreme Court held that a hospital may be held liable under the doctrine of apparent authority even when the patient was admitted by her own personal attending physician. In reaching this conclusion, the court noted that "[m]odern hospitals have spent billions of dollars marketing themselves, nurturing the image with the consuming public that they are full-care modern health facilities."[2] The holding in *Kashishian* is significant in part in that it makes a hospital potentially liable for the acts of physicians on its staff even when the patient was treated by the physician of her choice. This is a departure from liability premised on the acts of an emergency department physician where the patient "came to" the emergency department and not to the physician rendering care. This holding makes the institution, at least potentially, responsible for all care rendered within its walls.

Courts have recognized that modern health care services are purchased from institutional providers such as health maintenance organizations, whereas, in the past, such services were purchased from the individual physician who actually performed the services. In these changed circumstances, courts have found that it is reasonable for the patient to believe that the services are provided by the institution as opposed to the individual practitioner and have been receptive to vicarious liability for ostensible agents.[11] For example, a medical malpractice action against a health maintenance organization could be premised on: "(1) vicarious liability on the basis of *respondeat superior* or ostensible agency; (2) corporate negligence based upon the selection and negligent control of the physician; and (3) corporate negligence based upon the corporation's independent acts of negligence, e.g. in the management of utilization control systems."[12] Additionally, an action premised on healing arts malpractice could be brought against a health maintenance organization on contract and warranty theories.[12]

The law is not settled as to when a health maintenance organization may be held liable for its own conduct. For example, in Texas, health maintenance organizations are statutorily prohibited from engaging in the practice of medicine.[13,14] Acts or omissions alleged to constitute negligence in the delivery of health care services, such as diagnosis, have been held, in Texas, to constitute a "medical function" that health maintenance organizations are barred from performing.[15,16] In other jurisdictions, courts have recognized that health maintenance organizations may effectively engage in the practice of medicine, depending on the degree of control exerted on participating or employed physicians.[11,12] In such circumstances, a determination of the health maintenance organization's vicarious liability is fact specific.[11,12]

Courts have held that health maintenance organizations may be held liable for the negligence of physicians participating in their plans even where the health maintenance organization has only limited ability to control such physicians.[11,12] Thus, courts have allowed litigants to step around the barrier of "independent contractor status" and have effectively limited the ability of health care institutions to insulate themselves from liability for the actions of those who are not under their control.[7-10] This expansion of ostensible agency promises to become more significant with a shift toward health care being delivered by networks and associations instead of by individual physicians. Notably, President Clinton's proffered Health Care Security Act provides, among other things, for demonstration projects in which enterprise liability is the exclusive remedy in medical malpractice actions.[5] In these projects, the health plan would bear financial responsibility for most of the acts of individual health care providers.[5]

Corporate Negligence

Throughout the years, the hospital was not considered to be directly responsible for quality of patient care. If liability attached at all, it was derivative as a result of employee negligence. However, the 1965 Illinois Supreme Court case, *Darling v. Charleston Community Memorial Hospital*,[17] was the genesis for the concept of direct hospital accountability in the corporate boardroom for patient injury. This judicially recognized doctrine, known as "corporate negligence," reflects the public perception and expectancy of the modern hospital as a multifaceted health care facility responsible for the total quality of medical care and treatment rendered. "Corporate negligence" has been defined as a doctrine under which the hospital is held liable if it fails to uphold the "proper" standard of care owed the patient: to ensure the patient's safety and well-being while at the hospital.[1] "[H]ospital's duties have been classified into four general areas: (1) a duty to use reasonable care in the maintenance of safe and adequate facilities and equipment (*Chandler General Hospital, Inc. v. Purvis*, 181 S.E.2d 77 (Ga. App. 1971); (2) a duty to select and retain only competent physicians (*Johnson v. Misericordia Community Hospital*, 301 N.W.2d 156 (Wi. 1981); (3) a duty to oversee all persons who practice medicine within its walls as to patient care (*Darling v. Charleston Community*

Memorial Hospital): and (4) a duty to formulate, adopt, and enforce adequate rules and policies to ensure quality care for the patients (*Wood v. Samaritan Institution*, 161 P.2d 556 (Cal. App. 1945)."[1] This differs from ostensible agency/*respondeat superior* in that liability arises not from the agent's acts but from the hospital's own conduct. The hospital's liability, under a corporate negligence theory, is not vicarious.

Significantly, one of the justifications offered by the Wisconsin Supreme Court for expanding the scope of ostensible agency was that holding a hospital liable for a physician's negligent acts provides a stronger incentive to the hospital to monitor and control physicians.[2,18] Generally, in order for a hospital to be held liable under the "corporate negligence" doctrine, it must first be shown that the hospital had actual or constructive knowledge of the defect or procedures that caused the harm.[1]

The *Darling* decision recognized a hospital's obligation to provide overall surveillance of the quality of care a patient receives and rejected the notion of the hospital as an administrative shell in which independent practitioners render patient care. *Darling* and its progeny hold that a hospital has a duty to establish a mechanism to evaluate the quality of medical care provided by the hospital and its staff and to act to avoid unreasonable risk of patient harm. Thus, a hospital has an independent and direct duty to oversee patient care within its four walls, to exercise care to ensure that physicians selected as members of the medical staff are competent, and to continually review and delineate staff privileges so that incompetent staff members are not retained. The quality of care required is determined by reference to accreditation standards, medical staff bylaws, and licensing regulations.

In the 1980 Wisconsin case *Johnson v. Misericordia Community Hospital*,[18] the hospital failed to adhere to established procedures for checking a particular physician's credentials prior to granting him staff privileges. While on the staff, the physician negligently injured a patient. Had the hospital adhered to established procedures, it would have discovered that several other hospitals had investigated him and either denied or restricted his privileges. The court stated, "Misericordia's failure to adhere to established procedures with regard to the 'credentials process' involved a breach of the separate and distinct duty owed to potential patients and, therefore, created a foreseeable and unreasonable risk of harm to such patients."

In a 1986 Illinois Appellate Court decision,[19] a newborn was injured after being overoxygenated. Board of Health regulations required there be one registered professional nurse trained in the care of newborn and premature infants. The hospital's failure to have a specialty-trained nurse on duty at the time of injury was found to be a breach of a direct duty owed by the hospital to the newborn. Consequently, the hospital was held liable for the injury.

Although the doctrine of corporate negligence creates a direct duty between hospital and patient, it does not mean that a hospital is liable for individual acts of negligence occurring under its roof. The hospital is not a guarantor of adequate medical care. Isolated acts of negligence by an otherwise competent physician are that physician's sole responsibility. Again, expansion of vicarious liability for the acts of ostensible agents is eroding the wall insulating hospitals from liability for the acts of those practicing at the facilities. Moreover, if the qualification or competency of the hospital staff or overall hospital monitoring system becomes an issue (i.e., but for the physician's being on staff, the negligent act would not have taken place), the hospital may be held liable for violating an independent duty of care owed the patient.

Finally, while the screening, monitoring, and reviewing function may be delegated on a day-to-day basis to the medical staff, the duty and responsibility for those functions are nondelegable.[1-3,20] The medical staff that performs the oversight function acts as the agent of the governing board, which, under the doctrine of *respondeat superior*, remains fully accountable.[1-3,20] Thus, under certain circumstances, a hospital's own conduct may give rise to liability in addition to vicarious liability for the acts of physicians practicing within the hospital's walls.

Health Care Quality Improvement Act of 1986

On November 19, 1986, President Reagan signed into law the Health Care Quality Improvement Act of 1986.[21-22] This statute was premised on the finding by Congress that medical malpractice and the need to improve the quality of medical care are problems requiring intervention and monitoring on the federal level. Also, a need was found to restrict the ability of competent physicians to move from one state to another without disclosure or discovery of prior incompetent performance and to develop an effective professional peer review system.

This federal law mandates that every entity that makes a payment under an insurance policy (including self-insurance), or in partial or full satisfaction or settlement of a judgment, must report the following information to the Secretary of Health and Human Services (HHS) or to an appropriate private or public agency as the Secretary designates: "The name of any physician or licensed health care practitioner for whose benefit the payment is made; the amount of payment; the name (if known) of any hospital with which the physician or practitioner is affiliated or associated; a description of the acts or omissions and injuries or illnesses upon which the action or claim was based; and such other information as the Secretary determines is required for appropriate interpretation of information reported under this section."[21] Thus, a physician may choose to settle an unfounded action for economic or other reasons unrelated to the merits of the case, but, nonetheless, the settlement must be reported much the same as if the physician had been found liable from a jury's verdict.

The above information must also be reported to the appropriate state licensing board. Any entity that fails to report information of a payment required by the Act is subject to a $10,000 fine for each payment involved.

Next, the Act requires that a Board of Medical Examiners that takes adverse action against a physician for reasons relating to a physician's professional conduct or competence must report the name of the physician involved to HHS, along with a description of the acts or omissions that led to the adverse action and other information HHS deems appropriate.

Third, a health care entity or professional society of physicians that follows a formal peer review process that takes action adversely affecting the clinical privileges of a physician for longer than 30 days, or accepts a physician's surrender of clinical privileges, must report to the Board of Medical Examiners the name of the physician involved and the reasons for the action taken. A health care entity that fails to substantially meet the reporting requirement will not be protected under the provisions of the Act that prevent liability for professional review actions.

Fourth, on the following occasions, it is the duty of each hospital to request information reported under this law from HHS: "At the time a physician or a licensed health care practitioner applies to be on the medical staff or for clinical privileges at the hospital; once every 2 years for any physician or practitioner who is on the medical staff or has been granted clinical privileges at the hospital. A hospital also may request this information at other times."[21]

If the hospital does not request the information as required by the Act, it will be presumed to have had knowledge of any information reported under this law with respect to a physician or practitioner. Additionally, a hospital may rely upon information provided under this law and will not be held liable, in the absence of the hospital's knowledge that the information provided was false.

The Act also provides that the Secretary of HHS must, upon request, provide information requested under the Act to state licensing boards, to hospitals, and to other health care entities (including HMOs) that have entered, or may be entering, into an employment or affiliation relationship with a physician who has applied for clinical privileges or appointment to the medical staff.

The Act further requires confidentiality of disclosed information, provides penalties for breach of confidentiality, and contains a provision protecting the review body or its members from liability.

Antitrust and the Hospital

With the emergence of for-profit health care facilities and alternative health care organizations, general legal principles of competition have become an increasing concern for health care management. Various forms of joint ventures, mergers, and consolidations may result in exposure to allegations of antitrust violations.

One of the more common areas of antitrust exposure that is unique to the health care industry involves staff membership, privileges, and credentialing decisions. When a doctor's privileges are terminated or denied, the physician's practice no doubt will suffer direct economic harm. Given the fact that a successful antitrust suit can result in the award of triple damages, it is not uncommon for the injured physician to attempt an antitrust action.

There are several federal and state statutes that provide the underpinning of a health care professional's antitrust suit, although state rules generally parallel federal statutes. With reference to staffing issues, the primary federal law is the Sherman Act, which prohibits "every contract, combination...or conspiracy in restraint of trade or commerce." Section 1 of the Sherman Act applies to combinations and conspiracies to fix prices, allocate markets, and engage in group boycotts; it also covers tying and exclusive dealing arrangements.

Conspiracy, by definition, must involve an agreement between two or more entities. In view of the multiple layers of relationships in hospital care and administration, it seems that identifying two conspiring entities would be fairly straightforward. However, such is not the case. A basic rule of law states that a single entity cannot conspire with itself.[23] Therefore, if a hospital and its medical staff or peer review committee are treated as a single entity, there can be no antitrust violation. The claim of single identity is often the first line of defense asserted in an antitrust action. Depending on specific facts, some courts have accepted this defense while others have not.

Where individual members of an organization have a personal interest in the exclusion of the complaining party, a court is more likely to find the existence of separate and distinct entities. However, the court's acceptance of two entities is only one step in the analysis of an antitrust lawsuit. It does not mean that the plaintiff will prevail.

In a 1987 decision, *Mosby v. American Medical International*,[24-25] a federal court dismissed a lawsuit by a radiologist who alleged that the hospital and a second radiologist conspired to prevent him from maintaining his practice at the hospital. The plaintiff, a staff radiologist, was listed on the hospital's on-call roster of radiologists. The hospital contracted with the second radiologist to provide continuous radiology services for the physicians practicing at the hospital. The contracting radiologist used the on-call roster for referrals in order to meet his obligation to provide services during evening and weekend hours. However, he later decided to hire a full-time assistant and ceased using the on-call roster. The plaintiff applied for, but was denied, the assistant position. He later filed a lawsuit.[26]

Although it was clear the hospital and the contracting radiologist were two entities that were capable of conspiring, the court did not find evidence of an unreasonable restraint of trade. Because the contracting radiologist could have concluded he could better control the quality of services provided under the contract by hiring an assistant, the court determined the alleged restraint had justifications that outweighed possible anticompetitive effects. This line of defense is bolstered by the trend discussed earlier to broaden the reach of agency under principles of ostensible agency. In other words, if the radiologist is to be held liable for the assistant's conduct, he should be afforded some latitude in the selection of an assistant, even though this has some anticompetitive impact.

Had the above case involved an agreement among competitors, such as among several doctors, the result may have been different. Agreements among competitors have traditionally been treated more strictly by the courts than agreements among noncompeting entities. An allegation that several doctors are engaging in a concerted refusal to deal with a practitioner outside their group has a greater chance of success than an allegation that a hospital and a physicians' group are refusing to deal with another physician.

The difference in judicial treatment lies in the difference between the *per se* rule and the "rule of reason." Agreements among competitors, also known as horizontal restraints, have traditionally been subject to *per se* analysis. Under this reasoning, proof that the alleged conduct occurred is sufficient, the act itself is conclusively presumed to have an anticompetitive effect and is, therefore, illegal *per se*.

In *Arizona v. Maricopa County Medical Society*,[27,28] competing physicians who were members of a foundation for medical care agreed upon minimum prices as full payment for medical services rendered to policyholders of approved insurance programs. Finding that the physicians' conduct constituted horizontal price fixing, the court ruled it to be a *per se* violation of the Sherman Act. It was unnecessary for the court to receive evidence concerning the actual effect of the restraint.

Similarly, in *Weiss v. York Hospital*,[29,30] the court applied the *per se* rule to a horizontal group boycott. In *Weiss*, members of the medical staff agreed to disallow staff privileges to all osteopathic physicians. The court held that such concerted action automatically was presumed to have an anticompetitive effect in the marketplace.

In contrast to the *per se* rule, rule of reason analysis imposes a much more difficult burden on the complaining party. Not only must the plaintiff prove the alleged conduct occurred, but also that such conduct constitutes an unreasonable restraint of trade. In other words, rule of reason analysis allows the defendant to justify the challenged conduct and requires the court to balance anticompetitive effects against the claimed justifications. Only then can the court determine if the restraint was unreasonable.

Generally, a defendant hospital's pro-competitive justifications for excluding a plaintiff physician from the staff are accepted if the justifications foster legitimate hospital objectives. Pro-competitive justifications may include maintaining or improving the quality of care, efficiency, or staff harmony at the institution. For example, a hospital that has a management strategy for becoming a teaching and research institution may be justified in denying privileges to a physician who evidences no interest or background in such activities. In a majority of jurisdictions, courts adhere to a "rule of non-review," under which, as a matter of public policy, internal staffing decisions of private hospitals are not subject to judicial review.[31,32] In such circumstances, review is limited to whether the hospital adhered to its by-laws in making its decision.[31] With the broad justification for alleged trade restraint that courts find acceptable, it should be no surprise that, when rule of reason analysis is used in antitrust cases based on denial of privileges, the defendant invariably prevails.

There are several reasons for the health care institution's succeeding in denial of staff privileges lawsuits. First, because most state laws create some role for a hospital in establishing or overseeing staffing patterns and decisions, hospitals are invariably named as defendants. The net effect of this is to create an alleged vertical, rather than horizontal, restraint for which the rule of reason analysis generally applies. (A vertical restraint involves an agreement among noncompeting entities, such as between a hospital and a physicians' group.) Under the rule of reason test, the plaintiff will have great difficulty establishing more than minimal anticompetitive restraint. Conversely, much weight is given to justifications such as increased quality of care or efficiency in the delivery of health care services. Attainment of these objectives may improve the reputation of the hospital and, hence, improve its competitive position in the relevant market.

Another common situation involving denial of privileges that satisfies the conspiracy or combination requirement of the Sherman Act arises when a hospital enters into an exclusive contract with a group of physicians to supply specific services to the hospital. A physician who is denied staff privileges on the basis of not being a member of the exclusive contracting group may allege an antitrust violation under an "exclusive dealing" theory. If no other allegation accompanies that charge, courts very likely will treat the case as a vertical combination to which the "rule of reason" analysis applies. As indicated, defendant hospitals almost always prevail when this test is applied to such facts.

In an effort to persuade the court to apply the *per se* rule, plaintiffs will often claim a horizontal restraint in the form of a tying arrangement charge. A tying arrangement occurs when an entity or person sells a product, called the tying product, only on condition that the buyer purchase a second product, the tied product. Although all tying arrangements are horizontal restraints, not all tying arrangements are unreasonable *per se*. For the *per se* rule to apply, the plaintiff must demonstrate that the seller has sufficient market control over the tying product to force the buyer to purchase the tied product, which is not necessarily desired or price/quality competitive on the free market. For example, if a seller controls 70 percent of the apple market, but conditions the sale of an apple on the simultaneous purchase of a pear, an unlawful tying arrangement exists. If the seller does not possess sufficient market power over the tying product (i.e., the buyer can get his apples elsewhere), the arrangement will be subject to the rule of reason rather than *per se* analysis.

The seminal case involving a tying agreement and exclusive dealing contract in the context of medical staff privileges is the 1984 United States Supreme Court case, *Jefferson Parish Hospital v. Hyde*.[33] In *Hyde*, the plaintiff, an anesthesiologist denied privileges at the defendant hospital, alleged that an exclusive contract between the hospital and an anesthesiology group practice was an illegal tying arrangement because it required that every patient admitted for surgery use the services of one of four anesthesiologists in the group practice.

The court commenced its analysis by finding that two distinct services existed. It concluded that operating room services were tied to anesthesiology services, as a patient using the former automatically received the latter. Next, the court inquired whether the hospital had sufficient market control over operating room facilities to force patients to purchase the services of the anesthesiology group practice. The Supreme Court accepted the lower court's finding that the defendant hospital had a 30 percent market share, which the Court determined was insufficient to force patients to purchase the anesthesiology services provided by the hospital: patients always had the option to use another hospital. Therefore, the *per se* rule did not apply. After engaging in the rule of reason analysis, the Court found that the exclusive contract had no actual adverse effect on competition, and, therefore, the linkage in services did not violate antitrust prohibitions.

Subsequent cases[34-36] have held that exclusive dealing contracts between hospitals and physicians are not *per se* illegal and, in most instances, are not illegal at all. The physician executive should be aware, however, that, if the hospital in question is the only health care facility in the region or offers unique services, the requisite market power may be found to exist.

In fact, in a majority of states, courts do not engage in judicial review of the substantive issues associated with the staffing decisions made by private hospitals.[31-32] In a minority of states, courts do grant judicial review of the substantive issues associated with staffing decisions made by private hospitals. However, in a majority of these states, even that review is somewhat limited. Specifically, a majority of the states in which courts review the substantive basis for a private hospital's staffing decisions are relatively sparsely populated. In such cases, courts have noted that some oversight of staffing decisions is necessary because there is no economic mechanism to ensure that hospitals will make consumer-sensitive decisions.[37-39] In such sparsely populated states, a hospital is more likely to play a monopolistic role in the provision of health care services, and a hospital's decision to deny or terminate hospital privileges is likely to serve as an effective bar to a physician's practicing in that geographic area.

Staffing, Peer Review, and Health Care Relationships

None of this is to suggest that the staffing decisions by a private hospital will, in a majority of states, escape judicial scrutiny altogether. That is not the case. Instead, the courts engage in procedural rather than substantive review of the staffing decisions made by private hospitals. Specifically, the review is limited to the process followed by the hospital in granting, denying, or amending staff privileges to ensure that the hospital followed its bylaws and afforded the affected physician an opportunity to participate in the process, and to see that the decision was not predicated on actual bias.[32] In this regard, it is essential that hospitals follow their bylaws to the letter in passing on staffing decisions, because failure to do so may expose participants in the process to liability and may effectively cause the staffing decision to be overruled. For example, in Illinois, participants in the peer review process are immune from civil liability arising from or relating to those peer review actions except for actions involving willful or wanton misconduct.[40]

A majority of state legislatures have passed legislation limiting access to and disclosure of documents and reports relating to hospital self-evaluation and peer review.[41] Such legislation was enacted under the promise that external access to peer investigations conducted by staff committees stifles candor and inhibits objectivity and that such restrictions on disclosure elevates the quality of care.[42] This is not to suggest that all documents or reports of peer review committees are inherently privileged from disclosure, and, in fact, in some states, such materials are not privileged.[43,44] For example, in Kentucky, the statutory privilege of confidentiality for peer review committees is limited to suits against the peer review entities, not in actions premised on medical malpractice.[44,45]

Clearly, staffing decisions may have some impact on competition for health care services in large and small communities alike. However, such decisions rest in significant part on technical expertise, and the courts have demonstrated a willingness to defer to that expertise. Moreover, such decision making affords a mechanism by which health care professionals are able to police themselves and protect the public. Legislators have recognized that, absent insulation from liability, it is difficult to obtain qualified physicians to participate in peer review. A majority of state legislatures have passed legislation in the area of hospital committee confidentiality in an attempt to encourage physician self-evaluation.[41] As a consequence, hospitals and members of hospital peer review panels, in most but not all jurisdictions, have some degree of protection from liability for the anticompetitive impact of their actions in making staffing decisions, as long as they conform to institutions' bylaws and do not act in an arbitrary manner.

■ Hospitals

Most states have specific statutory exceptions permitting hospitals to employ physicians. These statutes allow hospitals to hire physicians as long as there is no interference by the hospital in the practitioner's exercise of professional judgment. Some jurisdictions distinguish between hospitals that are for-profit or not-for-profit, public or private, teaching or nonteaching, and emergency or general services facilities.

■ HMOs

The Health Maintenance Organization Act of 1973 provides that HMOs may do business in the corporate form and employ physicians. Additionally, some states have enacted HMO statutes that allow physician employment. However, the mere fact that a state authorizes HMOs does not necessarily mean that HMOs may circumvent the general corporate practice proscription. For example, in Texas, there are statutes that permit HMOs but that do not allow them to "employ or contract with physicians...in any manner which is prohibited by any licensing law...under which physicians...are licensed."[46] Again, medical decisions, in general, cannot be delegated by physicians to a corporate or lay entity.

■ Professional Corporations

A physician may practice in the corporate form pursuant to individual state professional corporation statutes. These acts preserve the professional's individual responsibility to patients by providing that the professional will be liable for professional services rendered despite the corporate shareholder or employee status. However, the corporate form shields the practitioner from liability for nonprofessional service debts, such as a contract to purchase equipment. Only persons licensed to practice in the particular profession can be shareholders in a professional corporation.

■ Independent Contractors

Often, a physician's "employment" contract states that the physician is acting in the capacity of an independent contractor. In order to avoid the charge that the professional is in fact an employee, the contract must state very clearly that the physician maintains complete control and responsibility over, and for the benefit of, patients. However, as discussed earlier, the fact that a contract provides that a physician is an "independent contractor" may not insulate a health care institution at which a physician provides services from liability under an ostensible agency theory.

■ Private Industrial Clinics

Some states permit corporations to hire physicians to treat their employees. For example, a Colorado statute provides that, "Any licensee...may accept employment from any person, partnership, association, or corporation to examine and treat the employees of such person, partnership, association or corporation."[47]

Although there are many exceptions to the rule against the corporate practice of medicine, and some consider the rule to be an anachronism, the general prohibition still exists. The physician executive should be aware of this prohibition and the potential threat it still poses to employment relationships between physicians and health care facilities.

Insurability/Alternative Risk Protection Mechanisms

A key area of concern for the physician executive is how to best protect the health care organization from exposure to financial loss emanating from liability lawsuits. Until fairly recently, the primary method a hospital used to protect itself was to purchase commercial insurance. As premiums soared and availability of malpractice coverage plummeted, many health care institutions turned to alternative funding and risk management methods. In addition to the inadvisable option of going bare (that is, maintaining no insurance), an institution has two basic choices: funding a self-insurance program or trust on a single - or multihospital basis or the formation of a captive insurance company, also known as a limited purpose insurance company.

Funded self-insurance is a mechanism that collects and disburses funds to cover liability losses. The trust amount is actuarially determined and is managed by a qualified trustee. Generally, a self-insurance trust on a single-hospital basis will not constitute the conduct of the business of insurance. The formation and operation of the trust is relatively simple, as it will not be governed by the applicable state insurance code. However, if the trust is formed for multihospital protection, compliance with a state's applicable insurance code may be required. Consequently, individual state laws must be consulted to determine precisely what activity constitutes the business of insurance. Self-insurance trusts are often considered attractive because they eliminate the profit element of commercial insurance, investment returns remain in the trust, and claims administration and loss prevention are controlled by the health care institution itself. The down side, of course, is that such trusts cannot spread risk as well as commercial insurance does.

The second alternative risk protection mechanism is the creation of a limited purpose liability company, referred to as a captive insurance company because its owners are the ones protected by its coverage. A captive insurance company is essentially a self-insurance program organized under the insurance code of a particular state. The company is in all respects a distinct insurance company that is wholly owned by its insureds. All the formalities required by the applicable insurance code must be complied with to form this type of entity. Generally, this includes capitalization, reporting, and reserve requirements, as well as limitations on risks that can be undertaken.

A bill allowing the formation of a "risk retention group" was passed by Congress in October 1986.[48] This law expanded a 1981 version of the law that only allowed risk retention groups to insure against product liability claims. The new law allows coverage for any kind of liability and has generated a great deal of interest and, thus, deserves more detailed treatment here.

To qualify as a risk retention group, a group must be exclusively owned by persons who are insureds of the company; the group must consist of similar or related businesses. Once a group is chartered under the law of any state in accordance with the provisions of the Risk Retention Act, it may do business nationally, subject to only minimal restrictions. These restrictions include certain administrative requirements, such as requiring the group to submit to each state in which it proposes to do business a copy of a feasibility study prepared for the group, a copy of certified financial statements, and a copy of an opinion of a qualified loss reserve specialist on the group's loss and loss adjustment expense reserves. In addition, state insurance commissioners retain authority to prevent companies operating in an unsound manner from doing business in their states.

The Act provides numerous incentives for the formation of risk retention groups. Once a group satisfies the regulatory requirements of its chartering state, it is virtually free to do business anywhere in the United States. This obviates the need for companies to obtain prior rate and policy form approvals in all 50 states and the need either to become licensed as an admitted insurer in all 50 states or to utilize a fronting insurer. Second, the Act facilitates the company's ability to raise capital by providing an exemption from state securities laws and from the registration requirements of the federal securities laws. Thus, the company may readily raise capital without incurring the substantial costs associated with a registered public offering. Third, the Act exempts risk retention groups from any state law requiring such groups to utilize a broker or agent resident in the state to countersign insurance policies.

A group will most likely be formed under the laws of the state of Delaware, although other states, such as Illinois, have authorized the formation of risk retention groups. There are numerous advantages associated with incorporating in Delaware. Delaware offers a positive business climate. It was the first state to incorporate a risk retention group and is widely respected by insurance commissioners as a state with experience in the formation and regulation of risk retention groups and other complex businesses. Delaware has enacted legislation to substantially broaden permissible director indemnification and to limit director liability. Because the company's board will most likely comprise owner/insureds who will direct the operations of the company, this additional protection is highly desirable.

The Act is potentially a boon to the medical and health care industry, which has suffered from the unavailability of adequate insurance at reasonable cost. However, the Act is no panacea. Many questions remain as to how individual state commissioners may interpret its provisions. As previously mentioned, individual states in which the group plans to do business retain some discretion in regulating the capitalization of risk retention groups. Although antithetical to the intent of the Act, a state commissioner may, for example, refuse to fully recognize assets represented by letters of credit as admitted assets of the group.

The right to form risk retention groups within the health care industry certainly portends a substantial increase in the availability and affordability of malpractice insurance. Because all insureds are owners and all owners are insureds, each insured has a direct incentive to employ effective risk prevention programs to minimize loss exposure. To the extent that certain insureds fall short of their responsibilities, owners of the group may redeem the shares of such insureds and thus eliminate them from the risk pool. The Risk Retention Act will not solve all insurance problems, but the physician executive should be aware of its potential and be mindful of future developments.

Civil Discovery and Risk Management

Incident reporting systems and patient care review committees are obviously an integral part of hospital risk management programs. While such programs are necessary to control and contain risk, the documents produced as a result of the programs are potential time bombs, just waiting to be discovered by a plaintiff's attorney in malpractice lawsuits. Additionally, such documents are certainly significant in litigation brought by physicians who have been denied privileges or had privileges modified or limited. Consequently, the physician executive must be aware of legal avenues available to protect the institution from unnecessary disclosure of hospital documents.

Data generated by, and for, hospital review committees may be protected against discovery by specific statutes that ensure the confidentiality of such records. For example, the Medical Studies Act of Illinois, states, in part, "all information, interviews, reports, statements, memoranda or other data...(but not the medical records pertaining to the patient) used in the course of internal quality control or of medical study for the purpose of reducing morbidity or mortality, or for improving patient care, shall be privileged, strictly confidential and shall be used only for medical research, the evaluation and improvement of quality care, or granting, limiting or revoking staff privileges...."[49,50] This has been held in Illinois not to affect discovery concerning actions taken with respect to a physician resulting from peer review or quality control studies. The extent of the "privilege" from disclosure varies from state to state.

In order to increase the likelihood that a hospital's records fall within the purview of the above act, the institution should state very clearly on each document that it has been prepared for purposes of internal quality control, for medical studies to reduce morbidity or mortality, or to improve patient care. However, labeling a document is by no means a fail-safe procedure.

The existence of a statute such as Illinois' does not guarantee that a plaintiff's attorney in an action premised on medical negligence will not succeed in obtaining many documents because state laws are subject to varying interpretations by the courts. For example, some state laws may only prohibit the admission of such records into evidence at trial, thereby allowing a plaintiff's attorney to review them during pretrial discovery. However, even where discovery is not prohibited by statute, some courts have prevented their disclosure on public policy grounds or have allowed a defense claim that such documents constitute privileged material.

Additionally, hospitals and physicians must comply with state regulations concerning retention of medical records or risk liability for the spoliation of evidence. Some states, such as Illinois, mandate that medical records be maintained by hospitals (not physicians) for a specified period. A person who claims to have been the victim of medical negligence and whose records have not been retained may potentially bring an action against the institution that failed to retain the records on the basis that such failure has adversely affected the patient's ability to succeed in a medical malpractice action.[51] To avoid potential liability in such a case, it is not necessary that a hospital retain all patient records *ad infinitum*. Instead, the institution must have a uniform retention policy that is uniformly applied and consistently executed. Such a policy must take into account the hospital's needs for such records as well as any applicable record retention mandates—either by statute or from governing bodies such as JCAHO.

Contracts and the Hospital[52]

Finally, hospital administrators must focus on a number of generic issues common to any type of health care contract, whether it is a service, a purchase, or some other type of contract. Although some issues, such as compensation and termination, are of utmost importance, any provision that is carelessly drafted or inadvertently deleted may result in later disputes between the parties, litigation, and loss of essential services and supplies required by the hospital to continue to provide high-quality health care services on an uninterrupted basis.

Starting literally at the beginning of any health care contract, the identity of any parties to the agreement must be clearly and unambiguously stated. Although this might appear to be a simple and noncontroversial matter, health care administrators and their lawyers must be alert for certain problem situations. For example, shortly before the execution of one lengthy multimillion dollar hospital-vendor contract, it was discovered that the initials of the vendor, which had been assumed to stand for the company name, in fact stood for a separate subsidiary of the parent company. This discovery was significant, insofar as the parent company was a nationally known corporation with significant assets whereas its subsidiary was a newly formed entity that had been recently capitalized and held far fewer assets. In other words, the various indemnification provisions within the contract were far less meaningful when made by the subsidiary entity as opposed to the parent with whom the client thought it was negotiating.

Another example for the health care executive is to obtain additional information when negotiating a contract with a "partnership" as opposed to a corporate entity. The health care executive must be careful to ensure that the party negotiating on behalf of the partnership has the authority to enter into the agreement and to commit the partnership to providing the services or goods specified in the contract and that the terms of the proposed agreement do not in some way violate the terms of that partnership agreement. For this reason, when negotiating with a partnership, the actual partnership agreement should be reviewed in advance. Furthermore, a provision should be included within the contract wherein the other party warrants and covenants that he or she is obligated to enter into the agreement on behalf of the partnership and that the terms of the contract do not exceed the powers of the partnership's organizational documents.

If a hospital is going to be providing services of a type that it will provide to other parties, the terms of the contract should make clear that the contract is being entered into on a "nonexclusive" basis. Conversely, if you are obtaining services from a party on an exclusive basis, it should be so stated in the agreement. For example, when hiring a full-time medical director, the hospital manager should specify that that person will provide such services on an "exclusive" basis. In that type of situation, the hospital administrator should consider incorporating additional safeguards, such as specifying the period during which the medical director must be on the premises performing the responsibilities specified in the contract.

In any situation where hospital administration is providing services of some type for another health care provider or business, the hospital should be indemnified from liability for the acts or omissions of the other party. For example, if a hospital contracts to provide the inpatient component of services for a local or national HMO, the hospital should be held harmless and indemnified from any and all risks of liabilities, claims, and judgments (including reasonable attorneys' fees) related to the HMO's discharge of its responsibilities under the agreement or its provision of patient care services. Additionally, the hospital should be listed as a named-insured on the HMO's professional liability policy, which, in itself, should be for adequate amounts. Those amounts would be determined by the nature and scope of services to be delivered by the hospital and the general demographics (i.e., age and health condition) of the HMO's patients.

Provisions regarding compensation are usually one of the two most important areas of any health care contract. After all, if it weren't for compensation, at least one of the parties would certainly not be entering into the contract. For that reason, it is essential that the contract clearly state how, when, and in what amounts compensation will be made, particularly in those instances where it is the hospital that will be receiving payment for providing services. Additionally, the contract should state what, if any, penalties may be assessed for late payments. Typically, a hospital that is not paid on a timely basis will be entitled to assess penalties in an amount not in excess of that allowed by applicable law. In many states, however, "penalty" provisions are largely unenforceable and must be included as an added payment needed to defray administrative expenses caused by the late payment. This avoids prohibition of payments otherwise described as "penalties."

In order to protect a hospital's long-term interests, any contract should require the other party to discharge its responsibilities in accordance with state and federal law, particularly regulations applicable to hospitals. For example, in contracts for goods or services costing in excess of $10,000 over a 12-month period, the vendor should be required to provide access to its books and records to the Secretary of the Department of Health and Human Services or the Comptroller General, or their designates, as may be needed by the federal government to audit those services furnished or goods supplied by the vendor. The hospital, under applicable federal regulations of the Department of Health and Human Services, is required to include this type of provision in any such contract. As a general rule, if the hospital fails to comply with federal statutes and regulations, such as the one described here, it could fall out of compliance with Medicare's Conditions of Participation or suffer adverse reimbursement determinations by state and federal regulators and payers.

Given the rapid evolution in the delivery of health care services and the various statutes and regulations applicable to hospitals and health care providers, contracts should generally provide what will happen if the law or reimbursement regulations should change during the term of the agreement. If the hospital would be seriously affected by a change in law or regulation, the facility should have the right to demand a renegotiation of the contract or to terminate the agreement. Absent such safeguards, the hospital could not only lose the benefit of an agreement, but could actually suffer very serious financial losses if it were obligated to continue to discharge its responsibilities under an agreement for which it could no longer continue to be reimbursed.

Hospital clients frequently inquire whether it is advisable to include an arbitration provision of some type in agreements. As a general rule, arbitration provisions usually benefit the party that has less leverage and is less likely to be able to afford protracted litigation and costly legal fees. Whether or not an arbitration provision should be included within a particular contract will depend on factual circumstances and can only be made on a case-by-case basis. However, in those situations where an arbitration provision is deemed suitable by the parties, an informal dispute mechanism should be drafted whereby a neutral third party will review oral and/or written briefs and make a determination based upon what he or she believes is just and equitable within 20 days of the commencement of the informal dispute mechanism. A dispute mechanism of this type is generally quick and inexpensive (for both parties) and draws less attention than if a dispute had to be litigated in a court of law.

Alternatively, parties may agree to arbitrate disputes pursuant to the rules of the American Arbitration Association (AAA) and to use an arbitrator approved by the AAA. Additionally, state law in many jurisdictions provides for arbitration procedures that may be specified to govern any dispute arising between the parties.

In order to minimize, if not completely avoid, liability by somehow being deemed to be "in business" with the other party to the contract, health care organizations should draft contracts that generally specify that the parties are acting as "independent contractors," and not as partners or joint venturers, for the purpose of carrying out the terms of the agreement. Further, such contracts should generally specify that one party is not acting as the agent or representative of the other party. Such clauses, while helpful, may not be dispositive in instances in which the institution is sued for the acts of an ostensible agent.

Additionally, in those cases where hospital management may be contracting with an individual, such as a medical director, on an independent contractor basis, even though the individual would traditionally be deemed an "employee" of the facility, the hospital should obtain separate written assurances from the individual wherein he or she covenants that he or she will pay his or her income taxes in full on a timely basis. Such separate written assurances will serve to protect the hospital's financial interests in the event that the administrator or other like contracting party subsequently fails to pay his or her income taxes, in which case the hospital could be liable for those payments plus interest and possible penalties.

The second (many would say the most) important provision within any health care contract is the termination provision. Parties usually are far more acrimonious when an agreement is prematurely terminated than when it is initially negotiated. For this reason, it is critical that the duties and responsibilities of the parties related to a contract's termination be clearly articulated within the document. For example, if one party terminates the agreement as a result of the breach of the other party, the agreement might define what constitutes "breach" within the meaning of the agreement. The contract should explicitly state which responsibilities of each party will continue following termination. For example, if the hospital is to receive payments on the fifteenth day of each month for services provided during the immediately preceding month, the hospital should be guaranteed payment for services provided during the last month of the agreement even though such payment may not be made until after the contract's termination.

As a general rule, hospitals should not enter into agreements wherein the term of the agreement is self-extending unless terminated upon 30 days' written notice prior to an anniversary date of the agreement. The danger of such self-extending agreements is that if the hospital should fail inadvertently to give the required notice within the required 30-day "window," it may be unable to terminate the agreement for an additional 12 months. Obviously, hospitals should avoid this situation and can be certain to prevent themselves from being locked into an automatic renewal if the term of the contract is not self-extending.

Caveat: Hospital executives should treat exhibits as seriously as the actual terms of the agreements to which they affix their signatures. Exhibits frequently contain key terms of the mutual agreement of the parties. Accordingly, never, under any circumstances, should an agreement be signed unless all exhibits are attached and agreed upon by the parties. Should it be necessary to execute an agreement before all exhibits are completed, at a minimum, a provision should be made that the agreement will take effect only upon completion and execution by the parties of the specified (and not yet completed) attachments.

Health care executives may be familiar with the term "time is of the essence" within a contract. This phrase has an exact legal meaning and should generally not be included within a health care contract. More specifically, a contract that makes "time of essence" means that either party will have breached the contract as a matter of law should it fail to perform each and every term and duty delegated to it thereunder on a timely basis and as fully specified within the agreement. In other words, if the hospital were obligated to make a payment on the first day of the month during the term of the agreement, the hospital would be in breach of that contract if it were to submit such payment one minute late, i.e., 12:01 a.m. on the 2nd of the month. Thereupon, the non-breaching party would be entitled to all of its rights specified thereunder resulting from the hospital's technical failure to make timely payments. In order to avoid severe repercussions for failing to comply strictly with a contract's terms, time should not be made "of the essence."

Last, goods and services being purchased by a hospital or those to be discharged by the institution must always be carefully and unambiguously articulated within the contract so as to avoid future disputes with respect to the actual duties and responsibilities of the parties under the agreement.

Each situation will present parties negotiating a contract with different difficulties and problems requiring creative solutions designed to accommodate the special interests and factual circumstances of those parties. However, as described above, most agreements will generally have certain key points regardless of the factual circumstances. Health care executives and other health professionals and personnel with a health care facility should, however, be alert to carefully negotiate those terms. If those terms are negotiated to the satisfaction and advantage of the hospital, the contract should generally be one that will protect the institution during the term of the agreement and, perhaps more important, upon its termination.

Self-Referral and Anti-Kickback Legislation

Studies have linked self-referral to the overutilization of diagnostic services.[53] In response, some states have enacted legislation prohibiting physicians from referring patients to health care facilities in which they are investors. Illinois, for example, has enacted what is entitled the Healthcare Worker Self-Referral Act.[54] Likewise, the federal government has enacted the Medicare and Medicaid Anti-Kickback statute as a means of combatting financial incentives to physicians of forwarding particular services that patients did not need.[55-57]

The purpose of Illinois' Self-Referral Act is to eliminate potential conflicts of interest that arise whenever a health care worker has an investment interest in an entity to which he or she refers patients. Under Illinois' Act, with certain limited exceptions "[a] health care worker shall not refer a patient for health services to an entity outside the health care workers' office or group practice in which the health care worker is an investor unless the health care worker directly provides health services within the entity and will be personally involved in the provision of care to the referred patient."[58] Illinois' Act provides for civil penalties of no more than $20,000 for each violative referral and also provides that any violation of the Act is grounds for disciplinary action by the applicable board or committee. The federal law provides for similar limitations on self-referral and similar exceptions. Additionally, the Medicare fraud statute makes violations a felony.

Courts construing the Medicare fraud statute have noted that Congress, in passing the legislation, expressed a concern that "physicians often determined which laboratories would do the test work for their Medicaid patients by the amount of kickbacks and rebates offered by the laboratory....Kickbacks take a number of forms, including cash, long-term credit arrangements, gifts, supplies and equipment, and the furnishing of business machines."[56] The Act was aimed at inducements to either order services or refer services to a particular provider.[56] Consequently, the Act has been found to be violated when compensation was paid to a physician both to induce a physician provider's services and to compensate him or her for professional services.[56]

Health Care Security Act of 1993 and Health Care Reform

In response to concerns about the ever increasing cost of health care and a concern that a significant percentage of the U.S. population lacks adequate health care insurance, President Clinton proffered the Health Care Security Act.[5] As of the writing of this chapter, the Act is still being debated and will surely undergo significant revision and amendment before it becomes law. The Act does propose what can be described, at best, as modest tort reforms. Specifically, the Act provides for arbitration and/or mediation of claims before any medical malpractice claim can be adjudicated. The Act also requires that a qualified health care professional certify the merit of the suit prior to the litigation of medical malpractice actions. It is doubtful that either of these proposed reforms will have a significant impact on the litigation of medical malpractice actions.

In contrast, the Act provides for two demonstration projects that are more likely to affect medical malpractice litigation. Specifically, the Act provides for a demonstration project to test the efficacy of enterprise liability. In that project, the enterprise, and not the individual physician, would be held financially accountable for malpractice actions. Additionally, the Act provides for a demonstration project to test the efficacy of practice guidelines in promoting better quality of care. Adherence by a practitioner to the practice guidelines would amount to a complete defense in a medical malpractice action.

Conclusion

Hospital liability has undergone expansive growth since the days when the hospital's only responsibility was to provide facilities in which independent health care practitioners plied their trade. Today, if a health care institution does not exercise effective control over how care is provided and who provides it, it runs the risk of liability for patient injury. Conversely, if the institution exercises too much control, it runs the risk of violating laws prohibiting the corporate practice of medicine as well as liability to practitioners for restraint of trade. To avoid liability, it is essential that the physician executive be aware of the legal environment in which he or she operates, such that an effective but not overly restrictive risk management course may be charted.

References

1. *Thompson v. Nason Hospital*, 591 A.2d 703, 706 (Pa 1991).

2. *Kashishian v. Port*, 481 N.W.2d 277, 282 (Wi 1992).

3. *Gilbert v. Sycamore Municipal Hospital*, 156 Ill. 2d 511(Ill.1993).

4. *Holger v. Irish*, 851 P.2d 1122, 1127-1128 (Or. 1993).

5. Health Care Security Act, ¶5311 (as of October 27, 1993).

6. *Brown v. Coastal Emergency Services*, 354 S.E. 2d 632 (Ga. App. 1987).

7. See, Phoenix, "Hospital Liability for the Acts of Independent Contractors: The Ostensible Agency Doctrine." *St. Louis University Law Journal* 30:875-93, 1985-1986.

8. "Hospital Liability May Be Based on Either Doctrine of Ostensible Agency or Doctrine of Corporate Negligence." *St. Mary's Law Journal* 17: 551-78, 1986.

9. Zaremski, M., and Spitz, M. "Liability of a Hospital as an Institution; Are the Walls of Jericho Tumbling?" *Forum* 16(2):225, Fall 1980.

10. Zaremski, M. "Hospital Corporate Liability: The Walls Continue to Tumble." *Medicolegal News* 9(2):13, April 1981.

11. *Chase v. Independent Practice Association, Inc.*, 583 N.E. 2d 251, 254-255 (Mass. App. 1991).

12. *Raglin v. HMO Illinois, Inc.*, 230 Ill. App. 3d 642, 646 (lst Dist. 1992).

13. Tex. Rev. Civ. Stat. Ann. art. 4495b, ¶3.04 (Vernon Supp. 1993).

14. *Williams v. Good Health Plus, Inc.-Health America Corp. of Texas*, 743 S.W.2d 373 (Tex. App. San Antonio, 1987).

15. *Pickett v. CIGNA Healthplan of Texas*, 1993 WL 209858 (Tex. App. Houston (lst Dist.)).

16. *Hunte v. Hinkley*, 731 S.W. 2d 570 (Tex. App. Houston (14th Dist.)).

17. *Darling v. Charleston Community Memorial Hospital*, 33 Ill. App. 2d 326 (1965), cert. denied 383 U.S. 946 (1966).

18. 97 Wis. 2d 521, 294 N.W. 2d 501.

19. *Northern Trust Co. v. Louis A. Weiss Hospital*, 143 Ill. App. 3d 479 (1st Dist 1986).

20. *Rohe v. Shivde*, 203 Ill. App. 3d 181, 199 (lst Dist. 1990).

21. 42 U.S.C. ¶11101 *et. seq.*

22. For cases interpreting the Health Care Quality Improvement Act, see *Goldsmith v. Harding Hospital, Inc.*, 762 F. Supp. 187 (S.D. Ohio 1991)—Legislative history of Act indicates intent to provide solely for immunity on the part of professional review bodies and does not provide private cause of action to physician claiming denial of due process by reason of his suspension from hospital's psychiatric residency program); *Teasdale v. Marin General Hospital*, 138 F.R.D. 691 (N.D. Ca. 1991)—Act gives qualified immunity from suit to officials who conduct peer reviews, but would not be applied to prohibit the production of peer review documents predating the effective date of the Act); *LeMasters v. Christ Hospital*, 791 F. Supp. 188 (S.D. Ohio 1991)—Act would not be construed to limit discovery in sex discrimination civil rights action filed by physician against hospital). For cases holding that the Act provides immunity to physicians and doctors from antitrust violations, see *Smith v. Ricks*, 798 F. Supp. 605 (N.D. Ca. 1992); *Fobbs v. Holy Cross Health System Corp.*, 789 F. Supp. 1054 (E.D. Ca. 1992); *Austin v. McNamara*, 731 F. Supp 934 (S.D. Ca. 1990).

23. *Copperweld Corporation et al. v. Independence Tube Corporation*, 467 US 752 (1984).

24. 656 F. Supp. 601 (S.D. Tex. 1987).

25. For cases citing the Mosby decision with approval, see *Kiepfer v. Beller*, 944 F.2d 1213, 1221 (5th Cir. 1991)—Antitrust plaintiff must show not just that the defendants' actions injured him, but that they unreasonably restrained competition; *Rockbit Industries USA, Inc. v. Backer Hughes, Inc.*, 802 F. Supp 1544 (S.D. Tex. 1991)—Antitrust laws protect competition, not competitors.

26. Because the hospital had an open staff policy that permitted physicians to request the services of any staff radiologist, the plaintiff retained full staff privileges at the hospital and continued to receive referrals. Under this open staff policy, the radiology contract was not an exclusive services contract; the contracting radiologist took only those cases where the attending physician did not designate a preference for a particular radiologist.

27. 457 U.S. 332, 73 L. Ed.2d 48 (1982).

28. For additional cases following the Maricopa reasoning, see *Boulware v. State of Nevada Department of Human Resources*, 960 F. 2d 793 (9th Cir. 1992); 698 F. Supp. 679 (E.D. Mich. 1988); 593 F. Supp. 892 (1984).

29. 745 F.2d 786 (3d Cir. 1984).

30. For decisions following the *Weiss* holding, see, *Fuentes v. South Hills Cardiology*, 946 F.2d 196 (3rd Cir. 1991); *Oksanen v. Page Memorial Hospital*, 945 F.2d 696 (4th Cir. 1991).

31. *Adkins v. Sarah Bush Lincoln Health Center*, 129 Ill. 2d 497 (1989).

32. *Barrows v. Northwestern Memorial Hospital*, 123 Ill. 2d 49 (1988).

33. 104 S. Ct. 1551 (1984).

34. *Beard v. Parkview Hospital*, 912 F.2d 138 (6th Cir. 1990).

35. *Ezpeleta v. Sisters of Mercy Health Corporation*, 800 F.2d 119 (7th Cir. 1986).

36. *Action Ambulance v. Altanticare* Health Services, 815 F. Supp. 33 (D. Mass. 1993).

37. *Kelly v. St. Vincent Hospital*, 692 P.2d 1350, 1353 (1984).

38. *Holmes v. Hoemako Hospital*, 573 P.2d 477 (1977).

39. *Bricfker v. Sceva Speare Memorial Hospital*, 281 A.2d 589 (1971).

40. 225 ILCS 60/5.

41. *Jenkins v. Wu*, 102 Ill. 2d 468 (1984).

42. *Cedars-Sinai Medical Center v. Superior Court*, 12 Cal. App. 4th 579 (Cal. App. 2d Dist. 1993).

43. *Bundy v. Sinopoli*, 580 A.2d 1101 (N.J. 1990).

44. *Appalachian Regional Health Care, Inc. v. Johnson*, 862 S.W.2d 868 (Ky. 1993).

45. *Sweasy v. Kings Daughters Memorial Hospital*, 771 S.W.2d 812 (1989).

46. Tex. Rev. Stat. Ann. Art 4495b, ¶3.04 (Vernon Supp. 1993).

47. C.R.S. sec. 12-12-117(m).

48. Risk Retention Act, 15 U.S.C. ¶3901 *et. seq.* For an example of a case interpreting and discussing the applicablity of the Risk Retention Act, see *Scales v. Memorial Medical Center of Jacksonville*, 690 F. Supp. 1002 (M.D. Fla. 1988)—Federal Risk Retention Act extempts rish retention groups from certain state regulation and clarifies state authority in other areas related to risk retention groups, but creates no implied cause of action in favor of risk retention groups.

49. 735 ILCS 5/8-2101. The statute reads in full: "All information, interviews, reports, statements, memoranda, or other data of the Illinois Department of Public Health, the Illinois Department of Mental Health and Development Disabilities Medical Review Board, Illinois State Medical Society, allied medical societies, health maintenance organizations and medical organizations under contract with health maintenance organizations, physician-owned inter-insurance exchanges and their agents, or committees of licensed or accredited hospitals or their medical staffs, including Patient Care Audit Committees, Medical Care Evaluation Committees and Executive Committees, Medical Care Evaluation Committees, Utilization Review Committees, Credential Committees and Executive Committees (but not the medical records pertaining to the patient) used in the course of internal quality control or of medical study for the purpose of reducing morbidity or mortality, or for improving patient care, shall be privileged, strictly confidential and shall be used only for medical research, the evaluation and improvement of quality care, or granting, limiting or revoking staff privileges, or in any judicial review thereof, the claim of confidentiality shall not be invoked to deny such physician access to or use of data upon which such a decision was based."

50. *Woodward v. Krans*, 234 Ill. App 3d 690, 600 N.E.2d 477 (1992)—Medical malpractice plaintiff would not be allowed limited discovery of anesthesiologist's medical records relating to diagnosis and treatment of anesthesiologist's tuberculosis as Medical Studies Act protected most, if not all, information sought from discovery.

51. *Fox v. Cohen*, 84 Ill. App. 3d 744 (lst Dist. 1980).

52. Acknowledgement is made for the assistance of Michael Roth, Esq., in the preparation of the material on hospital contracts.

53. Steiner, J., and Wagner, M. "A Primer on the Legal Pitfalls of Physician Ownership and Self-Referral Practices." *Journal of Health and Hospital Law* 25(9):257-64, Sept. 1992.

54. 225 ILCS 47/5 *et seq.* Florida has enacted similar legislation entitled The Patient Self-Referral Act of 1992. Fla. Sta. ch. 455.236.

55. 42 U.S.C. ¶1320a-7b(b).

56. 42 U.S.C. ¶1395nn.

57. *United States v. Greber*, 760 F.2d 68, 71 (3rd Cir. 1985).

58. 225 ILCS 47/5 *et seq.*

Miles J. Zaremski is a Senior Partner and David B. Goodman is an Associate with Arnstein & Lehr, Chicago, Illinois, and West Palm Beach, Florida. The authors wish to acknowledge the assistance of Frank Calabrese, Esq., Associate, Arnstein & Lehr, in the preparation of this chapter.